MAKING THE LAW

The
REPORT
of
The Hansard Society
Commission
on
THE LEGISLATIVE
PROCESS

November 1992

The Hansard Society for Parliamentary Government
St Philips Building North
Sheffield Street
London WC2A 2EX

Tel 071-955 7478
Fax 071-955 7492

ISBN 0 900432 24 1

Typeset by A.L. Publishing Services, London W3, England
Printed by A.L. Print Works, London W3, England

The Hansard Society
St. Philips Building North
Sheffield Street
London
WC2A 2EX
Tel 071-955 7478
Fax 071 955 7492

Table of Contents

Foreword

Rt Hon Lord Hayhoe, PC

Chairman, The Hansard Society for Parliamentary Government

Lord Aberdare, when Chairman of Committees in the House of Lords, first suggested that the Society should set up a Commission on the Legislative Process. The Council of the Society readily accepted this timely proposal was well worthy of development. First we had to seek financial backing, and the Society is grateful to the Nuffield Foundation for providing the major part of the funding, and to several corporate donors who ensured the resources for the Commission to do such a thorough job including publication of evidence.

In Lord Rippon of Hexham – a distinguished Parliamentarian and Privy Councillor – the Commission had an excellent Chairman with wide Ministerial experience in high office. He assembled a powerfully authoritative group of knowledgeable people covering not only those who make our laws, but also those who interpret and use them. The sheer weight of experience on the Commission should in itself ensure close attention to their views. Finally, Michael Ryle, former Clerk of Committees in the House of Commons and joint author of 'Parliament', brought his not inconsiderable experience of report-writing to the task of drafting this highly-readable outcome of the Commission's deliberations.

Coming at a time when there is considerable debate about the nature of citizenship, this Report is a valuable reminder of the fact that laws are made for citizens who should be able to understand them and thus more easily be able to benefit from them. The Report has both clarity and conviction, with many thought-provoking proposals for reform.

With all its Commissions the Hansard Society acts as catalyst rather than campaigner. The Council of the Society has seen this report prior to publication and, since the Society exists solely to promote education, research and discussion, it neither accepts nor rejects the Commission's findings. We do, however, warmly commend the Report to the public as a worthwhile contribution to the subject and hope it receives the widespread attention it undoubtedly deserves, not least within Parliament and Government.

Appointment of the Commission

The Commission was appointed by the Hansard Society for Parliamentary Government in October 1991 to examine how Government and Parliament produce legislation and to assess whether the system is in need of overhaul and change.

The members of the Commission are-

Rt Hon Lord Rippon of Hexham, PC, QC (Chairman)
Mr Vernon Bogdanor (Reader in Government, Oxford University)
Rt Hon Lord Browne-Wilkinson, PC (Lord of Appeal in Ordinary)
Ms Frances Crook (Director, Howard League for Penal Reform)
Sir Brian Cubbon, GCB (former Permanent Secretary, the Home Office)
Sir John Dellow, CBE (former Deputy Commissioner, Metropolitan Police)
Sir George Engle, KCB, QC (former First Parliamentary Counsel)
Mr David Falcon (former Director-General, Royal Institute of Public Administration)
Sir Michael Latham (former Conservative MP)
Mr Clive Lloyd, CBE (Cricketer and former Member, Commission for Racial Equality)
Mr Gordon McCartney (former Secretary, Association of District Councils)
Mr Robert Maclennan, MP (Liberal Democrat)
Mr Austin Mitchell, MP (Labour)
Mr Joe Palmer, CBE (former Group Chief Executive, Legal and General Group)
Mr Joe Rogaly (Associate Editor, The Financial Times)
Mr Michael Ryle (former Clerk of Committees, House of Commons) (Secretary)
Ms Elizabeth Symons (General Secretary, Association of First Division Civil Servants)
Mr David Tench (Director of Legal Affairs, The Consumers Association)
Mrs Clare Tritton, QC.

The work of the Commission has only been made possible by generous grants from the Nuffield Foundation and other bodies, and the Commission is grateful for all the help it has received from these sources.

The Commission is especially grateful to Mr Michael Ryle, the member of the Commission who acted as Secretary, who brought a momentum and vision to the drafting of the Commission's Report.

The Commission wishes to express its thanks to its Chairman and to the Association of First Division Civil Servants, who made rooms available for its meetings and provided refreshments, and to Members of both Houses of Parliament for arranging meetings in the Palace of Westminster. It is also grateful to the Director of the Hansard Society and his staff for the considerable and efficient administrative and secretarial support they provided.

References to Evidence

Wherever possible, statements or quotations in this Report based on written evidence, are identified by reference to the relevant memorandum or other paper as published in Appendix 1 (e.g. M 1, para.1).

Statements based on discussions held by the Commission with various bodies and people are not specifically identified as details of these discussions have not been published. If the evidence of a body or individual is referred to without an M number, it means that the relevant evidence was given during discussions.

Glossary of Acronyms

The Commission has used a number of acronyms in the Report, as follows:

ABI   Association of British Insurers
ACPO   Association of Chief Police Officers
BBC   British Broadcasting Corporation
BMA   British Medical Association
CAA   Civil Aviation Authority
CBI   Confederation of British Industry
CPAG   Child Poverty Action Group
DoE   Department of the Environment
DSS   Department of Social Security
DTI   Department of Trade and Industry
EC   European Communities
FDA   Association of First Division Civil Servants
GLC   Greater London Council
HMSO   Her Majesty's Stationery Office
ICA   Institute of Chartered Accountants
ILEA   Inner London Education Authority
ITC   Independent Television Commission
MAFF   Ministry of Agriculture, Fisheries and Food
SLD   Statute Law Database
SSAC   Social Security Advisory Committee
TUC   Trades Union Congress
VAT   Value Added Tax

Chapter 1 – Introduction

"I find it impossible to discern with any accuracy the spirit of section 35 (5) simply because I believe that in all the flurry of legislation, evasive action and counter-legislation, the point under review has not been fully thought out" (Lord Justice Mustill, 1991, when considering the meaning of s. 35 of the Local Government Finance Act 1988 regarding the powers of the Secretary of State to cap local authority expenditure).

"Legislation is becoming increasingly inaccessible...and...impossible to understand. Unintelligible legislation is the negation of the rule of law and of parliamentary democracy" (James Goudie, QC, The Times , 20 August, 1991).

Lawyers are constantly "trying to find out what [statute law] is in force, when it came into force.....and when they have found out, what the hell it means." (Jane Hern, the Law Society, The Independent , 30 March, 1992).

"If Departments and the National Audit Office find it difficult to interpret legislation, what chance has the man in the street?" (Sir John Bourn, KCB, Comptroller and Auditor General, in evidence (M 9)).

"The form and drafting of legislation gives rise to increasing concern." (The Association of Metropolitan Authorities, the Association of County Councils and the Association of District Councils, in joint evidence (M 37)).

The Challenge

1. The observations above from highly experienced people involved in one way or other in the legislative process in this country must be taken seriously. If such people find difficulties in accessing and understanding statute law, what hope is there for the ordinary citizen who is affected by that law? Perhaps the time has come for Government and Parliament, and all who take part in the legislative process, to heed the words of the Prime Minister, Mr John Major, in his Foreword to the Citizen's Charter –

   "The Citizen's Charter is about giving more power to the citizen......it is a testament of our belief in people's right to be informed and choose for themselves"

   and to apply these principles to the central process of making law for the citizen. It is in this spirit that we carried out our inquiry.

2. There is undoubtedly widespread concern about the way the legislative process works and about its final product, statute law. For some time many of those who make the law, many of those who have to apply the law and many of those who have to comply with the law have been unhappy about the way legislation is prepared, drafted, passed through Parliament and published. All the evidence we have received bears this out (see paragraphs 53 to 63). Some of the

criticisms of the final product obviously reflect dislike of the policies embodied in the legislation – we are not concerned with these – but many complaints are of defects which appear to result from failures in the processes by which that legislation was made. The two aspects – process and product – are interrelated. We have been primarily concerned with the process as it affects the product.

3. Criticisms of the products of the legislative process by judges, various official bodies and select committees are of long-standing[1]. In 1970 a committee chaired by Sir Desmond Heap concluded that "The root of the problem afflicting statute law users lies more in the system by which the law is made and expressed than in the substantive law itself"[2].

4. The Heap Report was followed by other critical studies. In 1972 the Stow Hill Committee, appointed by the Statute Law Society, recommended solutions to the problems outlined in the Heap Report[3]. In 1973, following further comments by a Procedure Committee of the House of Commons[4], the Renton Committee[5] was appointed by the Lord President of the Council "to review the form in which Public Bills are drafted" ; it reported in 1975, making 81 detailed and technical recommendations for change.

5. The sorry fact is that despite these critical but constructive reports almost nothing has been done to improve the situation. The time has come for a fundamental re-think of the whole legislative process – which is not confined to the details of drafting or the intricacies of Parliament's procedures – and which may lead to substantial change. That has been our challenge. It is also a challenge facing Government and Parliament.

The Commission's Approach

6. Previous inquiries on this subject have generally concentrated on drafting or procedure. Various features of the legislative process – policy decisions; drafting; public bill procedure; scrutiny of delegated legislation; publication – have been looked at piecemeal as if they were independent functions. Instead the process is a continuum; all its stages being interrelated, the process must be examined as a whole.

7. The emphasis on limited aspects has also tended to obscure the main issues. Of course those affected by legislation are primarily concerned with the specific rights or duties or benefits it conveys, but too often the user is left questioning how the law came to be made. **We are convinced that all the processes by which statute law is made and published should be governed by the needs**

---

1 For example, "The imperfections in the statute law arising from mere generality, laxity or ambiguity of expression, are too numerous and too well known to require particular specification" (The First Report of the Statute Law Commissioners, 1835); and see *Statute Law Deficiencies* (the Heap Report) published by Sweet and Maxwell on behalf of the Statute Law Society, 1970, pp. 10 - 13, and Report of the Committee on the Preparation of Legislation, 1975 (the Renton Report), Cmnd. 6053, paras. 2.8 - 2.10.

2 Heap Report, op. cit., para. 99.

3 Statute Law: The Key to Clarity (Sweet and Maxwell, 1972).

4 HC 538, para. 68.

5 See Note 1.

of users and not primarily by the needs of those who pass legislation. We have therefore started from and concentrated on the users' perspective – of those to whom the law applies and of those who have to apply it – and have sought to come at the problem in a new way by looking at it through their eyes. This stems naturally from the wide-drawn membership of the Commission and is reflected in the evidence we received and in the selection of those with whom we held discussions.

8.   We must make it plain that our concern in this inquiry has been solely with the legislative process itself, not with the content of legislation except in so far as any weaknesses, errors or ambiguities in bills or delegated legislation may have resulted from the processes by which they came to be made. We have not looked in detail at the substance of any statute law or at criticisms of the content of Acts.

9.   We must explain some limitations of our inquiry. We would have liked to be able to consider the legislative processes in all parts of the United Kingdom. However, much of Scottish law is contained in separate Scottish Acts or in separate Parts of UK Acts, and currently Northern Ireland legislation is made by Northern Ireland Orders approved by the UK Parliament. Separate Scottish and Northern Ireland Government departments have responsibilities for this legislation, using separate parliamentary draftsmen; different interest groups and legal and other professional bodies are involved; their law is adjudicated in different courts. If we had tried to examine in detail the special features of the legislative process in these other jurisdictions, it would have added considerably to the amount of evidence and the number of meetings we would have needed. For reasons of time and resources, such duplication was not possible.

10.   We have therefore confined our Report almost entirely to the process in relation to UK and English legislation, with a chapter on the impact of European Community legislation. We believe, however, that many of our recommendations may have application in Scotland and Northern Ireland and also that lessons may well be learned from legislative experience in those countries. **We recommend that the Government should look at the implications of the issues we deal with in our Report for all parts of the United Kingdom.**

11.   We have focused entirely on the legislative process for Government bills. There was little reference to private Members' bills in the evidence and we have not considered them in any detail. We have not examined the processes relating to private legislation, which have recently been reviewed by Parliament. Nor have we considered how Church of England Measures are enacted, although they are equally part of statute law.

The Commission's Inquiry

12.   We held 20 meetings, over a period of twelve months. At 14 of these we had discussions with a wide range of bodies and individuals (see paragraph 16 and Appendix 2).

13. In addition special sub-groups on the Preparation of Legislation and Drafting; Consultation; Parliamentary Procedure and Delegated Legislation; and European Community Legislation were appointed, held discussions with civil servants and other experienced people and prepared working papers on different aspects of the legislative process.

14. We appointed Professor Gavin Drewry as the Commission's Director of Research; we are grateful to the Centre for Political Studies, Royal Holloway and Bedford New College, for making his services available. He was greatly assisted by Mr Brian Tutt, London School of Economics, and we must thank the Library of the House of Commons for giving him access to various parliamentary papers and for the support and advice they gave him. The research included an analysis of Government bills introduced into the House of Lords (Appendix 4), case studies of the preparation and passage of the Broadcasting Bill 1989-90 and the Dangerous Dogs Bill 1990-91 (Appendices 5 and 6), details of the volume of legislation (Appendix 7) and statistics on the use of consultation documents (Appendix 8).

15. We received a considerable volume of evidence. A wide range of bodies involved in or affected by the making of statute law were invited to comment on the legislative process and to draw on their experience. Although not a scientific sample, those bodies which responded are reasonably representative. They included industrial and employers' bodies; employees' organisations; local authority associations; regulatory and consumer organisations; professional associations; bodies concerned with health and social welfare; environmental bodies; and other pressure groups and campaigning bodies. Many of these bodies had experience of recent legislation and cited examples of both good and bad practice. Members of both Houses of Parliament, academics, lawyers and other individuals also volunteered or agreed to submit written evidence. Altogether 57 letters or memoranda regarding the legislative process in this country are published with the Report, as listed in Appendix 1.

16. We also held discussions with representatives of 23 bodies, covering industry and commerce, the legal and other professions, statutory bodies, various pressure groups and certain Government departments. We met 19 Opposition and back-bench Members of both Houses of Parliament, drawn from all parties, and received advice from the Clerks of the two Houses. We had discussions with academic experts and with a few senior civil servants. A full list of those we met is given in Appendix 2.

17. No inquiry into how statute law is made by Government and Parliament would be complete without taking account of the views of Government itself, and of the experience of Ministers and their departments. We were able to examine some aspects of the preparation and drafting of legislation with the First Parliamentary Counsel and the Treasury Solicitor, and certain practical questions with representatives of the Lord Chancellor's Department, the Board of Inland Revenue and H.M. Customs and Excise. One of our special sub-groups also received a helpful briefing on the preparation of legislation from senior civil servants.

18. Before agreeing our Report, we discussed some of the main issues arising from our inquiry with Ministers. We met the Lord President of the Council (Rt Hon Tony Newton, MP) and the Lord Privy Seal (Rt Hon Lord Wakeham, PC), being the Leaders of the two Houses of Parliament and also the Ministers most directly concerned with the Government's legislative programme. These discussions were extremely helpful and we have been able to take full account of the points made by Ministers in coming to our conclusions and making our recommendations.

19. We also sought information from a number of other countries with comparable democratic systems and constitutions. We obtained descriptions of the ways bills and regulations are drafted in Australia, Canada and New Zealand, and information about the legislative procedures and practices in the parliaments of Australia, Canada, Denmark, France, Germany, Israel and New Zealand. A guide to this information is given in Appendix 3. The documents have been deposited with the Hansard Society, where they may be inspected by appointment.

20. We express our gratitude to all those, in this country and overseas, who have helped us in this inquiry. We are especially grateful to those bodies and individuals – often very busy people – who prepared memoranda and met us for discussions. Whatever we conclude, the very publication of their evidence should create a better understanding of the problems of the legislative process and lead to its eventual improvement.

The Need for Change

21. There have been profound changes in the nature and impact of legislation in the last few decades, not least the growing volume and importance of European Community law. These changes, amounting in the view of some people to a legislative overload, have affected the working of Parliament and other aspects of law making in this country. Changing circumstances require new responses. It has therefore been our objective to consider to what extent and in what ways the legislative process for the making of statute law for the United Kingdom should be changed to meet the needs of the country today. Based on evidence of widespread anxiety on the part of those most directly affected about the way things are working at present, we make a large number of proposals. These should act as a catalyst for change.

22. We believe that action is needed in many areas, but what is most needed is the will to accept change and the momentum to carry it through. There may be doubts and disagreement about the details of our proposals, but above all **we hope that our conclusions and recommendations may stimulate further debate, open up the argument, and get the thinking moving.** If our Report helps to bring this about, we will have achieved our objective.

Chapter 2 – The Overall View

Outline of the Legislative Process

23. The legislative process has been described and analysed in a number of academic works and legal text books[1]. Here we outline its main features which form the structure of our Report.

Primary and delegated legislation

24. Statute law which is made in this country (so excluding European Community law, which we consider in Chapter 8) is contained in two different basic sets of documents, made under differing authority, but with absolutely equal binding force as far as the citizens or bodies to which it applies are concerned. Primary legislation is contained in Acts of Parliament, enacted by the Queen in Parliament following passage by both Houses[2] and not subject to challenge by the courts[3]. Delegated legislation is made by Ministers under powers given by Acts of Parliament; it is (nearly always) set out in the form of a statutory instrument which may or may not be subject to parliamentary proceedings. The exercise by a Minister of his power to make delegated legislation may be challenged in the courts.

Stages in the legislative process

25. It is convenient to identify six stages in the legislative process for Government bills.

26. The first stage is the **initiation of legislation.** Bills may be initiated for many reasons and may emerge from a range of sources. It is not fruitful to define these too precisely – there is much overlap and mixing of parentage – but the origins of legislation include political commitments set out in election manifestos or stated at party conferences; ministerial responses to new political challenges or emergency situations; international requirements; proposals of the two Law Commissions; recommendations of Royal Commissions, select committees or other inquiry bodies; parliamentary debates; studies made within Government departments; decisions by courts or observations by judges drawing attention to some apparent defect in the law; and annual or other routine requirements (sometimes important, as is the Finance Bill). The origin

---

1　See, for example, S. A. Walkland, *The Legislative Process in Great Britain* (Allen and Unwin, 1968); David R. Miers and Alan C. Page, *Legislation* (Sweet and Maxwell, 2nd ed. 1990); F.A.R. Bennion, *Statute Law* (Longman, 3rd ed. 1990); and Michael Zander, *The Law-Making Process* (Weidenfeld & Nicholson, 1980).

2　Unless passed by the Commons alone and presented for Royal Assent under the Parliament Acts 1911 and 1949.

3　Except in respect of compliance with European Community law, see Case C 213/89 (Regina v Secretary of State for Transport , *ex parte* Factortame Limited (1990) 3 C.M.L.R. 867.

of any policy which requires legislation strongly influences the conduct of the various stages of the legislative process.

27. Once Ministers have agreed on the need for legislation, the second stage of the process – **the preparation of legislation** – can go ahead. A bill team is assembled and the details of policy are progressively developed within or between Government departments.

28. At this stage there may be consultations with outside bodies affected by the proposed legislation or with various pressure or interest groups that wish to influence its content. These may be largely informal, or more formally may require responses to Green Papers or other consultative documents. As a result of these consultations, or of new thoughts by Ministers and within departments, policies may be further refined; additional, more detailed policies may be grafted on to the original concept; and practical questions, such as the problems of implementing or enforcing the legislation, will come to the fore and produce still further matters for consideration. Many of these additions and refinements may be made at a late stage in the bill's preparation. In general the original simple policy proposal is liable to begin to look far more complex as time draws nearer for a bill's publication. This second stage has been well described as "putting the bones on the skeleton".

29. Approval for the inclusion of a bill in the Government's legislative programme has to be obtained from the Future Legislation Committee of the Cabinet. This approval gives the necessary authority for the third stage in the process, when the **drafting** of the bill is done. Preparation and consultations continue within the departments concerned (or in some cases, for shorter or more urgent bills, it may only start after the Future Legislation Committee's decision), but the departmental administrators can now give their departmental lawyers details of what they want to achieve and the lawyers can translate this into legal requirements for additions to or amendment of the current statute law. Their requirements are expressed in instructions to Parliamentary Counsel who actually draft the text of the bill.

30. There are 32 draftsmen in the Parliamentary Counsel Office, including those seconded to the Law Commission (Scottish draftsmen who draft Scottish bills are employed separately in the Lord Advocate's Department). The head of the Parliamentary Counsel Office is the First Parliamentary Counsel, who is directly responsible to the chairman of the Future Legislation Committee of the Cabinet (currently the Leader of the House of Commons) for delivering the Government's programme of legislation, as agreed by that Committee. Individual Ministers are ultimately responsible for the wording of the bills they present to Parliament, but it is rare for Ministers to insist on a form of words against the advice of Parliamentary Counsel.

31. When the drafting of a bill has been completed, the bill must be finally cleared by the Legislation Committee of the Cabinet before it is presented to Parliament and published. This Committee is now usually chaired by the Leader of the House of Commons; the Lord Chancellor, the Attorney General, the Lord Advocate and the Chief Whips of both Houses are also members.

32. Legislation now enters the fourth stage of the process, the **scrutiny and passage of bills by both Houses of Parliament.** The details of the parliamentary processes are well known[1]. The majority of Government bills (23 out of 39 in session 1991-92) and especially most politically important or controversial bills, are introduced first into the Commons, and published. Each bill has a general debate on second reading; individual clauses and amendments may be debated in committee and on report; and it is read the third time and passed. The bill is then similarly scrutinised and passed by the Lords. Any amendments made by the Lords have to be agreed by the Commons before the bill can be presented for Royal Assent and become an Act of Parliament[2].

33. Some bills (16 in 1991-92) are introduced first into the Lords, and these may include bills of considerable size and complexity, such as the Copyright, Designs and Patents Bill 1987-88 and the Children Bill 1988-89. We provide an analysis of the bills introduced into the House of Lords in Appendix 4. The procedures on bills in the Lords are broadly similar to those in the Commons. Again the agreement of the two Houses is needed before a bill can be given Royal Assent.

34. The fifth stage is the **publication** of Acts of Parliament by H.M. Stationery Office, on behalf of the Statutory Publications Office, as soon as possible after they have been given Royal Assent. Acts which have been amended by later enactments are sometimes re-printed as amended. The Law Commission has a continuing programme of consolidation of previous statute law and each session a number of consolidation Acts are passed which do not change the law (though corrections of apparent errors and minor improvements may be allowed). Statute Law Repeal Acts are also passed from time to time to help tidy up the statute book by removing matter which is spent or no longer of practical effect.

35. All the public Acts of each year are published in several volumes of Public General Acts and Measures. The Statutory Publications Office also publishes Statutes in Force, an annual Index to the Statutes and an annual Chronological Table of the Statutes. These arrangements are currently under review (see paragraphs 441-445).

36. When an Act is passed and published, the legislative process does not stop. Delegated legislation may be made under that Act. The new law has to be complied with; various bodies will be concerned with its enforcement; many people, and ultimately the courts, will be concerned with its interpretation. Our sixth stage is therefore **post-legislative review** in the light of experience. Are the policies applied by the bill still desired or acceptable; what problems have

---

1 The legislative proceedings in both Houses, and the relevant procedures, are summarised in J A G Griffith and Michael Ryle, *Parliament* (Sweet and Maxwell, 1989), pp. 227-244 and 480-490. For a detailed examination of how the examination of legislation worked in practice in the two Houses between 1968 and 1971, and for proposals for reform, see J A G Griffith, *Parliamentary Scrutiny of Government Bills* (George Allen & Unwin, 1974)

2 Unless it is pushed through by the Government under the Parliament Acts 1911 and 1949, with the agreement of the Commons, despite the disagreement of the Lords, as happened with the War Crimes Act 1991.

there been in interpreting, enforcing, administering and complying with the Act (all these matters have a direct bearing on the preparation and drafting of legislation); are the orders, regulations etc. made under the Act working effectively? Such questions need to be answered to complete the legislative cycle.

Delegated legislation

37. The legislative process for the production and review of delegated legislation is somewhat different. This legislation springs from the requirements of primary legislation and not from independent policy choices. Its preparation and drafting (in the form of statutory instruments) is conditioned by the contents of the parent Act. The parliamentary processes, if there are any (some minor instruments are not subject to any formal parliamentary scrutiny) are quite different – either to approve a statutory instrument (the affirmative procedure) or to annul it (the negative procedure) – according to the terms of the parent Act[1]. Motions for annulment of statutory instruments are usually called "prayers". Delegated legislation is published separately from primary legislation. And review is encouraged by the fact that it is much easier to amend delegated legislation in the light of experience than it is to amend Acts of Parliament.

The process seen as a whole

38. A central theme of our inquiry is that the legislative process must be seen as a whole. Although it is convenient to list separate stages in the process, these are interrelated and interactive. The origins of a bill have a profound affect on its preparation and passage through Parliament; a measure insisted on urgently by the Prime Minister has a different momentum from one that has been dug out of some departmental filing cabinet to fill a gap in the programme. The preparation and drafting stages often overlap and bills frequently have to be re-drafted as a result of continuing consultations. Sometimes Parliamentary Counsel will draw attention to a practical, legal or even policy problem revealed by the process of translating policy requirements into language that will stand up in a court of law. Consultations, further thoughts and consequential re-drafting are frequently influenced by parliamentary scrutiny, and outside bodies can still influence the preparation of legislation by lobbying Members of both Houses at this stage. Finally the review of legislation by Government, Parliament and outside bodies, to see whether new legislation is needed, starts almost as soon as a bill becomes an Act or a regulation is made. One cannot say where the legislative process starts; it is a seamless robe.

39. The whole process is held together by the Government's legislative programme. This is decided by the Future Legislation Committee, in about March of each year, for the forthcoming Parliamentary session; sometimes a bill for a later session may also be approved, so that the department can work on it knowing that their efforts will not be wasted. The main bills to be passed are mentioned

---

1   For a description of the procedures for scrutiny of secondary legislation in Parliament, see Griffith and Ryle, *Parliament* , op. cit., pp. 244-247 and 488-489.

in the Queen's Speech at the beginning of each session. It is then the task of the business managers – the Leaders of the two Houses, and the two Government Chief Whips, closely assisted by the Secretary to the Chief Whip in the Commons – to prepare a programme for the passage of all these bills by the end of the session, and to exercise party discipline to maintain this programme as far as possible.

40. Although we will look at each stage of the legislative process on its own, we are impressed by the need, sometimes overlooked we fear, to assess the process as a whole. **In particular, we take this first opportunity of emphasising the Government's prime responsibility to seek to get a bill right while the bill is being prepared and drafted, not leaving it to be done by substantial amendments of its own when the bill is before Parliament.** We will return to this central theme in more detail in later Chapters.

European Community legislation

41. Several bodies, particularly the CBI (M 22) and the Institute of Directors (M 30), impressed on us the growing volume and significance of European Community legislation. For many people in industry and commerce, agriculture, transport, the financial markets and some of the professions, the impact of EC legislation is as great as or even much greater than that of UK legislation. We appreciate the importance of this development and of the interrelationship of the two bodies of law.

42. Our Commission was not appointed to examine the legislative process in Europe itself, nor is it within our remit to examine the scrutiny of EC legislation in this country or in Parliament (where the procedures have recently been revised). We are concerned with the affect of EC legislation on the UK legislative process. In particular, we have examined the implications for that process (on drafting styles for example) of the requirement to give legal force to European Community legislation in this country. We consider these questions more fully in Chapter 8.

The Volume of Legislation

43. Lord Howe of Aberavon has drawn attention on several occasions, most recently in an Address to the Statute Law Society[1], to the overloading of the legislative process by the passage of too much law. Others drew to our attention the burden imposed on them by the volume of legislation. The CBI said that the quantity of legislation could adversely affect its quality (M 22). The TUC complained about too many and too frequent changes in the law. The CBI, the Magistrates' Association and other bodies emphasised the difficulties their members had in assimilating the incessant publication of Acts and statutory instruments. Members of both Houses, and of all parties, have emphasised the problems for Parliament in finding time to deal with the legislative workload.

44. Thus the volume of legislation – primary and secondary – bears on the legislative process at almost all stages. What are the facts? The following table

---

1 Address by Sir Geoffrey Howe, QC, MP (as he then was) to the Statute Law Society, 8 May, 1991, to be published in a forthcoming issue of the Statute Law Review, Vol.13, No. 3.

shows the growth in the total volume of public Acts put on the statute book in this century (and see Appendix 7).

Volume of all Public General Acts, 1901-1991

Year.	No. of Acts	Pages	No. of Sections and Schedules
1901	40	247	400
1911	58	584	701
1921	67	569	783
1931	34	375	440
1941	48	448	533
1951	66	675	803
1961	65	1048	1087
1971	81	2107	1963
1981	72	2276	2026
1991	69	2222*	1985

* Printed on A4 paper which was larger than the size previously used, so requiring fewer pages.

45. However consolidation Acts are included in the table above and distort the picture to some extent. Consolidation Acts are often large (the Income and Corporation Taxes Act 1988 had 1038 pages, with 845 sections and 31 Schedules) and our researches show that on average, in the sessions 1987-88, 1988-89 and 1989-90, consolidation Acts were approximately three times as long as other Government Acts (excluding Consolidated Fund and Appropriation Acts). A better indication of the volume of primary legislation in more recent years is therefore given by the following table which indicates the volume of *new* public legislation by excluding consolidation Acts (and see Appendix 7).

Volume of Public General Acts 1985-1991, showing effect of excluding consolidation Acts

Year	No. of Acts	Pages	No. of Acts excluding cons. Acts	Pages excluding cons. Acts
1985	76	3233	65	1860
1986	68	2780	64	2310
1987	57	1538*	56	1269*
1988	55	3385	49	2047
1989	46	2489	43	2399
1990	46	2391	42	1743
1991	69	2222	61	2012

* The statute book from 1987 onwards has been printed on A4 paper which is larger than the size previously used, so requiring fewer pages.

46. Other statistics show the growth of new UK and English primary legislation only[1]. -

---

1   HL Deb., 24 January 1990, col. 1157 (w).

**Number of Pages of Legislation
(excluding consolidation and Scottish Acts)**

1974*	1360	
1975	1690	
1976	1400	
1977	790	
1978	830	
1979*	580	
1980	1470	
1981	1330	
1982	1360	
1983*	660	
1984	1485	
1985	1558	
1986	2174	
1987*	1131**	(A4 - 943)
1988	2170**	(A4 - 1809)
1989	2581**	(A4 - 2151)

* Election years.   ** Converted from A4 format for purposes of comparison.

47. Fuller information relating to these statistics is given in Appendix 7, with explanations of the variations in the volume of legislation. In particular the annual volume of legislation varies according to the stage of a Parliament, the policies of Governments and the incidence of general elections.

48. The volume of delegated legislation is also important. The following table shows the growth since 1951.

Volume of Statutory Instruments

Year	No. of General SIs	Pages
1901	156	N/A
1911	172	N/A
1921	727	N/A
1951	2335	3523
1961	2515	4524
1971	2167	6338
1981	1892	6521
1983	1966	6405
1984	2065	6062
1985	2082	6476
1986	2332	9048
1987	2279	6266*
1988	2311	6294
1989	2510	N/A
1990	2569	N/A
1991	2945	N/A

* Statutory Instruments from 1987 onwards have been printed on A4 paper which is larger than the size previously used, so requiring fewer pages.

Again, some qualifications regarding these statistics are made in Appendix 7.

49. In general, the annual number of Acts has remained broadly constant over the last forty years, but (even allowing for consolidation Acts) the annual volume appears to have increased significantly over the last forty years and comparisons with years before the Second World War are even more striking. The number of statutory instruments has also not changed greatly in the years covered by the table, but their annual volume has increased markedly.

50. Those who have to prepare, draft, consider or assimilate new legislation are understandably concerned about the problems created by its volume. However we note that many bodies – including some of those who feel over-burdened by the present legislative load – are often pressing for more legislation in areas where they have special concerns. To quote Lord Howe of Aberavon again: "we are making too much law – the system is overloaded", but "we are making too little law – because urgent statutory needs are being neglected" (he instanced delay in bringing forward the Charities Bill and a Friendly Societies Bill and failure to implement proposals from the Law Commissions (see paragraphs 494-495))[1].

51. It is also not easy to reduce the volume of legislation. In this century Governments of all parties have moved, by legislation, into areas that were formerly largely outside the responsibilities of government – social security, health services and town and country planning come to mind, to say nothing of nationalised industries. Unless a Government were to abandon completely areas of public life in which it is now a major participant, further legislation will continue to be needed to alter policies as Governments change or to modify the law in the light of changing needs. And even retreat from these areas would need legislation to repeal the previous laws.

52. Most important, it is the right – indeed the duty – of Government to seek to legislate in whatever ways it thinks desirable in the interests of the people it serves. **One cannot say, in general, that there should be more or less legislation; that is for Governments to decide. If the present volume of legislation is causing problems at various stages of the legislative process – and all our evidence confirms that this is so – the first requirement is not a reduction in that volume, but improvements in the process at those stages where it is under strain.** The kitchen should be big enough and properly equipped to satisfy the legislative appetite.

The Criticisms Received

53. Before we examine the various stages of the legislative process in more detail, we outline the main criticisms we received – from a wide range of bodies – which have prompted our conclusions and recommendations.

54. **The weight and extent of the criticisms received is perhaps the most notable feature of our inquiry.** We are sorry to see that many of the complaints made to and by the Heap Committee twenty-two years ago are still being repeated. It should also be noted that although these criticisms mainly relate to defects in

---

1   Address to the Statute Law Society, May 1991.

the way things are done – which is what our inquiry is about – many of the critics also offered examples of what they believed to be defective legislation which resulted from weaknesses in the legislative process; in the end, it is the quality of the product that most concerns the user. We will refer to some of these examples in later Chapters.

Initiation of legislation

55. We received few criticisms regarding the first stage of the process, the initiation of legislation. The choice of what legislation the Government should introduce is largely a matter of political judgement which must be left to the politicians. The only criticism of substance that we have considered relates to the neglect of Law Commission proposals, which we consider in Chapter 7.

Preparation of legislation

56. Nearly all representatives of outside organisations which are affected by legislation criticised the way consultations are conducted. While it appears that in some areas there is now more consultation than there was in earlier years, there were complaints that consultations are often too late, too rushed, too narrow and not thorough enough. Some bodies said that insufficient attention was given at this stage to the practical problems of how to implement and enforce legislation.

57. As a result of inadequate or defective consultation, it is argued, bills are too often introduced to Parliament "half-baked" and with a lot of the detail insufficiently thought out, as evidenced by the large number of Government amendments that are needed.

58. Adverse criticism was not universal and some good practices were drawn to our attention. We seek to draw on these when we examine the consultative processes in more detail in Chapter 3.

Drafting

59. The main criticism of the drafting of bills – made by outside bodies and by some parliamentarians – was of lack of clarity. Some critics were also concerned that purposes and principles are not set out in the texts of bills. The courts may have difficulty in interpreting the "intention of Parliament". Several people thought that drafting started too late and was often too rushed. Opinions differed on the extent to which detail should be included in bills or left to delegated legislation. There was some concern that the Parliamentary Counsel Office might be under-staffed. We examine all these matters in Chapter 4.

Parliamentary processes

60. Members of both Houses, as well as organisations which had experience of legislation before Parliament, consider that parliamentary processes are not well designed to secure the passage of better legislation. Opinions in this area were far from unanimous, but common complaints were that debates in the Commons and in committees emphasised political confrontation rather than scrutiny of practicalities and detail (this was particularly stressed by outside bodies); that the stages of bills were too rushed; that the timing of debates was unpredictable; that there was need for more direct contact between Parliament and the

informed public; that insufficient use was made of select committees, with powers to hear outside and expert evidence, for the examination of bills; and that there was inadequate scrutiny of delegated legislation.

61. Some people thought that better use could be made of the expertise of Members of the House of Lords. Lack of attention by Parliament to monitoring how Acts were working in practice was criticised. Some bodies drew attention to the difficulties that they had in getting access to meetings of committees on bills and in obtaining parliamentary papers for bills which concerned them. In general, there was little support for the way legislation is handled by Parliament today. We return to this central question in Chapter 5.

Publication

62. Bodies which are affected by legislation and professional people who have to apply legislation in the courts or elsewhere need to have the law at their fingertips and to have ready access to all changes in the law. We received considerable criticism regarding the publication of bills and statutory instruments. The main complaints related to delays in publication; the inadequacy of official re-publications of Acts and statutory instruments after their amendment by later legislation; the cost of accessing statute law; and insufficient provision of explanatory material with new or reprinted Acts. There was also demand for more consolidation bills. We consider these matters in Chapter 6.

Legislative programming

63. At the heart of the matter, holding the whole legislative process together, is the Government's legislative programme. We became aware of general concern regarding the present practice and approach. A number of people feared that there was too much emphasis on the speedy passage of legislation rather than on getting it right. Others believed that there was too rigid adherence to an annual programme in Parliament. Some critics regretted the absence of systematic time-tabling of legislation in the House of Commons; others took a different view. We consider these matters in Chapter 7.

Guiding Principles

64. In the light of the evidence given to the Commission, and noting the Government's wish, as expressed by the Prime Minister, to give "more power to the citizen" (see paragraph 1), we have agreed five central principles which guide and govern all the recommendations we make:

- **Laws are made for the benefit of the citizens of the state. All citizens directly affected should be involved as fully and openly as possible in the processes by which statute law is prepared.**
- **Statute law should be as certain as possible and as intelligible and clear as possible, for the benefit of the citizens to whom it applies.**
- **Statute law must be rooted in the authority of Parliament and thoroughly exposed to open democratic scrutiny by the representatives of the people in Parliament.**

- Ignorance of the law is no excuse, therefore the current statute law must be as accessible as possible to all who need to know it.
- The Government needs to be able to secure the passage of its legislation, but to get the law right and intelligible, for the benefit of citizens, is as important as to get it passed quickly.

These principles provide the themes of Chapters 3 to 7 of our Report.

Chapter 3 – Consultation

Laws are made for the benefit of the citizens of the state. All citizens directly affected should be involved as fully and openly as possible in the processes by which statute law is prepared.

Primary Legislation

The evidence

The need for consultation

65. Many organisations emphasised the fundamental importance of consultation in the legislative process. As the CBI said –

> *"business is concerned that it may operate in the best legal framework. To achieve this, a proper partnership is required to balance the experience of parties affected, knowledge of experts in the particular field and the objectives of lawmakers....The key to this partnership is communication, with the objectives clearly set out and a thorough consultation as early as possible in the legislative process. The more thorough the consultation the better the drafting that results, the less Parliamentary time wasted and the better the law enacted" (M 22).*

The Law Society, which has considered these matters in considerable depth and over several years, recommended that –

> *"in all but exceptional cases there should be full consultation with all interested organisations and bodies on the policy of proposed legislation before a bill is drafted" (M 36, para. 5.3).*

The Association of First Division Civil Servants (FDA), representing the experience and perspective of senior civil servants charged with preparing legislation, told us that –

> *"it is also desirable that legislation should be preceded by full consultation and where possible should command consent"*, although this was not possible on some political issues *(M 5, para.2).*

66. More specifically, Consumers' Association identified four valuable functions of consultation . It should improve the efficacy of legislation by providing a check on whether the proposed measure is technically adequate for its purposes, and whether it might have unforeseen and unacceptable side effects. It should lighten Parliament's load in various ways. It implements the principles of "open government". And open consultation can identify the views of all interested parties and not just those of the richer and more powerful organisations who are in the best position to lobby (M 23, para. 1).

67. In the experience of Consumers' Association, the central characteristic of the current consultation process is its diversity. There can be much consultation,

some or none; it can be general or detailed; it can be formal, with Green and White Papers, or it can be informal, consisting of no more than a few "soundings" on the telephone. It can, said the Association, "be a genuine request for help, or merely an attempt to legitimise proposals that the Government has already made up its mind to pass into law". The Association believed that this variation in practice is not simply due to the differing nature of different bills, but results from the absence of a coherent policy regarding the role consultation should play in the legislative process; civil service guidelines do not appear to be followed; and there are inconsistencies of approach between, and even within, Government departments and agencies and other statutory bodies. "This results", it said, "in a mixture of good and bad consultation practice, and, more fundamentally, in a distortion of the whole consultation process" (M 23, paras. 2.1 and 2.2).

68. As we will show, this central assessment is confirmed by the varying experience of other bodies involved in consultation with different departments. More specifically, most of the bodies from whom we received evidence commented on the extent, nature, timing and conduct of consultations on bills.

Extent of consultation

69. Some bodies, for example English Heritage (M 24), the National Trust (M42) and the Bank of England (M 6) had few or no complaints about the extent of consultation. The Institute of Directors found the British Government to be "very open". "Its approach to pre-legislative consultation with interested organisations is a model" (M 30, para. 21). The Association of Chief Police Officers (ACPO) found that the mechanisms for consultation with the police in many respects operate satisfactorily, although they also recommended some improvements (see below) (M 4). Some examples of the benefits of good pre-legislation consultation were given, for example by the British Medical Association (BMA) in respect of the Nurses, Midwives and Health Visitors Bill in 1991 (M 12) and by the BBC in respect of the Copyright, Designs and Patents Act 1988 (M 11, para. 7).

70. Some of the people or bodies that gave evidence, including the CBI (M 22, para.1) and the Institute of Chartered Accountants in England and Wales (the ICA) (M 29, para. 8), welcomed the increase in the extent of consultation in recent years. For example, the National Consumer Council said that the MAFF had consulted widely on recent proposals and improved its record in this field considerably (M 41, para 2.1). And the local authority associations (the Association of Metropolitan Authorities, the Association of County Councils and the Association of District Councils, who submitted a most helpful joint memorandum) were glad to see, very recently, some increase in the willingness of Government to consult on local government matters (M 37).

71. In contrast, Consumers' Association (M 23, paras. 2.3 and 2.4), the TUC (M 55, paras. 2-6), Shelter (M 51) and the Scottish Consumer Council (M 49) were concerned about the failure of Government to consult at all on some legislation or about insufficient consultation. The BMA found an increasing reluctance on the part of Government to consult on matters which are seen as being of major

significance to the Government, and instanced the recent NHS changes which were based, without a preliminary Green Paper, on a White Paper which was produced without consultation with any interested parties (M 12). Consumers' Association recognised that Governments might properly be unwilling to consult on the political objectives of some legislation, but this objection should not apply to consultations on how such objectives could best be achieved. Complaint was made that although there were White Papers setting out the Government's proposals for both the community charge legislation and the NHS reforms, the consequential bills were introduced without any attempt to seek the views of those most directly affected (M 23 para. 2.3.2). The Association feared that on other occasions there appeared to be a covert failure to consult. "Government and other public agencies sometimes go through the motions of consultation but pay no attention to the results" it said, and instanced the consultations on the compulsory competitive tendering provisions of the Local Government Act 1992, where the bill was passed by the Lords before the end of the consultation period (M 23, para. 2.4). The TUC came to similar conclusions about the consultations that preceded the Employment Act 1990 (M 55, paras. 5 and 6).

72. The local authority associations were particularly critical of the limited extent of consultation. One hundred and forty-three Acts with a direct application to local government in England and Wales were enacted between 1979 and May 1992, of which 58 contained major provisions, so local government's interest in the legislative process had been enormous. Indeed, a notable feature of recent policy-making had been the increased pace of change, particularly relating to education, "as new developments are superimposed on others which have barely been implemented". "In recent years", the associations said, "there has been a serious decline in the extent and nature of consultations and inquiry undertaken before legislation is proposed in Parliament"; they had pressed repeatedly for improved consultative arrangements. They welcomed the establishment in 1990 of a Review of Local Government to which they had been invited to contribute, but even then the results had been disappointing. The papers were superficial; there had been no real interchange of views; and many of the questions they had agreed at the outset to consider remained unaddressed eighteen months later. In general, the associations concluded -

> *"representative bodies of local authorities and similar organisations should be included within an agreed process and timescale of consultation with central government on all proposals which will become the subject of legislation", and "major changes of policy should be proceeded by open debate, based on a Green and White Paper wherever practicable" (M 37).*

73. Lord Howe of Aberavon would also welcome more consultation with interested bodies when legislation was being prepared. There had been extended consultations on taxation for married women, and as a result when the provisions were introduced, they passed through Parliament without difficulty. On the other hand there had been considerable problems in getting right other bills, which would have benefited from earlier publication in draft form for

consultations. One of the problems was that most legislation was in gestation for longer than the period of office of a Secretary of State, which made it difficult to secure the continuing concern of a single Minister, and he instanced legislation relating to town and country planning and broadcasting. There was often extensive pre-legislative discussion of major topics, but when the actual legislation came it was often too rushed. Much of the legislation dealing with local government had suffered from being treated in this way. For example, a range of possible reforms of the system of local government finance, including the poll tax (as it had originally been called) and other local taxes had been considered at length, with extensive use of consultations, in the early 1980s, but when the later community charge was agreed on, the legislation was rushed through with little consultation with those in local government who would have to implement the proposals.

74. The Independent Television Commission made a similar point in noting that the Broadcasting Bill was introduced to Parliament in 1989 without the type of thorough inquiry that had been used for broadcasting legislation in the past thirty years. Consequently many details remained to be worked out in the Bill (the number of clauses was increased from 167 to 204, and the Schedules from 11 to 22, as the Bill went through Parliament) and consultation was largely confined to detailed points. "The Bill as it was eventually presented to Parliament", concluded the Commission, "would undoubtedly have benefited from a period of prior exposure to scrutiny as a totality, with the opportunity for informed opinion to comment on it". This process was used on the Broadcasting Service Bill in Australia (M 27, paras. 7-9). The BBC's experience was similar. The Broadcasting Bill "was another example of a bill prepared in haste, policy not properly thought through and it became a question matter of getting the policy right during the passage of the Bill rather than improving it and refining it" (M 11, para. 5). We commissioned a case study of the passage of the Broadcasting Act 1990, which examines these matters in greater detail (Appendix 5). We give some other statistics illustrating the growing practice of amending bills in Parliament, at a fairly late stage, in paragraph 173.

75. The TUC was also concerned about the pace of change, particularly in local government and labour law, with separate industrial relations Acts in 1988, 1989, 1990 and (potentially) 1992. It thought this symptomatic of failure to research a problem fully in advance and devise a comprehensive solution; "'step-by-step' approaches may have their political merits", it said, "but the consequences for many people in the real world can be devastating" (M 55, para. 10).

76. Other bodies, including the Equal Opportunities Commission (M 25) and the Commission for Racial Equality (M 19), wished to be consulted more regularly on certain aspects of all legislation on which they had special expertise. The ACPO wanted more time for the police to advise the Government on both the operational policing aspects of proposed legislation and on its implications for police resources in terms of manpower, finance, equipment and training requirements; it feared that the resource implications of the Police and Criminal

Evidence Act 1984 had not been considered carefully enough. Otherwise the Act had stood the test of time well; the second Bill (the first had been lost at the 1983 general election) was much better than the original Bill as a result of there being more time for consultation (M 4, paras. 4, 5 and 7).

77. There are of course special factors – especially the need for some degree of secrecy on some (but not all) aspects of the Budget – that affect the extent and nature of consultation on the intended provisions of the annual Finance Bill. Large organisations such as the Institute of Directors, with a major and continuing concern with tax legislation, are fully consulted on proposed tax legislation and work closely with officials on expected provisions of Finance Bills (M 30, paras. 5-7). The CBI said that consultation in the tax field had become more widespread, though by no means universal. The need for the fullest possible consultation on major tax changes, with the publication of Green or White Papers, was now widely accepted and consultation on lesser points by the Inland Revenue had become far more general in recent years. The CBI had drawn up detailed proposals for further improving the process (M 22, para. 1 and Appx. A). Its main complaint was that once the Finance Bill was drafted, the process became too rushed. The ICA told us that the representations it made in the fiscal field largely concerned the problems of implementation and other technical aspects. There was particular danger from long and complex legislation where, with the speed with which bills were passed, matters might slip through without adequate consideration. More top level consultation with experts was needed to get bills right.

78. Evidence from other quarters claimed that there was too much Budget secrecy. Mr Ralph Instone, QC, an expert on company and fiscal law, argued that failure to consult had led to nonsenses on the statute book and that consultations should start with the publication of tax legislation (excluding changes in tax rates) in provisional form at least four weeks before the Budget. He said that the Inland Revenue should recognise, as the DTI has long since done, the advantages of widespread consultation on proposed legislation (M 32). Consumers' Association complained of "a quite unnecessary degree of secrecy" (M 23, para. 2.3.3). The CBI told us that there was relatively open consultation at the earlier stages, but that was followed by silence until the Finance Bill was presented as a fait accompli ; more openness was needed the whole way through the process.

Stages of consultation

79. Opinions on the best stage for consultation varied. The Society of County Secretaries put it to us that there was a need for more advance notice of proposed legislation, on the lines of the consultations initiated by the Law Commission. The TUC argued that consultation should start at the earliest possible stage, even before a Green Paper was prepared, to identify the problems which legislation was designed to overcome. The BMA expressed a similar preference. The ABI and Lloyd's said that it would be helpful if departments were more open with trade associations on Government thinking. Consultation at an earlier stage, which had proved valuable when working on Law Commission proposals, would enable them to brief Government

departments on the insurance background to proposed legislation; they had been able to do this, at short notice, on the Dangerous Dogs Bill in 1991 (M 3, paras. 2.1 and 2.2).

80. Consumers' Association argued that if consultation takes place, as it sometimes does, only towards the end of the preparation of legislation, the scope for implementing consultees' suggestions is inevitably much diminished; it was important to have full consultation before drafting of a bill began. However consultation should not be terminated too early as examination of bills that are more or less fully-formed can result in improvements to details and reduce the need for numerous amendments in Parliament (M 23, para. 2.6). In effect, it (and the Law Society (M 36, para 5.1)) argued for two stage consultations – corresponding to the preliminary and final drafting stages of the preparation of a bill – with separate consultation documents being issued at both stages (M 23, para. 3.2.1 to 3.2.4). The National Trust emphasised to us that bills (for example the recent Charities Bill) were often much more detailed than White Papers and that present processes left little time for consultation on details. And the Society of County Secretaries spoke of their concern about new ideas being introduced at a late stage, as had happened on the Children Bill; this had left little time for consultations with interested parties.

81. The Equal Opportunities Commission would also like to see more consultation prior to the drafting stage (M 25). The Child Poverty Action Group warned of the dangers of consulting at an early stage in only very broad terms, but equally of the limitations of consultations which were confined to the White Paper stage, when representations were restricted to practicalities and did not affect policy (as happened, it said, in regard to child support proposals) (M 15). The Legal Adviser to the BBC, with previous experience as a Government lawyer with the Department of the Environment, said that White or Green Papers were frequently being prepared at the same time as instructions were being given to Parliamentary Counsel which made it difficult to accept proposals for change in the light of comments received, and that departmental lawyers were brought in at too late a stage to be able to advise effectively on whether policy was achievable in legal terms (M 48, paras. 5 and 6).

82. Much evidence favoured more consultation on draft bills or, recognising the pressures of time and the limited resources of Parliamentary Counsel, at least on some draft clauses. Consumers' Association welcomed the inclusion of a draft bill in the Commonhold consultation paper issued in 1990 (Cm. 1345) (M 23, para. 3.2.4). The BBC would also like to see the publication of draft bills for scrutiny by experts in advance of their introduction to Parliament (M 11, para. 8). The Director of the Community Council for Somerset supported this idea, saying that some "howling errors" had got into the Charities Bill and the poll tax legislation which could have been avoided if "those of us on the ground" had been able to see the proposed bill in draft form (M 20). ABI and Lloyd's had found, when consulted on Finance Bill proposals, that publication of draft clauses was of the utmost value (M 3, para. 2.2). The CBI said that although the DTI were good on preliminary consultation, there was not enough consultation

on the drafting of bills. It and the ICA favoured the publication of draft clauses, particularly on purely technical points, in advance of the Finance Bill (M 22, Appx. A, and M 29, para. 15). Both the Institute of Directors and the BMA would welcome the publication of draft bills, as was done by the Law Commissions.

83. Mr Tony Benn, M P (who had published a draft Electricity Bill when he was a Minister in 1979) said that where possible bills should be published in draft before their presentation to Parliament, and Lord Renton suggested that the departmentally-related select committees of the Commons might be encouraged to consider bills in draft at that stage (M 47, para (c)). Mr Alan Beith, M P, thought that more discussion on draft bills would be desirable, and that some of the clauses of the Finance Bill should be published in draft for discussion before the Budget. Mr Edward Mercer, a solicitor in private practice, wrote of the advantages he and others had experienced in being able to comment, without too much rush, on the draft clauses of the Copyright, Designs and Patents Act 1988 as they were published in advance of the Bill's presentation to Parliament. He contrasted this favourably with the way the Broadcasting Bill was hastily amended in 1990 without affected bodies having a proper opportunity to consider the content or drafting of the new provisions (M 39, paras. 2 and 3).

84. The Government Affairs Group of the Institute of Public Relations said that representations to MPs after a bill was published were not always satisfactory and could result in poor legislation being put on the Statute Book. It recommended that, for major bills, after preliminary consultations the Government should publish a "Green Bill", comprising the proposed legislation in draft form, for further scrutiny and consultation (M 31, para. 2 a). The Scottish Consumer Council made similar points (M 49).

Time allowed for consultation

85. Many bodies, including the TUC, the Law Society, the Magistrates' Association (M 38), the National Trust (M 42), Shelter (M 51), the BBC (M 11, paras. 5 and 8), the British Railways Board (M 13), the Community Council of Humberside (M 21), the National Consumer Council (M 41, para 2.3) and the Industry and Parliament Trust (M 28), criticised the way that consultations are often rushed. The National Trust gave two examples of bills having to be amended hastily in Parliament because of inadequate time for consultation at the preparation stage (M 43). The ICA, having commended the DTI and Inland Revenue for consulting on many matters, said that the increase in consultation had appeared to reduce the time allowed for consultation, especially on draft clauses, and instanced to us consultations on the Friendly Societies Bill 1991-92 (M 29, paras. 8 and 9).

86. Short deadlines are a real problem for many bodies, especially those which have to consult their members and experts or even conduct some research. The local authority associations and their members have long been concerned about the frequent failure of Governments to allow adequate time for this. One example of rushed consultations was on the Housing Act 1988, where the White Paper was published before consultation documents were issued and the bill was given

a second reading in the Commons before the end of a consultation period of only four weeks (M 37).

87. Consumers' Association had analysed 100 consultation documents issued in the first five months of 1991; most of these set a deadline for responses, but in about 10% of cases this was within three weeks or less (in four cases the time allowed was a week or less) and a further 20% of documents had a four week deadline. In its experience six weeks was a reasonable time to allow for responses, though smaller and less well resourced organisations might need a little longer; the three month consultation period allowed by the Lord Chancellor's Department for its proposals on Commonhold had been particularly welcomed as it gave time for research and surveys which enabled the Association to give a better response (M 23, para. 2.7).

88. The Scottish Consumer Council was concerned that the time allowed for responses to consultative documents was getting shorter; it usually found that a three-month deadline was needed to consult all those affected (M 49). The ABI and Lloyd's also complained of too tight deadlines in Government consultation papers (in contrast with those issued by the Law Commissions). Short deadlines should not be imposed merely for the sake of speed: "it is better for legislation to be clear and workable than for it to be enacted at the earliest possible opportunity and, before long, have to be changed by further legislation or interpretation by the courts" (M 3, para 2.1).

89. The ACPO gave recent examples of inadequate or rushed consultations, leaving little time for in-depth consideration, especially of the problems of implementing the legislation. The very short period for consultation on the Dangerous Dogs Act 1991 meant that the Home Office had had to issue further guidance on the operation of the Act (M 4, para. 7). And if there had been less hurried consultation on the Aggravated Taking Without Consent Act 1991, where the offence was already covered by existing legislation, "a more efficacious approach within that legislation might have been found" (M 4, para. 7). The ACPO said that Road Traffic legislation had often been rushed through Parliament and as a result further amending legislation was sometimes needed in a hurry; this left a period of uncertainty before the amendments were passed. The Department of Transport tried to be helpful in putting matters out for consultation, but a minimum of eight weeks was needed for considered responses and sometimes only eight days had been allowed, we were told. The ACPO also criticised the way important provisions were sometimes added to bills at a late stage, without enough consultation with the police, as happened with the Public Order Act 1989, when additional provisions relating to gypsies and travellers were hurriedly announced following disturbances at Stonehenge, and on the Road Traffic Act 1991 where a section was added in the Lords (placing a requirement on the police to vet prospective taxi drivers) without any warning to the police or any consultation (M 4, para. 8).

90. In contrast with some criticisms of inadequate time being allowed for preparation of responses, the CBI was happy to note improvement in the time allowed by the DTI in relation to company and consumer law (M 22).

91. Sometime consultations start too late. The British Railways Board complained that departments did not start consultations with affected bodies in sufficient time, although there had been some improvement recently; the DTI had been one of the worst offenders (M 13). The National Consumer Council said that consultation, on what information should be published relating to school league tables, took place after the Education Schools Bill 1991-92, setting out this information, had been published (M 41, para. 2.3).

92. Consultation can also be conducted at an inappropriate time, such as over a holiday season, as happened on the implementation of the Planning and Compensation Act 1991 (M 37) and in respect of the Education Reform Bill 1987 (M 12). The National Trust also made this complaint (M 42).

Breadth and balance of consultation

93. Consumers' Association was concerned about the danger of too much weight being given to the representations of well-established organisations that were in regular contact with their departments at all stages ; other groups and interests tend to be brought in at a much later stage. Government should compensate for the ability of some groups to advance their interests more effectively than others. A parallel concern was of unbalanced representation on advisory bodies that play an influential role in the early stages of the legislative process; producer interests tended to be over-represented (M 23, para. 2.9). The National Consumer Council made the same point (M 41, para 2.6).

94. The Law Society spoke to us of the need to ensure that all interested and affected parties were consulted, not just those most obviously involved. The National Consumer Council was concerned about smaller bodies, with something to contribute, being left out of consultations by the DoE on housing matters. It believed that the practices of departments should be more consistent and rigourous, and recommended a series of steps, including the compilation of lists of those interested in various fields, to ensure that bodies were not overlooked (M 41, para. 2.1).

95. Several bodies, including the CBI (M 22, Appx. A), the ICA (M 29, paras. 16 and 17), the Law Society (M 36, paras. 5.5 – 5.9) and the Bank of England (M 6) wished to see more consultation with technical experts at an early stage of a bill's preparation.

Methods of consultation

96. The local authority associations regretted that Royal Commissions or committees of inquiry were no longer appointed when major changes of policy were being considered; bills to reform local government finances and to abolish the GLC had been introduced without such prior inquiry (M 37). Lord Renton also pointed out the value of Royal Commissions and departmental committees in giving time to study problems in depth (M47, para (c)).

97. The local authority associations also regretted the decline in the use of the Green Paper/White Papers system which opened up consultative opportunities, with fewer White Papers being issued and the dropping of formal Green Papers in favour of looser consultative documents (see Appendix 8). For example there

had been no White Paper on any of the school-related proposals – such as the introduction of the National Curriculum, devolved school budgets and the abolition of the ILEA – in the Education Reform Act 1988 (M 37). The Independent Television Commission complained to us that the purposes of the Broadcasting Bill had not been adequately stated to those concerned; the Government should be required to explain such purposes in terms intelligible to laymen. They would also like to see publication of the proposed time-table for implementing legislation, and to be consulted on the practical consequences of such a time-table.

98. The local authority associations also regretted a change in the nature of White Papers; they had become multi-coloured glossy booklets promoting the policy concerned without reference to alternatives and with less discussion of the issues than in earlier years. They contrasted the "Rates" White Paper of 1983 (Cmnd. 9008), which gave much background information and discussed the pros and cons of the options, with the 1991 White Paper on "Education and Training for the 21st Century" (Cm. 1536) which was made up of assertions without relevant statistics or reasoning (M 37). The TUC was likewise critical of the 1989 Green Paper, "Unofficial Action and the Law", which was the basis for consultations on the Employment Bill of 1990; it was too vague (M 55, para. 5).

99. The National Consumer Council found that some consultation documents were not presented clearly and precisely (M 41, para. 2.2). Consumers' Association said that a consultative document should highlight the specific questions it wished consultees to address; this had been well done in the documents issued by the Department of Transport on Motorway Service Area Deregulation and by the DSS on Changes to the State Pension Age. It would also help if departments produced brief, clause by clause explanations of the proposed provisions in consultation documents relating to bills (M 23, paras. 2.5.4 and 2.5.5). The ABI and Lloyd's said that on occasions they found it difficult to understand the Government's intentions in consultative documents, as with the draft regulations on conveyancing under the Courts and Legal Services Act 1990 (M 3, para. 2.1). The Community Council of Humberside would like consultation papers to include summaries which are geared to the general public and could be used in newsletters (M 21). The National Trust was concerned about lack of co-ordination between sections of Government departments, who sometimes published separate consultation papers when one consolidated document would be preferable (M 42).

Openness of consultation and Government's response

100. Consumers' Association believed that lack of information added to the impression that some consultation was spurious; there should be more feedback from Government departments, with bodies being informed, before the end of the consultations, on the effect their representations had had on the proposed legislation or why their proposals had been rejected. However it welcomed the increasing practice of departments – MAFF in particular had started doing this – of seeking consultees permission for publication of their comments; this should

be normal practice. Another current example of good practice was the feedback consultees were receiving from the Home Office on the progress of negotiations on the EC Directive on Data Protection (M 23, para. 2.5). The ABI and Lloyd's also complained of lack of feedback; little information was published about the views of consultees, and little information was given of the departments' reactions to the representations they had received (M 3, para. 2.1).

101. Shelter (M 51), the CPAG (M 15) and the National Consumer Council (M 41, para. 2.4) argued that the Government should publish the results of consultation exercises, including the nature of the responses (unless the consultees objected) and the Government's replies, as is required for representations by the Social Security Advisory Committee (SSAC). The Scottish Consumer Council pointed out the value of Government departments publishing lists of those who had been consulted so that attention might be drawn to other bodies which might be invited to respond; this was not always done (M 49). Mr Maurice Frankel, Director of the Campaign for Freedom of Information, set out proposals for achieving more openness in the consultative process, which were designed to secure the early publication – subject to certain limited exceptions – of all inputs which the Government receives from outside bodies relating to proposed legislation, and the Government's own assessments of the likely impact of its proposals (M 14).

102. Others were less critical. The National Trust was "reasonably content" with Government responses to its recommendations on the details and technical aspects of proposed legislation; it had more difficulty on proposals stemming from major policy decisions or ideological presumptions (M 42). The CPAG said that its consultations with the Social Security Advisory Committee (SSAC) had proved useful and that in recent years – though not in the 1980s – the Government had decided to modify several proposals after consulting the SSAC (M 15).

Administration and expense of consultation

103. The local authority associations would like all bills affecting them to be supplied direct to local authorities; this would assist discussions with their members, speed the consultative processes and enable local authorities to begin considering how to implement the legislation several months earlier (M 37). The Magistrates' Association complained that Government departments often did not provide enough copies of bills and consultation papers; it had to buy additional copies from HMSO, at considerable expense, to send to its members (M 38). The Law Society drew our attention to the expense of papers, including bills and Acts; the Citizens Advice Bureaux had had to pay £400 for working copies of the Social Security Bill. The Community Council for Humberside, and other bodies in rural areas with no easy access to large libraries, had difficulty in obtaining relevant documents, including bills and Acts. Furthermore, consultation documents were not properly publicised or circulated (M 21).

104. The Scottish Consumer Council drew attention to the difficulties representatives of people affected by legislative change in Scotland had in lobbying effectively in London (M 49).

An overall view

105. The general approach of many of the bodies who gave evidence was that there was need for a careful, overall review of what consultations were intended to achieve and of how they could best be conducted. Consumers' Association expressed this most specifically. It believed that improvements would be brought about by the standardisation and promotion of good practice, rather than by introduction of radical changes. There was no need for rigid, multi-staged consultation procedures to be used in all cases – diversity of legislation and its preparation required flexibility – but a more planned approach related to the desired outcome was needed. The Association suggested that "the exercise of discretion as to when and how to consult should be subject to carefully considered guidelines, and the whole process of the preparation of legislation made more open to public scrutiny so that compliance with such guidelines can be monitored" (M 23, para. 3.1). It detailed what those guidelines should cover (M 23, para. 3.2).

The Government's and civil servants' experience

106. We received some indication of how Government departments and senior civil servants see the part that is, and should be, played by consultation within the legislative process.

107. We had a useful meeting with officials from HM Customs and Excise and the Board of Inland Revenue. Inland Revenue sought representations in response to consultative documents; they issued draft clauses for consultation if time permitted; and there was further more detailed discussion on technical matters. After the Finance Bill was published, they held an open day when they got specialists together from a wide range of bodies for a detailed explanation of the Bill. Subsequently many bodies made representations and as far as possible these were discussed with those bodies. Complex matters like taxation were not easy to describe and, even after legislation was passed, there would be further explanations issued by leaflet, on television etc. to affected bodies.

108. Inland Revenue had, with the approval of Ministers, tried to expand their consultations. Twenty-two clauses of the 1992 Finance Bills had been the subject of consultation, and there had been six consultative papers. There was a wide range of consultations on tax law, but it was impossible to generalise about the nature of consultations (for example, consultations with oil companies were very different from consultations on the taxation of husbands and wives). Inland Revenue recognised the problems for interested bodies, especially when consultations appeared to be rushed, but it was often important to close a loophole in tax law as quickly as possible and there was sometimes political urgency for other provisions.

109. Before the Second World War, Customs and Excise had historically dealt with few internal taxpayers (mainly excise traders) direct, but Purchase Tax had widened the range of bodies they had to deal with and VAT had extended it much further. Consultation with a wide range of trade and professional bodies on tax matters was now the norm. Changes in the law certainly caused problems

for tax payers; for example some of the legislation under the new single market was long and difficult and, when first published, was understood by very few people. They had not found it easy to get traders to understand the purposes of administrative changes in customs duties and taxes, but Customs and Excise's public relations had greatly improved over the years. They recognised the anxieties of a number of outside bodies regarding the processes of consultation and they had had discussions with some of these bodies, including the CBI, on the processes themselves.

110. The FDA, representing senior civil servants, was critical of the nature and quality of some of the responses that departments received when they sought to consult outside bodies. Proposed legislation that would adversely affect an organised and well-resourced interest group often drew few responses and these tended to concentrate on issues of principle, often at a political level, rather than on practicality. Even where the consultees included a large interest group, they often did not speak with a single voice and failed to present their views to best effect. "Ministers are liable to disregard responses to consultations if these are divided, if they clearly derive from an opposition party stance, or if they are ill prepared", the FDA said. By contrast, some trade and professional interest groups were able to be effective by working through a single organisation, commenting mainly on technical points and maintaining close contacts with Ministers and officials. Perhaps more time was needed, the FDA considered, for full evaluation of conflicting points of view (M 5).

111. For various reasons, the FDA concluded –

> "*frequently....when a firm policy proposal emerges, as a Green or White Paper or other ministerial announcement, any consultation with those affected will have made little impact on development of the policy, and little attention will have been given to how the policy is to be given effect in legislation*" *(M 5, para. 9).*

At the later stage when a bill is being drafted, consultation with outside interests is unlikely to be officials' top priority. Except where consultation is in effect mandatory, "consultation may be forgone or at best rushed", especially if consultees' views are seen as predictable (M 5, paras. 7-9 and 14).

Research findings

112. We commissioned a study of the extent to which Green Papers and other consultative documents have been issued by Government departments in recent years (Appendix 8). Although the statistics cover all types of papers, and not just those specifically concerned with proposed legislation, a clear picture emerges of a very considerable increase in the use of consultative documents, from 11 in 1976 to a peak of 288 in 1988 and 232 in 1991; the number of Green Papers issued up till 1988 ranged from 3 to 15 a year, but none have been issued since 1988.

Conclusions and recommendations

The need for consultation

113. Not all the people and bodies we received evidence from were critical of all

aspects of the consultation process in preparing Government bills, and our attention was drawn to good practices and successful products. However, **the overwhelming impression from the evidence is that many of those most directly affected are deeply dissatisfied with the extent, nature, timing and conduct of consultation on bills as at present practised.** We recognise that some of the adverse criticisms of the Government's handling of consultations on particular bills reflect disagreement with Government policies or disappointment that the representations made by the critical body were not accepted by the department concerned. But the criticisms cannot be discounted on these grounds. There is substantial, objective evidence of failure to consult, inadequate time for consultation and subsequent unworkability of legislation. **We believe that the Government must heed this criticism and seek to meet it.**

114. We also believe that it would be in the Government's own interest to respond positively to the criticisms. Ministers must wish their legislation to work as well as possible, whatever the policies; this is more likely to be achieved if they heed the experience and advice of those who will have to make it work. One of the most depressing aspects of our evidence was the repeated complaint by representatives of such bodies as local authorities and the police (see paragraphs 71, 72, 76 and 89) of insufficient or unsatisfactory consultation on how an Act would actually operate. It may well be that the collapse of the community charge legislation resulted largely from the Government's failure to ensure, by discussions with those most directly involved, that it would be workable in practice and that the charges could be collected (paragraphs 73 and 96). There were similar problems, for the same reasons, with the Dangerous Dogs Act 1991 (paragraph 88). **We recommend that the Government should always seek the fullest advice from those affected on the problems of implementing and enforcing proposed legislation.**

Getting the bill right

115. It would also be of great help to Governments if they could get a bill as right as possible before it is introduced into Parliament. That should be seen as their first responsibility, as well as reducing the need for amendment and re-drafting as the bill goes through the two Houses, and so minimising the amount of parliamentary time required. Many people have complained of bills being introduced "half-baked", with a lot of their provisions not fully thought through (see paragraphs 74 and 80-84).

116. We are convinced that a central problem of the legislative process is that far too many bills are introduced into Parliament in a state that is recognised – even, we suspect, by Ministers – to be less than perfect. Consultation is sometimes still continuing; detailed drafting has not been completed; further matter is yet to be added; many Government amendments are therefore required. And while the extent of parliamentary amendment to a bill is not necessarily an indication that the bill was introduced in a defective form – new points may be raised in Parliament or elsewhere, new situations may have arisen, parliamentary reactions to the original bill have to be heeded – all our evidence suggests that

in many cases Government amendments are necessary to remedy defects in the bill which were already known to those who prepared and drafted it. Therefore we also believe that too many bills are introduced half-baked.

117. At the heart of the problem is the inherent conflict between the need, for the assumed public good and for political impact, to get a bill on the statute book without unwanted delay – and some bills really are urgent – and the need to "get it right". In our view the latter is of first importance; defective or unenforceable legislation is of limited value to the citizens it is ultimately designed to benefit. As the Association of British Insurers and Lloyd's told us –

> *"it is better for legislation to be clear and workable than for it to be enacted at the earliest possible opportunity and, before long, have to be changed by further legislation or interpretation by the courts"* (M 3, para. 2.1).

We therefore note with some concern a statement by Lord Waddington, when he was Leader of the House of Lords, that –

> *additional or deeper scrutiny of bills in the Lords which succeeded in "improving the quality of the legislation eventually passed......would be unacceptable if this added to the overall time taken for the passage of a bill through the House."* [1]

We trust that this indication that, for the Government, speed has priority over quality in the passage of legislation (which admittedly was made in the limited context of the Lords' procedure) does not represent the considered view of Ministers in relation to the whole legislative process. **We believe that although some bills are inevitably required in a hurry, getting a bill right should always have priority over passing it quickly, and we recommend that the Government should publicly endorse this policy.**

118. In the search for "getting a bill right", we emphasise the great importance of the pre-parliamentary stages of the legislative process. It is not necessarily too late if defects have to be removed during the passage of a bill through Parliament, but it is highly undesirable to leave matters to that stage deliberately, and it is often not easy to tidy up or correct a bill in either House. It is even more undesirable for significant matter to be added at this late stage without proper consultation, as has happened too often, for example on the Broadcasting Bill 1989 (paragraph 74). 58 Government amendments were made to this Bill in committee in the Commons, and 503 on report; in the Lords a further 359 Government amendments were agreed in committee, 285 on report and 117 on third reading (Appendix 5). **We therefore recommend that the Government should make every effort to get bills in a form fit for enactment, without major alteration, before they are presented to Parliament; in the Government's review of the legislative process, this should be a first and overriding objective.**

119. In our view, getting legislation as right as possible at the pre-parliamentary stage must involve early and extended and full consultation with those most

---

1   Memorandum by the Lord Privy Seal to the Select Committee of the House of Lords on The Committee Work of the House (HL 35-II of Session 1991-92), Evidence, page 135.

experienced in the matters concerned or most directly affected by what the Government propose. As Lord Howe of Aberavon has recently said –

> *"we should do everything possible to promote advance identification, clarification and preparation of policy objectives, early instructions to Parliamentary Counsel and preliminary drafts. And we should accompany that by as much consultation as possible in the form of Green Papers, consultative documents, White Papers, draft bills and draft clauses"* [1].

These publications should be seen as a genuine exercise in consultation rather than opportunities for promoting the Minister's bill.

120. Several bodies from whom we took evidence spoke favourably of the work of the Law Commissions. We are also impressed by the quality of the work they do and by the way they do it. They consult widely and in depth. Their law reform bills appear to attract little criticism as far as their preparation and drafting is concerned – they seem to get their bill as right as possible before they report to Parliament – and they do important work on consolidating the statute law. Looking ahead, the time may come when the Law Commissions could play a more direct part in preparing less urgent and more technical legislation on behalf of Government departments. However that would be a significant change in their role and, as there are other problems relating to law reform bills and other work of the Law Commissions which need early attention (which we consider in Chapter 7), we do not make any recommendations on this matter at this time.

The extent of consultation

121. The value of proper consultation was emphasised by many of those who gave evidence. We are therefore greatly disturbed by some of the evidence we received. The three local authority associations, for example, said that –

> *"in recent years there has been a serious decline in the extent and nature of consultations and inquiry undertaken before legislation is proposed in Parliament"* (see paragraph 72).

Although we had evidence that in some areas consultation had sometimes been well conducted, and indeed had recently improved or increased in extent (see paragraphs 69-70, 77, 102 and 107-109 and Appendix 8), it is clear that elsewhere much more consultation – for the benefit of Government as well as of the bodies concerned – could be carried out.

122. We recognise that there is a price to pay for extended consultation. It is time consuming and could delay legislation; it requires more effort by departmental officials; it brings out differences of view which may be difficult to reconcile; it may raise expectations which later cannot be fulfilled and hence lead to disappointment and possible political criticism; it may provide a platform for political attacks on the policy. However none of these apparent disadvantages outweigh the advantages of "getting a bill right" and of establishing good working relations with those who are at the receiving end of legislation.

---

1   Address to the Statute Law Society, May, 1991.

Some Government departments, including the Inland Revenue and Customs and Excise, seem to have discovered the advantages, on balance, of consultation; others have practised it successfully on some bills; others have yet to make the same discoveries.

123. **We are convinced that proper consultation should play a central part in the preparation of bills, and we recommend that all Government departments should act accordingly.**

How should consultation be conducted?

124. The Government needs to give careful thought to how consultation should be conducted. Many of the critical comments we received related to the nature, staging, timing, content and administrative aspects of consultation, as well as to its extent. We realise that the best practices in each of these aspects must vary with the subject matter of the legislation, its urgency, and the degree of political commitment involved. Ministers and departments will wish to consult differently on each bill. Bodies involved in consultation also differ in their nature and approach – and in the resources on which they can draw – and will wish to make their own representations in different ways. The process will therefore have to be tailored to fit every bill.

125. We do not intend to recommend any precise pattern of consultation or to define steps that should always be taken. We do, however, suggest some guiding considerations, based on the evidence we have received, which we hope all departments would respect. We also realise that if the Government were to extend and develop consultation on the lines the bodies which gave evidence to us have urged, this would certainly require more time for the preparation of bills and would thus have major consequences for the Government's legislative programme. We only state our conclusions and recommendations on consultation itself at this stage. We return to the consequences for the legislative programme in Chapter 7.

126. As a starting point, we note the definition of proper consultation contained in a judgement delivered by Mr Justice Webster (quoted by the local authority associations (M 37)) –

> *"the essence of consultation is the communication of a genuine invitation to give advice and a genuine consideration of that advice.....to achieve consultation sufficient information must be supplied by the consulting party to the consulted party to enable it to tender helpful advice. Sufficient time must be given by the consulting to the consulted party to do that, and sufficient time must be allowed for such advice to be considered by the consulting party."*

Stripped of the legal foliage, this means that consultation should be open, honest, informed and un-rushed. How should these principles be applied in practice?

127. Broadly speaking, there are three levels of decision-taking during the preparation of bills. The first level is the identification of a problem that may require a legislative solution and determination of the relevant facts. The second level is the clarification of policy options and the choice of the policy to be followed. The third level is determination of the methods by which the policy

should be applied and of consequential practical questions such as appointment of administrative authorities, the expenses to be authorised, monitoring, enforcement and penalties. At this third level it will often be found that there are further policy decisions to be taken, and at all stages additional policy questions are liable to be raised or brought into the equation.

128. **Good consultation practice requires that when a bill is being prepared, bodies with relevant experience or interests – particularly those directly affected – should be given all the relevant information and an opportunity to make their views known, or to give information or advice, at each level of decision-taking.** Not all will wish to make representations at each stage – some bodies will be more concerned about policy; others with practical questions of application – but all should know what is going on and what the Government has in mind. This suggests that departments should be required to put out the fullest possible relevant information at each stage, together with invitations to comment. Possible steps would be: a Government statement that legislation was being considered on such-and-such a matter, and that comments and relevant information would be welcome; a Green Paper setting out policy options, with all the relevant facts, and arguments, and perhaps a preferred solution, and again requesting responses; and a White Paper setting out the Government's proposed policy and indicating how it is to be carried out, in both legislative and administrative terms, together with requests for comment on the practicalities, but not the policy.

More open consultation

129. We accept many of the points made by those who gave evidence on the need for broad, balanced and open consultation (see paragraphs 93-95 and 100-102). **Consultation should be as open as possible.** Normally public invitations to respond should be issued, so that all potential interests may be involved, not just the obvious ones or those known to the department. Or if certain bodies are specifically invited to respond to a consultation document, a list of all those invited should be issued so that any other body could ask to be included. Advisory bodies appointed by Ministers should be representative of all relevant interests. Government departments should be under an obligation to consult consumers as well as manufacturers

130. Some bodies, including the Law Society (M 36, paras. 5.5-5.7) and the Institute of Chartered Accountants (M 29, paras. 16 and 17) have argued for standing committees or advisory panels comprising organisations who are interested in certain areas of legislation and who would be automatically consulted on any bill being prepared in those areas. We recognise that these could be helpful in getting consultations going with minimum delay. However there are often some aspects of proposed legislation which directly affect a body outside the main stream of the bill, which would not be represented on such a panel; it would be important to ensure that consultation with members of a standing body did not become too exclusive and that other affected bodies such as consumers were not left out.

131. **Secrecy regarding the content and results of consultations should be minimised and feed-back maximised.** The Government should publish information of what consultations have been held at each stage, including lists of those consulted. The responses made to formal consultation papers should normally be published. Analyses showing the degrees of support for the various proposals put out by departments are desirable. The Government's own reactions to the responses they had received, including explanations why rejected ideas could not be accepted, should usually be published. Some of these steps are already being taken by some departments; they should become the norm. We return to this theme in paragraphs 148-152.

Better ways of consultation

132. Some major matters require fundamental consideration in depth of the basic policies concerned and of the need for and nature of further legislation. It was suggested to us that reform of local government finances, local government reorganisation and of changes of the law regulating broadcasting were cases in point; earlier Governments had appointed review bodies on these matters before introducing legislation but in the 1980s this had not been done . This is perhaps the most important form of consultation that can be held. **When major reviews are required of how the current law is operating and of the need for reform, we would welcome more frequent appointment of independent inquiries, including Royal Commissions. If the Government is not prepared to accept the advice of such inquiries, it would be expected to publish its reasons.**

133. Other earlier consultation will usually be based on Green and White Papers, or other formal documents. **Consultative documents should be as clear and precise as possible. They should be specific about the questions on which departments want responses, while leaving opportunity for bodies to put forward further ideas of their own on relevant points. Green Papers should set out the facts fully and, as far as possible, the options being considered. White Papers should normally be preceded by Green Papers. White Papers should, where possible, systematically detail changes from Green Papers, indicating why these changes had been made** (as was done in the White Paper preceding the Courts and Legal Services Bill (Cm. 740)). All this seems obvious, and is often done, but it seems that these basic ideals are not always achieved (see paragraphs 98 and 99).

Consultation on draft bills or clauses

134. An important issue to be considered is the extent to which Government departments should consult on actual drafts prepared by Parliamentary Counsel of bills or clauses, and the possibility of publishing such drafts before a bill is presented to Parliament. Before considering the pros and cons we must clear up one misapprehension.

135. The Law Society were under the impression that full consultation on a draft bill or clauses was in conflict with "parliamentary rules" which declare it a "constitutional impropriety" to disclose the precise contents of a bill before it

has been announced in the Queen's Speech and before MPs have had the opportunity to see it (M 36, para. 5.4). Indeed it was suggested that even some Government departments believed that there was such a rule, although others frequently do not observe it. The fact is that there is no such parliamentary rule. There is no standing order in either House which imposes such a restriction, and the laws of parliamentary privilege and contempt, which can apply to people outside Parliament, relate only to matters or actions which affect either House in the performance of its functions[1]. Erskine May's *Parliamentary Practice* describes the matters which have been declared to be contempts of the House of Commons, and makes it plain that prior publication of drafts of documents, such as bills, to be presented to Parliament by Ministers has never been held to be a contempt[2].

136. There is therefore no constitutional bar on Government departments circulating draft bills, or drafts of individual clauses which they are considering including in legislation, to interested bodies or experts and inviting their comments. Nor should Members of either House of Parliament resent such disclosures before bills are laid before Parliament; it would simply be designed as an aid to better consultation.

137. To what extent should such consultation be used? There are some obvious advantages in enabling bodies to look at the actual text of the proposed law and to see how it would affect them, and to draw attention, before the publication of a bill, to any problems which they detect in the light of their experience. Any improvements made to drafts on the basis of such representations obviously reduce the pressures for amendments during the passage of the bill through Parliament. These advantages are particularly apparent in respect of practical questions of implementation rather than policy; it is too late for outside bodies to raise policy questions at the drafting stage. In an ideal world, therefore, it might be desirable for all bills to be scrutinised in draft by interested bodies and outside experts before they go to Parliament, or indeed they might be published for everyone, including Parliament and its committees, to see. Some of our evidence pointed in this direction and there certainly was a widespread desire for more consultation on draft texts (see paragraphs 82-84).

138. The disadvantages are equally obvious. First, consultations on drafts would tempt some bodies to try to re-open questions of policy which had been resolved – or should have been – at earlier stages. Second, if departments were required to consult everybody on drafts, they might be tempted to defer all consultations to that stage to avoid duplication of argument, which would be contrary to our earlier recommendations. Third – and this disadvantage must

---

1 Erskine May's *Parliamentary Practice* , 21st edition, p.69 (London Butterworths, 1989).

2 It may be that the misunderstanding arises either from the Commons rule of contempt which prohibits the publication of proceedings of the House or its committees without the authority of the House, or from the way the Speaker has frequently (especially in recent years) deprecated some announcements of Government policy being made informally outside Parliament rather than to the House. Prior publication of *draft* bills or clauses are clearly outside these restrictions, as are publication of Green and White Papers.

weigh heavily with Ministers and officials, and indeed with those who are anxious for early change in the law – consultation on drafts would tend to postpone the presentation of the bill to Parliament, and so affect the parliamentary time-table and delay the bill's passage. Fourth, it could also cause problems for Parliamentary Counsel by extending the time that they spend on drafting before a bill's introduction; they have little time to spare.

139. We are not dogmatic. All bills are different and pose different problems. In some cases differences of view have been resolved, and problems solved, at earlier stages and there is nothing left to consult about at the draft stage. In other cases there may be many outstanding problems of detail or practicalities on which experienced bodies could profitably advise right up to the agreement of the final draft for presentation to Parliament. We note that the extent of consultation on drafts appears to be increasing. There was extensive consultation on the clauses of the Copyright, Designs and Patents Bill 1987-88. We were told that the Child Support Bill 1990-91 was first issued in draft for consultation, and this was welcomed by those involved. And there has been increasing consultation on draft clauses between the Inland Revenue and key financial and industrial bodies in respect of tax legislation; twenty-two clauses of the 1992 Finance Bills were circulated in draft for consultation (see paragraphs 77, 82, 83 and 107-109). However some of the bodies involved, including the CBI, would like this to be taken further.

140. In this, as in other matters, the Government should learn from experience and encourage departments to follow the best practice. We believe that, in principle, there should be as full consultation as is practicable on draft bills and clauses. Evidence suggests that this is now the time for a move forward. **We therefore recommend that departments should offer more consultations on draft texts, especially in so far as they relate to practical questions of the implementation and enforcement of legislation. We also recommend that the experience of the Inland Revenue in consulting on individual draft clauses of the Finance Bill be studied by other departments and adopted in other fields. And we further recommend that – as has sometime been done – where there is no great urgency for a bill, the whole bill might sometimes be published in draft in a Green Paper, as the basis for further consultation and possibly parliamentary scrutiny.**

Less hurried consultation

141. The biggest single complaint by bodies that are regularly consulted by Government departments was of consultation in a rush and of insufficient time being allowed for responses to consultation documents; requests for early responses sent out just before a holiday period were also criticised. There is a special problem for many national organisations, who have to consult member authorities, companies or other bodies all over the country, before they can respond properly (see paragraphs 85-92).

142. The Government must take these criticisms seriously. There is no point in consulting if you are not going to get the fullest possible information and well-considered advice; rushed consultations are almost inevitably going to

result in less helpful responses from those consulted. We fear that late and hasty consultation has sometimes suggested that the department concerned was simply going through the motions for public relations or political purposes – so that they could say that all relevant bodies had been consulted – without having a serious intention to pay much regard to the comments they received (see paragraph 71). We accept that in some cases the responses of some bodies may be predictable, or that their views will be contrary to Government policy and so not acceptable, but even here that is no excuse for not giving the body enough time to prepare its reply. The department may, after all, not have predicted the responses accurately, and even a body that is politically opposed to the policy of the bill may have useful points to make about how that policy should be carried out or on the details of the legislation.

143. We cannot say how much time should be given for consultation. It must vary from circumstance to circumstance. **We therefore recommend that Government departments should consult the main bodies concerned in each case and seek to agree how much time should be allowed for their responses to a consultation document.**

144. We have already recommended that there should be consultation at all stages of the preparation of a bill (paragraph 128). Enough time must also be allowed for departments to study the responses to consultations that they receive, to provide proper feed-back and to consider their own proposals in the light of those responses. All this means that consultation may have to start at an earlier stage than sometimes happens now. A flagrant example of lack of any real consultation as a result of delay was recently provided by what happened on the Civil Service (Management Functions) Bill 1992. The Council of Civil Service Unions was only told of the existence of this Bill eleven days before its second reading. When introducing the Bill in the Lords, the Minister, Earl Howe, admitted that the Council was informed of the Bill "as soon as it was finalised". But, as Lady Seear retorted, "consultation is not consultation if it takes place after the decisions have been made"[1]. Another recent example of belated consultation was the Education White Paper, published at the end of July 1992, which allowed only time for consultation during the summer holiday period on a major bill to be introduced into Parliament in the autumn. It is not acceptable, we believe, to defer consultation to such a late stage. However, when consultation should begin must depend on circumstances. **We simply recommend that consultation should not be delayed.** We consider in Chapter 7 one way in which earlier consultation could be made possible.

Government help for those consulted

145. If consultation is to be treated as a central part of the legislative process and as essential to "getting a bill right", as we believe it should, then the Government should give all possible practical help to those bodies whom it asks to participate in consultation and to other bodies who can contribute relevant experience, information or advice. A number of major organisations told us of

---

1   HL Deb., 15 June 1992, cols. 29-30.

the difficulties they sometimes had in obtaining consultation papers, or in obtaining enough copies to circulate to their members, and complained of the expense involved. The situation is worse for smaller and less well-funded bodies, especially those working outside London without access to big libraries (see paragraphs 103-104).

146. We believe that it is a democratic right of any body that plays a positive part in consultations designed to improve Government legislation to receive help from the Government in so doing. Such positive encouragement would also be in accord with the Government's desire to give more power to the citizen, as set out by the Prime Minister in the Citizen's Charter (see paragraph 1 of this Report). **We therefore recommend that bodies invited by Government departments to respond to consultative documents on proposed legislation, and other bodies with a *bona fide* interest, should be given, free of charge, as many copies of those documents as they can show they need.**

147. Furthermore, even after formal consultations on Green or White papers or other departmental documents have been completed, interested bodies will wish to see the results – they may wish to make further representations to departments or to lobby Members of Parliament – and again there was evidence of the difficulties and expense of getting hold of the documents (see paragraph 103). **We therefore recommend that bodies which have contributed to consultation on proposed legislation should be supplied, free of charge, with copies of the resulting bills, Acts and statutory instruments.**

Guidelines for Government departments

148. As Consumers' Association emphasised (M 23, para. 2.1), and as all our evidence brings out clearly, there is great diversity in the extent, staging, timing, nature and methods of consultation. Some departments on some occasions are very good; on other occasions consultation is totally inadequate or non-existent. We believe that the Government should seek to bring standards of consultation up to that of the best in recent years.

149. The first step in achieving this would be for a central department (perhaps the Cabinet Office) to study the evidence we have received and to consult with other departments, with those who have been critical about consultation, and with others who have long experience of the matter. A number of bodies praised the arrangements made by the Law Commissions for consultation. Although the Law Commissions operate on a much longer time-scale than most departments when preparing bills, and so can allow longer time for consultation (M 35, para. 2), the Government should also draw on their experience and ask themselves whether there are lessons they could learn from the Commissions.

150. **We recommend that**, on the basis of these consultations, **the Government should, drawing on best practice, prepare consultation guidelines which would be applicable to all Government departments when preparing legislation.** These guidelines should be influenced largely by the advice and experience of those most directly involved (we draw attention particularly to ideas on the content of guidelines submitted by Consumers' Association (M 23,

para. 3.2)), but naturally we hope that they would take account of our own conclusions in this Chapter.

151. We also draw attention to guidelines for consultation that have been drawn up in New Zealand by the Legislation Advisory Committee, a Government appointed body[1]. They are included in broader guidelines for the preparation of legislation published by the Committee and approved by the New Zealand Government[2]. Two features of these guidelines appear to us to be worth incorporating in any guidelines adopted in this country. First, the guidelines themselves are published so that all can see what sort of consultations departments are expected to carry out. Second the guidelines require that when a request is submitted to the Cabinet Legislation Committee for a bill to be included in the legislative programme, information has to be given of the consultations, within and outside government, that have been carried out or are planned, of the methods of consultation, of the results to date, and of by when consultations will be completed. And when a bill is finally submitted to the Committee the same information is again required, plus an explanation of why any consultations have not yet been completed.

152. It is important that compliance with the guidelines should be monitored. Publicity is the best way to achieve this (see paragraphs 129-131). **We recommend that:**

　(a) **the Government's guidelines on consultation should be published;**

　(b) **each department when applying to the Future Legislation Committee for inclusion of a bill in the Government's legislative programme should submit a check-list indicating how far it has been able to comply with the guidelines, and give details of the consultations it has already carried out or proposes to conduct; and**

　(c) **an up-dated version of the check-list and this information should be submitted with the draft bill to the Legislation Committee and published with the bill.**

Delegated Legislation

The evidence

153. Many of the bodies which gave evidence to us did not differentiate between consultation on bills and on delegated legislation, but the latter is especially important for some bodies (see for example the evidence of the Society of County Secretaries (M 53, para. 2) and the CBI (M 22, para.1)). Often it is the details of how an Act will be applied that concerns them as much as the broader policy, and such details are frequently included in statutory instruments making regulations, orders, schemes etc., rather than in the primary legislation. Specific comments on consultation on such documents are therefore worth examining.

1　For a description of the work of this body, see "The Responsibilities of the New Zealand Legislation Advisory Committee" by Walter Iles, Chief Parliamentary Counsel, New Zealand, in *Statute Law Review*, Vol. 13, No. 1 (Summer, 1992).

2　Legislative Change: Guidelines on Process and Content (revised edition), Report No. 6 by the Legislation Advisory Committee.

154. In some cases there was no or little criticism. For example the Civil Aviation Authority (CAA), which is concerned with the nuts and bolts of safety regulations which are contained in the Air Navigation Order 1989 made under the Civil Aviation Act 1982, welcomed this arrangement which had proved flexible and robust. Amendments to the Order were frequently initiated by the CAA, and consultations with the aviation industry worked well (M 17, paras. 2-4). The National Trust told us it was happy about consultations on planning regulations. The National Consumer Council welcomed the inclusion in some Acts of requirements to consult specified classes of people or bodies before regulations are made; it recommended that this should be the general practice (M 39, para. 2.5).

155. Many criticisms of failure to consult or of insufficient consultation on delegated legislation (as made by the CBI (M 22, para. 1), the Law Society (M 36, para. 6.2), the local authority associations (M 37), the CPAG (M 16) and the Commission for Racial Equality (M 19)), and of rushed consultations (as made by the Law Society (M 36, para. 6.2)) were on the same lines as the complaints made in respect of consultation on bills. There were some differences or additional points however. For example the BBC found it ironic that there was likely to be more consultation on delegated legislation than on primary legislation (M 11, para. 9). And the Community Council of Humberside said that there should be more effort to consult on the implications of regulations – for example those under the Food Act and the Children Act – at local level (M 21). The BMA and the ABI and Lloyd's were normally given enough time to consider and comment on delegated legislation, but there was insufficient consultation when their interests were peripheral (the ABI and Lloyd's instanced the Dangerous Dogs Bill).

156. Particular interest was shown in consultation on draft statutory instruments. Again the evidence varied. The CPAG had been consulted on the outline of regulations under the Child Support Act, but these were not always precise and it would have preferred to be consulted on the regulations themselves (M 15, para. 3(d) and M 16). On the other hand the Law Society said that consultation on draft regulations was more common – though not a standard practice – than consultation on their content before they were drafted and it wanted more consultation at the earlier stage (M 36, para. 6.2-6.3). The local authority associations would like to have consultations at both pre-draft and draft stages, with information on those who had been consulted being published for the benefit of Parliamentarians (M 37). The Inland Revenue gave evidence of significant consultation on draft statutory instruments before they were laid before Parliament; they consulted on twelve out of the seventeen less straight forward instruments introduced in the first half of 1992.

157. Some bodies, for example the BBC (M 11, para. 10), the Society of County Secretaries and the CBI (M 22, para. 1), believed that proposed delegated legislation should be published at the same time as the bill. We consider this in Chapter 6.

Conclusions and recommendations

158. The importance of proper consultation on delegated legislation should not be underestimated. For many bodies its importance is equal to- or even greater than – the importance of consultation on bills. And from the point of view of those directly affected, it is equally important to get delegated legislation right. Delegated legislation may be of secondary importance to Ministers and those in Parliament where it plays a subordinate part in the legislative process, but for those to whom the law applies or to the practitioners – lawyers, accountants, the police, the courts – who have to apply it, the method by which the law is made is of little significance. Primary and delegated legislation are equally part of the law of the land.

159. We therefore believe that the conclusions we have reached regarding bills apply almost equally to consultation on statutory instruments and other forms of delegated legislation, and that our recommendations designed to improve consultation on bills should, as far as possible, be applied to consultation on delegated legislation.

160. A different emphasis may be appropriate in one area. Most delegated legislation is concerned with practical questions of the application of legislation – administration, enforcement, adjudication etc. – and deal with these matters in considerable detail. For various reasons, it is desirable that those who are most experienced and affected should be able to study those details in as complete a form as possible. First, although there are advantages in consulting on the outline of proposed regulations and commenting on broader policy questions at an early stage, the experts cannot judge how the regulations will really work unless they see the full texts. Second, there is usually not the same pressure of time on statutory instruments as they, unlike bills, are not bound tightly by the requirements of a parliamentary time-table, and so it matters less if the final drafting is delayed by consultation at this late stage. And third, departmental lawyers do the drafting and not Parliamentary Counsel (who have to work to a tight schedule) and instruments can more readily be drafted and re-drafted to get them right before they are laid before Parliament – indeed they must be got right at this stage as they cannot be amended in Parliament. For these reasons, draft texts are often circulated to interested bodies – but by no means always. We believe it would benefit both the departments and those who have to apply the law if this was the general practice.

161. **We therefore recommend that there should be consultation where appropriate at the formative stage of delegated legislation, but that wherever possible departments should also consult outside experts and affected bodies on drafts of the actual instruments that they propose to lay before Parliament.**

162. **Finally, we recommend that the Government's guidelines that we have recommended regarding consultation on bills, should be applied with appropriate modifications to consultation on delegated legislation.**

Chapter 4 – Drafting

Statute law should be as certain as possible and as intelligible and clear as possible, for the benefit of the citizens to whom it applies.

How Bills and Statutory Instruments are Drafted

The evidence

The present system

163. Once a Government department has decided what it wants to put in a bill, and the approval of the Future Legislation Committee of the Cabinet has been obtained, instructions are prepared by the department's lawyers for the drafting of the bill by Parliamentary Counsel. This is a vital stage in the legislative process as, once a bill is drafted, the form of the final Act is substantially determined, although there may still be significant amendments and additions or (less often) deletions during its passage through Parliament. Drafting begins to set the Government's policies in legislative concrete; second and third thoughts become harder and harder.

164. There is an important difference in the way delegated legislation is drafted. Statutory instruments, containing regulations, orders etc., are not drafted by Parliamentary Counsel but are prepared by the departmental lawyers of the department concerned.

165. Instructions to Parliamentary Counsel and the drafting processes for bills and statutory instruments play an important part in the processes we have examined. They are also somewhat of a mystery. Drafting arrangements were summarised in Chapter III of the Renton Report, and have been described and commented on elsewhere[1], but it is difficult for anyone outside the system to understand properly how it works. Instructions and drafting are matters essentially internal within the machinery of government (see the evidence of the FDA (M 5, paras.13-19)). Neither outside bodies, nor practitioners nor Parliamentarians have much opportunity to observe the process. Parliamentary Counsel keep their cards close to their chests; apart from their contacts with departmental lawyers – and, as Lord Renton said, one does not know what goes on between them (M 47, para. (d)) – they do not normally (except indirectly through the instructing department) consult other people who might be interested in the texts to be produced, or might be able to suggest drafting improvements. There is no independent body which oversees the production of bills or can examine their drafting before they are presented to Parliament, as does the Conseil d'Etat

---

1 See, for example, Miers and Page, *Legislation* , op. cit., Chapter Five; Sir William Dale, *Legislative Drafting – A New Approach*, (Butterworths, 1977); Bennion, *The Drafting of Legislation*, 3rd Edition, op. cit., Chapter Two; and Michael Zander, *The Law-Making Process*,op. cit., pp. 1-18.

in France (see documents listed in Appendix 3). And, apart from Parliament itself and the courts, there is no systematic *ex post facto* scrutiny of the drafting of Acts.

Evidence on how the system works

166. It is therefore not surprising that we received very little evidence from outside bodies regarding the methods by which departmental instructions are prepared or on how Parliamentary Counsel draft bills, or departmental lawyers draft statutory instruments. We did however have a useful private discussion with the First Parliamentary Counsel and with the Treasury Solicitor (who has had considerable experience as a departmental lawyer). We also had discussions with the Chairman and an academic member of the Law Commission, who have experience of the drafting of Law Commission bills (they have their own draftsmen, who are seconded Parliamentary Counsel). The FDA also gave us the experience of the senior civil servants it represents (M 5, paras. 10-19).

167. Parliamentary Counsel are rightly proud of their highly specialist skills, and are reluctant to let others become too closely involved in the actual drafting of bills. An experiment with using outside lawyers in the 1970s was not considered a success, nor has been the occasional use of parliamentary agents (lawyers in private practice who draft private legislation). Some of the individuals and bodies we met would like to see people other than Parliamentary Counsel contributing to the drafting of bills. Lord Renton would like to see more consultation on early drafts of bills with practicing lawyers with relevant experience (M 47, para. (d)). Mr Edward Mercer made similar proposals (M 39, paras. 4-7). The police would also like to contribute to the choice of words for carrying the intentions of a bill into practice (M 4, para. 10). The CBI had similar aspirations (M 22, para. 2).

168. Lord Renton was concerned about the increase of detail in both bills and delegated legislation, and believed that this resulted from pressure from middle-ranking civil servants to ensure that every possibility contingency was covered. Civil servants, he told us, should be specifically instructed to keep down the details they put in bills.

169. The Bank of England had sometimes found that –

> *"difficulties are caused by each Government department having its own lawyers and there being no centralised legal view, as well as by the convention that communication with Parliamentary Counsel is only through the sponsoring department. This can sometimes result in pieces of legislation which have the same intent adopting different definitions of the same concept."*

The Bank gave an example of the problem to which it referred (M 6).

170. Lord Howe of Aberavon, in his address to the Statute Law Society in May, 1991, described how, before the 1970 election, he had personally prepared a draft of an industrial relations bill, which drew extensively on American and Commonwealth experience and drafting; when the Conservative Government came to power he had brought this out as the first draft of the Government's Industrial Relations Bill. He had looked forward to co-operating with

Parliamentary Counsel – in the way Gladstone had done when he was Prime Minister – in getting the bill right, but in practice he was told by the then First Parliamentary Counsel that this was not the way things worked and that the bill would be drafted by a draftsman in his Office. He understood that his own draft was never actually considered in the Parliamentary Counsel Office "because the idea of accepting such external input represented too revolutionary a notion for that to be tolerable". He told us that, with hindsight, he believed there could have been improvements in the way the 1970 Industrial Relations Bill was drafted if his ideas had been followed up, but he feared that Parliamentary Counsel, like other bodies, had "an enormous capacity to resist change".

171. Mr George Bednar, who had personal experience of what he considered to be ill-drafted legislation, emphasised the problems for Parliamentary Counsel caused by policy decisions that seek to provide for every possible contingency and so become unduly complicated, and by the need then to draft in a hurry (M 7).

172. The Law Society said that the style of drafting used for delegated legislation is on the whole worse than that for primary legislation, possibly because the departmental lawyers had not had the opportunity to build up the necessary skill and expertise. It recommended that delegated legislation should also be drafted by Parliamentary Counsel (M 36, para. 6.4). The local authority associations also complained of obscure drafting in statutory instruments (M 37). Lord Renton, on the other hand, found that for the most part delegated legislation was well drafted in Government departments; responsibility for its drafting should not be transferred to Parliamentary Counsel (M 47, para. (g)).

173. The overriding concern of many bodies, and of Members of both Houses of Parliament, is of bills being presented to Parliament "half-baked", that is to say with detail remaining to be worked out and consequently large numbers of Government amendments having to be tabled in Parliament (see paragraphs 115-119). The local authority associations illustrated this with statistics published by a House of Lords working group on the Workings of the House which had expressed its concern about a tendency to "legislate as you go" and about legislation which may have been introduced without adequate consideration; 2,401 amendments were made in the Lords in 1988-89 (606 of them to the Local Government and Housing Bill) (M 37).

174. Lord Howe of Aberavon drew our attention to further relevant statistics. Between 1979 and 1983, an average of 1,106 Government amendments were moved in the Lords each session; between 1983 and 1987 the sessional average was 1,609; and between 1987 and 1989, the sessional average rose to 2,668. The large number of Government amendments, in both Houses, has had a marked effect on the size of Acts compared with the original bills. For example. the total length of five key bills introduced in the 1987-88 session was 714 pages, but the Acts that resulted were 1,084 pages long – an increase of 53%; in session 1988-89, eight key bills, totalling 1,160 pages on introduction, increased

in length by 43% to 1,663 pages on enactment[1] Our research describes numerous Government amendments being made in Parliament to the Broadcasting Bill (paragraph 118 and Appendix 5).

The views of civil servants

175. Some of the reasons for bills being published in an unfinished state were revealed by the evidence of well-placed insiders. Although we received little formal evidence from civil servants, the FDA succeeded in lifting the veil slightly on the mysteries of the relations between departmental administrators and their lawyers on the one hand and Parliamentary Counsel on the other.

176. In theory administrators specify the policy objectives; the departmental lawyers act as interpreters between administrators and Counsel, clarifying legal problems; Parliamentary Counsel have full responsibility for drafting the text of the bill. In practice their roles are not as distinct as this textbook description suggests. Legal drafting to give effect to a policy can subtly change that policy, and –

> *"it is common for administrators to feel that Counsel is giving higher priority to ensuring that the draft is clear in its effect and immune from judicial reinterpretation, than to give precise effect to the Minister's intentions. Counsel, by contrast may feel that administrators are more concerned to get the bill on the statute book to demonstrate that the Government has achieved its political goals, than with the need of those who will have to work with the legislation."*

Compromise can leave both sides unsatisfied, with the administrators feeling that priority has been given to form over substance and Counsel regretting that the quality of the drafting falls short of his or her high standards. (M 5, para. 15-16).

177. Time pressures exacerbate the difficulties. "Frequently", said the FDA –

> *"the drafting timetable slips, because Counsel is overloaded or because agreement cannot be reached in time on whether Counsel's proposed draft achieves the desired policy objectives. It is also true on occasions that policy is still being formulated, and that 'goal posts' are moved on a fairly regular basis"*.

The target date for introducing the bill into Parliament is, however, seen as an absolute, and bills "are therefore commonly introduced with significant parts missing" which later have to be added by Government amendments at a later parliamentary stage. This makes it harder to ensure that the bill fulfils its intended purpose, risks damage to the drafting and limits the scope for proper parliamentary scrutiny (M 5, para. 17).

178. Summing up, the FDA said that "the outcome of the drafting process is, all too often, the introduction of what is no more than a first or second draft of the bill", with a lot more work to be done (M 5, para. 19).

---

1   Address to Statute Law Society, May 1991.

Responsibility for the drafting of bills

179. The ultimate responsibility for how a bill is drafted lies with the Minister in charge of the bill. First Parliamentary Counsel is directly responsible to the Chairman of the Future Legislation Committee (who is at present the Leader of the House of Commons) for delivering the Government's programme of legislation.

180. However some of those who gave evidence thought that this was not enough. Lord Simon of Glaisdale, speaking with long experience as a former Minister, Law Officer and High Court judge, told us that he would like to see the Legislation Committee of the Cabinet give closer attention to the way bills were drafted. He said that this Committee used to be chaired by the Lord Chancellor and acted as a scrutiny committee, looking carefully at constitutional points as well as drafting; now it was chaired by the Leader of the House of Commons and operated more as a business management committee. A return to the former approach would, in his view, be a remedy for some of the drafting ills he had experienced. The representative of the Bar Council also regretted that there was now no body charged with scrutinising the form, arrangement and language of proposed legislation before it was presented to Parliament, the Legislation Committee of the Cabinet having largely abdicated this function (M 26).

Staffing of the Parliamentary Counsel Office

181. The representative of the Association of Chief Police Officers told us that he was worried by what he saw as falling standards in the quality of drafting; he believed that the number and training of draftsmen needed to be reviewed. Lord Howe of Aberavon shared the same anxieties, and also believed that more drafting resources were required and better programming of the work of Parliamentary Counsel. Clarity, a body concerned particularly with standards of drafting, emphasised the importance of systematic training of draftsmen (M 18). Some information about the staffing arrangements in Australia, Canada and New Zealand, and on how their draftsmen work, is given in the papers listed in Appendix 3.

Conclusions and recommendations

182. We have referred in paragraph 173 to widespread concern about "half-baked" legislation being introduced into Parliament with consequential need for large numbers of Government amendments. We will examine the consequences of this for Parliament in Chapter 5. However the failure of all Governments "to get bills right" – or more nearly right – before they are presented to Parliament has been, in our view, the basic defect in the legislative process and a grave indictment of those Governments' approach to law-making. This partly results, we believe, from the way Parliamentary Counsel are required to work.

183. Parliamentary Counsel work under great pressure, and much of this stems from the demands of Ministers who in their turn are seeking to achieve the passage of all the legislation to which they are committed within the framework of a tight legislative programme. However it is not only the volume of legislation which causes the pressure. As Sir Henry de Waal, QC, a former First Parliamentary Counsel, has said, " the principal pressure on the draftsmen seems to flow from

late instructions, short deadlines and sudden and quite elaborate policy changes"[1].

184. Accepting Sir Henry's analysis, we conclude that part of the problem results from weaknesses in the consultation processes which we considered in Chapter 3. The solutions we there recommend should produce more settled and helpful instructions; it should certainly minimise late and elaborate policy changes. A large part of the problem flows from the tight nature of the Government's legislative programme, which results in late instructions and short deadlines. We review the programming and time-tabling of legislation in Chapter 7, and propose a new approach which should reduce the pressure on Parliamentary Counsel.

185. Finally much of the blame, we believe, rests with Ministers. They are responsible for deciding what legislation is needed. Here we endorse a proposition put forward by Lord Howe of Aberavon in his address to the Statute Law Society –

> *"it is essential to achieve sufficient clarity at a sufficiently early stage about the objectives of each piece of legislation. The alternative takes the form of policy making on the hoof, while the bill is going through Parliament; and the consequences of that are not acceptable."*

All the evidence we have received – from those who are affected by legislation and from those who make it – suggests that Ministers should follow this advice.

186. Although some of the main remedies of the problems in drafting bills therefore lie in other areas, the responsibilities, organisation and administration of the Parliamentary Counsel Office should also be examined. On most of these matters we received little evidence, but we consider several ideas that have sometimes been canvassed.

Responsibilities of Parliamentary Counsel

187. The existence in England and Wales of a central, highly professional, skilled and specialised drafting service, acting for all departments in the drafting of bills, differs from the arrangement in many other countries. In France, for example, and in some other European countries, bills are initially drafted in the various departments and in part by non-legally qualified draftsmen[2]. However we received no evidence of a desire to change the system in this country. We see advantages in entrusting the drafting of all Government bills to a single group of experts who can maintain a general consistency of method and style. This was the main reason for establishing the Parliamentary Counsel Office in the last century and, although there may be some disadvantages in over-specialisation[3], we make no recommendations for change in this matter. Indeed we believe that the skills and experience of the Office would contribute

---

1 Statute Law Review, 1989, p. 211.

2 For the arrangements in some other countries, with a discussion of the pros and cons of different systems, see Dale, *Legislative Drafting – A New Approach* , op. cit., Chapter 14; and see Appendix 3 of this Report.

3 Dale, op. cit., pp. 337-338.

greatly to the carrying through of many of the other recommendations in this Report. Further upheaval would not be helpful.

188. It has also been proposed – contrary to the idea of devolving the drafting of bills to departments – that drafting of statutory instruments should be transferred from departmental lawyers to Parliamentary Counsel. Again, we are not in favour of a change, in part for the reasons given at the end of the last paragraph.

189. There are also several advantages in keeping the drafting of delegated legislation in the departments. Much delegated legislation deals with practicalities and administrative details regarding the application of legislation; these are aspects with which departmental administrators and lawyers are much more familiar than Parliamentary Counsel, and the "legal" content of instruments is generally lower than in bills. The timing of the drafting of instruments after an Act is passed is closely related to administrative decisions regarding the bringing into force of the various provisions of the Act, and these are all departmental responsibilities. The rigid parliamentary time-table that applies to bills, by which Parliamentary Counsel are ruled, does not apply to statutory instruments, so leaving departmental lawyers more flexibility which might be lost if their work were to be transferred to Parliamentary Counsel. Finally, increased direct consultation with interested experts and bodies on draft texts of delegated legislation, which we have recommended, would be assisted by retaining their drafting in the hands of the departmental lawyers. We therefore make no recommendations for change in the responsibilities for drafting statutory instruments and other delegated legislation.

Oversight of drafting

190. Another radical idea which has sometimes been floated is that we should have in this country an independent or quasi-independent body which would scrutinise all draft bills before they were presented to Parliament to seek to maintain high drafting standards and to look at constitutional, legal and other non-policy matters. This is broadly how the Conseil d'Etat works in France (see papers listed in Appendix 3). Sir William Dale has recommended the setting up of a similar body, to be called the Law Council, comprising judges, other lawyers, and various lay people, to review bills as drafted by Parliamentary Counsel and to advise Ministers on whether and how the bill might be redrafted. He suggested that at first, on a pilot basis, this might be done by the Law Commission[1]. Others have suggested that the Law Commission might play a positive part in reviewing the drafting of all bills.

191. We are opposed to all these proposals. We received very little evidence either for or against them, but have come to our conclusion for three reasons. First, so long as drafting remains centralised in the Parliamentary Counsel Office (as we have recommended) the dangers of varying drafting styles and patchy quality, as experienced when bills are in the first instance drafted by a wide range of people in different departments as in France, are minimised; a second eye is therefore less needed. Second, the most skilled draftsmen work in the

1   Ibid., pp. 336-337.

Parliamentary Counsel Office; for an outside scrutiny body to be able to make constructive drafting criticisms, it would need some full-time and skilled draftsmen of its own (we do not believe such a detailed and technical job could be properly done by part-time judges, lawyers and laymen, however experienced) and it would not be easy to find them, except by weakening the Parliamentary Counsel Office. Third, the additional scrutiny suggested would introduce further delay in the legislative process; we prefer that any extension of the process that may be contemplated (see Chapter 7) should be devoted to better pre-legislative consultation, preparation and drafting or to better parliamentary scrutiny, rather than to an attempt to revise the drafting of Parliamentary Counsel. Therefore we do not recommend the appointment of any new body outside Government to review the drafting of bills.

192. However, the somewhat Olympian position of Parliamentary Counsel, their near monopoly of drafting responsibility and skills, and perhaps even their very specialist professional qualities, may pose a problem. The impression given is that Parliamentary Counsel will in no circumstances allow a single word to go into a public Act of Parliament unless they have drafted it or the wording has received their approval. This may or may not be so, but, to quote Lord Howe of Aberavon again –

> *"responsibility for the......state of the statute book overwhelmingly rests upon Senior Parliamentary Counsel.....and the Government of the day", and "neither Parliamentary Counsel nor Ministers.....are exactly notorious for their revolutionary tendencies."* [1]

There may be a danger of complacency. It might be a good thing for someone to look critically at drafting. There may be a need for someone to keep an eye on Parliamentary Counsel.

193. We see the solution in clarifying and strengthening the chain of command and accountability – within Government – for all Government drafting. It is not satisfactory for the ultimate responsibility for the drafting (as distinct from the policy content) of bills to rest solely with the Minister in charge of the bill. He or she will rarely have the personal training or skills to carry out such a function. His or her officials are unlikely to be able to appraise the details of a bill's drafting with objective detachment (the most qualified will have been closely associated with the drafting themselves, having instructed Parliamentary Counsel) or if objective, are unlikely to have the necessary skills. It is certain that neither the Minister or the officials (other than the administrators or lawyers directly working on the bill) will have the time to read each bill with the care required to test the drafting. Finally, maintenance of good drafting standards across the board will not be achieved by having each bill scrutinised in the department that is preparing that bill.

194. We believe that some central responsibility is required. As we will show, a number of significant issues arise on the drafting of a bill. It will be important that Government departments adhere to a co-ordinated Government line on such

---

1 Address to the Statute Law Society, May, 1991.

matters as the granting of delegated powers, and that they observe the spirit and the letter of the Government's consultation guidelines that we have recommended. A Cabinet committee should supervise this.

195. At present bills are submitted a few days before publication to the Legislation Committee, which is primarily concerned with them as a matter of business management. The Committee, as it operates at present, cannot be expected to give effective legal scrutiny to bills at the late stage at which it sees them. **We recommend that the Legislation Committee of the Cabinet should be given the wider and longer-term role of ensuring that bills conform with the best constitutional principles and, where appropriate, that they have been prepared after full and genuine consultation.** This wider role would mean that the Committee should not necessarily be chaired by the Leader of the House of Commons (as is often the case at present).

196. There remains the question of ministerial responsibility. **We recommend that ministerial responsibility for the work of the Parliamentary Counsel Office, and particularly for oversight of the drafting methods employed and scrutiny of the drafting of all Government bills, should be assigned to the Attorney General.** In our view, a legally qualified Minister with legal advisers is needed, for although a lay person may have sound ideas on clarity and other aspects of drafting style, for full appreciation of the legal complexities of a piece of drafting some legal skills – as well as a good feel for language – are indispensable. The Attorney General is already the Minister most closely in touch with the drafting of bills.

197. The Attorney General should also take over from the Cabinet Office responsibility for the establishment and expenses of the Office. However, the most senior appointments should continue to be in the hands of the Prime Minister. First Parliamentary Counsel would be accountable to the Attorney General for the day to day work of the Office but would remain responsible to the Chairman of the Future Legislation Committee for the delivery of drafted bills according to the agreed time-table.

198. **The Attorney General and his or her department should also keep an eye on, and where necessary seek to harmonise, the drafting styles of statutory instruments**, although clearly responsibility for these must remain with the Minister who makes the regulations etc.

Methods of working of Parliamentary Counsel

199. We received little evidence on how Parliamentary Counsel carry out their work or, apart from that given by the FDA (paragraphs 175-178), on their relations with departmental administrators and lawyers. However, there does appear to be some anxiety lest they are too cut off from other sources of expertise, and from the practicalities of administering the law, to appreciate properly the concerns of others involved in the legislative process. Some outside experts, for example the Bank of England (M 6), regretted that they were never allowed to talk to Parliamentary Counsel direct. We accept that the detailed structuring of a bill and the careful choice of precisely the right words are best left to Parliamentary

Counsel alone and may best be done in isolation and tranquillity; but Counsel must still work as a member of a team.

200. We do not wish to be too precise or dogmatic about this – and it may be that much of what we are going to suggest is already done – but we would see advantages in Parliamentary Counsel, where necessary and by arrangement with the instructing department, having direct discussions with outside experts from industry or the professions, especially on highly technical matters such as occur in the fiscal field.

201. We also wonder whether Parliamentary Counsel could with advantage, from a fairly early stage on some bills, be a more full-time member of a department's bill team, to enable him or her to note their intentions at the time they are being formed, and to enable them to note any points he or she may make about the drafting problems involved in giving effect to those intentions. It appears that Government draftsmen in Canada form part of mixed teams in this way, and that all original drafting is done by mixed teams in France (see documents listed in Appendix 3).

202. In general, **we recommend that Parliamentary Counsel study Canadian and other overseas experience and practices to see whether there are lessons that could be applied in this country regarding their working methods.**

Staffing of the Parliamentary Counsel Office

203. Good draftsmen are a rare species, and the Government needs to recruit enough of them, to train them to the highest standards and to retain them. We understand from the FDA and others (see paragraph 181) that there is cause for concern on each of these scores; for example there has recently been excessive turnover at the middle level of experience. We emphasise that the successful operation of the legislative process depends on there being enough draftsmen to draft the Government's bills in the time that is made available. If some bills have had to be drafted in a hurry because there were not enough sufficiently skilled or experienced draftsmen to start the work earlier; or if the drafting of others was defective because not enough drafting time could be spent on them; or, in general, if one of the reasons why many bills are introduced into Parliament "half-baked" is that there are not enough cooks to complete the culinary process on time; then it is Parliament and the public – and indeed the Government itself – who suffer.

204. Again we are not able to suggest detailed solutions of what could become a serious problem. Those responsible and who know all the facts must find the remedies. Recruitment and training may need to be reviewed. We note that much more formal and systematic methods of recruitment and training of Government draftsmen seem to be used in Canada than in this country and that there is a lot of cross-checking of the work of individual draftsmen by their colleagues (see documents listed in Appendix 3). **We recommend that the methods of recruitment and training of Government draftsmen in Australia, Canada and New Zealand be studied, with a view to seeing if there are lessons which could be learned and applied in this country.**

205. On the major question of the number of draftsmen that is needed, **we simply**

recommend that the Government review the number of draftsmen required to draft all Government bills with proper care, and take all necessary action to recruit and retain Parliamentary Counsel accordingly. There can be no excuse for not having enough tools to do the job.

Style of Drafting

The evidence

206. The Renton Committee found widespread and deep-seated concern about the style in which Acts were drafted, especially about lack of simplicity and clarity in their language. It made many detailed recommendations aimed to improve matters. Since 1975 there have clearly been improvements, especially increasing use of textual amendment for amending earlier statutes, which were welcomed by some of those who gave evidence to us. However the general tenor of most of the comments we received on this matter was of continuing dissatisfaction about the style in which UK Acts of Parliament are drafted. We do not set out these criticisms in detail, but they can be summarised under three heads.

207. Many people and bodies were critical of the complex or obscure language used in some Acts. These included Lord Howe of Aberavon, Lord Renton (M 47, para. (d)), the Bar Council (M 26), English Heritage (M 24), the National Audit Office (M 9), the BMA (M 12), Shelter (M 51), the BBC (M 11), the National Union of Mineworkers (M 44), the Association of Chief Police Officers (M 4, para. 12), the TUC (M 55, para. 9), the CBI (M 22), the Law Society (M 36, paras. 5.17 and 5.18), Mr George Bednar (M 7), the local authority associations (M 37), the Institute of Public Relations (M 31, para. 2b), the National Consumer Council (M 41, paras. 3.1 and 3.2) and the Community Council of Humberside (M 21).

208. Others were critical of various drafting practices, such as occasional failure to use textual amendment or lack of statements of principle. These included Lord Renton (M 47, para. (f)), Lord Simon of Glaisdale, the Bar Council (M 26), the Institute of Chartered Accountants (M 29, paras. 21-23), Mr Justice Paul Kennedy (representing the Judges' Council) (M 33), the CBI, the Institute of Directors and the Independent Television Commission.

209. Some bodies, including the British Railways Board (M 13, para. 2), the Equal Opportunities Commission (M 25), the Law Society (M 36, para. 6.4) and the ABI and Lloyd's, were specifically critical of the style or drafting of statutory instruments.

210. Clarity, a body devoted to the encouragement of the use of plain English in statutes, sent us a lengthy memorandum, solely on the methods and style of drafting (M 18). We do not summarise Clarity's arguments – which are both critical and constructive – at length, but the main points included the need for a purposive approach to drafting and interpreting legislation, the influence of European Community legislation on drafting style (which we consider in paragraphs 562-566), the importance of draftsmen having the right attitude and training, the need for bills to be drafted to help the most likely reader,

techniques for making texts shorter and simpler, and the value of using illustrations, typographical devices and formulae to help the reader.

211. Clarity concluded that "the best statutory drafting is now very good" (it instanced the Local Government Act 1988) but some drafting was still bad (the Leasehold Reform Act 1967 was an example); many problems remained with the style of statutory instruments (M 18, Part 4). Clarity welcomed the moves that Parliamentary Counsel have made in recent years towards clearer drafting but believed that they could still learn lessons from recent reforms in other Commonwealth countries. Clarity's memorandum is published with this Report. It is clear and thorough and, although we do not agree with all its conclusions, we commend it to all those interested in this aspect of the legislative process.

212. Documents describing some of the steps taken to improve the style of drafting in Australia, Canada and New Zealand are listed in Appendix 3. They include the use of non-lawyers in Canada to read the work of the drafters to try to eliminate obscure or confusing structures or forms of expression, and the move towards a simpler style initiated by the First Parliamentary Counsel in Australia, including the production of a Clear Drafting Manual for use by legislative drafters.

Conclusions and recommendations

Response to the criticism

213. The issue of drafting style is important and cannot be ignored. The complaints are real. We set out, at the head of this Chapter, a guiding principle that statute law should be written for the benefit of those to whom it applies. Most of the critics we have listed fall into that category – bodies affected by the law who should be able to understand it. It appears that our guiding principle is not always being followed. As the Comptroller and Auditor General asked, having expressed his concern about the complexity of some recent legislation which had led even Government departments to fail to comply with the law, "if Departments and the National Audit Office find it difficult to interpret legislation, what chance has the man in the street?" (M 9).

214. We will not attempt to match the detailed critique that the Renton Committee applied to the methods of drafting used at the time of its Report; some of its recommendations have been accepted; others are perhaps less relevant today. Nor indeed will we go into much detail about questions of style, such as those dealt with by Clarity, but we suggest some guidelines that we believe Parliamentary Counsel should seek to follow.

Drafting to help the users

215. We are convinced that statute law ought to be drafted primarily for the convenience of the user, and not primarily for the benefit of Ministers and other Members of Parliament who have to approve the legislation, or even for the "man in the street"; the Renton Committee took the same view (para. 10.3). For this reason we also welcome the move towards textual amendment of previous legislation, which means enacting the actual wording to be included in the amended statute (or subordinate instrument) rather than amending the law by

operating on the earlier legislation without amending its text[1]. Textual amendment is much more helpful to the user, who wants to have the law on any matter stated in as few texts as possible, and when an earlier Act is amended can then amend his or her copy accordingly. We recognise that it is not as helpful to those in Parliament, who cannot understand the effect of the changes without reference to the earlier legislation, but this difficulty can be alleviated by explanatory notes on clauses.

216. The question arises: who is the user? As Clarity said "Parliamentary Counsel and other writers of law don't write for themselves: they write for others. The essence of writing law is communication" (M 18). With whom should the draftsman be communicating? The answer in each case must determine the style of drafting and the language that should be used for each bill. There is no such thing as a "correct" drafting style; there is only a good style for a particular bill or provision.

217. We see four main sets of users. The first are those who are going to have to apply and administer the law, including Government departments, local and other public authorities, various inspectorates and the police. The second are those who have to comply with the law, including local government, many industrial and commercial bodies, other employers and ordinary citizens and tax-payers. The third are those who will benefit from or be protected by the law, including companies, farmers, employees, pensioners and again ordinary citizens and tax-payers. And the fourth are those who have to interpret or advise others on the meaning of the law, including lawyers, accountants, various charities, interest and pressure groups and ultimately – and most importantly – the courts.

218. Which of these are the main users in any case is something that only the Minister and departmental officials, and Parliamentary Counsel, can decide; but the decision must be consciously and deliberately taken. To achieve the best drafting style it is almost as important to be clear for whom you are drafting as it is to decide what should be in the bill or instrument. **We recommend that before Parliamentary Counsel begin drafting a bill, or a departmental lawyer drafts a statutory instrument, a definite decision be taken by the department and draftsman concerned on who are to be regarded as the main users of the legislation concerned, and that the draftsman then adopts an appropriate style of drafting for those users.**

Certainty, clarity, simplicity and brevity

219. The many critics did not sing the same song. Some wanted more certainty in the law; many wished for greater clarity of language; others wanted bills to be simple and brief. It is impossible to satisfy all these aspirations[2]. To achieve certainty the draftsman may have to deal specifically with a number of possible situations to which the statute could apply, and this militates against simplicity

---

1   For a fuller explanation, see Renton Report, pp. 76-77.
2   For an excellent exposition of this dilemma, see Sir Patrick Mayhew, QC, MP, "Can Legislation Ever be Simple, Clear, and Certain?", *Statute Law Review*, Vol.11, No. 1 (Summer 1990).

and brevity; it may also require elaborate wording that is not immediately clear. To achieve clarity, he or she may have to sacrifice some simplicity. Apparently clear and simple wording may not be so certain when it comes to interpretation by the courts in some unforeseen circumstance. As the FDA said –

> *"What appears clear to the layman may not be certain in meaning to the courts; and much of the detail in legislation, which can appear obfuscatory, is there to make the effect of the provisions certain and resistant to legal challenge" (M 5, para. 25).*

220. In many cases the law can be both clear, simple and certain. In other cases this combination is difficult or impossible to achieve. The choice must again depend on the subject and the expected users. Some provisions are not likely to require adjudication in the courts, so clarity and simplicity can be the prime aims; others almost certainly will, so certainty is more important.

221. The need for recourse to the courts for the interpretation of statute law should be minimised. It is slow, expensive and itself a cause of continued uncertainty. If a choice has to be made between simplicity and certainty in drafting, we agree with the Renton Committee, who said –

> *"the draftsman must never be forced to sacrifice certainty for simplicity, since the result may be to frustrate the legislative intention."* [1]

The courts, if required to adjudicate, might find the simple wording left matters obscure and might hold that the Act meant something other than that intended by the Government or understood by Parliament. **We therefore recommend that draftsmen should always seek for clarity, simplicity and brevity in their drafting, but that certainty should be paramount.**

Review of drafting styles

222. There has been much discussion over the years about drafting styles and methods[2]. Draftsmen in Australia, Canada and New Zealand have reviewed their styles and practice and have come up with some interesting innovations. Further constructive ideas have been put to us by Clarity and others. **We recommend that Parliamentary Counsel and departmental lawyers should take to heart the criticisms that continue to be made, by those most directly affected, of the style of drafting of statute law, and should review their own drafting styles accordingly.**

Statements of Principle and Purpose

The background and the evidence

223. We have considered two important drafting issues which affect the substance – as opposed to the style – of Acts of Parliament. Both relate to the question of how much detail draftsmen should put into their bills .

224. The first issue stems from the English legal tradition that the courts derive their interpretation of legislation from the text alone, and will not look beyond the text to construe statutory provisions; according to this view, the intention of

---

1 Renton Report, para. 11.5.
2 See, for example Bennion and Dale, op. cit. and of course the Renton Committee.

legislation is largely irrelevant. Recognising this tradition, draftsmen naturally seek to set out the proposed law as fully as possible, and to deal with every eventuality in considerable detail, so as to assist the courts by minimising uncertainty.

225. They have been encouraged in this approach by the attitude of Members of Parliament of all parties, including Ministers, who in many cases seem to be unwilling to entrust matters to the judgement of judges, do not want them to be drawn into making politically sensitive interpretations of the law, and are therefore anxious to minimise the discretion that is left to the courts. Evidence was given to us by Dr John Cunningham, representing the official Opposition, to this effect. Parliament therefore appears to favour having every detail spelt out in bills, and certainly amendments moved by Members are nearly always in the direction of inserting more detail rather than reducing detail to make a bill simpler. As a former First Parliamentary Counsel has said –

"Parliament may insist that the rights of the citizen should be spelt out precisely and may well refuse to accept the argument that the way the legislation is to be worked should be left to the courts." [1]

There is thus a demand from many quarters for what the Renton Committee called "immediate certainty", and Parliamentary Counsel respond to this demand.

226. The policy of the draftsmen of relying on detailed provisions designed to achieve certainty has been challenged from two quarters. The courts have frequently been willing to look beyond the words of an Act, and to seek to discover the parliamentary intention [2] and, if the words permit, adopt the construction which carries out that intention in preference to a possible literal construction which would defeat it.. This has been called the "purposive approach" to legal interpretation. Recognising this development, some people (Clarity, for example (M 18) and Sir William Dale [3]) have argued that the drafters of bills should also adopt a purposive approach and draw legislation up in more general terms which enact the law in the form of clearly expressed general principles, which would help the courts to interpret and apply that intention.

227. The second challenge to traditional English drafting practice comes from Europe. It has long been the practice in most countries in Western Europe to draft most (but by no means all) law in much more general terms, with reliance on broad objectives and statements of principle. This system has been followed

---

1   Renton Report, para. 10.6; and for the general discussion of this question, see Chapter X of that Report.

2   A somewhat misleading and notoriously difficult concept as it is the Government which has an intention as to the changes in the law that it wishes to make; Parliament, working through two separate Houses, whose Members are often divided in their wishes, can hardly be said to "intend" anything, although it agrees, with or without amendment, to some of the bills laid before it. For an interesting discussion of these matters, see A P Le Seur, "The Judges and the Intention of Parliament: Is Judicial Review Undemocratic?", *Parliamentary Affairs*, Vol. 44, No. 3 (July 1991).

3   Op. cit., pp. 339-340.

by the European Community, and much EC legislation is framed in such general terms[1]. We consider some of the implications this has for UK delegated legislation in Chapter 8, but here we note the implications for the drafting of bills in this country. Some people prefer the European approach for its own sake, as being simpler, more intelligible and briefer. Others, Clarity for example (M 18), have argued that we should now move over to the European method as in future so much of our law will be drafted in a style that is not purely English. In short, Clarity said, it means that Parliament must trust the judges; the link between drafting and interpretation must be given greater recognition, and there must be a "new form of partnership between Parliament and the judiciary".

228. The Renton Committee considered this problem at length. Certainty remained important and it was not prepared to recommend a wholesale move to European methods. The Committee concluded that -

> *"the adoption of the 'general principle' approach in the drafting of our statutes would lead to greater simplicity and clarity. We would therefore like to see it adopted wherever possible."*

It accepted however that this approach would mean some sacrifice of immediate certainty and would place greater reliance on the courts. It recognised that for certain types of legislation, such as fiscal, the new approach would not be acceptable to the Government or Parliament, and that bills should not be drafted in such broad terms that expensive recourse to the courts became necessary[2].

229. The Renton Committee therefore recommended –

> *"that encouragement should be given to the use of statements of principle, that is to say, the formulation of broad general rules", whether or not detailed provisions were also thought necessary (para. 10.13).*

It also recommended that bills should contain statements of purpose, either for the whole bill or for various parts, "when they are the most convenient method of delimiting or otherwise clarifying the scope and effect of legislation" (para. 11.8).

230. Lord Renton, in evidence to us, said that these were two of the most important recommendations in his Committee's report which had not been implemented; he still believed that bills should not attempt to cover every contingency and that they should be less detailed and more concerned with principles and purpose. Other evidence from the Bar Council (M 26), the BBC (M 11, paras. 10 and 11), the CBI (M 22, para. 2), the Institute of Chartered Accountants (M 29, para. 25), the Law Society (M 36, para. 5.18), the local authority associations (M 37), the Institute of Public Relations (M 31, para. 3b), Clarity (M 18), and the FDA (M 5, para. 26) supported this approach.

231. On the other hand, Parliamentary Counsel have in the past been sceptical about the value of the European approach and opposed to statements of purpose for reasons which the then First Parliamentary Counsel explained to the Renton

---

1 See Renton Report, Chapter IX.
2 Ibid., para. 10.13.

Committee[1].

232. Mr Justice Paul Kennedy (now Lord Justice Kennedy), representing the Judges Council, believed that, on balance, judges would take the view that if a problem cannot be dealt with in primary legislation in a simple and coherent way, it would be better if the Act were to confine itself to statements of principle, leaving the detail to statutory instruments or interpretation by the courts (M 33, para. C). In oral evidence he added that general statements of principle or purpose, leaving the precise meaning and application to interpretation by the courts would not be suitable in controversial measures. However it could be desirable, in some cases, both to set out the detail in a bill and to state the purposes in some other form, and he suggested how this might be done (see paragraph 245).

Conclusions and recommendations

233. Although the number of Acts passed each year remains relatively constant, the total amount of legislation produced each year has grown considerably (paragraphs 45 and 46). In the years 1950, 1951, 1960 and 1961, a total of 241 public general Acts of all sorts filled 3,900 pages of the statute book – an average of 16 pages per Act. In 1988, 1989, 1990 and 1991, 195 Acts (excluding consolidation Acts, see Appendix 7) took 8,201 pages – an average of 42 pages per Act. This indicates a very significant increase in the size of individual Acts over the last forty years. The main cause of that increase appears to be the inclusion in bills of more and more detail. Longer and more complex bills become increasingly difficult for all concerned – parliamentarians, practitioners, affected bodies and the courts – to comprehend and use. The aim should be to make statute law simpler and clearer; too much detail can be un-productive and confusing and frustrates that aim. It is therefore our belief that the growth of detail, especially in Acts of Parliament, needs to be halted and **we recommend that Ministers, civil servants and in particular Parliamentary Counsel do all they can to eliminate unnecessary and complicated detail in the bills for which they are responsible.**

234. The present method of legislative drafting seeks to cover by express words every set of circumstances intended to be regulated by the legislative provision; statutory provisions seldom contain a statement of the result sought to be achieved by the express words, i.e. the underlying parliamentary intention. This method, while effective to produce certainty in many cases, has disadvantages. First, in many cases a given set of words enacted by Parliament on the basis of ministerial statements or notes on clauses appear to the legislators to carry out the parliamentary intention; yet the effect of those words when read by the end users (the citizens, their lawyers and the courts), who are ignorant of the parliamentary intention lying behind them, may be obscure or ambiguous. Words take their colour from the intention lying behind their reference to events which they foresee. But no one can foresee every set of circumstances which may arise, and the unforeseen usually happens. When it does, there is doubt

---

1   Ibid., para. 11.7.

whether or not the statutory provisions cover the event unforeseen by the draftsman.

235. To deal with these problems, the courts have recently departed from a strictly literal approach to construction and adopted a purposive approach (see paragraph 226). This seems to us to be a desirable change in the approach to statutory construction. But at present this approach is inhibited by the fact that the parliamentary intention can only be gathered from the other provisions of the statute, the detail of which often obscures the underlying intention. Virtually every other legal system in the world permits the courts to gather from sources other than the words of the statute the intention underlying the enactment, although the means by which this is done varies from system to system. **We recommend that some means should be found of informing the citizen, his lawyers and the courts of the intention underlying the words of a statute.** We have no doubt that this would render the effect of statutory words both more comprehensible and more certain.

236. Whatever aids to understanding may be employed, we must emphasise that it remains the responsibility of Parliamentary Counsel to do everything possible to ensure that the words of an Act give the courts and other users all the material they need for certainty of construction; and the courts must play their part in deriving the maximum help from the Act as a whole. Admittedly there can sometimes be a grey area of unintended ambiguity or unforeseen circumstances, but it is Parliamentary Counsel's duty to restrict this grey area to a minimum.

237. However the question remains, when there is a residual grey area, of how best to enable users to discover the intention underlying the words of a statute, as we have recommended. We turn to consider various methods which have been suggested.

238. We begin by rejecting the idea that the European style of drafting should be generally adopted in this country. We see no reason why UK legislation, to be passed by the UK Parliament, applied to UK citizens and adjudicated in UK courts should necessarily follow the pattern of EC legislation (although we do see potential difficulties over the translation and application of EC directives into UK statute law, which we consider in Chapter 8). In any event we would be strongly opposed – as we believe most Members of Parliament would be – to making statute law as general as it often is in other European countries, with the almost certain consequence that there would have to be much more recourse to the courts to settle disputed interpretations of Acts. Court proceedings are expensive for all concerned and the need for people to go to court should not be expanded.

239. Although the Renton Report did not go wholly down the European path, but would have allowed the inclusion of detailed provisions in some cases as well as statements of principle and purpose (see paragraphs 228-229), we do not agree with its proposals for solving the problem of how to inform users of the intention underlying the words of a statute. We firmly believe that certainty in the law must be the paramount aim in the drafting of statutes, and we do not

believe that the automatic inclusion of statements of principle or purpose in the body of Acts would help to that end.

240. In the first place, statements of principle or purpose would still have to be interpreted by the courts, even if other detail remained in the Act, and their very generality would leave open the possibility of differing interpretations. All the suspicions of MPs about the judges, and their reluctance to leave matters to the courts, would remain. As Sir Patrick Mayhew has said –

> *"I confess to great difficulty in seeing how a general statement of principle or purpose could enable the law to be developed by the judges, and thereby affect the public's rights, in a way foreseeable with sufficient accuracy by that public"*[1].

241. Second, we see considerable problems in including in an Act two different formulations of what must be intended to be the same law on a single point – one in the form of a statement of principle or purpose (in some cases perhaps both) and the other in the form of detailed provisions, as the Renton Committee accepted would often be required. In some cases the two formulations would obviously produce the same result, but we fear that in many cases this way of drafting could be a recipe for confusion, with some people relying on one formulation and some on the other. This would lead to increasing disputes in the courts with the parties again differing on what the statute really meant. And the judges would be left with the difficult task of deciding which words – of equal legal status – should prevail.

242. There may be occasions where the inclusion in an Act of a statement of purpose would provide an indication of what is to be treated as the intention of Parliament – and sometimes draftsmen do include such statements. We accept that this matter must be left to the discretion of the draftsman or indeed the Minister (for sometimes the reason for including a statement of purpose will be primarily political), but we believe that the inclusion of statements of principle or purpose in Acts should not be adopted as a general practice.

243. Another possible solution that has often been advocated is that the courts should be allowed to refer to reports of ministerial speeches as reported in Hansard, and to other Government statements such as White Papers. This is being considered in the case of *Pepper v Hart*, currently before the House of Lords[2]. Mr Justice Paul Kennedy gave us several arguments against this proposal, and feared that adding to the material to which a court ought to have regard could increase the length and expense of litigation. His objections appear to be shared by other High Court judges (M 33, para. D). We also see difficulties in relying on Hansard. If a Minister nods his head in response to an interpretation of the meaning of a clause, is that a ministerial statement of the purpose of that clause? The possibilities for confusion – and for time-wasting argument and counter

---

1 Op. cit., Statute Law Review, Vol. 11, No. 1, p. 7.
2 Since the Commission agreed this Report, the House of Lords has decided that the courts should be permitted to refer to parliamentary material in certain limited circumstances (*Pepper v Hart*, judgement given on 26 November 1992).

argument in the court – are endless. References to Hansard could also result in clashes between Parliament and the courts and conflicts of privilege. Therefore, if some other way can be found of assisting all those concerned to discover the intention underlying the words of a statute, we would not wish to recommend that the Hansard record of ministerial statements in Parliament should be used by the courts.

244. The advocates of the Hansard idea have however put their finger on a vital part of the solution. It is not the "intention of Parliament" which is at issue, but the intentions of Ministers. It is Governments that decide what they want to achieve; decide how to achieve it; and secure the agreement of Parliament to the bills embodying those decisions. It is Ministers who can best state what their principles, purposes and intentions were in securing the passage of a statute in its final form. It is Ministers who can best state what, in their opinion, an Act or its individual provisions are intended to achieve. We believe, therefore, that, in cases where the meaning of the words of an Act is uncertain, the best guidance the courts could get would be from a considered ministerial statement.

245. As reported to us by Mr Justice Paul Kennedy (M 33, para. D), Lord Donaldson, when Master of the Rolls, proposed that after an Act was passed, a memorandum of the purposes of the Act should be prepared by some neutral person (he suggested the Speaker's Counsel), approved by Parliament and then used by the courts as an aid to construction. Mr Justice Kennedy also thought that this might be tried, at least on an experimental basis. Another judge thought that judges should be allowed to look at notes on clauses (M 33, para. D), as did Lord Aberdare, former Chairman of Committees, House of Lords (M 1, para. 1).

246. We believe that the solution lies in the last proposal. We see difficulties about a neutral person preparing statements of ministerial purposes; on this departmental officials and Parliamentary Counsel must be the authorities, and the latter must be assumed to have the best understanding of the legal import of the Act. We also see difficulties regarding the suggested need for parliamentary approval, which could be the cause of prolonged argument and debate. What is needed are properly up-dated notes on clauses, taking account of all amendments made to the bill since the notes were first prepared. We call these notes on sections.

247. Notes on clauses (and, as regards amendments, notes on amendments) were originally prepared for the use of Ministers to help them explain the provisions of a bill or amendment to Parliament. Notes on clauses are now often (though not always) made available to Opposition shadow Ministers and other members of committees on bills in both Houses. They are drawn up by departments, with some assistance from Parliamentary Counsel, and are generally accepted by MPs and others who see them as objective and accurate statements of what a provision is intended to achieve and thus of its purpose.

248. Quite apart from the problems faced by the courts in applying Acts of Parliament, we believe that notes on sections should be published in order to provide great help to other users of statutes, particularly as textual amendment

of existing Acts is not immediately intelligible without reference to those Acts; notes on sections would state the effect of the amended wording. We note that in 1975 the Renton Report recommended the publication of notes on clauses with bills in some cases, and that a minority view on the Committee favoured, as an experiment, publication of notes on sections with Acts. Another minority view (including that of a former First Parliamentary Counsel) was opposed to both proposals because of the difficulty of excluding argumentative matter[1].

249. Things have moved on since 1975. Notes on clauses are no longer seen as controversial. Notes on sections would be in similar style. We recognise that their preparation would have to be done with considerable care if they were to be of real value, and that this might well require additional deployment of resources by both Government departments and Parliamentary Counsel. But, in order to give as much help as possible to all users of the statute law, this would be well worth while.

250. **We therefore recommend that, for every Act of Parliament, notes on sections, explaining the purpose and intended effect of each section (and Schedule), should be prepared by Government departments, with the assistance of Parliamentary Counsel, by up-dating the notes on clauses (and notes on amendments) prepared for Ministers; that these notes on sections should be approved by Ministers and laid before Parliament, but should not require formal parliamentary approval; and that notes on sections should be published at the same time as Acts.**

251. Statutory instruments also need to be understood and may need interpretation by the courts. We received some complaint that the explanatory notes, which are helpfully placed at the beginning of each instrument, are not always informative (the Institute of Chartered Accountants drew our attention to a short note on an instrument relating to VAT which did not even indicate to which tax it applied). **We recommend that explanatory notes on statutory instruments should explain their purpose and intended effect in the same way as the proposed notes on sections.**

252. There remains the question of the use of notes on sections by the courts. The words of the statute must have prior authority and ministerial explanations of the purpose and intended effect of a provision, given in notes on sections, should only be called in aid if those words do not provide the answer. Notes on sections, approved by Ministers, would therefore not override an Act of Parliament, but they could help the court to understand and construe it. The courts would have to bear in mind at all times that the notes on sections were *ex parte* statements by the Government, and only an aid to ascertaining the underlying parliamentary intention. **We recommend that notes on sections (and Schedules) of Acts of Parliament, and explanatory notes on statutory instruments, should be allowed to be used by the courts as an aid to understanding an Act or instrument, but that the the words of the Act or instrument should prevail unless these are not sufficient by themselves for**

---

1   Renton Report, para. 15.10 and pp. 159-160.

determining its effect. If necessary, legislation should be introduced for this purpose.

The Balance of Primary and Delegated Legislation

The evidence

253. Given our conclusion that to achieve certainty statute law must where necessary deal with problems in detail rather than by general principles, the second drafting issue which affects the substance of Acts relates to the question of how much detail draftsmen should put into bills and how much should be left to delegated legislation. Our evidence on this was very divided.

254. Several people and bodies thought that the substantive provisions of statute law should be dealt with in Acts of Parliament, with only less important details being left to delegated legislation, or were unhappy about the extensive use of delegated legislation. Evidence to this effect was given in memoranda or orally by Lord Simon of Glaisdale, the Bar Council (M 26), Shelter (M 51, para. 2b), the CPAG (M 15, para. 1 and M 16), the Society of County Secretaries (M 53, para. 2), the TUC (M 55, para. 8), the CBI (M 22), the Law Society (M 36, paras. 5.19-5.23), the local authority associations (M 37, section B), the Institute of Public Relations (M 31, para. 2e), the National Consumer Council (M 41, para. 4), the Scottish Consumer Council (M 49), the Industry and Parliament Trust (M 28), the Institute of Directors, Dr John Cunningham, MP, Mr Andrew Bennett, MP, and Sir Peter Emery, MP.

255. The reasons for this critical view of the use of delegated legislation were numerous. They included objection to "skeleton bills"; the use of delegated powers to determine the principles rather than the detailed implementation of legislation (the local authority associations gave several examples of this (M 37, section B)); the increased power it gave to Ministers; the lack of parliamentary time for scrutiny of delegated legislation and inadequate parliamentary scrutiny; the difficulty of campaigning against bills that include extensive delegation of powers and against draft orders etc.; the fact that statutory instruments cannot be amended; the danger of the drafters of bills thinking they could rely on regulations to put matters right if there were a flaw in a bill (suggested to us by the Child Poverty Action Group); the fact that the drafting of statutory instruments was sometimes delayed till too near the time they had to be applied (noted by the FDA (M 5, para. 23)); the uncertainty of leaving things to regulations and waiting for them to be made; the difficulty of discovering the law on any matter if it is buried in a number of statutory instruments; and, as emphasised to us by many bodies, including the CBI and the Institute of Directors, the difficulty for Parliament and other bodies of appreciating the full effect of a bill before the relevant delegated legislation is available.

256. Others who gave evidence believed that only the policy elements and other major provisions of legislation need be included in bills, or saw some advantages in leaving more detail to delegated legislation. Supporters of these

views in written or oral evidence included Lord Howe of Aberavon[1], Lord Renton, Lord Aberdare (M 1, para. 3), the Association of British Insurers and Lloyd's, the BBC and the Institute of Chartered Accountants.

257. The main arguments advanced in favour of greater use of delegated legislation were also weighty. The included the advantage of keeping primary legislation uncluttered; the fact that delegated legislation is not subject to the same constraints of the parliamentary time-table as is primary legislation and that therefore there can be more time for consultation; the greater flexibility it permits (because it does not involve the passing of a bill through Parliament) in up-dating the law to match changed circumstances and in correcting or amending it in the light of experience; and its value for VAT and other fiscal legislation.

258. Others, including Mr Justice Paul Kennedy representing the Judges' Council (M 33, para. E), appeared to be content with the present balance between primary and delegated legislation.

259. The Renton Committee recommended that general principles should be set out in the body of an Act, with details of a permanent kind in its Schedules rather than its sections, and that only details liable to frequent modification should be dealt with by statutory instruments (para. 11.25).

260. Certain particular uses of delegated legislation were strongly criticised. Lord Renton (M47, para. (g)), Lord Simon of Glaisdale, the Law Society (M 36, paras. 5.19 and 5.23) and Mr Bob Cryer, MP, were strongly opposed to the increasing use of "Henry VIII clauses" which empower Ministers to amend primary legislation by statutory instrument.

Conclusions and recommendations

261. There has been a considerable increase in the volume of delegated legislation over the last thirty years, despite no great change in the annual number of statutory instruments. For example, in 1960 there were 2,496 instruments covering 2,820 pages; in 1988, 2,311 instruments required 6,342 pages (Appendix 7); figures for later years are not available. It is clear that more detail is being included in delegated legislation as well as in Acts. It may be that the use of delegated legislation for some purposes has decreased in some areas, which would explain the fairly stable number of statutory instruments each year, but it is still heavily used in some other areas. For example the Child Support Act 1991 contains over 100 regulation-making powers.

262. As we have shown, there are strong differences of view on whether there should be more use of delegated legislation or less. There are good arguments each way. Opinion within our Commission was also divided. **On balance however, we believe that the main advantages of making greater use of delegated legislation outweigh the very real disadvantages.**

263. In particular we emphasise the merit of keeping bills as clear, simple and short as possible. This not only makes Acts easier for the user to follow, but it helps Parliament to focus on the essential points, and on policy and principle, in its

---

1   Address to the Statute Law Society, May 1991.

debates on bills. Above all we find advantages – for the Government and for those affected by legislation – in keeping the legislative process flexible so that statute law can be kept as up-to-date as possible. If significant changes in the way the law is to work – in the light of experience of how it is operating, or following changed circumstances – can only be made through an Act of Parliament, then, given the pressures on the parliamentary time-table, such changes may have to wait several years before a bill can be introduced. It is much easier to bring in amending statutory instruments with less delay. Less rigidity in procedures and timing should also facilitate improved consultations.

264. We recognise the disadvantages of extensive use of delegated legislation, but many of them could be overcome. The scrutiny of statutory instruments in Parliament is inadequate and unsatisfactory, but it need not be. We make recommendations for improving this in Chapter 5. There are problems in debating bills before Members and those advising them know what is to be contained in the delegated legislation. Again we suggest a solution to this in Chapter 5 . Difficulty is undoubtedly experienced in accessing statute law when it is set out in a number of different documents – both Acts and statutory instruments. We examine this matter in Chapter 6.

265. A dividing line must be drawn somewhere; someone must decide what should be put in a bill and what left to delegated legislation. At present it appears rather haphazard, with Ministers, departmental officials and Parliamentary Counsel all having a say and differing solutions being adopted. Lord Renton has suggested various guidelines for what should be put in bills and what excluded[1].

266. We see great difficulty in laying down precise demarcation rules – the political needs, content, legal import and urgency of each bill differ – but we accept that some standard treatment, which does not appear to exist at present, would be desirable. We ourselves are not in a position to suggest what this might be. We welcome, however, the setting up by the House of Lords of the Delegated Powers Scrutiny Committee (see paragraph 406 below), which has been given, as its first task, the consideration of ground rules and criteria on what matters can appropriately be left to delegated legislation[2].

267. We emphasise that statutory delegation should never leave an Act bare of everything except a framework of ministerial powers, with all real substance being left to ministerial regulations etc. This has been done (see the legislation on student loans in the Education (Students Loans) Act 1990, for example); it should not be repeated. The main principles of the legislation and its central provisions should appear in the Act itself. Subject to that, and in the expectation that the new Lords Committee will be able to work out helpful ground rules, on balance **we recommend that the main provisions of statute law should be set out in Acts of Parliament, but that most detail should be left to delegated legislation, provided that much more satisfactory procedures are adopted**

1   See his article in *The House Magazine*, February 11, 1991.
2   HL Deb., 10 November 1992, col. 91; and see Report from the Committee of the House of Lords on The Committee Work of the House (HL 35-I of 1991-92), para. 133 (vii).

by Parliament for scrutiny of delegated legislation and that improved arrangements are made for the publication of all statute law.

Henry VIII clauses

268. We comment on one particular use of delegated legislation. There has been growing concern recently about the use of Henry VIII clauses[1] (see paragraph 260). Henry VIII clauses (so named, it has been said, "in disrespectful commemoration of that monarch's tendency to absolutism") have been used from time to time since the Local Government Act 1888, but originally on a very limited scale and in strictly limited ways. When the Donoughmore Committee on Ministerial Powers reported on this practice in 1932 (Cmd. 4060), it recommended that it should be abandoned in all but the most exceptional cases, and indeed it was not used again till after the 1939-45 War.

269. In recent sessions however there have been several examples of Ministers being given these powers in very wide terms indeed. Section 147 of the Local Government Finance Act 1988 empowered the Secretary of State, by order, to "make such supplementary, incidental, consequential or transitional provisions as appear to him to be necessary or expedient for the general purposes or any particular purpose of the Act...." and then provided that such an order might amend, repeal or revoke any provision of any Act of the same or any earlier session. There had been similar provisions in other Acts of 1985, 1986, 1987, and such powers were again included in the Local Government and Housing Act 1989, the Companies Act 1989 and the Children Act 1989. As one Minister has said, "these order making powers are not novel, they are part of the accepted form"[2].

270. Henry VIII clauses are, of their nature, undesirable. Unless absolutely necessary, a single Minister should not be given power to change the law made by Parliament as a whole. In some cases – to up-date penalties in line with inflation, for example, or to make some transitional provision or consequential amendments – such a power may be useful and not unreasonable. However Parliament should always have to approve any amendment of its own Acts, and we welcome an undertaking given by the Lord Chancellor during the Committee stage of the Courts and Legal Services Bill 1990, that in future he would see that the affirmative resolution procedure would normally be used for all orders of this kind. We also welcome the appointment of a Delegated Powers Scrutiny Committee (see paragraph 406) which would be able to keep an eye on any further use of these powers. **We recommend that future Acts of Parliament should not normally include Henry VIII clauses.**

---

1   Particularly in debates in the House of Lords, see HL Deb., 31 January 1990, cols. 382-407 and 14 February 1990, cols. 1407-1437; see also Lord Rippon of Hexham, "Henry VIII Clauses", *Statute Law Review* , Vol. 10, No. 3, 1989, and Lord Rippon of Hexham, "Constitutional Anarchy", *Statute Law Review*, Vol. 11, No. 3, 1990.

2   See Lord Rippon of Hexham, "Henry VIII Clauses", op. cit.

Chapter 5 – Parliamentary Processes

Statute law must be rooted in the authority of Parliament and thoroughly exposed to open democratic scrutiny by the representatives of the people in Parliament.

How Parliament Deals with Legislation

The evidence

271. Many of the bodies who gave evidence were critical of the way Parliament handled legislation. The broadest criticism was simply that Parliament's processes were not well designed to handle the mass of legislation that came before it, and that parliamentary scrutiny did not usually succeed in improving bills. Those who appeared, from specific points or the general tenor of their evidence, to take this view included Lord Aberdare (M 1, para. 2, and M 2), the ABI and Lloyd's (M 3, para. 2.3), the Law Society (M 36, paras. 5.11, 5.21 and 5.30-5.40), the local authority associations (M 37, section C), the Study of Parliament Group (M 54, paras. 4-7), Professor Philip Norton (M 45), the FDA (M 5, paras. 20-33), and Dr John Cunningham, MP. Professor Page said that the greatest defect in the way bills were at present examined by Parliament was the lack of commitment by MPs to effective scrutiny of legislation.

Evidence of outside bodies

272. Some bodies would like to see Parliament involved in an earlier stage of the legislative process. The British Railways Board suggested that there should be more use of pre-legislative inquiries by select committees (M 13, para. 4). Lord Aberdare favoured such inquiries by joint committees of the two Houses (M 1, para. 2).

273. Many complaints were received about the parliamentary processes being too rushed. Some bodies that lobby Members of both Houses on bills and amendments – for example the ITC (M 27, para. 17), the ABI and Lloyd's (M 3, para. 2.3), the Institute of Chartered Accountants (M 29, para. 28), the Law Society (M 36, paras. 5.31-5.33), the TUC, the CBI, the local authority associations (M 37, section C), the Magistrates' Association, the BBC, the ITC and the Association of Chief Police Officers – would like to have longer or fixed intervals between the stages of bills or more time to study Government amendments and to brief Members. The Institute of Chartered Accountants told us of difficulties it experienced as a result of rushed proceedings on the Finance Bill, especially when much new matter was added at a late stage (there were 69 clauses in the first Finance Bill of the 1992-93 session, but 83 sections in the ultimate Act).

274. A complaint expressed by some bodies who are involved with the application of legislation, such as the local authority associations (M 37, section C) and the

CBI (whose representatives were particularly concerned about the deteriorating quality of debate in Finance Bill committees), was that parliamentary debates tended to concentrate too much on policy matters and did not give enough attention to practicalities and detail. The National Association of Health Authorities and Trusts regretted that later clauses of bills tended to be neglected because of protracted debate on earlier clauses (M 40). Shelter criticised the quality of debate in standing committees when the whips were applied (M 51, para. 3c).

275. Several bodies, such as the ITC (M 27, paras. 11-13), would like to see more recognition by Parliament of the interests of outside people and bodies or more direct contact between Parliament and informed representatives of the public. For this and other reasons the BMA (M 12), the CBI (M 22), the Law Society (M 36, paras. 5.36-5.40), the local authority associations (M 37, section C), the Institute of Public Relations (M 31, para. 2c), the ABI and Lloyd's and the Association of Chief Police Officers believed that experts and bodies from outside Parliament affected by the legislation should be able to give evidence to committees on bills. The ABI and Lloyd's, the Society of County Secretaries and the National Trust were all sympathetic to the suggestion that select committees might also examine bills at an early stage, before the political debates in Parliament, perhaps after the first but before the second reading, as in New Zealand.

276. Some bodies, including the Law Society and Shelter (M 51, para. 3b), would like to see regular post-legislative review of the working of major Acts after they have become law. The Institute of Public Relations suggested that this should be done systematically for major Acts, except Finance Acts, by the appropriate Commons select committees (M 31, para. 2g) and the TUC made a similar point to us. The National Union of Mineworkers would like a Select Committee for Legislative Review to consider complaints about the administration of legislation (M 44, paras. 2 and 3). By contrast, the FDA believed there should be a process of post-enactment review of legislation, but thought it should be conducted outside Parliament, possibly by the Law Commission (M 5, para. 31). The Association of Chief Police Officers and the Institute of Chartered Accountants both advocated special procedures for correcting, without delay, ambiguities and other drafting defects which are discovered after an Act is passed (as had happened with legislation dealing with flick knives).

277. There was fairly widespread concern, reflected by the Bar Council (M 26), the CBI (M 22), the Law Society (M 36, paras. 6.6-6.8), the National Consumer Council (M 41, para. 4), the Society of County Secretaries, Shelter and the FDA (M 5, para. 32), about the inadequacy of parliamentary scrutiny of delegated legislation. The Law Society urged Parliament to recognise that delegated legislation (sometimes called secondary legislation) –

"is not 'secondary' in importance, but is as important, if not more important in some cases, than primary legislation, and therefore should be accorded the necessary time for full and detailed scrutiny" (M 36, para. 6.7).

278. Some bodies, including the Bar Council (M 26) and Shelter (M 51, para. 2c), preferred use of the affirmative procedure for scrutiny of most statutory instruments. The Child Poverty Action Group drew our attention to the problem of "sub-delegated legislation" (it instanced directions relating to categories of need which could be met by the social fund established by the Social Security Act 1986) which the Secretary of State was under no duty to publish and are not subject to any parliamentary process or debate (M 16). Mr Justice Paul Kennedy believed that certain statutory instruments, especially those pursuant to Henry VIII clauses, should be amendable by Parliament (M 33, para. E)

279. There were some particular comments on the work of the House of Lords. Mr Vernon Bogdanor, a member of this Commission, has argued that the main role of the House of Lords ought now to be to act as a chamber of experts, bringing its expertise to bear on bills through the establishment of special standing committees which could examine evidence, rather than a legislative revising chamber as traditionally conceived[1]. However, the National Trust found the legislative arrangements of the Lords superior to those of the Commons (M 42, para. 13), and the Institute of Public Relations favoured the Lords committee procedures on the floor of the House, and noted with concern suggestions that some bills should go to special committees upstairs. It also proposed that the Lords could be used more for debates on Green or White Papers (M 31, para. 2f).

280. Some bodies were concerned about the practical problems they experienced in obtaining access to Parliament and following business on bills. For example the Magistrates' Association (M 38) and the National Trust (M 42. para. 11), would like to have more information about when particular sections of a bill were to be debated. Others, including the BMA (M 12), the local authority associations (M 37, section D) and the BBC (M 11, para. 13), drew attention to the difficulty and cost of getting bills and amendment papers and other relevant documents. The ITC complained of various difficulties in following legislation in Parliament and about access to committee rooms and the embargo on note-taking in the public galleries of the Commons' chamber (M 27, paras. 19-22).

Evidence of Members of Parliament on the Commons legislative processes

281. Members of Parliament approach these matters with a different perspective, and they drew attention to different problems. Inevitably they were not unanimous.

282. Mr Alan Beith, representing the Liberal Democrats, suggested to us that select committees might examine matters of social interest before legislation was introduced. Mr Dafydd Wigley believed that there should be more careful scrutiny of bills before second reading, and Mrs Margaret Ewing would like to see pre-legislative consideration of proposed Scottish bills by a committee of Scottish MPs. Lord Howe of Aberavon, on the other hand, was less sure that pre-legislation committees would help to improve the drafting of legislation.

---

1 Evidence given to the Select Committee of the House of Lords on The Committee Work of the House (HL 35-II of 1991-92), pp. 216-220, paras. 1-13.

283. Dr John Cunningham, representing the official Opposition, said that the Government were very reluctant to accept amendments to many of its bills, and he criticised the way some measures, such as the community charge bill and the football spectators bill, had been steam-rollered through; the Lords had had more success in getting their amendments accepted. Sir Peter Emery, Chairman of the Commons Procedure Committee, and Mr Wigley believed there should be more time between the presentation of bills and their committee stage, so that interested bodies could be consulted.

284. Lord Renton (M 47, para (j)), Lord Howe of Aberavon, Dr John Cunningham[1], Mr Tony Benn (M 8), Mr Graham Allen, Mr Andrew Bennett, Mr Bob Cryer, Sir Peter Emery, Mr Beith and Mr Wigley all told us that they would like to see more use of evidence-taking committees – special standing committees were particularly favoured by most of these Members – for examination of the details of some bills. Mr Wigley also suggested more use of informal seminars to brief MPs. However Sir John Wheeler said that special standing committees had not been a great success and did not want to see them further used. Sir Robert Rhodes-James, then a member of the Chairmen's Panel, said that ordinary standing committees often worked well. However, from his experience of chairing the special standing committee on the Matrimonial and Family Proceedings Bill in 1984, he also believed that special standing committees would be useful for some bills, provided that adequate time was allowed for taking evidence (it had not been, in his view, in 1984).

285. Sir John Wheeler, then Chairman of the Home Affairs Committee, was particularly opposed to sending bills to the departmentally-related select committees who should concentrate on examination of policy and expenditure in a dispassionate way, without the pressures from the Whips that taking the committee stages of current bills would inevitably attract. On the other hand, Mr Allen believed that these committees should look at all bills after first reading for a period of not more than six weeks; this would be a valuable learning process for MPs, and the Members concerned would then deal with the bill at all its later stages. Both Mrs Ewing and Mr Wigley supported the idea of bills going to select committees after first reading.

286. Mr Cryer, as Chairman of the Joint Committee on Statutory Instruments, drew attention to the fact that between 1500 and 2000 instruments a year were laid before Parliament; it was impossible to control these effectively. He recommended that affirmative instruments should never be debated until the Joint Committee had reported on them. There should be many more debates on "prayers" against statutory instruments (see paragraph 37), to be held after the Joint Committee had reported; in 1990-91, 114 "prayers" had been tabled, but only 25 had been debated. Dr Cunningham was critical of present procedures for scrutiny of statutory instruments; because they could not be amended, MPs had little interest in debating them. Mr Alan Beith agreed and proposed that

---

1   And see evidence given to the Select Committee of the House of Commons on Sittings of the House (HC20-II of 1991-92), pp. 51-55, para. 33.

instruments should be debated on substantive motions and that it should be possible to move formally that instruments should be amended in a specific way. He also found it totally unacceptable that the great majority of "prayers" against statutory instruments were not debated.

287. Mrs Ewing complained that statutory instruments were hurried through with far too little attention being paid to them. Mr Bennett drew attention to the fact that there was no scrutiny of Ministers' failure on occasions to use delegated powers; Ministers should be required to explain why they had decided not to use these powers. Mr Wigley made the same point about failure to make commencement orders for parts of Acts.

288. Mr Cryer believed that the remit of the Joint Committee on Statutory Instruments should not be widened, as the Committee should not get into policy matters, but its powers should be strengthened by ensuring that in all cases where it called special attention to an instrument, that instrument was debated. Sometimes the Committee had believed an instrument to be ultra vires, but that instrument had gone through Parliament without debate. Mr Bennett recognised that orders were sometimes withdrawn following criticisms by the Committee, but the Committee was very dependent on professional advice and he believed more assistance was needed, especially for the non-lawyer members.

289. Dr Cunningham, Mr Benn and Mr Allen wanted better research and information facilities for MPs. Mr Bennett would welcome the appointment of a legislative draftsman to help back-benchers. Sir Peter Emery said it would be helpful if Ministers always supplied their notes on clauses to committees on bills.

Evidence of Members on the Lords legislative processes

290. On the broader issues, Lord Williams of Elvel, representing the Labour Peers, said that he feared that the Lords was in danger of loosing its legitimacy as a revising chamber for Commons legislation; the balance of the parties had been damaged in recent years and the influence of the Opposition had been weakened. Lord Tordoff, representing the Liberal Democrat Peers, shared these fears and thought the situation was getting worse. As a politician, Lord Williams could not accept (as was sometimes suggested) that the Lords should ignore political issues and only look at the administrative or practicality aspects of legislation.

291. Turning to specifics, Lord Renton welcomed the fact that more bills now start in the Lords (M 47, para. (i)). Lord Williams would like to see earlier involvement of the Lords in the legislative process so that it could be more effective in revising legislation coming to it from the Commons; too many changes were made to bills in the Lords at a very late stage (he instanced fifty substantial new amendments which were made to the Financial Services Bill at Report stage without warning or prior consultation with Members). There could be useful prior consultations with interested parties, as there had been on the Copyright, Designs and Patents Bill, but the ability of Members to play a helpful part had been limited, he said, by the failure of the Government to circulate their proposals to the Opposition parties. Lord Tordoff was also concerned about time pressures; there was too much rushing of legislation without time for

effective discussions to help Peers to understand the bill or proposed amendments properly.

292. Lord Aberdare suggested that too much time was spent in committee in the Lords on probing amendments, designed to discover what a bill was intended to mean. It would be better to arrange an informal meeting, after second reading, between the Minister and his officials and Opposition front-bench representatives, interested back-bench peers and representatives of outside interest groups (this had occasionally been done after the committee stage). They would go through the bill clause by clause, clarifying its purposes and meaning and identifying possible objections. Such a meeting would also bring together the Ministers' advisers and those advising other Members, which could be fruitful in seeking agreement. Lord Tordoff welcomed this proposal, but Lord Williams emphasised the importance of public debate of controversial issues; the Electricity Bill had been changed extensively as a result of debate, he said.

293. Lord Williams would like to see more use made of special standing committees, with power to take evidence, even on controversial bills; there was much waste of time in committees of the whole House. Special standing committees should also be used for Law Commission bills. He would also welcome greater use of public bill committees for debating the committee stage, although he saw difficulties (as did Lord Tordoff) if there were to be many divisions in these or other committees; he was opposed to taking all debate on probing amendments off the floor of the House. Lord Aberdare was sceptical about using more select committees at any stage – pre-legislative, after first reading, or post-legislative – because of the difficulties (of which he had had direct experience as Chairman of Committees) of finding Members to man them – a view shared by Lord Tordoff.

294. Lord Tordoff would like to see a longer interval between second reading and the committee stage, so that outside bodies would have more time to brief Members. Lord Williams thought that too many amendments were debated at short notice; Members should be given more time to study them.

295. Lord Williams would like to see post-legislation select committees scrutinising the operation in practice of one or two Acts each session. This would be a natural part of the Lords revising function; it should not be done by joint committees of the two Houses.

Northern Ireland, Scottish and Welsh legislation

296. Some MPs from Northern Ireland were highly critical of the way Northern Ireland legislation is made by Northern Ireland Orders rather than by Acts and statutory instruments (Mr David Trimble (M 57) and Rev. Ian Paisley (M 46)). The Scottish Consumer Council drew attention to difficulties for Scottish organisations wishing to lobby Members of both Houses when important changes in Scottish law are appended to English bills, and to failure to find time to put Scottish Law Commission bills through Parliament (M 49). Mrs Margaret Ewing believed that the scrutiny of Scottish legislation by Scottish Members at Westminster could be greatly improved. Mr Dafydd Wigley thought that a

special Welsh committee should be set up to examine the administrative application of those parts of bills which apply to Wales or where the Secretary of State for Wales has responsibilities.

Evidence of academic students of Parliament

297. Professor David Miers and Professor Alan Page, representing the Study of Parliament Group, analysed many of the proposals that have been made for reform of the legislative processes in Parliament, and set out clearly the arguments for and against them. Starting from the reality that the legislative process is first and foremost a political process, noting the long-standing complaints about how it operates, recognising the Governments opposition to any reforms or additional scrutiny that could threaten its control of the parliamentary time-table or delay its legislation, they concluded that –

"*procedural reform by itself can achieve very little. The solution to the dissatisfaction currently being expressed lies with the Government and.....also with the Opposition who seldom display any real commitment to the effective scrutiny of legislation. For a Government committed to citizens' charters, performance standards and quality control, it may be thought odd that it should not be equally prepared to take steps to improve the quality of legislation and its scrutiny*" *(M 54, para. 13).*

298. Professor Philip Norton, who has written extensively on the workings of the UK Parliament and of other legislatures, submitted a long and helpful memorandum (M 45), which is too comprehensive to summarise here. He made a number of positive recommendations for change in Commons procedures, the main ones relevant to this chapter being: much more use of special standing committees to take evidence on bills; the appointment of a core of specialist Members for legislative committees in various areas, possibly drawing in the departmentally-related select committees which would need to be enlarged; the acceptance of regular time-tabling of bills; longer intervals between the stages of bills; improved research and other facilities for Members; better explanatory material to be published with bills; a review of procedures for scrutiny of statutory instruments; and linking of procedural reforms in the two Houses.

Previous inquiries

299. There have been a number of previous inquiries into the legislative procedures of both Houses, and our findings must be seen against this background. Many of these went into details of procedure with which we are not concerned; we paint on a wider canvass and are concerned with parliamentary processes and procedures as part of the whole legislative process. We took particular note of five more recent inquiries – four in the Commons and one in the Lords.

300. The Select Committee on Procedure reported on Public Bill Procedure in 1984-85[1]. The findings relevant to our inquiry were –

    (i) the departmentally-related select committees should not be used principally for considering legislation, but they could carry out some pre-legislative

---

1   Second Report of the Select Committee on Procedure of 1984-85 (HC 49).

work and could examine Green Papers or conduct inquiries linked to forthcoming legislation – as some had already done (para. 7);

(ii) the occasions for sending bills to select committees were strictly limited (para. 10);

(iii) the 1977-78 Procedure Committee had recommended that all bills should be committed to special standing committees unless the House otherwise ordered. This had not been accepted and in practice little use had been made of these committees, but the 1984-85 Committee said that nearly all the evidence it received, including that of the Solicitor General (Sir Patrick Mayhew), was enthusiastic about their operation. It recommended that the special standing committees be made a permanent part of the House's procedure and hoped that they would be used for a wider range of bills in future, including parts of Finance Bills (paras. 11-13);

(iv) to avoid taking up time at Report stage, Government amendments to fulfil ministerial undertakings given in standing committees should be considered by the original committee (para. 19);

(v) all Report stages should be kept on the floor of the House (para. 20);

(vi) minimal intervals between the stages of bills should be required (para. 23);

(vii) ordinary public bills should be dealt with in one session and their carry-over should not be allowed (para. 24); and

(viii) there was a pressing need for more balanced consideration of controversial bills and this required formal time-tabling. A Legislative Business Committee, set up for each Parliament, should propose a time-table for bills which were likely to need more than 25 hours in standing committee; the Committee would also propose time-tables for the remaining stages of the bill (paras. 26-44).

301. The Government did not accept the Procedure Committee's recommendations on time-tabling. The Procedure Committee of 1985-86 returned to the charge[1]. It recognised some objections to the proposed Legislative Business Committee and recommended that the time-table for a bill in a standing committee should be worked out by a Business Sub-Committee of that committee, representing those who best understood the bill, including back-benchers.

302. In 1990 the Procedure Committee surveyed the working of the departmentally-related select committees[2]. It considered what legislative role they should perform, and in particular whether bills should be formally committed to these committees for their committee stage. It concluded –

(i) "There is widespread dissatisfaction with the way the standing committee system operates" and "there is some validity in the argument that the questioning approach of select committees could lead to better thought out, and ultimately more workable, legislation" (para. 312);

(ii) there were, however, a number of practical difficulties in creating a formal legislative role for the departmentally-related select committees. It would

1 Second Report of the Select Committee on Procedure of 1985-86 (HC 324).
2 Second Report of the Select Committee on Procedure of 1989-90 (HC 19-I).

distract them from their inquiries into policy, administration and expenditure; there was a problem about the position of the Minister if his bill was committed to an existing select committee, of which he was not a member, for its committee stage; and "a formal involvement by select committees in legislation, including the power to make amendments to bills, would be bound to attract increasing attention from the Whips, which in its turn would place at risk the consensual approach adopted by select committees to the rest of their work". For these reasons the Committee did not favour a greater legislative function for these select committees (paras. 313-315);

(iii) it agreed, however, that the departmentally-related select committees should pay more attention to the ways in which legislation is implemented – how Acts and relevant delegated legislation are working in practice – a few years after it comes into effect (paras. 311 and 315); and

(iv) it repeated the support of earlier Procedure Committees for special standing committees; the procedure already existed and "all that is lacking is the necessary will on the Government's part". It recommended that "a reasonable proportion of the legislative programme" should be referred to special standing committees (para. 315).

303. The Select Committee on Sittings of the House (the "Jopling Committee")[1] reported in 1992 on the time-tabling of bills. Its evidence, including that from the Leader of the House (who suggested "the more widespread use of time-table motions, at Report stage for example") and the spokesmen for the Opposition parties, was almost without exception in favour of its more general use. Views varied on how extensive and comprehensive time-tabling should be. The Committee concluded that time-tabling should be applied after second reading to all bills committed to a standing committee, but that "existing practice" (the use of the guillotine) should continue for bills taken in committee of the whole House; the details of time-tables should be worked out by some kind of business committee as recommended by the Procedure Committee (paras. 63-69).

304. The Jopling Committee also reported on procedures for scrutiny of statutory instruments. It wished to reduce late night debates and recommended that affirmative instruments should normally be referred automatically to standing committees, although more important and controversial instruments should still be debated on the floor of the House. The maximum time allowed for standing committee debates should be extended to two and a half hours for each instrument (paras. 73-76).

305. The Select Committee of the House of Lords on The Committee Work of the House (the "Jellicoe Committee")[2] also considered the legislative role of committees. It concluded that:

---

1   HC 20-I of 1991-92.
2   HL 35-I of 1991-92.

(i) "the time has come for the House to consider a limited amount of legislation off the floor to improve the quality of legislation and save some time on the floor" (para. 181);

(ii) the use of Public Bill Committees (debating committees like the Commons standing committees), which had recently been revived experimentally with the Charities Bill, should be continued for one or two suitable bills each session (paras. 131 and 182); and

(iii) there should be an experimental use of special standing committees, taking a limited amount of evidence from interested parties, like those in the Commons, before considering a bill clause by clause; such committees would initially consider less controversial bills starting in the Lords. This procedure, the Committee believed, would be well suited for certain legal and technical bills, such as Law Commission bills or those concerning company law, which might otherwise not find a place in the legislative programme (paras. 132, 183 and 184).

306. The Jellicoe Committee also recommended the appointment, as an experiment, of a Delegated Powers Scrutiny Committee (as first suggested by the Chairman of this Commission) on the lines of the Scrutiny of Bills Committee of the Australian Senate. The Committee's scope should be narrower than that of the Australian committee (which also considers the effect of legislation on personal rights and liberties) and should initially be directed to the appropriateness of delegated powers and whether subsequent delegated legislation will be sufficiently subject to parliamentary approval. A first task of the Committee would be to see whether it was possible to devise ground rules and criteria as to what must be dealt with in primary legislation and what could properly be left to delegated legislation (see paragraphs 265-266 of this Report). The Committee would examine all bills before the Lords and report its findings before their committee stages. Its reports would be purely advisory and would not seek to amend bills (paras. 132 and 185).

Research findings

307. We commissioned two case studies. The lengthy proceedings of both Houses on the Broadcasting Bill 1989-90 are analysed in detail, including statistics of amendments moved etc., in Appendix 5. The much briefer proceedings on the Dangerous Dogs Bill 1990-91, which was guillotined in the Commons before any debate and passed all its stages in that House in one day, but which was more fully considered in the Lords, are analysed in Appendix 6.

Legislative processes in other parliaments

308. We have found comparisons with practice in other parliaments in the Commonwealth and elsewhere to be stimulating and helpful. Although some of their legislative processes would not be suitable for the Westminster system, we believe that lessons can be learned from some of their experience – both how things might be done, and how not. Documents describing the practices and experience of some other parliaments are referred to in Appendix 3.

Conclusions and recommendations

The legislative functions of Parliament

309. Legislation comprises a large part of Parliament's business. In Session 1990-91, 32% of the time on the floor of the House of Commons was taken up with Government bills, motions on statutory instruments and other proceedings related to legislation. Proceedings related to bills and Government motions on delegated legislation absorbed 58% of the total time spent on business initiated by the Government[1]. This takes no account of the large amount of time spent in various committees on Government bills and delegated legislation. In the Lords, 59% of floor time was spent on Government bills in 1988. It is important that this time is well used.

310. We begin by setting out our conception of the legislative functions of Parliament and of its two Houses. Parliament does not "make the law". That is essentially done by the Government which performs the decision-taking role in the constitution, and secures the approval of Parliament for its legislative decisions through its control over the majority party in the House of Commons[2]. **In practice, Parliament's main role in relation to UK legislation is to call Ministers to account for their proposals for changing the law by close and detailed scrutiny of both bills and delegated legislation.**

311. For its fulfilment, this requires opportunities in Parliament, in both Houses, to require information and explanation; to argue the policy; to press alternative policies and solutions; to examine how the law will be applied or implemented; to identify obscurities, ambiguities and other drafting problems; to seek to improve bills; and in general to carry out effective scrutiny of legislation.

312. The particular role of Members of the House of Commons is to speak for the people and to articulate the concerns of their constituents and of other affected groups, bodies or interests, including the policies, doctrines and interests of the political party they represent. This means there will always be an emphasis on the political aspects of legislation – seeking to highlight and publicise Governments' successes and failures – rather than simply trying to improve bills.

313. The particular role of the Lords is less political, with greater emphasis on constitutional issues and legal points. The Lords can also draw attention to matters not fully considered in the Commons, and can bringing forward new matters (often raised by interest groups) to be considered for inclusion in legislation. The Lords may be more concerned in seeking to improve the terms of a bill, and in generally acting as a revising chamber. An analysis of the bills which are introduced into the House of Lords is given in Appendix 4.

314. We have judged the present procedures and practices of the two Houses by their suitability and success in enabling the Houses to fulfil the legislative functions we have described. We have asked, are Members given the opportunities and procedures they require to exercise effective scrutiny of bills and delegated

---

1   Calculated from House of Commons Sessional Information Digest, 1990-91, Section A1.

2   See Griffith and Ryle, *Parliament*, op. cit., pp. 5-17.

legislation? **From the evidence received and our own impressions, we have concluded that both Houses fail to fulfil their legislative functions as effectively as they could do. In particular, the House of Commons as a whole should consider more deliberately for each individual bill how its scrutiny can be as effective as possible in the time available.**

315. We see a need, if parliamentary scrutiny of legislation is to be effective, for the House of Commons to move away from the largely party-political confrontation, substantially orchestrated by the front-benches and Whips on both sides, that at present characterises debates on bills, and to move towards a more considered approach whereby Members, from all parts of the House, could be enabled better to inform themselves and to look collectively, in a more systematic way, at the Government's legislative proposals.

316. More specifically, we have come to the following broad judgements:

- **Parliament could play a greater part by pre-legislative inquiry in the preparation of legislation.**
- **Both Houses could make better use of inquiry techniques, as used in select committees, to establish direct links with outside experts and affected interests, to get information and to probe the details of legislation.**
- **In debates on bills, particularly in committee, there has been too much emphasis on policy issues and inadequate attention to the practicality of what is proposed.**
- **In both Houses, legislative business is often too rushed.**
- **Scrutiny of delegated legislation is badly neglected in both Houses.**
- **There is not enough post-legislative review of the working of Acts.**
- **Public access to legislative proceedings is unduly restricted.**

317. We consider in the following sections what should be done to meet these criticisms. We recognise that much of what we propose would involve still further detailed and time-consuming work for Members of both Houses whose time is already heavily committed in standing committees, select committees and other parliamentary activity. But this need not freeze out better ways of handling bills and delegated legislation in the interests of the user. It is a question of priorities. We believe that our proposals for new procedures will help to focus Members' scrutiny of legislation more effectively.

318. Before turning to our specific proposals in relation to Government legislation, we mention one other feature of Parliament's legislative functions. Members in both Houses can also initiate legislation by private Members' bills. However we took little evidence on this subject and we received few criticisms of the use of these opportunities and procedures. They were welcomed by some bodies (for example the CBI (M 22)) and indeed some people would like to see the use of these bills expanded, but, as we have not examined the system of private Members bills, we make no recommendations for change.

Proceedings in the Commons

Conclusions and recommendations

Pre-legislative proceedings

319. We summarised the little evidence we received on pre-legislative proceedings in paragraphs 272, 282 and 300. Documents describing the practice in other parliaments are listed in Appendix 3.

320. The main responsibility for preparing legislation for presentation to Parliament lies with Governments. Members – and some outside bodies – sometimes complain about Parliament's lack of influence at the crucial formative stage when legislation is being prepared. However, as we have said, it is not a prime function of the British Parliament to "make the law" and Members are not necessarily expert in advising how the law should be framed. On the whole they should leave the initiative to Government but look critically at what Ministers produce.

321. On the other hand, there are occasions, and topics, on which some broader political input at the stage when legislation is being considered and prepared could be helpful to all those concerned. For example, parliamentary debate or inquiry could promote more public discussion of the policy options, could encourage consultations or could help create a consensus approach to a problem. All of this in time might help smooth the passage of the legislation through Parliament. General debate is obviously valuable, but often a more detailed fact-finding inquiry is needed, drawing on outside experience. We note that a few such pre-legislative inquires have been carried out in recent years by select committees in the Commons[1].

322. The mechanisms and opportunities already exist for carrying out pre-legislative inquiries. They should be more fully used. **We believe that departmentally-related select committees might helpfully examine Green and White Papers and other published consultative documents relating to proposed legislation and make reports which would assist the preparatory work on the legislation and inform parliamentary debate.**

323. Evidence was received of major changes in policy involving legislation being embarked on without adequate public airing and investigation (see paragraphs 71-74). Parliament could play a part here, as it has done in the past, for example when select committees were appointed to look at proposals for corporation tax (1970-71), tax credits (1972-73) and a wealth tax (1974-75. Although this last inquiry was not a success – the matter was too political – it is generally felt that the first inquiry, in particular, was helpful to both Government and Parliament in getting the legislation right. **On occasions, when a fuller inquiry is required into aspects of proposed legislation on which the experience and reactions of MPs would be relevant, and when the legislation is not needed in a hurry, select committees should be specially appointed to carry out**

---

1   See Gavin Drewry, ed. *The New Select Committees*, 2nd edition (Clarendon Press, Oxford, 1989); and Griffith and Ryle, *Parliament*, op. cit., pp. 424-428 and 430-433.

pre-legislative inquiries. This might sometimes be done by joint committees of the two Houses.

Scrutiny of bills

324. We have summarised the main evidence we received on the way bills are considered and scrutinised by the Commons in paragraphs 271, 273-274, 283-285 and 297-303.

325. Various Procedure Committees have attempted to achieve improvements in the way the House deals with legislation. On the whole their less important reforms have been adopted, but more important recommendations, particularly on the use of special standing committees, have not been accepted by Ministers. Members of all parties who gave evidence to us, and outside bodies with direct experience of bills before the House, were critical of present arrangements, and few were content with the way bills are now scrutinised. We believe that it is time for a fundamental re-appraisal of these processes, with more radical solutions than hitherto proposed.

326. We leave for the moment the important and disputed question of whether or not proceedings on bills should be systematically time-tabled. We consider this, as part of the broader question of the programming of legislation, in Chapter 7. However we must make one broad point at this stage. **We recognise that it would be difficult for the Government's business managers to accept some of our recommendations for more effective scrutiny of bills unless there were to be some compensating assurance, through time-tabling, that these would not cause unacceptable delays in the passage of legislation.**

327. Our recommendations are addressed both to Governments and to Parliament. Parliament itself has a collective responsibility to ensure the quality of the legislation it enacts, and therefore to give full and effective scrutiny to the practicalities involved, as well as to the policy and the politics. The Opposition of the day has a key role in this, because of its bargaining power with the Government over the business and procedures of the Commons. Furthermore, although the Government brings forward its legislation, the Opposition is largely in command of the way bills are examined, and of how debating time is used; it has a heavy responsibility to ensure that these opportunities are not wasted and that legislation is properly scrutinised.

328. **We fear that over the years Oppositions, of all parties, have too often failed to live up to these responsibilities**. Much time has been wasted in standing committees, especially on long filibusters on the early clauses of contentious bills. And too much time has been spent on repetitive debates of policy aspects which should have been settled – and accepted as settled – at second reading.

329. Although a major part of the House's debates on many bills must consist of political fighting and the clash between the parties on policies, the importance of also looking at the practical questions of how the eventual Act will work, and whether there are snags that could be avoided or better ways of achieving the same objectives, should not be neglected (see paragraph 274). We fear that this is increasingly ignored. The emphasis in committee should be on improving the

bill and not just on discrediting the policy and the Government (although those are legitimate Opposition objectives).

330. Broad assaults on policy are also counter-productive; it is much easier for a Minister to use political arguments to fend off an amendment which has been given a political flavour, rather than to deal with a carefully argued amendment on its merits. Overmuch concern with broad political points leads to poor scrutiny of legislation, and Ministers and their officials are not properly tested. The Opposition and Members from either side will naturally decide what they should debate, but for all the reasons we have given, **we believe it is important that debates on bills in committee should not concentrate too much on policy but deal also with practical questions of the bill's operation.**

331. **We see a need for a two stage approach to the examination of bills in the House of Commons.** At the first stage Members should be able to brief themselves about the purpose, meaning and intended application of the bill. At this stage there should also be an opportunity for outside bodies and people to give the House their views and information on the proposed legislation. No formal decisions on the content of the bill would be taken at this stage. After the House had thus briefed itself, it would proceed to the second, decision-taking stage – the second reading, committee, report and third reading – when the bill would be formally considered, amended and passed.

332. We first set out our proposals for **the preliminary briefing stage.** Only a select committee, with power to take evidence from civil servants as well as from outside experts, affected parties and the wider public, could undertake preliminary exploration of a bill in this way. We also see some advantages in the practice of referring bills to committees before they are debated in the House itself, as in most European parliaments. The procedure we envisage is derived from – but not the same as – that which has been developed and appears to work well in the House of Representatives of New Zealand, where committees examine nearly all bills after they are presented to parliament and before second reading (a description of this procedure is referred to in Appendix 3)[1].

333. Immediately after a bill's first reading and publication a select committee could be appointed to examine the bill. It should have some twelve to sixteen members, drawn from all parts of the House; as usual there would be a majority of Government supporters. These committees would be completely distinct from the departmentally-related select committees, although overlapping membership with the select committee that covers the department responsible for the bill would be helpful in many cases.

334. In order to avoid premature political commitment and not to restrict their freedom to adopt, at a later stage, a different stance from that reflected in the

---

1   And see Austin Mitchell, "The New Zealand Way of Committee Power", to be published in a
    forthcoming issue of *Parliamentary Affairs*. For similar proposals for reforming committee
    procedures, but involving select committee examination of bills after second reading, see J A G
    Griffith, *Parliamentary Scrutiny of Government Bills*, op. cit., pp. 246-252.

bill, Ministers and Opposition shadow-Ministers should not be on the committee. As the committees would not be required to vote on the policies incorporated in the bills before them, they might, in many cases, adopt a consensual approach to their work (as do the departmentally-related select committees today); it would therefore not be desirable to appoint Government or Opposition Whips.

335. It would not be the function of the committee to hold Ministers to account or to attack the Government or its policies expressed in the legislation. It might, however, expect to persuade Ministers to look again at some of the proposed provisions of the bill, and to consider sympathetically improvements suggested by the committee. The Chairman should therefore be a senior Government back-bencher who has a good working relationship with the relevant Ministers.

336. The committee would issue a public invitation to all interested or affected bodies or individuals – and indeed to the wider public – to make written submissions on the bill. If the consultation processes had worked well and all the provisions of the bill had been carefully thought out, there might be few representations at this stage. In other cases – or where there were strong policy differences – many bodies might want to press their arguments further with the select committee. It would be for the staff of the committee to sift and analyse the submissions and for the committee to decide who should be invited to attend for public hearings of evidence. Civil servants from the departments concerned (but not Ministers) and other experts would be invited to give evidence to clarify the purpose, meaning and intended application of the bill.

337. Having considered the evidence, the committee would deliberate in private and agree a report, which could draw attention to ambiguities in purpose or meaning, apparent problems in the application or implementation of the legislation, possible consequences of the proposed policies and other practical, technical or drafting points that have emerged. The committee would have power to recommend improvements in the bill but would not be able to amend the text.

338. The committee would have to work hard and fast, meeting at least as often as standing committees do today. And it would have to have adequate staff, including in some cases specialist advisers – those assisting the corresponding departmentally-related select committees might be suitable appointments, if available.

339. The procedures we have outlined would not be suitable for bills required in a hurry, or for many simple bills with few problems of application. Preliminary examination by a committee would however be appropriate for many other bills. **We recommend that in most cases the more complex bills – even if controversial – should be referred to a select committee immediately after their presentation to the House.** We refer to these committees as "first reading committees".

340. We see real advantages in the use of first reading committees at the briefing stage. Clarification of ambiguities and intent at the very beginning, before the Minister is fully politically committed by the debate on second reading – before

the political concrete has set – could well save time later on by reducing the need to debate probing amendments in committee. Areas of disagreement could be clearly identified at this stage and, except on major political issues, possible means of compromise explored, especially on practical questions of application and administration. In general, if Members could explore the bill and brief themselves in this way, they would come to the specific debates on the bill much better prepared than they are now; and the Minister would have a better idea of what matters are troubling Members. The committees' hearings would also create a direct link between the pre-parliamentary preparation of legislation and the scrutiny of the bill by Parliament, and provide a natural progression from consultation with affected bodies to public debate.

341. Although the additional examination of bills that we propose would require more time, and extra work by Members, there should be benefits to all the participants in the legislative process. It would stem the headlong legislative rush which troubled many of those who gave evidence to us. It would make the House of Commons the ultimate focus of the widespread and growing desire to be heard and thus enhance Parliament's standing. It would give Opposition Members a much more constructive and interesting legislative role than the frustrating and negative job of seeking to obstruct proceedings in standing committees. It would enable Government back-benchers to play a more positive part in the scrutiny of bills. And it would be of value to the Government by drawing attention at the first parliamentary stage to practical problems in the application of its proposals that may have been overlooked, by helping to avoid mistakes in statute law, and finally by making legislation more acceptable to those to whom it will apply. In general, improved parliamentary scrutiny of legislation should lead to improved quality of statute law.

342. We now turn to the second, decision-taking stage of the parliamentary processes.

343. **The second reading** is the main occasion for debating the policy of a bill and for the big political arguments, if the bill so requires. Once a bill is read a second time, the main policies of the bill should be taken as approved. We see no need for change in the nature of the debate itself. **However prior examination by a first reading committee could reduce the need for long second reading debates in many cases. We also believe that Second Reading Committees could more frequently be used for bills on which a division is not expected.**

344. We turn to the **formal committee stage** (leaving aside committees of the whole House, on which we make no observations). Standing committees do a vast amount of work. Taking a recent normal length session, in 1989-90 27 Government bills were considered at their committee stage at 437 meetings of standing committees; a total of 620 Members were appointed to serve on standing committees of all types (not only Government bills), with many Members attending at least twenty meetings and 33 attending on more than 40 occasions. Many bills required only a few sittings, but the Broadcasting Bill was considered at 38 sittings (see Appendix 5), the Environment Protection Bill at

32, the National Health Service and Community Care Bill at 30 and the Law Reform (Miscellaneous Provisions) (Scotland) Bill [Lords] at 21[1]. As the average length of a sitting is some two-and-a-half to three hours (depending on the extent of afternoon and evening sittings), and as about twenty Members are usually appointed to each committee, attendance at standing committees absorbs a large amount of Members' time.

345. It is essential to try to ensure that all this time and effort is used effectively. The present standing committees can do a good job, as an experienced Member reminded us (paragraph 284), and some of their debates are excellent. However, as the 1990 Procedure Committee reported, "there is widespread dissatisfaction with the way the standing committee system operates" (see paragraph 302 above), and much of our evidence bears this out (paragraphs 274-275 and 284). Certainly many Members appear to find committee work on bills to be largely a waste of time under present procedures; Government back-benchers are discouraged by their Whips from making any contribution; the Opposition side feels frustrated because it can make so little impact on the bill; Ministers are forced to make few concessions of any significance at this stage[2]; the public, say some Members, are alienated by the whole process. On the other hand, the importance of requiring Ministers to explain and defend their bills publicly, even if in the end no amendments are made, should not be ignored. The important question is: how can this accountability best be achieved?

346. Much of the problem, we believe, results from the procedures used in standing committees. The very process of two sides confronting each other, and of every amendment requiring a "yes" or "no" at the end of the debate (if it is not withdrawn), tends to highlight the policy content of debates. The decision on the main policies at second reading should restrict policy debates at later stages, but we fear that this principle is not always respected and that the Opposition too frequently returns at the committee stage to the broader policy questions. This approach tends to play down the more consensual approach needed for consideration of practical questions.

347. Furthermore, both sides are dependent on advisers, but they must sit at opposite ends of the room, they must brief Ministers and other Members privately (often by passing scribbled notes), and they cannot explain their points direct to the committee or be questioned by them. The process is too hidden from the public and officials and interested bodies and pressure groups cannot readily be challenged (by other groups as well as Members) on the advice they give. The whole process is inefficient and highly unsatisfactory for Members and for all

---

1   House of Commons Sessional Returns, 1989-90 (HC 218). For a fuller analysis of the work of standing committees, especially on Government bills, see Griffith and Ryle, *Parliament*, op. cit., pp. 270-279 and 315-329.

2   See J A G Griffith, *Parliamentary Scrutiny of Government Bills*, op. cit., Chapter 6; Griffith and Ryle, *Parliament*, op. cit., pp. 315-317; and Andrew Adonis's case study of the Water Act 1988 in *Parliament Today* (Manchester University Press, 1990).

concerned[1].

348. In our view – and that of many people, including a succession of Procedure Committees – the present procedures in standing committees are no longer acceptable for scrutiny of many bills. They are particularly unsatisfactory for debates on more complex bills or those where information or advice from outside experts and affected bodies would be relevant. In the Australian Senate and in the Canadian House of Commons bills are often sent to committees which call evidence as well as deliberating on the clauses of the bill, and we understand that this works well (documents relating to these procedures are listed in Appendix 3). **The conclusion that the time has come to make it possible to receive direct evidence on bills in committee flows overwhelmingly from our own evidence.**

349. We see some difficulties in going over to a complete select committee system for all committee stages of bills, not least in their time-tabling. In particular we would not favour sending bills to the departmentally-related select committees for the reasons given by the Procedure Committee (paragraph 302). However the special standing committee system, as advocated by the Procedure Committee (paragraphs 300 and 302), enables committees to examine witnesses and to publish their evidence at the beginning of their examination of a bill before turning to more formal debates (and party disciplines) for the decision-taking processes on proposed amendments and on the clauses of the bill. This system, which was used on five occasions between 1980 and 1984, has been strongly supported by Sir Patrick Mayhew, who as Solicitor General had direct experience of the working of this kind of committee, and who has described the procedures as "a real advance in our treatment of statute law".[2] It was also supported many bodies and Members who gave evidence to us (paragraphs 275 and 284), **We therefore recommend that after second reading a bill should normally be committed to a special standing committee.**

350. The committee should comprise the members of the first reading committee (if there was one) and in any event should include members of the relevant departmentally-related select committee. Ministers, Opposition shadow Ministers and Whips would also be members of special standing committees.

351. As far as possible, special standing committees should carry out detailed scrutiny of all parts of the bill, and look particularly at the practical problems of implementation etc., and at matters where the purposes, meaning or intended application of the bill are not clear. Although after the evidence hearings, all the clauses of the bill would be debated in the usual way, it might be convenient, by agreement between the parties, to defer major policy debates to the Report stage, as is sometimes done at present. Government amendments, including

---

· 1   For an examination of the inefficiency of proceedings in standing committees, see J A G Griffith, *Parliamentary Scrutiny of Government Bills*, op. cit., pp.244-246.

2   Rt Hon Sir Patrick Mayhew, QC, MP, "Can Legislation Ever be Simple, Clear, and Certain", *Statute Law Review* , Vol. 11, No. 1 (Summer 1990).

amendments responding to criticisms or suggestions made by the first reading committee, if there was one, would also be debated at this stage.

352. Subject to any time-tabling, special standing committees should be free to decide for themselves how to spend their time; they should not be restricted (as they are under the present standing order) by limits on the number of days on which evidence may be heard. Indeed the committee should not be obliged to hear any further evidence. It would be important to avoid duplication of evidence, and if the bill had already been considered by a first reading committee then the proceedings in the special standing committee might be considerably shorter, as much of the relevant evidence would already have been heard and agreement might have been reached on many matters. The time spent on debating clauses and amendments should also be reduced by deferment of big policy debates, and because clarifications of purposes, meaning or intended application at the evidence-hearing stage should considerably curtail the need for probing amendments.

353. There are two subordinate points about the committee stage which we wish to commend as helpful to Members. First, **circulation of notes on clauses and, where appropriate, of notes on Government amendments, as prepared for Ministers, has become fairly general in recent years. We recommend that this should now become the standard practice.**

354. Second, **it would be a useful preparation for debates on a technical or complex bill if the Minister and his civil servants were to hold a pre-committee informal factual briefing for all Members.** This was done recently on the Fisheries Bill 1992.

355. **The report stage** should be primarily concerned with debates on areas of policy disagreements and on other major matters deferred from the special standing committees. And, as at present, there should be further detailed debate on problems discovered at earlier stages but not yet resolved, in particular following Government undertakings in committee. **We recommend that, if there are many detailed points to be further debated at report stage, bills should be re-committed to the special standing committee for this purpose.** This would save time on the floor of the House.

356. We make no proposals for changes in the procedure on **third reading**.

357. House of Commons **consideration of Lords Amendments** is often concerned with detailed points, for which expert explanation would be helpful. **When there is no great rush** – as there often unfortunately is – **and there are large numbers of Lords Amendments, we recommend that they be committed to the special standing committee for consideration.**

358. Several people and bodies complained to us about proceedings on bills being too rushed. There was particular concern about insufficient time being allowed between publication of a bill and its committee stage for interested bodies to brief Members, and Members would also like more time to conduct their own research and seek advice. Complaint was also made of not enough time being allowed for Members and interested bodies to study Government amendments (paragraphs 273 and 283). Frequently, very little time is allowed for Members

to study Lords Amendments before they are debated in the Commons. Procedure Committees have recommended that there should be not less than two weekends between first and second reading; ten days between the second reading and the start of the committee stage; and ten days between report from committee and the start of the report stage.

359. However, as the Procedure Committee of 1984-85 discovered, these minimum intervals between stages have frequently not been complied with. In 1983-84, 7 out of 43 bills had their second reading after less than the recommended interval; 14 out of 36 bills were considered in committee too early; and 8 out of 34 bills were considered on report after less than the recommended interval[1]. As an example of a rushed bill, the Dangerous Dogs Bill 1991 stands out. It was published on 4 June, 1991; it was taken through all its stages in the Commons, under a guillotine, on 10 June (Appendix 6).

360. Furthermore, Government amendments have often been tabled very late. For example, the 1986 Finance Bill was reported from committee on 19 June and reprinted as amended on 26 June; 156 Government amendments were tabled between 30 June and 4 July, the last bunch, including 5 important new clauses were tabled on a Friday and so were not readily available till Monday 7 July; the report stage was due to be held on 8 and 9 July (in the end the second day was postponed till 17 July when the new clauses were debated)[2].

361. These are not very recent examples, but continuing complaints of late tabling of Government amendments suggest that matters have not improved. Our own researches bear this out. During the committee stage in the Commons on the Broadcasting Bill in 1990, complaint was made that not enough time had been given for consultation on 21 new clauses and Schedules tabled only a week to ten days before the end of the committee stage, and the Opposition complained again at the Report stage about the time constraints under which they had to operate. On the same bill in the Lords, the Government tabled 46 pages of technical amendments (including new clauses and Schedules) on the afternoon of Friday 20 July, which were due to be considered on Tuesday, 24 July. Following criticism, Ministers promised to table as many of their further amendments as possible by 19 September for the Report stage starting on 9 October. In the event, out of 294 Government amendments, 203 were tabled by the promised day, but many other important amendments were not tabled until 28 September, and further substantial amendments were tabled as late as 4 October. Ministers explained these delays in part by reference to the need for lengthy consultations[3] ; this was 10 months after the publication of the Bill (Appendix 5).

362. In our view it is essential that there should be enough time for bills and amendments to be properly considered and for the desirable partnership between Parliament and the public in responding to legislation to be made

---

1   Second Report of 1984-85, op. cit., para. 23; see also Griffith and Ryle, *Parliament*, op. cit., p. 242.
2   Griffith and Ryle, ibid., p. 243
3   HL Deb., 9 October, 1990, cols. 154-156.

effective. We believe that this problem could be alleviated by the systematic time-tabling of all bills (see Chapter 7), and we point out that there would be more time to study bills if they were referred to first reading committees, as we have proposed. **However, to avoid legislation being unduly rushed, we recommend that the minimum intervals between the stages of bills be increased and that longer notice should be required for amendments on report.**

Northern Ireland, Scottish and Welsh legislation

363. We have considered the evidence we received from Northern Ireland MPs and from Members representing the Scottish Nationalist Party and Plaid Cymru regarding procedures for bills relating to their jurisdictions (paragraph 296). We hope that their special problems will be considered sympathetically – especially the case for returning to legislating for Northern Ireland by Acts rather than Orders – though we recognise serious political and constitutional implications of any change in respect of most of the matters drawn to our attention.

Delegated Legislation

364. Few, if any, people are satisfied with the attention the Commons pays to delegated legislation, although some think that the problem results from the sheer number of statutory instruments and can see little that could be done about it. The evidence from interested bodies (paragraphs 277-278), Members of Parliament (paragraphs 286-288) and academics (M 45) was almost universal: the present arrangements for debate and scrutiny of statutory instruments are inadequate and ineffective.

365. Following reports by various Procedure Committees, opportunities for debate of statutory instruments have been provided, both on the floor of the House and in standing committees, but time is not provided for debate on many of the instruments subject to the negative procedure ("prayers" – see paragraph 37) that Members wish to debate (paragraph 286). Furthermore, these debates are time limited and those in committee take place on a technical motion that does not permit the expression of any views on the merits of an instrument – not even on whether it should be approved or not[1]. The only changes proposed in recent years have been those recommended by the Jopling Committee (paragraph 304).

366. **Law contained in delegated legislation is no less the law of the land than the law contained in Acts of Parliament, and must be treated as seriously.** In our view, the main flaws in the way Parliament treats delegated legislation at present derive from the fact that Ministers, the Opposition and Members generally treat nearly all delegated legislation as less important than primary legislation. Of course most delegated (or secondary) legislation is less important than most bills, but many statutory instruments are of more than "secondary" importance, as the Law Society reminded us (paragraph 277) and should be given equally serious consideration. Present procedures do not encourage this. **We consider the whole approach of Parliament to delegated legislation to**

---

1 For the procedures and practices in debating secondary legislation in the Commons, see Griffith and Ryle, *Parliament*, op. cit., pp. 244-247, 275, 331-334, 345-350 and 406-407.

be highly unsatisfactory. The House of Commons in particular should give its procedures for scrutiny of statutory instruments a thorough review.

367. We aim to make a start on such a review. We suggest a number of ways by which scrutiny of delegated legislation could be improved. We recognise that, without time-tabling, some of the reforms we recommend would not be acceptable to Ministers ; this we consider in Chapter 7. We also recognise that additional scrutiny requires additional commitments by Members, including Ministers, and that a balance has to be struck between total accountability and practicability. Overall, however, we are convinced that the balance of parliamentary attention to delegated legislation needs to be be shifted in the direction of improved scrutiny and fuller accountability.

368. Members, it is said, are little interested in statutory instruments (paragraph 286). However, one of the problems for Members in getting to grips with delegated legislation is simply discovering what there is to examine or debate. 2,000 or more statutory instruments are laid before Parliament each year; there were 2,945 in1990 (Appendix 7); many of these are very minor but among them are some important and interesting ones. Of course affected bodies lobby Members on regulations etc. that they are unhappy about, but even then it is difficult to identify those that most merit debate; this applies particularly to "prayers". Members need some more detached, parliamentary appraisal of the importance of instruments, similar to that given to EC documents by the European Legislation Committee. Members would also find delegated legislation more interesting, we believe, if they were able to take a closer look at what was coming forward.

369. We do not propose any new formal procedures. The machinery already exists for drawing the attention of the House to important delegated legislation; it only needs to be used. **We recommend that the departmentally-related select committees might review statutory instruments in their field when they are laid before Parliament, and report on those that raise matters of public importance.** They could, for example, identify matters that required further clarification or justification by Ministers in debate.

370. Some experienced Members expressed concern about the powers and functions of the Joint Committee on Statutory Instruments (paragraph 288). This Committee does valuable work in examining all instruments to ensure that they are properly made under the powers given to Ministers by Act and are clear in their drafting, etc.[1] However, some of its critical findings appear to be ignored by Ministers. We heard from the Chairman of the Committee that some instruments on which his Committee had reported adversely had not been debated. We also understand that debates on affirmative resolutions, approving instruments, are quite often held before the Committee has had time to report[2].

---

1   For a description and analysis of the work of this committee, see Griffith and Ryle, *Parliament*, op. cit., pp. 444-446.

2   First Report from the Procedure Committee, 1977-78 (HC 588-I), para. 3.8.

371. We find this very unsatisfactory, If the Joint Committee is to be effective, its reports must be heeded and Ministers should be required to answer its criticisms in debate. We recommend that, except in cases of emergency (which a Minister would have to explain to the House) no statutory instrument should be debated until the Joint Committee on Statutory Instruments has reported. Furthermore, where the Joint Committee has reported that it considers an instrument to be ultra vires or otherwise defective, a motion to approve that instrument should not be made without a resolution to set aside the findings of the Committee. This, in effect, is what happens in Australia (see documents listed in Appendix 3).

372. We turn to debates on statutory instruments. First there is the question of where the debates should be held. We see little merit in short debates late at night on the floor of the House with few Members taking part, as often happens now. We agree with the Jopling Committee that it is desirable to free the time of the House itself by sending most delegated legislation to standing committees for debate[1]. We also see positive advantages in debating such business in smaller committee, with their more relaxed procedures, in the morning at a time when the media, if interested, can cover the proceedings more easily and interested bodies can attend and brief Members. This should improve the appeal and effectiveness of these debates. **We therefore recommend that, unless the House otherwise orders** (as might be agreed by the parties for occasional instruments raising major policy issues or for totally routine instruments on which no debate is desired) **all statutory instruments requiring affirmative resolutions, and all "prayers" for the annulment of other statutory instruments, should automatically be referred to standing committees for debate.**

373. **Longer or more complicated statutory instruments, which do not have to be approved in a hurry, could sometimes be sent to a special standing committee which could hear evidence.**

374. A prime objective must be to make it possible for Members to play a more constructive part in the work of standing committees on statutory instruments than they do at present, so that they will find it more worthwhile to spend time on them. Only then will they scrutinise delegated legislation properly. Drawing on suggestions made to us by Members (see paragraph 286), we propose three improvements to present procedures in standing committees on statutory instruments.

375. First, **we recommend that before a committee starts debating a statutory instrument, it should be able to question Ministers on the purpose, meaning and effect of that instrument**. This follows the procedure now used for the debates on European Community documents in standing committees, which we understand has proved helpful.

376. Second, the motions on which debates are held must be made more meaningful and interesting (not least to the media) than is the present motion (for the

---

1   HC 20-I of 1991-92, op. cit., paras. 72-73.

chairman to report that the committee has considered the instrument), which conveys no view on the merits of the instrument and does not even permit a meaningful vote. If Members are asked to debate an instrument they must be able to record – with a meaningful vote if so desired – their opinions on the matter, or at least their willingness or not to approve the instrument or to accept the "prayer" for its annulment, as the case may be. **We recommend that the debate on a statutory instrument in standing committees should be held on a substantive motion approving, rejecting or otherwise expressing opinions on the instrument.**

377. Third, many people have often complained that debates on statutory instruments are somewhat pointless because the House has no power (in the great majority of cases) to amend the instrument (paragraph 286). We see great difficulty in empowering the House or its committees to amend the text of instruments. If amendments were made in committee, there would have to be a report stage for the House to look at the instrument again; if amendments were agreed in the Commons, then, unless identical amendments were made in the Lords, there would have to be some procedure, as with bills, for seeking to resolve differences between the two Houses. Indeed, amendable statutory instruments would be very like bills, and all the advantages of the greater flexibility of delegated legislation would be lost.

378. However, the formal power to make amendments is not so important. In standing committees on bills, amendments are often moved, debated and then withdrawn on the Minister's undertaking to look at the matter again, and frequently the Minister moves the desired amendments to the bill at a later stage. It is the proposing and debating of the amendment that is important, not the immediate decision, provided that there is an opportunity for the bill to be amended at some stage. In the case of statutory instruments this could be achieved by allowing Members to suggest amendments to the text of the instrument, and if the Minister was persuaded that the wording might be improved, he would agree to withdraw the instrument and re-lay it in an amended form (if he was not so persuaded, the committee would still be able to vote on the suggested amendments). The revised instrument would again be examined in committee after it was re-laid, and the Minister would still have to persuade Members that he had got the wording right.

379. In order to enable Members to suggest amendments to statutory instruments, without actually amending the instrument, **we recommend that amendments be permitted to a substantive motion moved in a committee on a statutory instrument, either relating to the merits of the whole instrument or recommending that it be approved subject to specified amendments being made to the instrument itself.** To prevent abuse, the chairman of the committee would have the usual power to select amendments to the motion.

380. We do not like artificial restrictions on the length of debate on a matter, unrelated to the importance of or interest in that matter (such as the maximum of an hour-and-a-half at present allowed for debates on statutory instruments in committee, whatever their content). **We recommend that, subject to more**

general time-tabling (see Chapter 7), there should be no time limits on debates on statutory instruments in standing committees.

381. We have not described in detail the procedures that would be needed to implement our recommendations for debate of statutory instruments, but we set out in Annex A an outline of a system that the Procedure Committee may wish to consider.

382. One specific point that arose in evidence gives us cause for concern. The CPAG drew our attention to certain directions made by the Minister which regulated peoples claims for assistance out of the social fund established by the Social Security Act 1986 (paragraph 278 and M 16). Although these directions are obviously a serious matter for those concerned, they are apparently not subject to any parliamentary procedure – they are a species of "sub-delegated" legislation – and apparently could not be debated in Parliament. This is not acceptable. **We recommend that Acts and delegated legislation should always be so drafted that all important regulations and other delegated legislation may be debated in Parliament.**

383. There remains one problem about scrutiny of delegated legislation that is of considerable importance. As pointed out to us by the Chairman of the Joint Committee on Statutory Instruments, no time is provided for debating many "prayers" against statutory instruments ; only 25 out of 114 "prayers" that were tabled in session 1990-91 were debated. The inclusion in an Act of provision for motions to annul statutory instruments is a formal recognition of Parliament's rights to scrutinise such legislation. This statutory right is taken away if time is not provided for debates on "prayers".

384. Studies have shown that the 1990-91 situation was not un-typical. This has been a problem for many years and the percentage of prayers on which no action was taken is growing (from 28% in 1978-79 to 69% in 1985-86 and 78% in 1990-91)[1]. Although the official Opposition may suffer less than back-bench Members, as time is usually provided for the "prayers" they are really anxious to debate, the generally unsatisfactory arrangements for debates on "prayers" has troubled many people – including the Procedure Committee[2] and some of those who gave evidence to us (paragraphs 277 and 286) – for a long time.

385. Yet nothing has been done. Although, when procedures were changed in the 1950s to prevent unlimited debate in the House on an almost unlimited number of "prayers", and time restrictions and debates in standing committees were introduced, Ministers indicated their intention to ensure that time would always be provided for all serious "prayers" to be debated[3], in practice, as we have seen, these assurances seem to have been increasingly forgotten.

---

1   Griffith and Ryle, *Parliament*, op. cit.,give details of the numbers of "prayers" against statutory instruments in more recent years, and of their use by the official Opposition and by back-benchers, pp.345-350 and 406-407.

2   Second Report from the Procedure Committee, 1986-87 (HC 350), paras. 12 and 29.

3   For example, Captain Harry Crookshank, as Leader of the House, promised that "if honourable Gentlemen put down prayers, time will be found for prayers", HC Deb.(1951-52), Vol. 497, col. 1519.

386. The solution in the end must lie with the House of Commons, and particularly with Ministers and the Whips, to ensure that enough committees are appointed for "prayers" (other than those that are clearly trivial or designed to block other business) to be debated. No House time would be lost by debates in committee. The fact that under our proposals, all "prayers" would automatically be referred to committees, and so would form queues while awaiting debate, should act as a spur to the appointment of enough committees.

387. We have emphasised this problem because it involves a major erosion of Parliament's rights and a potential weakening of the scrutiny of delegated legislation. We again recognise that a balance may have to be struck between accountability and practicability – not every prayer can always be debated – but **we recommend that, as a matter of principle, "prayers" against statutory instruments should, as far as possible, be debated. We further recommend that the Legislation Steering Committee which we propose should be appointed (paragraph 507 and Annex B) should seek to agree the arrangements for standing committees to consider "prayers" and for selecting the "prayers" to be debated. This would ensure that the arrangements were not abused and that all parties, and back-benchers from both sides, were given a fair share of the opportunities to debate their "prayers".**

Post-legislative Review

388. We received evidence from several bodies on the part the Commons might play in review of legislation on the statute book (paragraph 276). The Procedure Committee believed that the departmentally-related select committees could profitably pay more attention to the ways in which legislation had been implemented (paragraph 302).

389. One source of information about how statute law is working in practice is the courts who, day in and day out, observe how some parts of the the law are being applied when trying cases, both civil and criminal, that come before them. These cases may reveal some weaknesses in the law, and judges have frequently drawn attention to ambiguities or apparent errors in the drafting of statutes or have suggested changes that may be required as a result of their interpretation of the law as it stands. On other occasions, Ministers or Government departments have had to consider changing the law as a result of a decision by the courts.

390. However this is a somewhat haphazard process, greatly dependent on what cases happen to come before the courts. In some other countries the courts play a more systematic role in reviewing statute law. In France, for example, the Cour de Cassation reviews contentious decisions of other courts and, when necessary, draws the attention of Parliament to the need to clarify the law. Improvements recommended by the Cour de Cassation are from time to time brought together in what might be called a "Law Reform (Miscellaneous Provisions) Bill" (see documents listed in Appendix 3). We considered whether the courts in this country could perform a similar more systematic and formal role in reviewing statute law, but Mr Justice Paul Kennedy, representing the Judges' Council, did not see our courts working in this way, though there could

be some merit in the courts giving advisory opinions in hypothetical cases (subject to there being enough judges to do the additional work) (M 33).

391. We also noted suggestions from the CBI (M 22, section 3) and from the FDA (M 5, para. 31) that the Law Commission, working closely with the responsible Government departments, might carry out reviews of the statute book in agreed areas on a systematic basis. We agree with the CBI that the present arrangements within Government for review of how Acts are working are ad hoc, with a variety of means being used. This may not be satisfactory, but it must be for Government to decide whether more systematic reviews by departments would be feasible or desirable. The Law Commission does sometimes identify errors and can seek to correct them. Perhaps, if its resources were increased, it could do more along these lines, but we make no recommendations on this matter.

392. A strong feeling ran through much of our evidence, however, that Parliament itself could do more to review systematically how legislation – both Acts and delegated legislation – is working out in practice. This is a task for which MPs are particularly well qualified because of the feed-back they get from constituencies and interested bodies.

393. **We recommend that the operation of every major Act (other than Finance Acts and some constitutional Acts), and all the delegated legislation made under it, should be reviewed some two or three years after it comes into force.** With the Procedure Committee, we believe that such reviews could best be done by the relevant departmentally-related select committee, and indeed some of the committees have carried out inquiries on these lines[1].

394. However the work-load of these committees is already heavy and we have proposed additional matters – Green and White Papers and delegated legislation – for their attention. It might be possible to appoint sub-committees to carry out post-legislative reviews, but this would not lessen the responsibilities of individual Members. It might therefore be necessary, at the instance of the relevant departmentally-related select committee, which could make a simple assessment of whether a fuller review was required (after all many Acts work well and provoke few criticisms), for a detailed examination of the working of an Act to be undertaken by a select committee on legislative review specifically appointed for this purpose. We note a proposal from the National Union of Mineworkers for something on these lines (M44, paras. 2-3). For review of the operation of some Acts – for example on law reform or the courts – a joint committee of the two Houses might be appropriate.

395. **We recommend that the committees carrying out post-legislative reviews should also examine, in the light of experience with the Act, the adequacy of the consultative process developed in accordance with our recommendations in Chapter 3.** The possibility of such review would

---

1   See Gavin Drewry, ed. *The New Select Committees* , 2nd edition (Clarendon Press, Oxford, 1989); and Griffith and Ryle, *Parliament*, op. cit., pp. 424-428 and 430-433.

encourage full compliance with the spirit as well as the letter of the Governments consultation guidelines that we have proposed.

Proceedings in the Lords

The evidence

396. Few outside bodies commented specifically about the legislative processes of the House of Lords. The evidence we did receive was mostly complimentary (paragraph 279). A former Chairman of Committees, and other Peers representing Opposition parties, were more critical (M 1 and M 2; and see paragraphs 290-295). The main theme of their evidence was a desire for the Lords to play a more active and constructive part in the legislative process and to be more effective as a revising chamber. They were concerned about important legislation coming before them at a late stage and about legislation being too rushed.

397. We welcome the report of the Jellicoe Committee which was published towards the end of our inquiry and dealt with a number of matters of interest to us. We note the initial reactions of Ministers to the report, and we welcome the statement by the Leader of the House in which he recognises "that the House must try to develop new methods of dealing with legislation if we are to reduce what, on occasions, can be considerable pressure on your Lordships"[1].

Conclusions and recommendations

398. Our task in considering the legislative processes of the House of Lords was considerably helped by the Jellicoe Committee's report. We largely endorse the Committee's recommendations relating to legislative proceedings, and this is reflected in our specific recommendations. It also means that we can set out the arguments more briefly as most of them were rehearsed by the Committee or its witnesses, or in the debate on the report[2].

Committee stages of bills

399. As in the Commons, it is important for Peers to come to the debates on a bill as well informed as possible. In the Lords, being a less political chamber, much is done by informal agreement. We are attracted by the idea put to us by Lord Aberdare, a former Chairman of Committees (who took a great interest in our inquiry and was most helpful on a number of matters), that sometimes it would be helpful if a Minister arranged an informal briefing on a bill (more fully described in paragraph 292). Lord Aberdare believed that such briefings would considerably reduce the need for long debates on probing amendments in committee (M 2). This proposal was also welcomed by Lord Tordoff, on behalf of the Liberal Democrat Peers.

400. We suspect that such briefings would be of less use on shorter, highly political bills, but for other bills, even if controversial, pre-debate clarification could lead to more constructive amendments which concentrated on practical issues, and could speed the committee stage. Briefing of this kind has already been tried on

---

1   HL Deb., 3 June, 1992, col. 907.

2   Ibid., cols. 899-1017.

a few bills, and we understand it has proved useful. **We recommend that informal briefings for Members and their advisers be offered by Ministers on all longer and more complex bills as soon as possible after second reading.**

401. Legislation is becoming increasingly complex and detailed. Even if more detail is left to delegated legislation, as we have recommended, the clauses of bills still need careful scrutiny. When they are introduced "half-baked" as sometimes happens, there is a resulting need to consider a large number of Government amendments, often in the Lords, and often at a late stage in that House (see paragraphs 173-174). A number of bodies, especially the local authority associations, expressed concern about bills being heavily amended in this way.

402. All this makes it extremely difficult to give a bill effective scrutiny by the simple process of debate on the floor of the House. It is also important in the less political House, with a highly experienced membership, for emphasis to be placed on the scrutiny of the practicality of legislation. This often requires information and careful deliberation rather than debate. As in the Commons, a more sophisticated procedure is required in the Lords which would enable evidence to be received direct from experts.

403. We therefore welcome the Jellicoe Committee's recommendation for the occasional appointment of special standing committees in the Lords, and we note the Government's support for the idea that they might be used for consideration of Law Commission bills (see paragraph 499)[1]. We do not believe their use need be so limited. These committees would be particularly appropriate for consideration of non-controversial departmental bills such as those dealing with company law and some of the more technical legislation in the trade and industry field. They could also be used for looking at the details of many long, complex bills – often, like the Charities Bill, the Copyright, Designs and Patents Bill or the Courts and Legal Services Bill, not particularly controversial between the parties – which at present take up much time on the floor of the House. **We therefore recommend that, whenever appropriate, bills should be committed to special standing committees in the House of Lords.**

404. If it is thought necessary to reduce the time spent on legislation on the floor of the House, then we can see a use for purely debating committees (Public Bill Committees as they are called in the Lords) for less contentious bills on which there will be few divisions. However we do not recommend them as a means of improving scrutiny of legislation as the nature of their debates must be similar to those of a committee of the whole House.

Scrutiny of delegated powers, etc.

405. Concern about delegated legislation is widespread. We have considered the scrutiny of such legislation in the Commons. We believe that the Lords, on the other hand, could do more to scrutinise provisions in bills conferring on Ministers delegated powers to legislate.

---

1 And see ibid., cols. 1010-1012

406. **We warmly welcome the decision of the Government to move for the appointment of a Delegated Powers Scrutiny Committee in the House of Lords.** It will be set up on an experimental basis for one session[1]. Such a committee was originally proposed by the Chairman of this Commission and was recommended by the Jellicoe Committee (paragraph 306). We understand that a similar committee, although with wider powers, works well in the Australian Senate (see the relevant documents listed in Appendix 3). The appointment of such a committee was also recommended by the Law Society (M 36, para. 5.12).

407. We see this Committee having the following functions -

    (i) examining every Government bill introduced into the House of Lords to see how it proposes that legislative powers should be delegated to Ministers; reporting its findings on whether such delegation is appropriate; and making recommendations for amendments where desirable;

    (ii) clarifying the proper use of Henry VIII clauses and monitoring their future use;

    (iii) examining proposals for further delegation under delegated powers, namely sub-delegated legislation, such as rules and codes;

    (iv) looking at the nature and extent of delegated legislation and attempting to draw up guidelines to indicate what sort of matters should be treated in primary legislation and what matters can appropriately be left to delegated legislation; and

    (v) monitoring the operation of such guidelines.

408. As we understand it, the Committee would not be concerned with policy or the merits of the regulations to be made under delegated powers. It should have no power to amend bills, but would report its findings on each bill before the committee stage in the Lords.

409. The Committee will be assisted by legally qualified staff; it may wish to take evidence from Parliamentary Counsel and departmental civil servants but not normally, in respect of individual bills, from outside bodies.

410. We believe that there is a real job that needs to be done by this Committee and not left to individual Peers raising these issues on the floor of the House. We are confident that the experimental appointment of a Delegated Powers Scrutiny Committee will prove a success and that the Committee will be set up on a permanent basis. It will strengthen quasi-legal scrutiny by the Lords; and it will nicely complement improved political scrutiny of delegated legislation in the Commons.

411. There are certain questions of a legal nature, not involving political judgements, which this Committee (with enlarged terms of reference) could also monitor, if thought appropriate.

412. First, Dr David Kinley, of the Australian National University, Canberra, drew our attention to the problem of conflict between provisions of bills and delegated legislation and the provisions of the European Convention on Human

---

1   HL Deb., 10 November, 1992, col. 91.

Rights (M 34). This is not just theoretical. The European Court of Human Rights has found in twenty cases that legislation passed subsequent to the United Kingdom's ratification of the Convention in 1951 was in breach of that Convention. Whatever one may think of the merits of these cases, legislation in conflict with a Convention, to which this country is party, is clearly undesirable; apart from other considerations, it means the United Kingdom is faced with adverse decisions by the Court and may feel obliged to amend our law accordingly.

413. All this could be avoided, as Dr Kinley pointed out, if the offending provisions had been identified before the legislation was passed. He recommended two joint parliamentary committees, one to examine all bills and the other all statutory instruments, to detect legislative conflicts with the Convention at the earliest possible stage and to report accordingly to both Houses. The very existence of such committees would, he believed, bring "considerable preventative pressure to bear on the Government to amend draft legislation so as to ensure its conformity to the Convention" (M 34). We do not recommend additional committees for this purpose but **the question of whether the powers and resources of the Delegated Powers Scrutiny Committee should be enlarged at some future stage, to enable it to detect potential legislative conflicts with the European Convention on Human Rights, is worth considering.**

414. **Another similar function which the Delegated Powers Scrutiny Committee might take on at some stage – again with increased resources – would be to detect prima facie conflict between provisions in proposed legislation and the requirements of European Community law.** Such conflict has always been a possibility; the *Factortame* case[1] has made it a reality, and the need for advanced vetting to avoid it has now been proved. No doubt Government lawyers always try to ensure that all the bills and statutory instruments they draft do not conflict with the requirements of European Community law, but additional parliamentary vetting does appear to be a proper function for the House of Lords. It might give this task to the new committee (see also paragraph 558).

General legislative functions

415. In general we see the role of the House of Lords as distinct from that of the Commons, and it should not be expected to examine legislation in the same way as that House. It should not just duplicate political scrutiny but should make a contribution, drawing on the rich reserves of talent and specialist experience possessed by its Members, to a wider and more long-term review and appraisal of Government legislation. For example, in addition to the necessary scrutiny of bills before the House, the Lords might look, through select committees, at matters more peripheral to current legislation though clearly relevant in the long term. We think particularly of such questions as those of civil rights or of

---

1   Case C 213/89 (Regina v Secretary of State for Transport , *ex parte* Factortame Limited (1990) 3 C.M.L.R. 867.

central/local government relations or of the environmental impact of new legislation. We recognise however that these are matters for the Lords themselves to assess, having regard to their limited resources for manning committees. We make no recommendation as to the priority to be given to our proposals.

Access to Legislation in Parliament by the Public

The evidence

416. Somewhat to our surprise, several bodies drew to our attention a range of problems which we had not originally envisaged. These were all bodies which had, from time to time, to come to Parliament, to attend committees and follow the progress of bills or to lobby MPs. They were concerned about various difficulties they had had in accessing the legislative processes in both Houses of Parliament, including getting hold of relevant papers; the cost of parliamentary papers; getting information on progress of business; and even occasionally in getting into committee sittings (paragraph 280).

417. These concerns were most fully set out by a relatively new body, the ITC (M 27, paras. 11-13 and 17-22). In general, it argued "it may be that......the public and the lobbyist may need to be accorded recognition as direct participants with their own legitimate role in the parliamentary process" (M 27, para. 11).

Conclusions and recommendations

418. We agree with the ITC. Bodies which are accustomed to the hassle and bustle of the Committee Corridor – who have been trading for years in the main street of parliamentary legislative business – may well be able to find their way around without great difficulty. Others who are new to the business or only come occasionally, and many individual citizens wishing to follow a particular bill, are not so street-wise. Following legislation can also be expensive, especially if the services of professional consultants are employed to find the way through the mysteries and maze of amendment papers. No doubt the bigger fish can manage – for example by using sympathetic MPs to get bills and other documents – but smaller or newer fry may need some help.

419. We sense that there is a question of principle here that goes wider than the practical convenience of a few organisations. We believe that the public should be welcomed to Westminster, not treated as a nuisance or kept at arms length, as we fear they sometimes are. Some of the departments and officers of the two Houses are as helpful as possible – the Public Information Office in the Commons was praised by some (M 27, para. 13) although criticised by others (M 38) – and no doubt most do their best within the rules each House has laid down. Also, many of the documents and procedures are inevitably difficult to follow; legislation itself is not easy reading.

420. However we fear that some of the present practices, official rules, and procedures in both Houses do give the impression that the interests of the public have a fairly lowly priority. Clearly the interests of Members and of the working of the two Houses must normally come first, but it would often be to the interests of Members to give more positive help to the public who come to

Parliament to meet them or follow their work. More important, many of the public coming to Parliament are there to assist Parliament in improving statute law. They need to know what is going on and to have access to Members involved in legislation. **We therefore believe that both Houses of Parliament should recognise the proper rights of the public, and especially of interested bodies, to be informed about, and to able to make a proper contribution to Parliament's scrutiny of legislation.**

421. We do not wish to go into detail on how the public could be better served. We only indicate the main changes we believe should be made to help those from outside Parliament who are involved in the legislative process. We hope that our approach will be approved by both Houses and that the practices and rules will be amended accordingly by the committees and officers concerned. We also point out that some of the other recommendations we make, for example regarding the use of special standing committees and time-tabling of legislation, go some way to meet the complaints we received.

422. The first step is to identify those who need more help. **We believe that bodies and people with a direct and sufficient interest in a bill or statutory instrument should be able to register their interest when that legislation is published by or laid before Parliament.**

423. Although bills can be readily bought from HMSO, and can now be purchased at the Parliamentary Bookshop on the corner of Whitehall, it is much harder for anybody to buy separate daily issues of amendment papers, and almost impossible (except through a Member) to get other relevant documents such as that which gives a chairman's selection and grouping of amendments. **We recommend that registered bodies and people should be entitled to free copies of all parliamentary papers relating to the legislation with which they are concerned.**

424. There is sometimes a problem for those most directly involved with bills that affect or interest many people in getting into crowded committee rooms in the Commons (M 27, para.22). **We recommend that the House of Commons authorities should issue passes giving registered bodies and people priority admission to committee rooms for legislation with which they are concerned.**

425. **We suggest that the public should also be able to buy sound or video recordings of committee proceedings.**

426. It is ridiculous that the public attending debates on bills in standing committees or in the House of Commons are not given the amendment papers and selection of amendments; it is impossible, for those who want to follow debates in detail, to do so without these papers. Following a recommendation of the House of Commons (Services) Committee in its 1977 report on Relations with the Public[1], amendment papers used to be put out in standing committees for the public, but this lapsed after a short while, perhaps on grounds of cost. We believe, however, that the rights of any citizen to follow intelligently the

---

1   Eighth Report of 1976-77 (HC 509), para. 28.

debating of the law that affects him or her must be respected – even at some cost. Not all of those in the public gallery will want all such papers, but **we recommend that a reasonable supply of amendment papers and other relevant parliamentary documents should be available to the public, on request, for each bill in committee in the Commons and, together with the reprinted bill, at the report stage.** We understand that this might be harder to achieve in the Lords, but we hope that the same principle will be applied as far as possible in that House.

427. Finally we received some complaints about difficulty in following the progress of bills. Information about what has happened – what clause and amendments were dealt with yesterday, for example – should be readily available from the Public Information Offices of the two Houses. Forecasts are less easy however; Members are the best advisers here. **In general, we believe that as much information as possible should be published regarding progress on amendments and clauses of bills in committee, and on expected timing of future debates.**

Chapter 6 – Access to the Statute Book

Ignorance of the law is no excuse, therefore the current statute law must be as accessible as possible to all who need to know it.

Publication of Acts and Delegated Legislation

The problem

428. Our evidence revealed considerable concern about how to find out what the statute law is on any given matter. There is of course no difficulty about a new Act which deals with a new problem on which there is no previous legislation. That Act is published soon after it is passed and states the law in one document. But that is not typical. Usually an Act amends at least one previous Act and often many more, and those previous Acts will have amended even earlier Acts. That is not the end of the story. To obtain a full statement of the law, one also has to look at the delegated legislation, and this is also made up of a web of regulations etc., amending other regulations etc. To make matters even more complicated, sometimes Acts will be amended, under "Henry VIII sections", by delegated legislation. Finally, different parts of some Acts are brought into effect at different times by commencement orders made by Ministers (without any parliamentary proceedings), and so to discover what the law is at any time, one needs to check whether the relevant part has yet been brought into force; occasionally some parts of legislation are never brought into force.

429. Therefore, especially in areas where the law is frequently amended, such as housing, social security, company and tax legislation, it is extremely difficult to discover the whole law on a topic; many documents have to be referred to. In lawyers offices up and down the country and in those of other people who have most frequent need to consult the statutes, previous Acts and delegated legislation are being kept up-to-date by crossing passages out and sticking other bits in. It is very unsatisfactory.

430. The problem can be greatly eased by the preparation and publication of consolidation Acts. Even then, however, reference may have to be made to several documents, as delegated legislation is not usually consolidated at the same time as Acts are consolidated. However consolidation has been of great assistance when it has been done – until another Act amends the consolidation Act.

431. Another aid has been the publication of Statutes in Force, which started in 1972, containing newly enacted Acts, revised re-issues of amended Acts, and Supplements showing the effect of later changes. However, the last group of Acts in this edition was published in 1982 and much of the statute book has never been revised in this edition. Statutes in Force has always had difficulty in keeping up with the rate of amendment, as we were told by the Head of the

Statutory Publications Office, and there has been no issue of revised Acts in this series for the last three years; the Office have concentrated in producing up-dated supplements, rather than editing revised texts of whole Acts for Statutes in Force. There are also private publications, such as Halsbury's Statutes, which publish up-dated texts of statute law. What is still lacking – and what many users require – is immediate access to the complete statute law on a given matter at any given point in history.

The evidence

432. Anxieties and criticisms of the present position came from a range of bodies. The Working Party of the Law Reform Committee of the General Council of the Bar on "Access to the Law" (here referred to as the Bar Council) was particularly unhappy about the situation; a combination of factors, it said, made statute law hard to find to a scandalous extent. (M 2). We summarise the evidence under several heads.

Original publication of Acts and statutory instruments

433. The Statutory Publications Office said that there was an average of eight to ten days' delay in publishing Acts of Parliament after Royal Assent and about the same delay in publishing individual copies of statutory instruments. However both the Bar Council and the local authority associations complained of delay in publishing Acts; recent examples were the the Local Government and Housing Act 1989 and the Education (Schools) Act 1992. The Bar Council believed that publication should always be before the date upon which the legislation takes effect (M 26 and M 37, section D). The ACPO said that sometimes the police were not in possession of legislation before it came into force (M 4, para. 12 (1)).

434. The British and Irish Association of Law Librarians said that in the last two years there had been delays of up to six weeks in publishing some Acts, especially the larger and more complex ones, which also tend to be the most important. Such delay was most unfortunate when some provisions came into force on Royal Assent, so before the new law was published. It suggested either delaying commencement or delaying Royal Assent until the Act was printed and ready for publication. There were occasional, though less serious, problems from delayed publication of statutory instruments, but more difficulty was experienced here from insufficient copies being printed (M 10).

Amendment of previous Acts

435. The Bar Council (M 26) and the Law Society (M 36, para. 5.28) drew attention to the difficulties caused when one Act is almost immediately amended by another Act, as happened with the Criminal Justice Act 1987 and the Criminal Justice Act 1988; the former was misleading without the latter and the latter incomprehensible without the former. Even consolidated legislation may be subject to immediate change, as the Town and Country Planning Act 1990 will be by the proposed Planning and Compensation Bill. The Bar Council was also concerned about primary legislation being changed by delegated legislation

made under later primary legislation, making it harder to identify the changes (M 26).

Commencement orders

436. The Bar Council (M 26), the ABI and Lloyd's (M 3, para. 2) and the Law Society (M 36, para. 7.2) all referred to difficulty in discovering what the law was on some date in the past (which is often relevant to lawyers and their clients), or even the current state of the law, when parts of Acts have been brought into force at different dates over a period of years; for example, the final commencement date for the Consumer Credit Act 1974 was not made till 1989. The Society of County Secretaries pointed out that certain provisions of the Children and Young Persons Act 1969 (for example section 4, which changed the age of criminal responsibility) had never been brought into effect and certain provisions of the Children Act 1975 were only implemented after 10 years; "these constitute examples of the executive (or a new Government) acting in contravention of the will of Parliament" it argued (M 53, para. 3). A similar point was made by Mr Andrew Bennett, MP, who was concerned by Ministers failure on occasions to use delegated powers; such failures should be explained to Parliament, he said.

Consolidation

437. The Bar Council welcomed consolidation on a comprehensive and on-going basis (M 26). The ACPO were not happy about partial consolidation or amendment leaving parts of old Acts still in force; it would prefer to see the new statute as the sole source of the relevant law. For example, the Road Traffic Act 1988 is the principal Act covering road traffic matters, but a few provisions of the Road Traffic Act 1960 and even of the Road Traffic Act 1930 remain in force, and now major changes have been made to the 1988 Act by the Road Traffic Act 1991. It would have been far simpler to have one comprehensive Road Traffic Act. The ACPO believed that such a procedure might well have avoided the problems found in implementing the law relating to passenger seat belts (M 4, para. 12 (3)). The ABI and Lloyd's said that the need for consolidation Acts had increased now that statutes were frequently amended by statutory instruments, following the European Communities Act 1972 (M 3, para. 2).

438. The CBI also wanted more regular and speedy consolidation and more resources devoted to this work by the Law Commission (M 22, section 2) as did the Law Society (M 36, para. 5.29 and 7.1). The local authority associations complained that a very low priority seemed to be accorded to consolidation legislation, including delegated legislation (M 37, section D). On the other hand, the Institute of Chartered Accountants welcomed increased consolidation in recent years, especially of fiscal legislation. It commended particularly the Companies Act 1985, but still further consolidation was needed after the changes made by the Insolvency Act 1986 and the Companies Act 1989. It would also like to see a "once and for all consolidation" of tax legislation, and continuous up-dating consolidation thereafter, as in the USA. It had put these

proposals to the Statute Law Committee, chaired by the Lord Chancellor in May 1990 (M 29, paras. 20 -21). Lord Renton told us he would like to see more use of "consolidation with simplification" bills.

Publication of up-dated statute law after amendment

439. The Bar Council (M 26), the Law Society (M 36, para. 5.26), the ICA (M 29, para. 30) and other bodies complained of the difficulty and expense of discovering the state of earlier statutes after their amendment. Even judges found the tracing exercise to discover the wording of a statutory provision at the relevant time to be a problem (M 33, para. B), and the Magistrates' Association spoke about the difficulty its members had in getting information about delegated legislation and its relevance to cases before them. The ABI and Lloyd's pointed out the great difficulty of tracing amendments to Acts made by statutory instruments which were not arranged in any identifiable series (M 3, para. 2).

440. The ICA said that legislation would be more accessible if Acts were regularly re-published in their textually amended form, as had been done commercially with the Companies Acts (M 29, para. 33). Shelter complained that statutes were not up-dated and remained on sale in their out of date form (M 51, para. 4a). The British Railways Board thought that much more needed to be done to keep Statutes in Force up-to-date; it was years behind schedule (M 13, para. 3).

Proposals for new publications

441. The Head of the Legal Group, Lord Chancellor's Department, described to us the Government's plans to achieve significant improvement in statutory publications. The printing of statutes and related information by traditional or present methods was taking too long; a new method had to be found and therefore his Group was planning to put the statute book on a computer database called the Statute Law Database (SLD). It was hoped to make the database available to users by September 1993. By 1993 all the statutes up to February 1991 would have been up-dated to the 1991 date, and and the database would then build up an historical record of each day's state as from that date. It was also hoped that the historic database would have caught up with the current state of statutory text by 1997. It was proposed that statutory instruments made in 1987 and thereafter would be loaded onto the SLD together with selected earlier instruments.

442. Once it is operating the SLD will be the only official means by which up-dated text of statute law would be prepared and made available to users. Work on editing revised re-issues of Acts for Statutes in Force had been stopped for the time being. However, new Acts and statutory instruments would still be published by HMSO, and the annual volume of the Statutes would continue to be produced, together with its Index and Chronological Table.

443. Users would have to be satisfied that the database was accurate, but the Head of the Legal Group was confident that it should provide a more accurate up-to-date product than printing. It was proposed that the database should be accessed on line and could be displayed on screen or printed-out on a local terminal. The

database would also be available to HMSO for the printing of statutes. The Index to the Statutes would also be on the database, as would helpful footnotes showing relevant statutory instruments, commencement dates, etc. The SLD would also be able to show historical versions of the statute law from 1991 onwards.

444. The SLD would initially be available only for Government departments and Parliament (including the Law Lords), but the planning Group also had requests for it to be made available to practitioners. None of the possible further extensions had been fully costed and Ministers had not stated their policy as to whether and when the database might be made available to other users; the Group did not plan to make the SLD openly available until its success had been proved within the public services. However the Head of the Legal Group believed that ultimately it was desirable that the SLD should be available in public libraries, to Citizens Advice Bureaux, in solicitors' offices, etc. and not just in Whitehall. Such users would find on-line access to a statute law database extremely valuable. Indeed, said the Head of the Statutory Publications Office, "ideally statutes should be available on database to everybody".

445. The Government were not in favour of the SLD being subsidised for outside users, we were told, and therefore a market would have to be found, but the Head of the Legal Group believed there would be such a market outside Whitehall and Westminster – indeed throughout the United Kingdom. A detailed pricing policy for outside users had not yet been adopted, but they were seeking some guarantee from potential users that there would be financial support for making the SLD more widely available. Eventually, apart from user charges, access to the SLD by outside users could prove comparatively cheap.

446. The Law Society welcomed the Government's proposal to set up the SLD, but noted that it was initially intended for Government use only; it thought it odd not to allow access to the database by others outside Government (M 36, para. 7.3). The ICA would be willing to pay for access to this database, if the price was right.

447. The Bar Council would like to see all legislation on a particular subject, including statutory instruments, contained in its latest form and comprehensively in one place; it made a number of detailed proposals to that end (M 26). The ACPO would welcome the computerisation of the statute book and its publication in loose-leaf form so that it could easily be kept up-to-date. The ICA also advocated the increased use if information technology to help accessibility; it welcomed the sale by HMSO of discs with up-dated pension and superannuation rules – a technique which it suggested could be extended to other areas of law (M 29, para 34).

448. Mr Francis Bennion, an academic lawyer and former Parliamentary Counsel, drew to our attention his proposals, as set out in his book *Statute Law*, for composite restatement of the law[1]. This would involve a restatement of the whole statute law on any topic, whether it be in Acts or statutory instruments,

---

1 Bennion, *Statute Law* ,op. cit., pp. 334-340 and 346-349.

by bringing together all the original wording in its entirety but presenting it in a logical order and in a style that would be as "user-friendly" as possible. He claims that a restatement is –

> " *far easier to understand than the source material it processes; it is far more reliable than any summary, precis, digest or abridgement" and would be "far more useful than consolidation."* [1]

He proposes that restated law would not replace the original statute law and that amendments would continue to be made by Parliament to the official texts, but restatements should be officially produced, perhaps by the Law Commission, as a tool for practitioners.

Supply of copies of Acts, etc. to interested bodies

449. The local authority associations made a strong plea for those who are charged with the implementation of legislation to be provided by Government with copies of all relevant documents that affect them (local authorities at present each get one copy of each Act of Parliament, but no copies of statutory instruments or of EC directives or regulations) (M 54, section D).

Publication of statute law in other countries

450. We have received some information about the publication of legislation and the use of a computer database for statute law in France (Appendix 3). The French aim to publish Acts and decrees within a few days of Presidential Assent. Printed publication is in the *Journal Officiel* and is highly subsidised. The *Journal* also includes interpretation of new laws in the form of instructions to enforcement officers prepared by the Government department concerned. These are not citable in the courts except in respect of tax laws.

451. Major advances have been made in France on the automated publication of texts, both statutes and decrees. A basic database permits the publication of a daily list of new texts. Other more sophisticated systems enable the public to access full texts on publication, old texts or up-dated texts of the law as amended by new texts. These databases, among others, are available throughout France on Minitel, which has over 5 million subscribers. There is no Government subsidy for the statute database as it is paid for by Minitel users through their subscriptions and according to use.

Conclusions and recommendations

452. As the statement of principle at the head of this chapter indicates, we believe that it is not only of great benefit to users but it is also their democratic right to have as full and easy access to the statute law as possible. For various reasons, as our evidence makes plain (paragraphs 428-440), this ideal is not being met. At present the accessibility of statute law to users and the wider public is slow, inconvenient, complicated and subject to several impediments. To put it bluntly, it is often very difficult to find out what the text of the law is – let alone what it means. Something must be done.

---

1   Ibid., pp. 334 and 340.

Printing of Acts and statutory instruments

453. We note concern about delays of up to six weeks in printing some Acts after they receive Royal Assent and about the consequences. It is particularly undesirable for new laws to come into effect before they are published, and for bodies like the police not to have copies of an Act that they are required to enforce – as appears to have happened (paragraphs 433-434). We hope that the computerisation of printing and the new Statute Law Database will considerably reduce the delay between Royal Assent and publication. We recognise that some Acts must come into force as soon as they are enacted, but the coming into force of other Acts can be deferred by the use of commencement orders. **We recommend that as far as possible Acts should not be brought into force until they are published.**

A Statute Law Database

454. We are glad to hear that the Government is taking the problem of access to statute law seriously, and has concluded that reliance on routine up-dating of the law in printed form has proved unsatisfactory. Statutes in Force is years out-of-date on some topics; speedier and more comprehensive methods are needed. The proposed computer database for publishing and systematically up-dating statute law (paragraphs 441-445) is a major development, and one which we warmly welcome. **We recommend that the Government should press ahead as fast as possible with the Statute Law Database.**

455. Although we understand the Government's desire to get the new system working properly before making it more widely available, and while appreciating the benefits it will bring for users within the civil service and Parliament, we must emphasise that this new system will be of very limited value unless it is also opened up to the many people throughout the country – from solicitors, barristers, other professionals, officials of advisory and charitable bodies, officers of local authorities, and legal staff in industry, to the judges in the High Court – who need full, accurate and speedy access to statute law in all its forms. **We recommend that the Statute Law Database should be made available to all potential users – outside as well as inside government – as soon as possible.**

456. Obviously outside users should make a contribution to the costs of the database, from which they will certainly benefit. However many users would not be wealthy bodies or individuals – we think particularly of charitable bodies and advisory organisations such as the Citizens Advice Bureaux and local law centres, or indeed some smaller solicitors firms – and for them access to the law should not be too expensive. In the early days at least, the full cost charges for use of the SLD could be rather high. **We believe that some Government subsidy to keep down charges to outside users for access to the Statute Law Database would be appropriate.**

Pricing of legislative documents

457. We have received a number of complaints about the prices HMSO charge for legislative documents or about other limitations on their availability (paragraphs

103, 280 and 449) . The documents that various bodies need to play their part in the legislative process at one stage or other include Green and White Papers, other consultative documents, bills, amendment papers, Hansards, statutory instruments and Acts. We have already recommended that bodies directly involved in consultations on legislation, and people attending debates in Parliament, should be given some of these documents free of charge (paragraphs 146,147 and 426). However there are many other users of legislation who will not benefit in this way, and some of those who get a few free copies of these documents may wish to buy others. The prices are certainly high, especially if numerous copies are needed for all members of some organisation. For example, we note that the published price of the original Broadcasting Bill was £11.30 and of the Act was £15.60.

458. We believe that everything possible should be done to make the statute law – and the legislative process itself – as freely accessible as possible to all citizens. Given present prices of documents, this should include subsidised publications, as in France, and **we recommend that the Government should enable HMSO to price their legislative publications, and especially bills, Acts and statutory instruments, at well below cost.**

Consolidation bills and other restatements of the law

459. We found the case, as argued by Mr Bennion (paragraph 435), for composite restatement of statute law, bringing Acts and statutory instruments together in one text, to be attractive in many ways. In theory restatement would be helpful to many users in giving them a sight of the whole law on a topic in a form which should be easy to follow. On the other hand there are many practical objections. To be useful, the restatements would need constant and frequent revision, and we understand that the preparation and revision of these publications would be very costly and difficult to do; recruitment of skilled restaters would not be easy, and we are concerned that the the rare skills of Parliamentary Counsel should not be diverted.

460. The immediate access to be provided by the SLD to the statute law at any point, which would be much quicker than periodically published restatements, greatly reduces the case for their additional preparation. In our view, the first priority at this stage should be getting the SLD off the ground; other solutions to the problem would be an undesirable diversion.

461. On the other hand we are struck by the fairly widespread evidence of the value of consolidation bills, and of the need to continue and indeed speed up the programme of consolidation (paragraphs 437-438). This need will not be diminished by the creation of the SLD. Consolidation is still necessary when extensive textual amendment has distorted or wrecked the structure of the original Act. However, when the SLD is in operation it will be less necessary in respect of statutes that have been textually amended, and we recommend that priority should be given to consolidation of those Acts or remaining parts of Acts which were passed before textual amendment became the usual practice, for example the law on stamp duty which is currently being consolidated by the Law Commission.

462. In general we welcome the valuable use of consolidation in recent years, and its growth. **We recommend that the pace of consolidation should continue to increase and that if necessary the drafting resources of the Law Commission be strengthened to make this possible.**

Explanatory Material

The evidence

463. The difficulties that users – and the wider public – have in understanding legislation and in following the inter-relationship of Acts and statutory instrument to one another has prompted a fairly widespread desire for more explanatory material to be published with Acts.

464. There were a number of specific suggestions. Shelter would like to see notes on clauses attached to bills and up-dated notes attached to Acts; they should also be up-dated when Acts are amended (M 51, para 4b). The Independent Television Commission recommended publication of more comprehensive explanatory memoranda with bills, stating, clause by clause, the purpose of the legislation (M 27, para. 14). The Law Society said that all the delegated powers contained in a bill, together with the enacting procedures in each case, should be set out in an explanatory memorandum (M 36, para. 5.23). It also wanted full explanatory notes on draft statutory instruments (M 36, para. 6.5).

465. Some 8,000 amendments are made each year to earlier legislation and are listed in the Table of Effects published with the bound annual volumes of the statutes which are published a year or more after the end of the year concerned. However some bodies want earlier explanatory matter of this kind. The local authority associations said that an aid to understanding would be for the original Explanatory and Financial Memorandum attached to a bill to be up-dated and published with the Act, and to show the affect of the Act on other legislation (M 37, section D) A similar proposal was made by Shelter (M 51, para 4b) and the ACPO (M 4, para. 12 (3)).

466. More generally, the ACPO thought that the Government should seek to keep the public better informed about new legislation and the reason for its introduction –

> "*Public understanding of the law would to some extent at least make the task of the police and other enforcement agencies easier*" *(M 4, para. 15).*

The ICA commended the production of simple explanatory leaflets by the Inland Revenue, DSS and Customs and Excise for the help of the general public; it would like to see similar explanation of company law for the many companies in the UK (M 29, para 35).

467. The National Consumer Council were concerned about the impact new legislation can have on independent advice services, such as Citizens' Advice Bureaus, law centres and neighbourhood advice centres, who have to advise on the meaning, requirements and consequences of much statute law. It recommended that advice services should be consulted on the "information and advice" implications of new legislation and should be given help in preparing for inquiries (M 41, para. 3).

Conclusions and recommendations

468. We are impressed by the wide desire for more explanation of the meaning and implications of legislation. The practitioners and users need it. The wider public may need it even more. Furthermore, we agree with a fundamental point made by the local authority associations when they wrote –

    "ultimately, an attempt better to explain the purpose of legislation may be more fruitful than attempts, however desirable, to simplify the drafting of legislation itself" (M 37, section D).

    This accords with our conclusions on drafting (paragraphs 213-222) and points the direction to be taken. Our specific recommendations are to that end.

Notes on clauses and sections

469. We have already drawn attention to the value of notes on clauses and notes on Government amendments which are prepared for Ministers and summarise the purpose and effect of each clause or amendment. They are particularly helpful when a clause contains textual amendment of an earlier Act which is largely meaningless without the text of that Act. These notes have proved useful for Members of both Houses when debating a bill in Parliament and we have recommended that they should always be made available for this purpose (paragraph 353). They should also be available to others who request them to enable them to follow the legislative process or to understand a bill. We have already recommended that notes on sections should be published with Acts (paragraph 250).

Delegated legislation

470. Several bodies were anxious about the relationship between debates on a bill and consideration of the regulations etc. to be made under it. Their concern was that if much of the detail of how an Act should work is left to delegated legislation, as we have recommended (paragraph 267), it is often difficult for interested bodies to appreciate the full effects of a bill before the related delegated legislation is available (see paragraph 255). We fully appreciate these anxieties; debates on bills without understanding of what the new law will really require are somewhat meaningless.

471. There is no easy solution for this. Ministers cannot be precise about how they will use their delegated powers before there is agreement, in the course of debate on the bill, on what those powers should be. However **we believe it essential that, as soon as possible after a bill is introduced which is going to be implemented substantially by delegated legislation, the Government should indicate the general nature of the regulations and other instruments they propose to make to bring the bill into effect, and their proposed time-table for implementing the legislation.** We suggest that his might be done in a White Paper, or in an explanatory statement published with the bill. On occasions, when matters are sufficiently advanced, Ministers could publish draft instruments for information at this stage, though this should not be formally required.

472. Many bodies have difficulties in keeping up with delegated legislation (paragraph 439). There have also been particular problems in finding what the state of the law is at any given time when an Act has had a number of commencement dates for different provisions, often spread over a number of years (paragraph 436). Although the SLD will go a long way to clarify the position, the user of a printed Act still needs help. **We recommend that statements should be published periodically in relation to individual Acts to show what regulations etc. have been made under the Act, and when they came into force, and also the commencement dates of various parts of the Act.**

Help for the public

473. In the end, laws are made for the citizen. Technical and detailed explanatory material, as we have recommended, is needed for the practitioner and other users of the statute law, but it would often be of little help to ordinary people or even to those most directly affected. As we have seen, the police and other professional bodies believe that more should be done to explain new laws to the wider public in language that the lay person can understand (paragraph 466). We share this view. We recognise that many good explanations of this kind are already published, but more could be done and the successful examples and experience should be followed. **We recommend that the Government should do all it can to explain new law to the public, and especially those most affected, in terms that are readily intelligible.**

474. Finally there is the position of bodies such as the Citizens Advice Bureaus, law centres and neighbourhood advice centres who have to advise the public on the meaning of new laws (paragraph 467). Such advice plays a real part in the legislative process. Ultimately the Government must wish its laws to be understood. But mastering new legislation and giving advice can be expensive. **Accordingly we recommend that the Government should give additional financial help to bodies who have to incur significant extra expense in explaining new laws to the public.** We understand that this has sometimes been done.

Chapter 7 – Programming and Time-tabling of Legislation

The Government needs to be able to secure the passage of its legislation, but to get the law right and intelligible, for the benefit of citizens, is as important as to get it passed quickly.

The Overall View

475. We now look at the broad implications of our conclusions and recommendations in the previous chapters for Governments' legislative programmes. We begin with two apparent conflicts of interest.

476. First, we have made recommendations designed to increase the involvement of outside experts and interested or affected bodies in the consultative processes and to give more time for consultations. We have recommended that more time should sometimes be allowed for the preparation and drafting of bills. And we have made recommendations to increase and extend the scrutiny of bills and delegated legislation by Parliament.

477. Bills vary, not least in their size, complexity and urgency. For some bills our recommendations would add little to the time it takes to put them on the statute book. For bigger and more complicated bills it would appear difficult to achieve the reforms that we, and many outside bodies, believe to be important, within the present annual framework for Governments' legislative programmes.

478. Second, we have also made recommendations to increase and improve parliamentary scrutiny of bills and delegated legislation, especially in the Commons, that threaten a clash with the wish of all Governments to get their legislation through Parliament without undue delay. Again we believe that our proposals are important, and they are broadly supported by both the parliamentary and outside evidence we received. On the other hand we fully accept that Governments must have means of ensuring that increased scrutiny will not be abused by filibustering or result in unacceptable delay in the eventual passage of the legislation.

479. In our view, the reconciliation of these conflicting interests requires acceptance by all concerned of a package deal. **Preparation and scrutiny of legislation should be improved, but its passage in reasonable time should also be assured.**

480. We are glad that we were able to have some discussions with Ministers on these matters, and we have taken account of their points of view in coming to our conclusions. We have also noted the indications of the Government's position as given by the then Lord President of the Council in evidence to the Jopling Committee[1] and by the then Lord Privy Seal in evidence to the Jellicoe

---

1 HC 20-II, op. cit., pp. 1-28.

Committees[1], and by their successors and by the Lord Chancellor in the debates on the Committees' reports[2]. We set out our considered conclusions in the following sections.

The Legislative Programme

The present annual programme

481. We have already described the present arrangements for the preparation and drafting of legislation and the role the Future Legislation Committee of the Cabinet plays in deciding the Government's legislative programme in March each year for the following session (paragraphs 27-31). Although earlier authority is occasionally given for the preparation of a bill to be introduced into Parliament two or more sessions ahead, the standard programme extends over some eighteen to twenty months, from about March in one year till the end of the parliamentary session in the following year, and deals with the parliamentary business for one session only. For simplicity we call this the one-year legislative programme. Its annuality is reinforced by the practice of both Houses of Parliament in dealing with all public legislation within one session and not allowing public bills (other than hybrid bills) to be carried over from one session to the next.

Conclusions and recommendations

Programme for preparation of bills

482. Many bills can easily be prepared, drafted and passed within a year; others are routine and take little time; others are required urgently to meet some emergency; Ministers wish to hurry others through for political reasons. There are, however, many bills which are not required in a hurry, which require a lot of consultation and careful preparation and drafting, and which involve lengthy parliamentary debate – we have in mind such recent bills as the Charities Bill, the Courts and Legal Services Bill, the Children Bill and the Copyright, Designs and Patents Bill. In our view, a one-year legislative programme is generally inadequate for such bills, and does not allow the full consultations that we have recommended to be started early enough (although we recognise that some less formal or committed consultations and departmental studies may have been begun under the present system long before the content of the one-year legislative programme is fixed).

483. There is a particular problem about the drafting stage. Authority for drafting to begin is deemed to be given when the Future Legislation Committee approves the inclusion of the bill in the legislative programme, and is not normally given earlier. Drafting of bills to be introduced into Parliament at the beginning of the next session in October, November or December has therefore to be done in some six to eight months, which is not a lot of time for a big or complex bill, especially when it is remembered that, in the period from April to September,

---

1 HL 35-II, op. cit., pp. 103-119, 132-139 and 146-153.
2 HC Deb., 2 March, 1992, cols.116-118 , and 13 July, 1992, cols. 833-844 and 904-907; and HL Deb., 3 June, 1992, cols. 904-908 and 1010-1015, respectively.

Parliamentary Counsel will usually still be occupied with the bills of the then current session. Certainly once drafting has begun on a big bill, there is little, if any, opportunity for taking account of continuing consultations between departments and outside bodies (see the evidence of the Association of First Division Civil Servants (FDA) (M 5, paras. 10-19).

484. The whole process at present is cramped and hurried, with the result, as we have seen, that bills are often introduced into Parliament "half-baked" (as it has been called) or not fully drafted. It certainly leaves no time for extending, as we have recommended, consultation on draft bills and clauses (paragraphs 137-140). **In our opinion, the one-year legislative programme both delays and compresses the drafting stage in some cases, and leads to some under-prepared bills being presented to Parliament.**

485. **The solution, we believe, is for Governments to move towards the adoption of a two-year legislative programme,** as is done in some other countries. Longer programming was also favoured in some of the evidence we received (see, for example the FDA (M 5, para. 28) and the Law Society, which actually suggested a five-year programme (M 36, para. 5.15)). We suggest that it should be done as follows –

(i) **each March the Future Legislation Committee should decide on the main content of the legislative programme for two years ahead, and authority should be given for drafting to begin on the larger, longer-term bills to be introduced in the second session as well as for the drafting of other bills for the first session; and**

(ii) **each year the Government should announce its legislation for the coming session and the bigger, longer-term bills for the session after that.**

486. It would probably be unacceptable for the announced programme for the last session before an election to include bills for the first session of the new Parliament. Otherwise it should be possible for Governments to adopt a public two-year legislative programme in this way, since this would only mean publicly authorising work to be begun on bills which are at present privately planned and often the subject of speculation in the media. The increased and improved consultations we have recommended could only be fully achieved within such an extended time-scale.

The legislative programme in Parliament

487. Many bills have to go through Parliament without delay. In other cases there are no problems in getting a bill through within a single session. However in some cases it may be difficult to complete proper scrutiny of a bill within the session. This may happen if it is introduced rather late in the session and then proves more complicated or controversial than originally thought, or if its progress is blocked by extra time being required for other business, or if new matters arise, or new representations are made which require additional time for consideration, or indeed if Government policies change or parliamentary support becomes fickle. These situations are more likely to arise on large complex bills, such as those we have already cited.

488. In all these circumstances, we would reiterate the fundamental principle stated in paragraph 117, that, if it comes to a choice, getting a bill right must always have priority over passing it quickly. It is wrong to hurry a bill through with inadequate debate and scrutiny simply because the end of the session is approaching.

489. We realise that the possibility of carrying over bills from one session to another has been considered on many previous occasions and that the Procedure Committee of 1984-85 recommended against it[1]. However previous arguments against this idea have usually been based on purely parliamentary considerations and particularly the preservation of the annual session (a practice which other parliaments, including that of Canada, have abandoned). We take a broader view, having regard to the whole legislative process, and particularly the value of deliberately programming some bills over a longer period than one year.

490. Our evidence was divided. Lord Howe of Aberavon said it should not be necessary to carry over bills if they were prepared properly and were in the right form when introduced to Parliament, but the Law Society (M 36, para. 5.30), the FDA (M 5, para. 30), the ABI and Lloyd's, the Study of Parliament Group (M 54, para. 11), Professor Norton (M 45) and Mr George Bednar (M 7) all favoured the option of carry over. We ourselves see no objection to its use in appropriate circumstances. **We therefore recommend that if a bill requires extended parliamentary time, and is not required in a hurry, it should be permissible to defer completion of that bill in the current session and to carry it over for completion in the following session.**

491. We see particular advantages in being able to carry over bills which have passed through the Commons towards the end of a session. Rather than having to rush them through the Lords – a practice which some Peers told us they found unacceptable (paragraph 291) – such bills could be carried over to be considered by the Lords at the beginning of the next session when the Lords are normally less busy. Indeed such carry-over could be planned for and announced in the Queen's Speech.

492. It would be harder to carry bills over a general election into a new Parliament, as normally the Opposition would not agree, but it might sometimes be done by agreement between the parties. Such agreement might be reached in respect of a long and technical bill which all parties favoured and did not wish to lose by an early dissolution. Rather than dropping the bill or rushing it through with inadequate scrutiny (as appears to have happened with the Charities Bill before the 1992 election), agreement might be reached to carry such a bill over to the first session of the new Parliament.

493. We envisage that the procedure for carrying over some public bills would be much the same as that used at present for suspending private bills from one session to the next. The carry over would be proposed on a Government motion,

---

1   HC 49-I of 1984-85, op. cit., para. 24.

and, for many uncontroversial bills, we believe that this motion might be acceptable to the Opposition for it would provide extra time to consider the bill.

Law Commission Bills

494. The Chairmen of the Law Commission and of the Scottish Law Commission drew our attention to a matter of some concern to them, namely the apparent neglect of Law Commission bills in Governments' legislative programmes in recent years. The statistics are striking. By February 1992, the Law Commission had published 113 law reform reports with draft bills appended; 38 of these had not been implemented. Since the end of 1984, it had produced 41 such draft bills; 28 of these had not yet been implemented. Of the 38 unimplemented reports, the Commission was only aware of two having been specifically rejected by the Government (M 35, para. 5). The number of unimplemented law reform reports grows longer and longer; not a single law reform bill prepared by the Commission was enacted in 1990 and no such bill was included in the Government's legislative programme for 1991-92 (although two bills prepared by the Law Commission were introduced by private Members into the House of Lords)[1]. The evidence from the Scottish Law Commission was of similar neglect (M 50).

495. Both Law Commissions regret that bills which have been drafted by skilled parliamentary draftsmen after long and careful consultations and preparation, and which are not party-politically controversial (although there was considerable public interest in some of their bills, such as those relating to children and divorce), are not enacted more readily. They looked for procedures which would ease their passage through both Houses and thus encourage Governments to include them in their legislative programmes. They welcomed some suggestions which had been made by the Lord Chancellor on this matter (M 35 and M 50). Mr Justice Paul Kennedy said that it seemed to many of the Judges of the High Court to be deplorable that Law Commission bills were neglected in the way they were; he too recommended some separate procedure to assist their passage (M 33, para. G).

496. The problem of Governments not being able to find time for Law Commission bills in their legislative programmes – even the majority of such bills to which they have no objection – is serious, especially after much time has been spent on consultations, and much attention has been given to their preparation and drafting. Many bodies would like to see more law reform measures on the statute book; we note, for example, the regret of the Society of County Secretaries that these bills do not have an easier passage (M 53). In our view, Law Commission bills are probably among the most carefully prepared of all bills; these legislative cakes are properly baked. Conflicting views have usually been reconciled and objections overcome. Therefore, unless they arouse opposition on political, moral or social grounds (a divorce bill, for example), they should be ready for a simple passage into law.

497. The main reason this has not happened in recent years appears to be because

---

1 Twenty-sixth Annual Report of the Law Commission, for 1991 (HC 280), para 1,2.

law reform bills tend to lack positive political appeal and Governments' business managers find it difficult to fit them in to tight programmes packed with bills – often controversial and therefore time consuming – that Ministers consider politically important. To put it bluntly, we suspect that the Whips do not want to waste precious time on Law Commission bills.

498. This is not satisfactory. Most of these bills, by general agreement, ought to become law. **Unless they actually disagree with the Commissions' proposals, we believe that Governments should normally give time for the consideration and passage of all Law Commission bills.** Anything that can be done to encourage this would be welcome.

499. If, as appears to be the case, Governments' anxieties about including these bills in their programmes are because of the time they will take on the floors of the two Houses, then arrangements for debating them in committees should help overcome this resistance. It might therefore facilitate passage of Law Commission bills through the Lords if they went to special standing committees, as suggested by the Lord Chancellor and recommended by the Jellicoe Committee[1]. Although we find this slightly curious – since these bills probably need less evidence than most because of the extensive consultations by the Law Commissions – it may be that such special procedures would reassure any critical Peers and enable later stages of the bills to be unimpeded and to require little time. **We therefore recommend that Law Commission and Scottish Law Commission bills be committed after second reading in the House of Lords to special standing committees, and that further debates in the Lords be as limited as possible.**

500. The use of special standing committees in the Lords would not of itself speed the passage of Law Commission bills through the Commons. Members would still want an opportunity to examine and debate them and to ask for ministerial assurances on any matters that concern them. They would not be content to leave all scrutiny to the Lords. Special procedures in the Commons would not help and any suggestion of short-cutting would be resisted. It would be perfectly normal for uncontentious Law Commission bills to go to a second reading committee (as they often have in the past), but we would not expect them to be referred to first reading committees or to be committed after second reading to special standing committees as there would seem to be no need to hear further evidence on these bills. In general, Governments might be able to rely on time-tabling (see Chapter 7) to ensure no undue delay of Law Commission bills in the Commons.

Technical Taxes Bills

501. We have also considered another case for including a special type of bill in Governments' legislative programmes. We received a considerable amount of evidence, mostly from the Law Society (M 36, paras. 5.5 and 5.6 and unpublished Annexes), the CBI (M 22), the Bank of England (M 6) and the Institute of Chartered Accountants (M 29, paras. 28 and 29), and in several

---

1 HL 35-I, op. cit., para. 132 (ii).

papers and reports published by these and other organisations, in favour of an annual Technical Taxes Bill or Taxes Management Bill to deal with the more technical and less political or revenue-raising provisions at present contained in the Finance Bill.

502. This was a proposal put forward by Sir Geoffrey Howe, as he then was, in 1977. As Chancellor of the Exchequer he had the idea examined carefully but it was decided not to pursue it because, as he explained in his address to the Statute Law Society in May 1991, of the extra draftsmen and other staff that would be required and the additional pressure on parliamentary time. In his evidence to us Lord Howe of Aberavon stuck by this later view. The Inland Revenue also saw problems with the proposal, especially the difficulty of separating the technical and revenue-raising aspects of the Finance Bill; the Budget and all that was in it was a seamless robe and had to be treated as a whole.

503. We see considerable attractions in the proposal, not least because it would enable those more technical aspects of the present Finance Bill to be given closer scrutiny – perhaps by a special standing committee or even a select committee – than is possible during the rather rushed proceedings on the Finance Bill as at present drafted. It would also shorten the length of the Finance Bill, and the debating time it required. If resources could be provided, and the technical problems overcome, the additional bill would, in our view, be desirable.

504. However the matter is highly complex and we do not make a positive recommendation. **We believe that the possibility of having a Technical Taxes Bill should be reconsidered in the light of our other recommendations regarding the procedures of the Commons and the programming and time-tabling of Government legislation.**

Time-tabling of Legislative Business in Parliament

The evidence

505. The question of whether to have general and systematic time-tabling of all legislation is thorny and much disputed. It is essentially a problem for the Commons; in the Lords informal agreements appear to work well and we received no evidence in favour of change. In the Commons, time-tabling of debates on bills ranges from none at all, through a considerable measure of voluntary time-tabling by agreement between the parties, through the use of the closure (a declining practice) to the imposition of a formal guillotine imposed after lengthy time-wasting debate (a growing practice)[1].

506. The question has been examined by several Procedure Committees, and most recently by the Jopling Committee, which have all recommended more general and systematic time-tabling of bills, especially in standing committees (see paragraphs 300, 301 and 303). We also received substantial evidence on the

---

1 For a description of the procedures and of how they have been used, see Griffith and Ryle, *Parliament*, op. cit., pp. 222-227 and 302-307.

subject. Views from all sources were divided but the majority view was in favour of systematic time-tabling.

507. The National Trust (M 42, paras. 11-12), the ABI and Lloyd's (M 3, para. 2.3), the Institute of Public Relations (M 31, para. 2c) and the CBI pointed out the unpredictability of parliamentary business; they would like to have more precise time-tabling, as would the Institute of Directors to ensure that all important clauses are debated.

508. The Child Poverty Action Group believed that early time-tabling would be helpful, but not the late imposition of guillotines, as at present. However the TUC was concerned about the use of guillotine procedures to curtail debate that might embarrass the Government, and so had reservations about time-tabling of bills (M 55, para. 7) as had Shelter. The local authority associations feared that time-tabling of bills could –

> *"simply become another means for the Executive to streamline consideration of its bills.....Time-tabling of any bill should proceed only by agreement through the Whips,"*

and they suggested some ways in which this might be done (M 37, section C).

509. MPs were divided on the merits of time-tabling all significant legislation in the Commons. Dr John Cunningham, both in evidence to the Jopling Committee[1] and in discussions with us, Mr Tony Benn, Mr Graham Allen and Mr Wigley were all in favour of formal time-tabling. We received little evidence on how it should be done, but Sir Peter Emery, who was a particularly strong supporter of time-tabling, urged the merits of the proposals worked out by his Procedure Committee for time-tabling bills in standing committees[2] (see paragraphs 300-301 above). Mr Beith was strongly opposed to the way guillotines had been applied without any safeguards for the rights of minorities or back-benchers, and to the way they had been used by the official Opposition to squeeze out representatives of the smaller parties. There was much misuse of time, and he would welcome proper allocation of time with the constraints proposed by the Procedure Committee.

510. Lord Howe of Aberavon told us that he would welcome the adoption of the Procedure Committee's proposals for the standard time-tabling of bills in committee provided it was seen in the context of a wider and more general approach to management of legislation.

511. Sir Robert Rhodes-James, Mr Andrew Bennett, Sir John Wheeler and Mr Bob Cryer were all opposed to more formal time-tabling, though welcoming informal time-tabling by agreement between the parties.

Conclusions and recommendations

The need for time-tabling of legislation

512. **We are convinced that the time has come for the House of Commons to recognise that if parliamentary scrutiny of bills and delegated legislation is**

---

1   HC20 of 1991-92, paras. 30-32, and Qs 226-238.
2   Second Report of 1985-86 from the Select Committee on Procedure, Allocation of Time to Government Bills in Standing Committees (HC 324).

to be improved, as many **Members wish, much more extensive formal time-tabling of all legislation will have to be accepted**. It will be impossible to refer bills to first reading committees, or to commit most bills to special standing committees, or to accept fuller and less restricted scrutiny of statutory instruments, as we have recommended, unless Ministers are given a real assurance that there will not be undue or unlimited debate and that they will be able to get their bills passed in the end. This must mean extensive time-tabling.

513. We do not believe that this would result in any real loss of influence for the Opposition, as research indicates that in very few cases, if any, has the so-called time weapon actually succeeded in making a Government change its mind[1]. All that the weapon has usually achieved is long, boring, time-wasting filibusters on the early clauses of controversial bills, followed by guillotines that normally result in many of the provisions of the bill escaping all scrutiny or debate (and see proceedings on the Dangerous Dogs Bill 1991 (Appendix 6)). We agree completely with the Procedure Committee that formal and regular time-tabling of all but the less controversial bills is necessary to ensure that all clauses are considered in committee.

514. The main danger we see from time-tabling is that of back-benchers being squeezed out of time-limited debates by a carve-up between the two front benches, who would concentrate debate on issues of their choosing, to the detriment of the smaller parties and more independent back-benchers who wish to debate other matters. This is a problem that must be heeded in considering how time-tables should be imposed.

Methods of time-tabling

515. We do not wish to go into detail on the best methods of time-tabling. That is a question for the Procedure Committee and others to answer, and it is not of direct relevance to the legislative process. We simply indicate the broad lines of what we think would work best to secure optimum scrutiny of legislation.

516. Possible methods include more use of the present guillotine system; allocation of time for committee and other stages by a committee of Members, including back-benchers, as proposed by the Procedure Committee; time limits on speeches and on debates on amendments (as in the US House of Representatives); broad programming of legislation and allocation of time to individual bills by a committee (as is done by the Bureau in the French National Assembly); and precise allocation of time in all debates to amendments and parties (again as in the French National Assembly).

517. Comprehensive time-tabling would have to operate at two levels, covering first the broad allocation of time between the various stages of every bill, and second the more detailed allocation of time for scrutiny of the provisions of a bill. Our proposals are intended to meet these objectives.

518. We believe that the time has come to take time-tabling out of the sole control of Governments (sometimes tacitly backed by the Opposition front-bench) as is the case with the guillotine, and to give it to broader-based bodies representing all

---

1 See HC 49-I of 1984-85, op. cit., paras. 27-29; and see Professor Norton, M 45.

sections of the House. Of course Governments would have a major part to play on such bodies, and, as nothing could finally be imposed against the wishes of the majority of the House, Governments, through their control of that majority, would have ultimate control of the decisions. However the need to operate through wider bodies would bring those decisions more into the open and would render Ministers more accountable.

519. **We therefore recommend that the House of Commons should consider a system of formal time-tabling of all its legislation on the lines set out in Annex B.**

520. Sceptics may doubt whether any Government would ever relinquish its direct control over the timing of its business in the way we have recommended. They may be right. However we believe that a scheme on these lines could be made to work, given good will. Ultimately all parties, and Members individually, would benefit from the House as a whole making better use of its time. And in so far as better use of time means more effective scrutiny of legislation, it should also mean better statute law for the benefit of all the citizens of this country.

Chapter 8 – The Impact of European Community Legislation

Introduction

521. In this Report we have so far dealt exclusively with the legislative processes in respect of statute law (Acts and delegated legislation) prepared by the UK Government, passed by the Parliament of the United Kingdom or made by Ministers under powers granted by that Parliament, published by the UK Government and enforced, if necessary, through the courts of this country. That was the matter we were appointed to consider. We are very conscious, however, that since 1972 an increasing amount of statute law affecting the citizens of the United Kingdom has been prepared by the Commission of the European Community, scrutinised and frequently amended by the European Parliament, scrutinised by our own national Parliament, enacted by the Council of Ministers and in some cases by the Commission, and adjudicated on referral by the European Court of Justice.

522. This applies all over the field. For example, all users of water – that is everyone – are now paying higher water charges due to the requirements of the Water Act 1988 as a precurser to the Water Act 1991, which was enacted as a result of a European Community directive. However, as this case and others to which we will refer show, much of the Community legislation has a direct impact on the preparation of UK statute law. No study of the legislative processes in the United Kingdom would be complete, therefore, without taking account of European Community (EC) legislation.

523. Although the EC legislative processes are quite different from those in the United Kingdom, and although EC legislation comprises a distinct code of law, it would be a serious error to treat the two codes as though they were totally separate and had no affect on each other. The fact is that an increasing amount of UK law is directly influenced by EC legislation. Not only do EC directives normally require to be brought into effect by the passage of UK statute law (see paragraphs 533-534), and not only may directly effective EC regulations require amendments to UK statute law or condition the preparation and passage of further UK law (see paragraphs 530-531), but more generally and with increasing importance, the whole corpus of EC law is influencing the development of UK law in many fields. The requirements, demands and implications of EC law must be fully considered at every stage. No doubt to some extent the reverse is also true; the preparation of EC law by the European Commission takes account of the existing laws of the member states. We can not afford to treat national law – nor national legislative processes – in isolation from EC law.

524. This inter-relationship can be illustrated by the Acts passed by Parliament – the sort of legislation which we have considered in this Report – which appear to be purely UK statutes but which are greatly conditioned by EC law, even if not specifically required to implement EC legislation. We have in mind such specific Acts as the Water Acts and the Consumer Protection Act 1987. The various Banking and Company Directives have led to substantial new UK legislation over the last 19 years. Or, to take current legislation, the Criminal Justice Bill, whilst appearing to be a purely English criminal law reform measure, in reality also enacts the Insider Dealing Directive.

525. We recognise of course that the prediction by the President of the European Commission that 80% of law in this country will be EC law does not apply in all areas. Much of the staple legislative diet of our Parliament – criminal law, education and children, local government organisation and finance, health services and much fiscal (but not VAT) legislation, for example – remain wholly or largely within national jurisdiction. Nevertheless there are major areas of legislation in which EC law is of increasing importance, particularly – but not exclusively – trade, industry, agriculture, employment, environment and financial services. In some areas, for example external trade, the European Community has exclusive competence.

526. All of this was brought home to us by much of the evidence we received, and most strongly in the memorandum from the Institute of Directors, which concluded –

> *"the Institute sees the legislative process as much wider than Parliament. It is a long drawn out process involving interactions at many levels and today, particularly with the growing scope of the competence of the European Community, the Westminster Parliament (Ministers apart) is a residual, last-stage focus of pressure. This conclusion must have very serious implications for our traditional views of Parliament as a legislator" (M 30, para. 24).*

527. In this Chapter, we do not examine in any detail the consultation and other processes whereby EC legislation is prepared by the Commission and enacted by the Council of Ministers, nor do we examine the scrutiny of EC legislation by either the European Parliament or by the two Houses of the UK Parliament. These are not the direct concern of our inquiry and we did not invite evidence on these matters. In addition the work of the House of Lords European Communities Committee has recently been reviewed by the Jellicoe Committee[1] and, following an inquiry by the House of Commons Procedure Committee[2], the processes by which the Commons examines and debates EC legislation and other business have been considerably improved. Judgment of these developments should await further experience. We do however draw attention to some of the main points that certain bodies made to us regarding the

---

1   HL35-I of 1991-92, paras. 20-23, 66-77, 137-147 and 188-193.
2   Fourth Report from the Select Committee on Procedure, 1988-89, HC622; and see Government Response, Cm 1081.

preparation, scrutiny and enactment of EC legislation and we comment in more detail on the impact that EC legislation has on the preparation, drafting and enactment of UK statute law.

The Processes of European Community Legislation

528. It is first necessary to identify the mechanics of EC legislation. As the Law Society said –

> *"One of the main problems with EC legislation involves distinguishing between different types of legislation: regulations, directives and decisions; working out when they are effective in this country (i.e. is it automatic, or is an implementing Act needed) and to what extent they override domestic law. To an extent knowledge of EC legislation can be improved by training, but it is submitted that the Government has a vital role to play in ensuring that adequate information on EC law is disseminated and ensuring that it is implemented in the correct manner at the correct time" (M 36, para. 6.16).*

Types of legislation

529. Both the Council and Commission have power under Article 189 EEC to "make regulations, issue directives, take decisions, make recommendations or deliver opinions". For reasons of brevity, we cannot consider the last three categories. Suffice it to say that decisions, which are of a more private legislative scope, are binding in their entirety upon those to whom they are addressed, normally undertakings and individuals. Recommendations and opinions have no binding force, but are frequently the precursor to a legislative measure, where the more informal approach fails to achieve the desired effect and compliance.

Regulations

530. A regulation "shall have general application. It shall be binding in its entirety and in all member states"[1]. Such regulations, which can dramatically change national legislation do not require national enactment, but are automatically part of a member state's laws. The direct effect of this type of legislation is not fully appreciated even now, nearly twenty years after we joined the Community. For instance, the Merger Control Regulation removed jurisdiction from the Monopolies and Mergers Commission of all mergers having "a Community dimension". A regulation adopted by the Council has the power to impose anti-dumping duties upon all importers of goods of a specific category from non-member states. Regulations control agricultural levies and subsidies, and can be changed on a daily basis.

531. No action is required in Parliament in respect of these regulations. However they can have a direct impact on UK legislation. In the first place, UK statute law may have to be amended to avoid conflict between EC law and UK law. In addition, future UK legislation will have to take account of the requirements of the EC regulations. Neither Government nor Parliament can ignore these implications, and should have regard to them both when considering proposals for EC regulations and when scrutinising UK legislation.

---

1   Act 189 EEC.

532. In the case of regulations, the only ways of influencing proposals is by scrutiny by Government departments, by sectoral interests or by Parliament (especially the European Communities Committee of the House of Lords and the European Legislation Committee of the House of Commons, although other select committees can also play a part). Such scrutiny must be done prior to adoption. Whether this is best achieved by directing lobbying through UK Government departments or directly with the Commission is a matter which will vary from proposal to proposal.

Directives

533. "A directive shall be binding, as to the result to be achieved, upon each member state to which it is addressed, but shall leave to the national authorities the choice of form and methods"[1]. It must be emphasised at this stage that a directive may have a direct effect in certain circumstances, even though it has not even been implemented into national law. The European Court has held that exceptionally a change in national law may not be necessary where general principles of that country's laws may render implementation of a specific directive superfluous. There are conditions attached to this doctrine of "direct effect". The legal position must be sufficiently precise and clear and the persons who are effected by the directives must be made fully aware of their rights and given the possibility to rely upon those direct rights before the national courts. Those individual rights must equally be given to nationals of other member states[2].

534. Normally, however, a directive requires to be given effect by some form of national legislation and the implementation of any directive must ensure that its obligations are rendered into national law with sufficient clarity and legal certainty. It is now widely acknowledged that the United Kingdom Government failed to implement properly the Equal Pay and Equal Treatment Directives. The minor amendments made to the Equal Pay Act 1970 and the Sexual Discrimination Act 1975 were held by the European Court to be quite inadequate[3].

535. National courts are required to interpret their national law in the light of the wording and purpose of the directive in order to comply with the requirements of Article 189(3). The courts are increasingly giving a purposive construction to directives and to regulations made for the purpose of complying with directives.

536. However, the discretion allowed member states as to the implementation of directives has given rise to considerable case law. In general terms, this European case law has held that where a member state has a discretion the directive is not directly effective if the member state acts within the scope of the given discretion. In the absence of implementation of any material obligation, the directive becomes directly effective, thereby creating rights by individuals against the state for its failure to implement Community law. Thus if it refuses

---

1 Act 189 (3) EEC.
2 Case 29/84 Commission against Germany (1985) E.C.R.1661.
3 Pickstone v Freemans plc (1989) A.C.66.

to exercise its discretion or abdicates it, it can be held accountable to both the Commission and to individuals adversely affected[1].

Consultation and scrutiny

537. It has been recognised by many, but in particular by the CBI (M 22) and the House of Lords Select Committee, that the most effective way to influence Community legislation is by consultation and scrutiny of it before its adoption. Most of those giving evidence on the impact of Community legislation have stated this very forcibly.

Consultation

538. We note evidence given to us on the importance and nature of consultation during the preparation of EC legislation, but we have not examined this question fully as it was outside our remit; we ourselves make no conclusions or recommendations on this matter.

539. The CBI (M 22), the Institute of Directors (M 30) and others emphasised the need not only for scrutiny but also for consultation prior to adoption of legislation by the European Community. There is no substitute for the investment of time and input at that stage. Everything that comes thereafter can only be "fine tuning". The representative of the TUC, in his oral evidence, said that the TUC was consulted properly by the European Commission in relation to directives, but there was inadequate consultation by the British Government. In particular, too much discretion was left to the national Governments, for example on the implementation of the Public Procurements Directive. The TUC, referring to the Social Action Programme, was also concerned that the Department of Employment would pay little regard to the TUC's concerns relating to implementation of directives into national legislation (M 56). In general it was suggested that the European Commission takes more care than the UK Government in its consultation process; this may be attributable to the need for the Community to acquire at least majority agreement.

540. Objections were put forward by the National Union of Mine Workers to the ability of the Government of the day to use European legislation as an excuse or lever to effect controversial national law changes. It cited the well-known controversy of the EC Directive on Working Time being used by the Department of Energy as a means of repealing the Coal Mines (Regulations Act) 1908. It believed it should have been consulted by the Government on the likely impact of the Directive on the coal industry (M 44), although in the event the 1908 Act remained in force.

541. Some bodies find advantages in the opportunity to make representations at an early stage in the preparation of EC legislation and in the comparative openness of consultations in Brussels. The CBI told us that it welcomed the opportunity to study texts of draft legislation when involved in consultations with the European Commission. However the Association of British Insurers and Lloyd's, and the BMA, were worried about inadequate consultation in Brussels

---

1 Joined Cases C-6/90 and C-9/90 A. Francovich and Others v Italian Republic. European Court of Justice. Judgment given 19.11.91.

on the details of EC legislation. The Institute of Directors told us that European consultations worked well at the earlier stages, but not once a proposal had gone to the Council of Ministers; the TUC made the same point.

542. The local authority associations felt that they were consulted by the Government too late in the process – on both draft regulations and draft directives – to be able to make effective representations (M 37). They had overcome this problem by participating in a local government international bureau which acted as a channel to and from central Government as well as the European Community Institutions and which allowed Government to involve local authority associations at a formative stage in European policy making. The associations were highly critical of Whitehall and felt that it had problems in co-ordinating its input to European legislation. The associations had become expert lobbyists in Brussels and Strasbourg as they felt that the Government was too slow to protect UK interest. They gave an example of their activities in safeguarding British interests in the disposal of waste, which is currently being harmonised at a European level. They pointed out, as others have done, that they are involved in the debate in Europe long before the UK Government has become involved at the Council of Ministers level.

543. We note the view of Consumers' Association that there is usually a lack of balance between affected interests in the European consultation process (M 23, para. 2.8). This arises either because major producer interests have close relationships with their Government departments (for example, airlines with the Department of Transport), or because –

> *"major 'producers' have the ability to influence the formulation of EEC proposals, since they can afford to have representatives in Brussels. The national Government encourages such involvement to protect British interests. Due to the costs involved, representation of consumer interest is comparatively weak, and, in some cases is not even invited". (M 23, para. 2.8.2).*

Consumers' Association also felt it would be of assistance if Government would provide more explanatory material when consulting on draft directives and regulations (M 23, para. 2.5.5).

Parliamentary scrutiny

544. As far as EC legislation is concerned, the Government alone has the freedom to act, in conjunction with the governments of other member states, without the necessity to subject European legislation for parliamentary approval, scrutiny or consultation. In short the executive itself, in agreement with other member states, assumes the normal constitutional function and powers of the Parliament. It is an inescapable consequence that Parliament strictly speaking has no role to play in the Communities' legislative process, except where marginal discretion is left in the implementation of directives. However Parliament retains the function of scrutinising all acts of Ministers and this gives it the opportunity to examine proposed EC legislation (and other European policies) on which Ministers are required to decide in the Council of Ministers. To a considerable

extent this scrutiny is carried out in both Houses of Parliament (and, indeed, to a greater extent than in some other European parliaments).

545. Evidence regarding parliamentary scrutiny of proposed EC legislation was largely complimentary of the work done by the European Communities Committee of the House of Lords. The CBI were quite certain that scrutiny by itself of European legislation is not sufficient, especially on the "fine points", but added –

"The House of Lords European Communities Committee and its sub-committees perform a valuable role in the scrutiny of European legislation, since they look at directives while they are still in draft form. They often question Commission officials responsible for them, testing the need for the legislation and assessing its compatibility with existing UK legislation. The Lords are thus a preparing, as well as a revising, Chamber" (M 22).

546. Comments on the Commons' scrutiny of European legislation have been more critical. We were told that the Bar Council wished to see more and better select committee scrutiny of European legislation; EC directives should be looked at much more carefully at any early stage. The Institute of Directors told us that it was essential to seek to influence proposed EC legislation at as early a stage as possible, in the way that the Lords' European Communities Committee can do at present. The Commons did not play nearly as effective a part in this area, but would have to take scrutiny of EC legislation seriously if it was to remain an influential body. The CBI stated that they would welcome more use of select committee procedures which would give them and other bodies an opportunity to comment before firm decisions were taken in the European field.

547. More generally, Mr John Biffen, MP, has said –

"It is quite remarkable the extent to which we have not undertaken any fundamental alteration in our procedures to take account of what I think to be something almost without precedence in significance over the last generation or so." [1]

and Mr Vernon Bogdanor, a member of this Commission, has described the same problem as follows –

"Europe was seen as a discrete and separate issue which could be tacked onto Parliament's traditional business as a kind of optional extra. It was seen as something extraneous, as a separate and insulated political system whose points of contact with the UK Parliament would be very few. This attempt, to continue with business as before, as if Europe could remain a self-contained system, seems doomed to failure" [2].

548. The House of Commons has recently strengthened its procedures for scrutiny and debate of EC legislation and other European Community matters. Improvement is certainly needed. We await the results.

---

1   Evidence to the Procedure Committee, 1988-89 (fourth report, HC622, Minutesof Evidence, Q1).

2   Paper to be published on Parliamentary Scrutiny of Community Legislation in Britain by the European University Institua in Florence.

Enactment of Directives

Implementation

549. We described in paragraphs 533 – 537 the scope and form of directives. We only consider here those directives which require implementation by national parliaments or governments. It is not necessary that the provisions be enacted in exactly the same words but the full application of the directive must be given with sufficient legal clarity. The European Court has amplified this by holding –

"the principles of legal certainty and the protection of individuals require an unequivocal wording which would give the persons concerned a clear and precise understanding of their rights and obligations and would enable the courts to ensure that those rights and obligations are observed." [1]

In general it is necessary that directives are enacted by statute law, but the European Communities Act, section 2 (2), does not lay down the method to be used, and the choice of the means (for example by primary or delegated legislation) whereby a directive is to be implemented into national law will vary from case to case.

550. The United Kingdom Government undoubtedly failed previously, for example, when it made only minor amendments to the Equal Pay Act 1970 and the Sex Discrimination Act 1979 rather than promulgating new laws based specifically on the Equal Pay and Equal Treatment Directives. Chaos and confusion was the result with frequent recourse to litigation. The Law Society referred to the problems of implementation and interpretation by quoting the Transfer of Undertaking Regulations 1981. These Regulations were made under pressure from the EEC to implement a 1977 Directive that was overdue for implementation and the House of Lords gave its decision on them in *Lister v Forth Estuary Engineering Company Limited*[2]. The Court held –

"The regulations received little or no scrutiny, they make no attempt to clarify the relationship between the directive and to parallel domestic provisions and, in addition do not conform with the directive in a number of respects."

The Law Society felt that some of these difficulties could have been overcome if primary and secondary legislation were subjected to increased scrutiny.

551. The problem of inadequate implementation of European directives has been the subject of evidence to the House of Lords European Communities Committee[3]. Public authorities are particularly concerned by inadequate enactment of directives as the case law of the European Court of Justice has established that they are bound by the terms of the directives in certain circumstances even though the requirements have not been translated into national law.

552. In general, directives commence with a preamble giving the background to the necessity for the adoption of the directive, and stating the purpose of the directive. For example the political desire to achieve the single market would

---

1   Case 143/83 Commission v Denmark (1985) E.C.R. 427 at 435
2   1990(1) Appeal Cases, pp. 546-578.
3   Implementation and Enforcement of Environment Legislation – HL53, 1990-92.

explain the need to introduce harmonisation of standards. The operative part of the directive is the part that is required to be implemented into national law.

553. Thus a difficulty arises because UK statute law is not used to such interpretative aids as a preamble gives and therefore the transposition in drafting terms from the generalised wording of the operative part of the directive to strict UK drafting techniques gives rise to difficulties, not least in achieving legal certainty. There are also difficulties of interpretation. The courts are increasingly giving a purposive construction to directives and to regulations made for the purpose of complying with directives (see the House of Lords decision in *Lister v Forth Estuary Engineering Company Limited*[1]).

554. It is not reasonable to expect users to consult the underlying European directive, although lawyers practising in this field do get used to carrying out this double research. Also problems of translation occur if the original directive was not drafted in English, as is frequently the case.

555. The result of this dichotomy or dilemma has been that there has been a tendency either to over-implement or to under implement directives. The directives dealing with Food Safety appear to have been incorporated into UK law with far greater precision and regulation (to the detriment of the affected industries), than may have been conceived by the original Community draftsman. Critics of the Consumer Protection Act 1987 would argue that the Directive on Product Liability has not sufficiently been enacted into English law. At least the UK implemented the directive, albeit in part, whereas some member states, e.g. France and Spain, had not implemented it by mid-1992. Some directives like the Directive on General Product Safety[2] will require particular care in implementation as they impose extensive obligations not only upon suppliers to produce safe products, but also to provide relevant information to enable users or consumers to assess the acceptable risks associated with the use of the product. Further they must take precautions against those risks throughout the product's foreseeable life-span and there is a duty re recall the product from the market if it is unsafe. Obligations are imposed upon member states to take appropriate powers to monitor and control all products on the market. This Directive will lead to extensive and powerful regulatory organisations within the UK and is likely to have considerable impact on commerce.

556. It will be seen that both primary and delegated legislation may be required to implement this Directive and the question of how to avoid inadequate or excessive implementation is not an easy one to answer. If previous examples of incorporation were to be followed, implementing legislation will be built up over the next few years, and it will become essential to return to the basic principles in the Directive for interpretative guidance. Lawyers specialising in community law always need to return to the basic foundation directive and, in many cases, other previous directives in order to see whether national law interprets and implements the Community law requirements adequately. This is

---

1   1990(1) Appeal Cases, pp. 546-578.
2   Adopted 29th June 1992.

necessary without the further problem of considering the position if one member state implements the law differently and inadequately, causing an uneven playing field.

557. We have already identified a need for statements of purpose and intended effect to be published with Acts and statutory instruments (paragraphs 250-252). There is a particular need for such aids to understanding for all users, including the courts, in respect of legislation implementing EC directives. **We therefore recommend that all Acts and statutory instruments implementing European Community directives should be accompanied by explanatory memoranda giving the essential Community background.**

Scrutiny

558. It is essential that any new legislation, whether it implements Community legislation or appears to be purely of a national dimension, is vetted by experts to see whether it complies with Community law at whatever level. The problems of Factortame[1] could well re-occur, if the present scrutiny and vetting procedures are not improved and if compliance measures are not undertaken to remove potential conflicts.

559. We have considered how best to avoid these difficulties. It would be unrealistic to expect the House of Commons European Legislation Committee to vet bills or delegated legislation in such detail; these are questions for lawyers rather than politicians. Outside Government and Whitehall, such vetting could however be carried out in the House of Lords, and we have already suggested one way in which it might be done, namely by an extension of the remit of the new Delegated Powers Scrutiny Committee (paragraph 414).

560. Whatever external or parliamentary vetting is carried out to avoid conflicts between EC and national law, it is essential that such checks are applied systematically within Government. It is not the task of Parliamentary Counsel to do this job; they work on the basis of departmental drafting instructions and this type of scrutiny is not within their remit. We do believe, however, that each Government department should ensure that its own lawyers have a thorough training in Community law, so that they can scrutinise proposed legislation emanating from their department before it is promulgated even for consultation purposes. Another possibility would be for such vetting for conflicts and evaluation as to the required legal level of implementation to be undertaken by a special department.

Consultation

561. Evidence indicated significant concern about the lack of Government consultation when community law is enacted into national law. **We believe that the evidence we received and the recommendations we have made for greater consultation on texts of bills, clauses and statutory instruments (paragraphs 137-140 and 160-162), and also our recommendations for earlier and more informed parliamentary scrutiny of proposed legislation**

---

1 Case C 213/89 (Regina v Secretary of State for Transport ex parte Factortame Limited (1990) 3 C.M.L.R. 867; and see paragraph 24 of this Report.

(paragraphs 320-323 and 331-341) are equally, if not more, applicable in principle to consultation on and scrutiny of implementation of Community legislation. In contrast with some adverse criticism we heard, consultation on the Insider Trader Dealing Directive, to be enacted in the Criminal Justice Bill (drafts of which are currently being circulated) has been highly praised. The draft Bill with its explanatory memorandum demonstrates the value of such an approach.

Drafting

562. The ABI and Lloyd's believed that –

> *"The implementation of EC directives presents special problems which require study. In theory, directives do not prescribe national law in detail, but only lay down objectives to be achieved. In some cases the UK legislator has taken advantage of this theory to attempt a restatement in traditional British statutory language of the principle of a directive. This has sometimes led to trouble; for example, the dispute over the implementation of the Product Liability Directive by the Consumer Protection Act 1987" (M 3, para. 2.5).*

This approach is confirmed by the Renton Report –

> *"the European legislative tradition has been to express the law in general principles; in this country the tradition has been to specify in detail the application of the law in particular circumstances"*.[1]

563. The Bank of England has found on occasions that the desire of UK lawyers to be more precise than the generally vague wording of the directive, has led to unintended or illogical results when domestic legislation has been amended to reflect EC directives (M 6).

564. The Civil Aviation Authority also had deep concerns about how Community legislation, which is very different from UK domestic legislation in style, content and method of preparation, is absorbed into the domestic legal system (M 17). It quoted by way of reference EC Regulations on the "Harmonisation of Technical Requirements, Administration and Procedures in the field of Civil Aviation".[2] It referred to a particular problem relating to Joint Aviation Requirements, drawn up by European aviation authorities. The European regulation will provide that these requirements are applied throughout the Community. One difficulty is that the requirements are drawn up by teams of technical experts speaking in a variety of languages. The problem is particularly acute in the case of EC Air Transport Regulations because in order to achieve compromise the CAA believed the wording was deliberately obscurely drafted. The legal effect of such unclear and ambiguous drifting, according to the CAA would have some knock-on effect on the enforceability of safety regulations under English law. (The CAA also complained that there had been insufficient public debate on this issue which could have a detrimental effect on the safety of national aircraft passengers). It felt that assimilation of the Community

---

1   Renton Report, op. cit., para. 9.14.
2   These came into force 1 January 1992.

legislation into the national legislative process was going to involve radical change which would be painful and difficult. There was –

> *"risk that during the transitional period serious mistakes will be made and that some of the legislation will prove to be both unworkable and unenforceable, and therefore incapable of achieving its objectives" (M 17, para. 12).*

565. On the other hand ABI and Lloyd's felt the present tendency was going the other way –

> *"More recently, there has been a tendency for directives to become increasingly detailed and for implementing legislation to reproduce them verbatim. The results can be unhelpful in terms of producing legislation which can be readily understood. For example, Schedule 3A, paragraph l(1) to the Insurance Companies Act 1982 simply parrots the words of the EC directive, to the effect that member states may allow a greater freedom of choice of law than that given in the first sentence of the paragraph, but fails to say whether the UK does or does not allow that freedom" (M 3, para 2.5).*

566. **The problems we have referred to in the above paragraphs underline, in our view, the essential need for all departmental lawyers to be trained in European Community law.**

Accessibility

567. The British Medical Association (M 12) criticised the paucity of information about European Community legislation about to become enacted in the United Kingdom. It felt that the absence of a central reference point giving such information was a serious shortcoming. UK Members of Parliament were also often unaware of legislation being planned in Europe.

568. Mr Edward Mercer suggested that the European Commission should be obliged to send all proposals, including draft directives and other regulations to anybody who registers an interest in that particular area with them (M 39, para. 8).

569. Local authorities do not receive copies of EC directives or regulations or bills in draft form. The small number of academic libraries which retain complete sets of statutory provisions implementing European legislation is inadequate. The few documentation centres, e.g. Exeter University, are not sufficiently widespread geographically to redress this problem. It was felt by many that it was the Government's job to ensure that relevant legislation is made more readily available to all interested bodies and we have made recommendations to that end (see paragraphs 145-147) . We believe that the same approach should be applied to EC legislation, both before its final adoption and after enactment.

570. Many witnesses testified to their impatience for the secret law-making process of the Council of Ministers. Mr Tony Benn felt that –

> *"because of the ease with which laws applying to the UK can be made through the Council, civil servants are tempted to use this mechanism rather than wait for a place in the Government's own legislative programme. Neither the public nor Parliament itself has any formal role in the making of these laws" (M 8).*

Whilst we do not approve of this lack of openness in law-making, matters could be remedied by improving access and creating more transparency of the legislative process.

571. **We recommend that there should be available in all reference libraries in major cities, and on request from HMSO, a complete update of legislation emanating from Brussels both in draft forms and in that recently adopted.** This should be categorised under subject matter as well as cross-referenced to facilitate easy access to the data. **We also recommend that local authorities and other selected bodies should receive copies from the relevant Government departments of all EC directives and regulations.**

Conclusions

572. Any attempts by a government to try to mould Community legislation to its own wishes are doomed to failure, following the extension of policy areas now subject to majority voting, thus almost eliminating the use of the veto. Member states can now be more readily out-voted, inevitably weakening their ability to change the direction of Community legislation. If that government's individual Minister in the Council of Ministers is out-voted, parliamentary control of legislation is irredeemably weakened. It still has not been sufficiently recognised that the Single European Act has eroded the power of Parliament even further than was the case in 1972. The European Court of Justice's judgment in the *Factortame* case[1] has further eroded any illusions of national legal supremacy.

573. With the exception of the excellent system operated at the pre-legislative stage by the House of Lords Select Committee on European Communities, Parliament has little, if any impact upon the process of European law-making. Where successful changes are introduced from the UK, these are usually done by various interested sectors and bodies.

574. The need for interested bodies to monitor legislative processes at all stages from the Commission to Westminster, and also to monitor the interpretation of Community legislation and decisions on the validity of Community measures by the European Court of Justice, was recognised by the Institute of Directors (M 30). The Institute no longer primarily focuses on the Westminster Parliament but shifts its focus depending on whether the primary legislation originates in Brussels or Westminster. The Institute is particularly active in the Community proposal for a European Company Statute as well as on a proposed Directive regarding liability for suppliers of services. The Institute felt that by the time the European Company Statute came to be debated by the House of Commons, its work would have been largely completed. It relied upon this experience to show how the House of Commons is really unimportant in the European legislative field; it was highly critical of its scrutiny procedures. **It is our belief that if the Commons' scrutiny of EC legislation was improved, this could lead to a greater chance of arousing public concern which of**

---

1   op. cit.

itself would lead to more successful influence upon the Community legislative process.

575. The European legislative process is a lengthy process whether such laws are directly applicable or not, and inevitably the preparation of Community law encompasses procedures in Brussels, Strasbourg and Luxemburg as well as in Parliament. In our opinion, this must have serious implications for the traditional view of Parliament as a legislative body. **Parliament and the Government must abandon the "head in the sand" approach that is sadly characteristic of too many Members and adjust their response to European Community legislation so that consideration is given to it in ways that are more effective than those at present employed.** If this is not done, the legislation originating in the Community could be seriously detrimental to the British people. Some changes have been made, but we greatly fear that they are not enough.

576. We have not been able in this inquiry to carry out a comprehensive study of how EC legislation is prepared by the Commission, of how the consultation processes are conducted in Brussels, of the role of national governments at that stage, of the examination of legislation by the European Parliament, of the scrutiny given to EC proposals by national parliaments (particularly by the Lords and Commons) or of the working of the Council of Ministers in adopting Community legislation. These are major matters which have a direct impact on the legislative processes in this country, and are of growing importance. They merit further study. **We recommend that the Hansard Society consider appointing another Commission to examine the whole legislative process within the European Community.**

Chapter 9 – Conclusions and Recommendations

General Conclusions

577. We have made many detailed recommendations to improve the way statute law is made in this country. These must be seen as a whole. Our central aims have been to involve the people, and their representatives in Parliament, more directly in the making of the law and thus to seek to improve the quality of statute law that applies to all citizens.

578. Changes as wide-ranging, and in some cases radical, as those we propose will not be easy for Ministers and civil servants to accept but, as our evidence shows, public anxiety about the present system is great and demand for change is strong.

579. The legislative process in this country has been unsatisfactory for a long time and Ministers have not, up till now, shown a willingness to change it. We believe a change of heart and of attitude is required on the part of Ministers, of the Opposition and of back-bench Members of Parliament on both sides – and indeed of Parliament itself – if things are to be put right. As Lord Howe of Aberavon has said "It is the politician who must bear the responsibility for changing the system, whether as Ministers or as parliamentarians. It is we who are in charge. Only we can change the system"[1].

580. We are convinced that changes on the lines we recommend are essential to improve the ways of making the law. That is the challenge before Parliament and Ministers today as they consider this Commission's Report.

Main Conclusions and Recommendations

581. The main conclusions we have reached and the recommendations we have made are as follows:

Chapter 1 – Introduction

1. The Government should look at the implications of the issues we deal with in our Report for all parts of the United Kingdom. (Paragraph 10).

Chapter 2 – The Overall View

2. One cannot say, in general, that there should be more or less legislation; that is for Governments to decide. If the present volume of legislation is causing problems at various stages of the legislative process – and all our evidence confirms that this is so – the first requirement is not a reduction in that volume, but improvements in the process at those stages where it is under strain. (Paragraph 52).

---

1   Address to the Addington Society, May, 1977.

3. We have agreed five central principles which guide and govern all the recommendations we make:
   - Laws are made for the benefit of the citizens of the state. All citizens directly affected should be involved as fully and openly as possible in the processes by which statute law is prepared.
   - Statute law should be as certain as possible and as intelligible and clear as possible, for the benefit of the citizens to whom it applies.
   - Statute law must be rooted in the authority of Parliament and thoroughly exposed to open democratic scrutiny by the representatives of the people in Parliament.
   - Ignorance of the law is no excuse, therefore the current statute law must be as accessible as possible to all who need to know it.
   - The Government needs to be able to secure the passage of its legislation, but to get the law right and intelligible, for the benefit of citizens, is as important as to get it passed quickly. (Paragraph 64).

Chapter 3 – Consultation

Primary Legislation

4. The overwhelming impression from the evidence is that many of those most directly affected are deeply dissatisfied with the extent, nature, timing and conduct of consultation on bills as at present practised..... the Government must heed this criticism and seek to meet it. (Paragraph 113).
5. The Government should always seek the fullest advice from those affected on the problems of implementing and enforcing proposed legislation. (Paragraph 114).
6. Although some bills are inevitably required in a hurry, getting a bill right should always have priority over passing it quickly, and we recommend that the Government should publicly endorse this policy. (Paragraph 117).
7. The Government should make every effort to get bills in a form fit for enactment, without major alteration, before they are presented to Parliament; in the Government's review of the legislative process, this should be a first and overriding objective. (Paragraph 118).
8. Proper consultation should play a central part in the preparation of bills, and we recommend that all Government departments should act accordingly. (Paragraph 123).
9. Good consultation practice requires that when a bill is being prepared, bodies with relevant experience or interests – particularly those directly affected – should be given all the relevant information and an opportunity to make their views known, or to give information or advice, at each level of decision-taking. (Paragraph 128).
10. Consultation should be as open as possible. (Paragraph 129).
11. Secrecy regarding the content and results of consultations should be minimised and feed-back maximised. (Paragraph 131).
12. When major reviews are required of how the current law is operating and of the need for reform, we would welcome more frequent appointment of

independent inquiries, including Royal Commissions. If the Government is not prepared to accept the advice of such inquiries, it would be expected to publish its reasons. (Paragraph 132).

13. Consultative documents should be as clear and precise as possible. They should be specific about the questions on which departments want responses, while leaving opportunity for bodies to put forward further ideas of their own on relevant points. Green Papers should set out the facts fully and, as far as possible, the options being considered. White Papers should normally be preceded by Green Papers. White Papers should, where possible, systematically detail changes from Green Papers, indicating why these changes had been made. (Paragraph 133).

14. Departments should offer more consultations on draft texts, especially in so far as they relate to practical questions of the implementation and enforcement of legislation. (Paragraph 140).

15. The experience of the Inland Revenue in consulting on individual draft clauses of the Finance Bill should be studied by other departments and adopted in other fields. (Paragraph 140).

16. Where there is no great urgency for a bill, the whole bill might sometimes be published in draft in a Green Paper, as the basis for further consultation and possibly parliamentary scrutiny. (Paragraph 140).

17. Government departments should consult the main bodies concerned in each case and seek to agree how much time should be allowed for their responses to a consultation document. (Paragraph 143).

18. Consultation should not be delayed. (Paragraph 144).

19. Bodies invited by Government departments to respond to consultative documents on proposed legislation, and other bodies with a *bona fide* interest, should be given, free of charge, as many copies of those documents as they can show they need. (Paragraph 146).

20. Bodies which have contributed to consultation on proposed legislation should be supplied, free of charge, with copies of the resulting bills, Acts and statutory instruments. (Paragraph 147).

21. The Government should, drawing on best practice, prepare consultation guidelines which would be applicable to all Government departments when preparing legislation. (Paragraph 150).

22. We recommend that –
    (a) the Government's guidelines on consultation should be published;
    (b) each department when applying to the Future Legislation Committee for inclusion of a bill in the Government's legislative programme should submit a check-list indicating how far it has been able to comply with the guidelines, and give details of the consultations it has already carried out or proposes to conduct; and
    (c) an up-dated version of the check-list and this information should be submitted with the draft bill to the Legislation Committee and published with the bill. (Paragraph 152).

Delegated Legislation

23. There should be consultation where appropriate at the formative stage of delegated legislation, but wherever possible departments should also consult outside experts and affected bodies on drafts of the actual instruments that they propose to lay before Parliament. (Paragraph 161).

24. The Government's guidelines that we have recommended regarding consultation on bills, should be applied with appropriate modifications to consultation on delegated legislation. (Paragraph 162).

Chapter 4 – Drafting

How Bills and Statutory Instruments are Drafted

25. The Legislation Committee of the Cabinet should be given the wider and longer-term role of ensuring that bills conform with the best constitutional principles and, where appropriate, that they have been prepared after full and genuine consultation. (Paragraph 195).

26. Ministerial responsibility for the work of the Parliamentary Counsel Office, and particularly for oversight of the drafting methods employed and scrutiny of the drafting of all Government bills, should be assigned to the Attorney General. (Paragraph 196).

27. The Attorney General and his or her department should also keep an eye on, and where necessary seek to harmonise, the drafting styles of statutory instruments. (Paragraph 198).

28. Parliamentary Counsel should study Canadian and other overseas experience and practices to see whether there are lessons that could be applied in this country regarding their working methods. (Paragraph 202).

29. The methods of recruitment and training of Government draftsmen in Australia, Canada and New Zealand should be studied, with a view to seeing if there are lessons which could be learned and applied in this country. (Paragraph 204).

30. The Government should review the number of draftsmen required to draft all Government bills with proper care, and take all necessary action to recruit and retain Parliamentary Counsel accordingly. (Paragraph 205).

Style of Drafting

31. Before Parliamentary Counsel begin drafting a bill, or a departmental lawyer drafts a statutory instrument, a definite decision should be taken by the department and draftsman concerned on who are to be regarded as the main users of the legislation concerned, and the draftsman should then adopt an appropriate style of drafting for those users. (Paragraph 218).

32. Draftsmen should always seek for clarity, simplicity and brevity in their drafting, but certainty should be paramount. (Paragraph 221).

33. Parliamentary Counsel and departmental lawyers should take to heart the criticisms that continue to be made, by those most directly affected, of the style of drafting of statute law, and should review their own drafting styles accordingly. (Paragraph 222).

Statements of Principle and Purpose

34. Ministers, civil servants and in particular Parliamentary Counsel should do all they can to eliminate unnecessary and complicated detail in the bills for which they are responsible. (Paragraph 233).

35. Some means should be found of informing the citizen, his lawyers and the courts of the intention underlying the words of a statute. (Paragraph 235).

36. For every Act of Parliament, notes on sections, explaining the purpose and intended effect of each section (and Schedule), should be prepared by Government departments, with the assistance of Parliamentary Counsel, by up-dating the notes on clauses (and notes on amendments) prepared for Ministers; these notes on sections should be approved by Ministers and laid before Parliament, but should not require formal parliamentary approval; and notes on sections should be published at the same time as Acts. (Paragraph 250).

37. Explanatory notes on statutory instruments should explain their purpose and intended effect in the same way as the proposed notes on sections. (Paragraph 251).

38. Notes on sections (and Schedules) of Acts of Parliament, and explanatory notes on statutory instruments, should be allowed to be used by the courts as an aid to understanding an Act or instrument, but the the words of the Act or instrument should prevail unless these are not sufficient by themselves for determining its effect. If necessary, legislation should be introduced for this purpose. (Paragraph 252).

The Balance of Primary and Delegated Legislation

39. On balance, the main advantages of making greater use of delegated legislation outweigh the very real disadvantages. (Paragraph 262).

40. The main provisions of statute law should be set out in Acts of Parliament, but most detail should be left to delegated legislation, provided that much more satisfactory procedures are adopted by Parliament for scrutiny of delegated legislation and that improved arrangements are made for the publication of all statute law. (Paragraph 267).

41. Future Acts of Parliament should not normally include Henry VIII clauses. (Paragraph 270).

Chapter 5 – Parliamentary Processes

How Parliament Deals with Legislation

42. In practice, Parliament's main role in relation to UK legislation is to call Ministers to account for their proposals for changing the law by close and detailed scrutiny of both bills and delegated legislation. (Paragraph 310).

43. Both Houses fail to fulfil their legislative functions as effectively as they could do. In particular, the House of Commons as a whole should consider more deliberately for each individual bill how its scrutiny can be as effective as possible in the time available. (Paragraph 314).

44. We have come to the following broad judgements:

- Parliament could play a greater part by pre-legislative inquiry in the preparation of legislation.
- Both Houses could make better use of inquiry techniques, as used in select committees, to establish direct links with outside experts and affected interests, to get information and to probe the details of legislation.
- In debates on bills, particularly in committee, there has been too much emphasis on policy issues and inadequate attention to the practicality of what is proposed.
- In both Houses, legislative business is often too rushed.
- Scrutiny of delegated legislation is badly neglected in both Houses.
- There is not enough post-legislative review of the working of Acts.
- Public access to legislative proceedings is unduly restricted. (Paragraph 316).

Proceedings in the Commons

45. Departmentally-related select committees might helpfully examine Green and White Papers and other published consultative documents relating to proposed legislation and make reports which would assist the preparatory work on the legislation and inform parliamentary debate. (Paragraph 322).

46. On occasions, when a fuller inquiry is required into aspects of proposed legislation on which the experience and reactions of MPs would be relevant, and when the legislation is not needed in a hurry, select committees should be specially appointed to carry out pre-legislative inquiries. (Paragraph 323).

47. It would be difficult for the Government's business managers to accept some of our recommendations for more effective scrutiny of bills unless there were to be some compensating assurance, through time-tabling, that these would not cause unacceptable delays in the passage of legislation. (Paragraph 326).

48. Debates on bills in committee should not concentrate too much on policy but deal also with practical questions of the bill's operation. (Paragraph 330).

49. In most cases the more complex bills – even if controversial – should be referred to a select committee immediately after their presentation to the House. We refer to these committees as "first reading committees". (Paragraph 339).

50. Prior examination by a first reading committee could reduce the need for long second reading debates in many cases. We also believe that Second Reading Committees could more frequently be used for bills on which a division is not expected. (Paragraph 343).

51. The conclusion that the time has come to make it possible to receive direct evidence on bills in committee flows overwhelmingly from our own evidence. (Paragraph 348).

52. After second reading a bill should normally be committed to a special standing committee. (Paragraph 349).

53. Circulation of notes on clauses and, where appropriate, of notes on Government amendments, as prepared for Ministers, has become fairly general in recent years. We recommend that this should now become the standard practice. (Paragraph 353).

54. It would be a useful preparation for debates on a technical or complex bill if the Minister and his civil servants were to hold a pre-committee informal factual briefing for all Members. (Paragraph 354).

55. If there are many detailed points to be further debated at report stage, bills should be re-committed to the special standing committee for this purpose. (Paragraph 356).

56. When there is no great rush, and there are large numbers of Lords Amendments, they should be committed to the special standing committee for consideration. (Paragraph 357).

57. The minimum intervals between the stages of bills should be increased and longer notice should be required for amendments on report. (Paragraph 362).

58. Law contained in delegated legislation is no less the law of the land than the law contained in Acts of Parliament, and must be treated as seriously........We consider the whole approach of Parliament to delegated legislation to be highly unsatisfactory. The House of Commons in particular should give its procedures for scrutiny of statutory instruments a thorough review. (Paragraph 366).

59. The departmentally-related select committees might review statutory instruments in their field when they are laid before Parliament, and report on those that raise matters of public importance. (Paragraph 369).

60. Except in cases of emergency (which a Minister would have to explain to the House) no statutory instrument should be debated until the Joint Committee on Statutory Instruments has reported. (Paragraph 371).

61. Furthermore, where the Joint Committee has reported that it considers an instrument to be ultra vires or otherwise defective, a motion to approve that instrument should not be made without a resolution to set aside the findings of the Committee. (Paragraph 371).

62. Unless the House otherwise orders, all statutory instruments requiring affirmative resolutions and all "prayers" for the annulment of other statutory instruments, should automatically be referred to standing committees for debate. (Paragraph 372).

63. Longer or more complicated statutory instruments, which do not have to be approved in a hurry, could sometimes be sent to a special standing committee which could hear evidence. (Paragraph 373).

64. Before a committee starts debating a statutory instrument, it should be able to question Ministers on the purpose, meaning and effect of that instrument. (Paragraph 375).

65. The debate on a statutory instrument in standing committees should be held on a substantive motion approving, rejecting or otherwise expressing opinions on the instrument. (Paragraph 376).

66. Amendments should be permitted to a substantive motion moved in a committee on a statutory instrument, either relating to the merits of the whole instrument or recommending that it be approved subject to specified amendments being made to the instrument itself. (Paragraph 379).

67. Subject to more general time-tabling (see Chapter 7), there should be no time limits on debates on statutory instruments in standing committees. (Paragraph 380).

68. Acts and delegated legislation should always be so drafted that all important regulations and other delegated legislation may be debated in Parliament. (Paragraph 382).

69. As a matter of principle, "prayers" against statutory instruments should, as far as possible, be debated. (Paragraph 387).

70. The Legislation Steering Committee which we propose should be appointed (paragraphs 518-519 and Annex B) should seek to agree the arrangements for standing committees to consider "prayers" and for selecting the "prayers" to be debated. (Paragraph 387)

71. The operation of every major Act (other than Finance Acts and some constitutional Acts), and all the delegated legislation made under it, should be reviewed some two or three years after it comes into force. (Paragraph 393).

72. The committees carrying out post-legislative reviews should also examine, in the light of experience with the Act, the adequacy of the consultative process developed in accordance with our recommendations in Chapter 3. (Paragraph 395).

Proceedings in the Lords

73. Informal briefings for Members and their advisers should be offered by Ministers on all longer and more complex bills as soon as possible after second reading. (Paragraph 400).

74. Whenever appropriate, bills should be committed to special standing committees in the House of Lords. (Paragraph 403).

75. We warmly welcome the decision of the Government to move for the appointment of a Delegated Powers Scrutiny Committee in the House of Lords. (Paragraph 406).

76. The question of whether the powers and resources of the Delegated Powers Scrutiny Committee should be enlarged at some future stage, to enable it to detect potential legislative conflicts with the European Convention on Human Rights, is worth considering. (Paragraph 413).

77. Another similar function which the Delegated Powers Scrutiny Committee might take on at some stage – again with increased resources – would be to detect prima facie conflict between provisions in proposed legislation and the requirements of European Community law. (Paragraph 414).

Access to Legislation in Parliament by the Public

78. We believe that both Houses of Parliament should recognise the proper rights of the public, and especially of interested bodies, to be informed

about, and to able to make a proper contribution to Parliament's scrutiny of legislation. (Paragraph 420).

79. Bodies and people with a direct and sufficient interest in a bill or statutory instrument should be able to register their interest when that legislation is published by or laid before Parliament. (Paragraph 422).

80. Registered bodies and people should be entitled to free copies of all parliamentary papers relating to the legislation with which they are concerned. (Paragraph 423).

81. The House of Commons authorities should issue passes giving registered bodies and people priority admission to committee rooms for legislation with which they are concerned. (Paragraph 424).

82. The public should be able to buy sound or video recordings of committee proceedings. (Paragraph 425).

83. A reasonable supply of amendment papers and other relevant parliamentary documents should be available to the public, on request, for each bill in committee in the Commons and, together with the reprinted bill, at the report stage. (Paragraph 426).

84. As much information as possible should be published regarding progress on amendments and clauses of bills in committee, and on expected timing of future debates. (Paragraph 427).

Chapter 6 – Access to the Statute Book

Publication of Acts and Delegated Legislation

85. As far as possible Acts should not be brought into force until they are published. (Paragraph 453).

86. The Government should press ahead as fast as possible with the Statute Law Database. (Paragraph 454).

87. The Statute Law Database should be made available to all potential users – outside as well as inside government – as soon as possible. (Paragraph 455).

88. Some Government subsidy to keep down charges to outside users for access to the Statute Law Database would be appropriate. (Paragraph 456).

89. The Government should enable HMSO to price their legislative publications, and especially bills, Acts and statutory instruments, at well below cost. (Paragraph 458).

90. Priority should be given to consolidation of those Acts or remaining parts of Acts which were passed before textual amendment became the usual practice. (Paragraph 461).

91. The pace of consolidation should continue to increase and if necessary the drafting resources of the Law Commission should be strengthened to make this possible. (Paragraph 462).

Explanatory material

92. As soon as possible after a bill is introduced which is going to be implemented substantially by delegated legislation, the Government should indicate the general nature of the regulations and other instruments they

propose to make to bring the bill into effect, and their proposed time-table for implementing the legislation. (Paragraph 471).

93. Statements should be published periodically in relation to individual Acts to show what regulations etc. have been made under the Act, and when they came into force, and also the commencement dates of various parts of the Act. (Paragraph 472).

94. The Government should do all it can to explain new law to the public, and especially those most affected, in terms that are readily intelligible. (Paragraph 473).

95. The Government should give additional financial help to bodies who have to incur significant extra expense in explaining new laws to the public. (Paragraph 474).

Chapter 7 – Programming and Time-Tabling of Legislation

The Overall View

96. Preparation and scrutiny of legislation should be improved, but its passage in reasonable time should also be assured. (Paragraph 479).

The Legislative Programme

97. The one-year legislative programme both delays and compresses the drafting stage in some cases, and leads to some under-prepared bills being presented to Parliament. (Paragraph 484).

98. Governments should move towards the adoption of a two-year legislative programme. We suggest that this should be done as follows:

(a) each March the Future Legislation Committee should decide on the main content of the legislative programme for two years ahead, and authority should be given for drafting to begin on the larger, longer-term bills to be introduced in the second session as well as for the drafting of other bills for the first session; and

(b) each year the Government should announce its legislation for the coming session and the bigger, longer-term bills for the session after that. (Paragraph 485).

99. If a bill requires extended parliamentary time, and is not required in a hurry, it should be permissible to defer completion of that bill in the current session and to carry it over for completion in the following session. (Paragraph 490).

100. Unless they actually disagree with the Commissions' proposals, Governments should normally give time for the consideration and passage of all Law Commission bills. (Paragraph 499).

101. Law Commission and Scottish Law Commission bills should be committed after second reading in the House of Lords to special standing committees, and further debates in the Lords should be as limited as possible. (Paragraph 500).

102. We believe that the possibility of having a Technical Taxes Bill should be reconsidered in the light of our other recommendations regarding the

procedures of the Commons and the programming and time-tabling of Government legislation. (Paragraph 504).

Time-tabling of legislative business in Parliament

103. The time has come for the House of Commons to recognise that if parliamentary scrutiny of bills and delegated legislation is to be improved, as many Members wish, much more extensive formal time-tabling of all legislation will have to be accepted. (Paragraph 512).

104. The House of Commons should consider a system of formal time-tabling of all its legislation on the lines set out in Annex B. (Paragraph 519).

Chapter 8 – The Impact of European Community Legislation

105. All Acts and statutory instruments implementing European Community directives should be accompanied by explanatory memoranda giving the essential Community background. (Paragraph 557).

106. The evidence we received and the recommendations we have made for greater consultation on texts of bills, clauses and statutory instruments (paragraphs 137-140 and 160-162), and also our recommendations for earlier and more informed parliamentary scrutiny of proposed legislation (paragraphs 320-323 and 331-341) are equally, if not more, applicable in principle to consultation on and scrutiny of implementation of Community legislation. (Paragraph 561).

107. All departmental lawyers should be trained in European Community law. (Paragraph 566).

108. There should be available in all reference libraries in major cities, and on request from HMSO, a complete update of legislation emanating from Brussels both in draft forms and in that recently adopted. (Paragraph 571).

109. Local authorities and other selected bodies should receive copies from the relevant Government departments of all EC directives and regulations. (Paragraph 571).

110. Parliament and the Government must abandon the "head in the sand" approach that is sadly characteristic of too many Members and adjust their response to European Community legislation so that consideration is given to it in ways that are more effective than those at present employed. (Paragraph 575).

111. The Hansard Society should consider appointing another Commission to examine the whole legislative process within the European Community. (Paragraph 576).

Annex A – Outline of Suggested Procedures for Debating Statutory Instruments in the House of Commons

1. Instruments subject to the affirmative procedure

(a) Unless the House otherwise orders on a non-debatable motion, all statutory instruments requiring affirmative resolutions should be automatically referred to standing committees for debate.

(b) Occasionally longer or more complicated instruments should go to a special standing committee which could hear evidence.

(c) Before a committee starts debating an instrument, it should be able to question Ministers on the purpose, meaning and effect of that instrument.

(d) Debate should be held on a motion moved by the Minister recommending approval of the instrument.

(e) Amendments to that motion should be permitted recommending that the instrument be not approved or that it be approved subject to amendments being made to the instrument itself.

(f) The chairman of the committee would have the power to select amendments to the motion.

(g) Subject to general time-tabling, there would be no time limit on debates.

(h) When a committee has recommended the approval of an instrument without amendment, the formal motion to approve the instrument would be put in the House without debate.

(i) When a committee recommends that an instrument be not approved, or approved subject to amendments, a Government motion in the House to approve the instrument would be debatable; debate would be time-limited.

2. Instruments subject to the negative procedure

(a) Unless the House otherwise orders on a debatable motion, all "prayers" for the annulment of a statutory instrument subject to the negative procedure should stand referred to a standing committee .

(b) The procedures in committee for debates on "prayers" would be as for affirmative instruments except that the Member who tabled the "prayer" would either move a motion for annulment of the instrument concerned or a motion recommending its amendment; the Minister could move amendments to such motions.

(c) If a motion for annulment of an instrument or recommending its amendment were negatived in committee, no further proceedings would be required.

(d) If a motion for annulment of an instrument or recommending its amendment were agreed in committee, the Member who moved that motion (or another Member on his behalf) would have the right to move a formal motion in the House for the annulment of the instrument; debate would be time-limited.

Annex B – A Possible Scheme for General Time-tabling of Legislation.

(a) a Legislation Steering Committee, to be chaired by the Speaker, including representatives of the parties and of back-benchers, should meet from time to time to seek to agree the legislative calendar for the main bills of the session and the total time to be available for each of those bills;

(b) the detailed allocation of time for the various stages of each bill, within the total time agreed by the Legislation Steering Committee, should be agreed by a Business Committee appointed for each bill;

(c) the Legislation Steering Committee should seek to agree the the arrangements for standing committees to consider "prayers" and for selecting the "prayers" to be debated.

(d) the allocation of time for considering individual statutory instruments in standing committees should be agreed by a Statutory Instruments Business Committee, with varying membership for each group of instruments being considered;

(e) decisions of the Legislation Steering Committee and of the Business Committees would be published and could be varied from time to time in response to changing circumstances and requirements; and

(f) the decisions of the Legislation Steering Committee and of the Business Committees would not need the sanction of the whole House if they were agreed unanimously, but if there was disagreement a debatable order of the House would be required.

Appendix 1 – Selected Written Evidence

M1. Aberdare, Rt Hon Lord, KBE
M2. Aberdare, Rt Hon Lord, KBE (supplementary letter)
M3. Association of British Insurers and Lloyd's
M4. Association of Chief Police Officers of England, Wales and Northern Ireland
M5. Association of First Division Civil Servants
M6. Bank of England
M7. Bednar, Mr George
M8. Benn, Rt Hon Tony, MP
M9. Bourn, Sir John, KCB (Comptroller and Auditor General)
M10. British and Irish Association of Law Librarians
M11. British Broadcasting Corporation
M12. British Medical Association
M13. British Railways Board
M14. Campaign for Freedom of Information
M15. Child Poverty Action Group
M16. Child Poverty Action Group (supplementary Memorandum)
M17. Civil Aviation Authority
M18. Clarity
M19. Commission for Racial Equality
M20. Community Council for Somerset
M21. Community Council of Humberside
M22. Confederation of British Industry
M23. Consumers' Association
M24. English Heritage
M25. Equal Opportunities Commission
M26. General Council of the Bar, Working Party of Law Reform Committee
M27. Independent Television Commission
M28. Industry and Parliament Trust
M29. Institute of Chartered Accountants in England and Wales
M30. Institute of Directors
M31. Institute of Public Relations: Government Affairs Group
M32. Instone, Mr Ralph, Q.C.
M33. Kennedy, Hon Mr Justice Paul (now Rt Hon Lord Justice Kennedy)
M34. Kinley, Dr David,
M35. Law Commission
M36. Law Society
M37. Local Authority Associations (AMA, ACC and ADC)
M38. Magistrates Association

M39. Mercer, Mr Edward
M40. National Association of Health Authorities and Trusts
M41. National Consumer Council
M42. National Trust
M43. National Trust (supplementary letter)
M44. National Union of Mineworkers
M45. Norton, Professor Philip
M46. Paisley, Rev. Dr Ian, MP, MEP
M47. Renton, Rt Hon Lord, PC, KBE, TD, QC
M48. Roscoe, Mr Gareth,
M49. Scottish Consumer Council
M50. Scottish Law Commission
M51. Shelter
M52. Simon of Glaisdale, Rt Hon Lord, PC
M53. Society of County Secretaries
M54. Study of Parliament Group
M55. Trades Union Congress
M56. Trades Union Congress (supplementary memorandum)
M57. Trimble, Mr David, MP

M1   The Rt Hon Lord Aberdare, KBE

I would like to put forward three ideas, which appeal to me, although not all original.

1. There is and always has been criticism of the drafting of Bills and the word "gobbledegook" is not infrequently used. Even the Judges sometimes confess that they are unable to understand the wording of a particular Clause.

   I think that we should reconsider allowing the Courts to interpret Bills in the light of what has been said by Ministers in Parliament and by notes on Clauses. Parliament has enacted the legislation as explained to them by Ministers and often with the aid of notes on Clauses. I cannot see therefore why the Courts should not equally be guided by the same. I know this has always been resisted but I hope you will reconsider it in order to obtain less complicated drafting.

2. Legislation at present imposes an enormous burden on Members and is ill-considered. There is often a guillotine in the House of Commons, followed by late nights in the House of Lords. Yet time is frequently wasted on aspects of Bills that are not of prime political interest.

   Hoping that any idea might be useful, I would suggest that before a Bill is published it should be considered by a Joint Committee of both Houses which could hear evidence from the promoting Ministry and interested parties. It could seek to remove misunderstandings and obtain agreement on less important proposals. It could also recommend to each House which matters were of major political importance and each House could then devise its own procedures to give maximum time at reasonable hours to such matters.

3. I know from your [Lord Rippon's] debate in the House of Lords of your concern about delegated legislation. However in my opinion if legislation is to be simplified and if the load on Parliament is to be eased, it seems inevitable that we shall find more, not less, delegated legislation. As I see it, Parliament would be wise to accept this fact and to seek greater control over such legislation.

   I suggest a Joint Committee with much wider terms of reference than the present Joint Committee to examine statutory instruments on their merits. The ideal would be to allow both Houses to amend such instruments, but I recognise that this would never be acceptable to Government. However, I believe that reports from a select committee would carry great weight.

3 December 1991

M2   The Rt Hon Lord Aberdare KBE: Supplementary Letter

I am in full agreement with the general consensus on the problems highlighted by the Commission so far and also with the constraints imposed by the need to pass Government legislation in a single session. As you say, the latter constraint is at the heart of the matter and in the hope that any idea is welcome, I would like to contribute one of my own so far as the House of Lords is concerned.

By far the greatest commitment in terms of time is to the Committee stage of major Bills. However, in my opinion, that time is not used as productively as it might be. Often amendments are considered at a very late hour with few people present other than the main participants from the front benches. Frequently, time is wasted in discussing probing amendments when, at the end of the debate, the Government accept the amendment or at least undertake to introduce an amendment of their own to cover the point at a later stage. Other amendments do not need to be pressed at Committee stage and left to the Report stage.

My suggestion is as follows: after the Bill has received a Second Reading, a meeting should be arranged at the promoting department, attended by the Minister and his civil servants, the spokesmen from the Opposition parties and their advisers, some representatives of interested outside organisations and some interested Peers – perhaps limited to two from each party and two from the cross benches.

No formal amendments would be considered at this meeting but the Bill would be discussed, clause by clause. The Bill's intention would be fully explained and objections expressed. Where an acceptable case has been made, hopefully the Government would make concessions. The time allotted for the consideration of the Bill would be agreed by the usual channels, and at the end of its deliberations the meeting would identify the main areas of major disagreement to be referred to the House itself.

There would then follow a Committee stage on the floor of the House, mainly confined by convention to the main areas of disagreement identified by the previous meeting and to Government amendments resulting from discussions at that meeting.

I believe that this arrangement by itself would accomplish a great deal in leaving only matters of fundamental importance to be discussed and decided at the Committee stage. It might be further worthwhile considering whether the Report stage and Third Reading should be taken together as they are in the House of Commons.

The idea underlying this proposed procedure is to save a lot of time spent on non-controversial issues at the Committee stage and to limit that stage to discussion and divisions on matters of major disagreement. Hopefully this would save a lot of time on the floor of the House and allow more time for other priorities.

I would emphasise that this is entirely my own idea and I have not had an opportunity of consulting any of my colleagues.

27 April 1992

M3 Association of British Insurers and Lloyd's

1. General Comments

There is a fundamental conflict between the necessity for a Bill to complete all its stages within one Parliamentary session and the complexities of some legislation. This enforced timetable may assist the efficient management of Government time, but does not take account of the complex nature of some Acts such as the Insolvency Act and the Financial Services Act. The adversarial nature of Committee Stage means that even then it is difficult to get informed debate; some parts of Bills are effectively never debated at all. By contrast, we have found the discussion in Select Committees, particularly on European matters, very helpful and are often asked to give evidence (see 2.3 below).

Complex legislation would benefit from more consultation before Bills are introduced into Parliament, or from earlier introduction of Bills. We would prefer the second alternative as it is only when proposals are transformed into draft legislation that many of the difficulties emerge. For example, it could be helpful if Select Committees were given the chance to consult widely on complex Bills, take evidence and suggest amendments, leaving the actual process of amendment to the customary Parliamentary procedures.

2. Detailed Comments

2.1 Extent and Nature of Government Consultation
The Association and Lloyd's are frequently invited to comment on consultation documents published by Government departments and other bodies, most notably the Law Commission and the Scottish Law Commission.

Law Commissions
Consultation documents published by the Law Commissions tend to be substantial pieces of legal research, which have been prepared by people who have had a considerable amount of time to familiarise themselves with the issues to be addressed and, in general, their recommendations are of a highly technical nature.

Unless the proposals in such consultation documents have direct application to insurance companies, ABI/Lloyd's comments are likely to be of a relatively general nature, whether supportive or opposed to the proposals under consideration, rather than to address the proposals in the detail which the issues might merit from a technical point of view. Examples include the Law Commission's Consultation Paper No. 120 on restitution of payments made under a mistake of law and the Scottish Law Commission's Discussion Paper No. 87 on statutory fees for arrestees.

Government Departments
On occasion, we have found it difficult to understand from consultation documents what are the Government's intentions underlying the proposals; it is not always clear at what the proposals are directed or how they fit in with the policy previously announced by the Government. This is the case with the draft Regulations on conveyancing to be made under the Courts and Legal Services Act 1990 (also mentioned at 2.2 below). In some cases the proposals may reflect a change or development in Government thinking but again this is not always made clear. This can make it more difficult to comment constructively on the proposals.

It would be useful for departments to be more open with trade associations on Government thinking, in order that trade associations and the Government could work together in developing legislation which could be easily complied with. We have found that unfamiliarity with technical insurance issues can lead to misunderstanding in Government departments as to the feasibility of proposed legislation. We would welcome consultation at an earlier stage so that we can brief the relevant department on the insurance background.

On certain issues, Government departments consult interested bodies at an early stage (see 2.2 below). For example, ABI has been working with the Law Commission, the Lord Chancellor's Department and the DTI since July 1986 on the insurance implications of the commonhold concept of property ownership. This consultation has resulted in the Lord Chancellor's Department putting forward draft legislation which, insofar as it concerns insurance requirements for commonhold property, should not present difficulties for insurance companies.

Deadlines
Formal consultation documents issued by the Law Commissions often have long deadlines, which is realistic given the sometimes lengthy and technical nature of the proposals. Consultation papers produced by Government departments often have tight deadlines, and it is occasionally not possible to give issues the full consideration they warrant. We appreciate that some deadlines are short because the department is itself subject to a deadline imposed, for example, by the timing of meetings in Brussels. This is not always the case, however; short deadlines should not be imposed merely for the sake of speed if this is not actually necessary. It is better for legislation to be clear and workable than for it to be enacted at the earliest possible opportunity and, before long, have to be changed by further legislation or interpreted by the courts.

Reporting on Consultation
Quite often little indication is given of what the general view of consultees was or the extent to which ABI's and Lloyd's own representations have been taken on board.

We are sometimes disappointed that, when commenting on matters of specific interest to insurance companies, we may not always receive a reply to our representations, even though they point out fundamental deficiencies and/or impracticalities in the proposed legislation.

Feedback would be particularly helpful concerning the development of EC draft Directives (see also 2.4 below). For example, ABI was sent a detailed consultation paper by the Home Office on the draft Data Protection Directive, yet apart from some helpful progress reports by the Home Office we have heard very little about the Government's views. Most of what we have learnt has been gleaned from presentations given by civil servants at seminars and conferences. The Government's thinking should be made more accessible at an earlier stage to enable interested parties to comment most effectively.

2.2 Form and Drafting of Bills and Instruments
We endeavour to scrutinise draft insurance legislation so as to identify inherent defects and weaknesses. ABI is regularly consulted by Government departments on technical matters relating to the insurance aspects of draft legislation.

For example, in the course of the passage through Parliament of the Courts and Legal Services Bill in 1990, we were able to explain to the Lord Chancellor's

Department the implications of Section 16 of the Insurance Companies Act 1982, which prohibits insurance companies from carrying on any business not connected with insurance business.

Similarly, we were able to assist the Government in understanding the limitations of various insurance contracts for the purpose of the Dangerous Dogs Bill in 1991. ABI provided briefings at short notice so that the legislation could be introduced with all possible haste to meet the concern of the public at the time.

In some cases Budget secrecy means that it is difficult for consultation to take place before the introduction into Parliament of legislation to be included in the Finance Bill. Where this constraint does not apply, the ABI and Lloyd's has found prior consultation and publication of draft clauses to be of the utmost value. We believe that this process has also assisted the Inland Revenue and HM Customs and Excise and urge that it should apply whenever possible.

2.3 Parliamentary Scrutiny of Legislation

Select Committees

Select Committees are regularly appointed by the House of Commons and the House of Lords to enquire into particular matters or consider draft legislation. We are often asked to give evidence on issues concerning the insurance industry. We consider that these Committees perform a thorough and valuable job, particularly the House of Commons Select Committee on European Legislation and the European Communities Committee of the House of Lords.

Scrutiny of Bills

Due to the considerable volume of legislation, its complexity, and the fact that MPs and Peers have other duties to perform outside Parliament, we feel that it is often difficult for legislation to be scrutinised properly.

For example, on the Second Reading in the House of Commons on 12th June 1990 of the Law Reform (Miscellaneous Provisions) (Scotland) Bill, MPs expressed concern that five weeks, the maximum period over which the Committee Stage could extend, would not be sufficient for scrutiny of the Bill and that it would be a pity if debates had to take place through the night when they should be taken at a reasonable pace and hour so that the general public could follow them as well as Members of the Committee. (Hansard, Columns 176, 196 and 219). Similarly, having to embark on a large miscellaneous provisions Bill in the middle of June was described as "an imposition and an unfairness, principally on Members of Parliament, but infinitely worse on the public..." (Hansard Column 186).

Again, on the Second Reading in the House of Lords of the Courts and Legal Services Bill on 19th December 1989, Lord Hailsham of St. Marylebone said that the House was discussing a Bill about 120 pages long with 13 schedules, dealing with a large number of quite separate issues; the Bill had been generated entirely inside the Government machine after consultation on Green Papers which had been followed by a White Paper on which both Houses were denied the possibility of debate. He continued, "Now we are discussing the Second Reading of a Bill of these proportions dealing with this important subject which was printed, I think, on 6th

December. It is now 19th December. This is no way to carry out serious law reform."

We are particularly concerned that in the case of a number of pieces of major Government legislation in recent years, Bills have grown dramatically in size in the course of their passage through Parliament and large numbers of Government amendments have been tabled at a late stage in the Bills' passage. Cases in point are the Financial Services Act 1986 and the Companies Act 1989. Significant Government amendments were made to the Companies Bill at Report Stage in the House of Commons concerning, inter alia, the execution of contracts by companies (Hansard, 26th October 1989, Column 1172) and changes to the ultra vires rule (Column 1191). When the House of Lords considered the Commons amendments on 7th November, Lord Williams of Elvel referred (Column 548) to the fact that the Bill had left the Lords containing 240 pages and that the Lords had received 531 amendments from the Commons consisting of 180 pages of printed text and including a great deal of new material in all sections of the Bill. He continued, "Many government amendments were not discussed in another place because the Report stage was guillotined.... We on these Benches are tired of this House being used as a sort of legislative sausage machine and I hope that I speak for the whole House when I lodge the strongest objection."

In other words, members of the House of Lords have gone on record as saying that their job was impossible; they were not being asked to review Commons' amendments but to consider a totally different Bill from the Bill as introduced into Parliament.

Some amendments are tabled only a day or so before the debate making it impossible, in reality, for interested parties to brief MPs or members of the House of Lords on points of concern or drafting errors. Sometimes the amendments are not available from HMSO until after the debate has taken place.

Informed debate in the House of Commons and the House of Lords is necessary if legislation is to fulfil its intended purpose. This debate can be assisted by briefings supplied by interested parties such as trade associations. It is also necessary, however, for MPs or members of the House of Lords who have been briefed to attend the House at the relevant time. We feel that all concerned would be assisted if an estimated timetable were available publicly in advance of debates as to how many clauses were likely to be dealt with at a particular sitting. While in the event it might be that fewer or more clauses were dealt with, a timetable might assist in improving attendance and might help avoid the problem of the last parts of a Bill to be discussed having to be rushed through, without proper debate, because Parliamentary time is running out because too much time has been devoted to other parts of the Bill.

The free House of Commons/House of Lords telephone information service is extremely useful in updating interested parties on the progress of individual Bills.

ABI and Lloyd's scrutinise Hansard for matters of interest to insurers. Hansard is not published, however, until the day after the debate has taken place, or even later in the case of Select Committees. Although members of the public can attend debates in person, there would not be sufficient room for everyone interested in learning the progress of a particular Bill on the actual day of the debate to be present, particularly at Committee Stage. It would therefore be of considerable benefit if dedicated TV channels to televise proceedings in both chambers and in Committee Rooms were commercially available for subscribers.

2.4 EC Directives – Consultation

Matters dealt with by EC Directives present special problems as regards consultation. Consultation by the EC Commission at an early stage, before a Directive is proposed, can be very valuable, but it is difficult to discern any consistent policy on the part of the Commission as a whole towards such early consultation and the number of persons consulted in the United Kingdom is likely to be limited. (We would except the Insurance Division of DG XV from this general stricture.) Consultation at a later stage by the Government should be accompanied by adequate explanation of the Community legislative process. Otherwise, consultees may fail to grasp the fact that to ensure victory for their cause it is not sufficient to convince Her Majesty's Government.

The stage at which proposed Directives are effectively scrutinised and often heavily amended is that of the Council Working Party. The major defect in the process lies in the fact that the proceedings of these working parties are, in theory, confidential. Nobody has the right to be told anything about them and if this rule of confidentiality were strictly observed, effective consultation would become impossible. In practice, to an extent which varies between government departments and indeed between individual officials, confidentiality is breached and trusted consultees are kept informed of what is going on. Only a few persons can be thus favoured and anybody who wishes to make the proposed Directive a matter of public debate is inevitably excluded. This represents a crucial aspect of the Community's "democratic deficit".

2.5 Implementation of EC Directives

The implementation of EC Directives presents special problems which require study. In theory, directives do not prescribe national law in detail but only lay down objectives to be achieved. In some cases the United Kingdom legislator has taken advantage of this theory to attempt a restatement in traditional British statutory language of the principle of a Directive. This has sometimes led to trouble; for example the dispute over the implementation of the Product Liability Directive by the Consumer Protection Act 1987.

More recently, there has been a tendency for directives to become increasingly detailed and for implementing legislation to reproduce them verbatim. The results can be unhelpful in terms of producing legislation which can be readily understood. For example, Schedule 3A, paragraph 1(1) to the Insurance Companies Act 1982 simply parrots the words of the EC Directive, to the effect that member states may allow a greater freedom of choice of law than that given in the first sentence of the paragraph, but fails to say whether the United Kingdom does or does not allow that freedom.

2.6 Accessibility to the Public of Legislation passed by Parliament

In theory, the public can acquire legislation from HMSO or can consult it at large libraries. In practice, unless a consolidating Act has just been passed, or reference is made to a looseleaf, updated version of the legislation, legislation is not really accessible to the layman because it very often consists of amendments to earlier legislation. It does not make sense unless this earlier legislation is also consulted, together with any related delegated legislation. It does not seem right that the complexity of law means that the public is probably unable to understand it without professional assistance. We cannot see any easy answer to this problem. We urge, however, that new legislation should be prepared as carefully as possible and that unnecessary complexities in drafting and structure should be avoided.

Deferred Commencement and Amendment by Statutory Instrument

The accessibility of legislation to the public has undoubtedly suffered in recent times from the lavish use now made of the techniques of deferred commencement and of amendment of statutes by statutory instruments. Too often, the law on a given topic consists of a mosaic of old statutes which have been prospectively repealed, a new statute which is only partly in force and a clutch of statutory instruments amending either the old or the new statutes. The Consumer Credit Act 1974 took ten years to be brought completely into force. The Financial Services Act 1986 had twelve commencement orders. These at least constitute a distinct, numbered series, so that a researcher who has discovered the existence of No. 12 knows that there are eleven others. Statutory instruments amending the Act began to appear a few months after Commencement Order No. 12. These do not constitute an identifiable series. The researcher simply has to find them, one by one, not knowing how many he is looking for.

The amendment of statutes by statutory instrument used to be a comparatively rare phenomenon but the European Communities Act 1972 has produced a major new category of cases. The need for consolidating Acts has accordingly increased but the resources available to produce them have not.

3. Conclusion

It is hoped that the Commission will find these comments helpful. We consider that our suggestions, if implemented, would improve the public accountability of Parliament and also enhance its reputation as a representative and democratic body.

14 February 1992

M4   Association of Chief Police Officers of England, Wales and Northern Ireland

1. The Association welcomes the initiative of the Hansard Society in appointing a Commission to examine the legislative process in England and Wales, and the opportunity to offer comments to it. The Police Service is as concerned as any organisation that any piece of legislation enacted by Parliament should be clear

as to its purpose and intent; capable of being readily comprehended; and capable of sensible enforcement.

Consultation

2. ACPO supports wholeheartedly the concept of wide consultation before legislation is drafted and, indeed, at other stages before enactment in some cases.

3. The mechanisms for consultation with the Police Service are in fact well-established and in many respects operate satisfactorily – but experience suggests that there are a number of aspects of the consultative process where change would be welcomed.

4. First, there is the need for an adequate period of time to ensure that the process is meaningful, and not merely a token exercise. The Association recognises the political imperative which drives some legislation, and the need of Government on occasions to respond urgently to public demands, but ACPO believes firmly that the timing of consultation should be such that the Police Service is able to advise Government fully, not only on the operational policing aspects of the issue in hand, but also on the implications for police resources in terms of manpower, finance and equipment. Importantly, information should be available to Government also on the police training implications of new legislation, including in some cases the extent of significant abstractions of officers from duty to enable necessary training to take place.

5. This lesson has been learned particularly through the implementation of the Police and Criminal Evidence Act, 1984, where the resource implications were perhaps not considered in as much depth as they might have been – though the Act itself, introduced as a result of a Royal Commission and several years of consultation between Home Office and the Police Service, has stood the test of time well, with relatively little amendment required.

6. In the recent past The Dangerous Dogs Act, 1991 and The Aggravated Taking Without Consent Act, 1991 provide examples of legislation on which there was little time given for in-depth consideration. In the case of the former, the very short period of consultation resulted in the need subsequently for Home Office to issue further guidance on the operation of the Act. In the latter case, the offence was covered by existing legislation, and a more efficacious approach within that legislation might have been found.

7. ACPO would wish to place considerable emphasis on the point raised in paragraph 4 relating to resource implications. At a time of continuing financial constraint; demands for value for money; and the emphasis on the need to produce a quality service, it is vitally important that the resource implications of proposed legislation for those who will have to enforce it are sought by and taken account of within Government.

8. ACPO is equally concerned that adequate consultation should take place if, in the course of the passage of a Bill through Parliament clauses are added or other amendments made which might considerably alter the Bill's effect. Two cases in point are S.39 of the Public Order Act 1989 relating to gypsies and travellers,

which was announced hurriedly following disturbances at Stonehenge, and the Road Traffic Bill 1991, where in the Lords a further clause was added placing a requirement on police to vet prospective taxi drivers. In this latter case there was no consultation; no warning; and no apparent regard taken of the already well publicised views of ACPO that requests for the vetting of prospective taxi drivers or any other groups simply could not be met from existing resources.

9. In recent times too we have faced problems where legislation has stemmed from EC Directives, with little or no regard being paid to advice from the Police Service, and no opportunity given to press the case further.

10. Greater consultation at the drafting stage with those who were to be responsible for enforcing the piece of legislation under consideration might assist to ensure that the intentions of the provisions, through the words used, were carried into practice.

11. To assist the consultative process might there be merit in the establishment of a number of working groups, consisting of members of appropriate professional associations and the general public who could be available to sit at short notice to work through the practicalities of proposed legislation? Each group might specialise in particular aspects of the law. Would such a suggestion commend itself to the Commission?

Drafting

12. Whilst recognising the problems of the Parliamentary draftsman (not least of which must be the sheer volume of legislation), the Police Service as enforcement authority – and indeed all those with the duty to comply with the law – would obviously welcome legislation drafted in plain, modern English, avoiding complex syntax as far as possible. We believe the following measures could also assist:

(1) There is a need to ensure that the enforcement agencies are in possession of legislation before it is in force: problems have been found in this regard particularly with road traffic legislation.

(2) Those tasked within the Service with the responsibility of maintaining up-to-date legal records would find it helpful if legislative documents could be compiled and indexed in loose-leaf format, so that amendments might readily be inserted and the need to keep a succession of associated papers obviated.

(3) It would be helpful if, when a statute consolidates or replaces part of existing legislation, the old legislation might be totally repealed, leaving the new statute as the sole source. By way of example, the Road Traffic Act, 1988 is the principal Act covering road traffic matters but a few provisions of the RTA, 1960 remain in force, as do a few sections of the RTA, 1930. And major changes have now been made to the 1988 Act by the Road Traffic Act, 1991. Matters would be far simpler if there were but one comprehensive Road Traffic Act. Such a procedure might well have avoided the problem found in implementing the law relating to children's seat belts and rear passenger seat belts, where the revocation of the original

legislation and drafting of comprehensive new legislation might have avoided enforcement problems with passengers aged between 14 and 17 years. At the very least, it might be helpful if each new piece of legislation was accompanied by an addendum to show how it affected the prior legislation.

(4) Reference often has to be made to other statutes to discover the definition of terms: this can be particularly time-consuming if the other documents concern a subject not related to the one in hand. Cannot the definition be repeated in each piece of relevant legislation?

The Parliamentary Process

13. We have referred to the political imperative which means that on occasions some laws are passed with speed – but others can be overly delayed because Parliamentary time cannot be found. The Association will be interested to see any recommendations the Commission might feel able to put forward which address this issue.

14. The Courts, using the rules of interpretation, determine the meaning of legislation. Whilst we have expressed the hope (paragraph 11 above) that drafting changes might serve to reduce the scope for ambiguities, might there be a procedure available to Parliament to pass "correcting" legislation? For example, there might be a Committee of Parliament empowered to amend legislation without delay if it became apparent that there was a defect in drafting which was causing confusion, or where a statute had been construed by a Court in a way which did not reflect Parliament's original intention.

15. Finally, there could be merit in Government giving consideration to means by which the general public could be kept better informed about new legislation and the reasons for its introduction. Public understanding of the law would to some extent at least make the task of the police and other enforcement agencies easier.

January 1992

M5   Association of First Division Civil Servants

Introduction

1. The Association represents senior civil servants, including administrators responsible for policy advice to Ministers on the preparation of Government Bills, departmental lawyers, responsible for drafting instructions to Parliamentary Counsel and for secondary legislation, and Parliamentary counsel responsible for the drafting of Bills.

2. The Association shares the concern of the Commission to improve the working of the legislative process and thereby the quality of the resulting legislation. Particular objectives are to make legislation more accessible to users, not only lawyers but also laymen, and to reduce the incidence of defeats in litigation that need to be remedied by amending legislation. It is also desirable that legislation should be preceded by full consultation and where possible should command

consent, though it has to be recognised that much legislation is political in content and will not secure consent from the governing party's opponents.

3. This submission focuses on issues where officials working within Departments may have special knowledge not available to others giving evidence. The Machinery of Government Sub-Committee of the Association has had the benefit of reading much of the evidence submitted to the Commission by other bodies.

Development of policy leading to legislation

4. The process of preparing legislation within Departments is conditioned by four factors:

   i) the concern of the Government to implement their political agenda, which largely determines the content of the legislative process;

   ii) the pressures on Parliamentary time that regulate the flow of legislation;

   iii) the constraints on public expenditure and civil service manpower that rule out use of resources for contingent purposes.

   iv) lack of resources generally.

5. Proposals for major substantive legislation generally originate from two sources: commitments in the governing party's manifesto, and the recommendations of internal policy reviews when endorsed by Ministers. More rarely they arise externally, for example to implement an international convention, or on the initiative of outside bodies, including private members' Bills (not discussed further here); and, increasingly, to implement E.C. directives.

6. Officials are more or less involved in the development of policy leading to legislation according to its source. With a manifesto proposal, policy may have been developed wholly by party headquarters or external advisers. Where a proposal derives from an internal policy review, officials will have been closely involved throughout; but the focus of such work is on setting the objectives of the policy rather than on how the policy is to be given legislative effect. Lawyers need to be involved at an early stage in the formulation of policy.

7. At the stage of the policy review, consultation may take place, according to the nature of the subject, the preference of the Minister and the extent of external pressure. However, experience shows that amongst organised and well-resourced interest groups, such responses concentrate on issues of principle, often at a political level, not on practicality.

8. Even where the prime consultees include a major interest group, for example local government, industry at large, or the academic world, consultees often do not speak with a single voice, focus on objections or principle, and fail to present their views to best effect. Ministers are liable to disregard responses to consultation if these are divided, if they clearly derive from an opposition party stance, or if they are ill-prepared. By contrast, in a small number of policy areas, trade and professional interest groups operate effectively by working through a single organisation, commenting mainly at the technical level, and maintaining close contacts with ministers and officials. Perhaps one conclusion is that more

time is needed to take conflicting points of view into account, so that proper evaluation is given to the varying weights of the points made.

9. Frequently, however, at the point when a firm policy proposal emerges, as a Green or White Paper or other ministerial announcement, any consultation with those affected will have made little impact on development of the policy, and little attention will have been given to how the policy is to be given effect in legislation. If the quality of legislation is to be improved, there is a clear need – though it is hard to see how this can be enforced in practice – for early thought to be given to how a policy can be encapsulated in statutory concepts that will not present problems of interpretation to the courts.

Preparation of legislation

10. As the Commission knows, collective ministerial consideration of the legislative programme for the following session takes place around February. At that stage, the list of bids for major bills almost always exceeds what can be accommodated in the Parliamentary timetable, and some proposed bills have to be dropped and others pruned. (In practice, more bills could sometimes be accommodated if they were ready for early introduction, but for reasons explained below, that can rarely be guaranteed).

11. In consequence, except for bills which are essential, e.g. Finance Bills, to implement a treaty commitment, and a very small number of bills of high political priority, Departments cannot be confident until the next session's programme is settled in March whether a particular bill will be included and what it will be permitted to include. Commonly, until that point no staff will be added to the policy division handling the issues to help prepare the bill, and there will be no dedicated lawyer; because of overall pressures on staff resources, even after a bill's inclusion in the programme, weeks or even months may elapse before a dedicated bill team is set up.

12. To produce a bill ready for introduction by November requires intense activity over the following six months. (The business managers press for major bills to reach second reading before Christmas, to avoid crowding the later stages of the session.) Commonly, major policy decisions, subsidiary to the broad thrust of the bill, will need to be taken by ministers and cleared inter-departmentally. Because departments see a bill as a rare opportunity to amend existing legislation, and often have a "shopping list" of desirable reforms independent of the main thrust of the bill, proposals are put to ministers to expand the scope of the bill to deal with other outstanding issues. Each of these, if agreed, has be cleared centrally; there is commonly resistance from the business managers to inclusion of additional material, however desirable, because the problems of Parliamentary handling of a Bill are in large part proportional to its length and scope.

13. Officials must then advise departmental lawyers on precisely what the bill is designed to achieve. Lawyers seek to turn this advice into instructions to Parliamentary Counsel; their principal functions are to tell Counsel what the objectives are, to consider the legal workability of the proposals, and to explain

the relationship with existing legislation. Instructions to counsel are often longer than the eventual bill. Counsel expects to receive them by July at the very latest if a bill is to be ready for November; Counsel in turn then has to work to a very compressed timetable for production of drafts and clearance with Departments.

14. During the period, consultation with outside interests is unlikely to be officials' top priority. On some issues consultation with other public bodies is effectively mandatory: no criminal justice bill would be introduced without consultation with the police and the judiciary. Elsewhere, especially if consultees' views are seen as predictable, consultation may be forgone or at best rushed.

15. The Commission will have some familiarity with the respective roles of Departmental administrators, Departmental lawyers and Parliamentary Counsel in the process of turning policy into draft legislation. In very broad terms, administrators are responsible for specifying the objectives of the policy with the necessary precision; Departmental lawyers for acting as interpreters between administrators and Counsel, including clarifying the relationship with existing law and any purely legal problems that the bill is designed to redress; while Counsel has full responsibility for drafting the actual text of the legislation.

16. In practice, the roles are not as distinct as a textbook description might indicate. The words chosen to give legal effect to a policy can more or less subtly change the policy. It is common for administrators to feel that Counsel is giving higher priority to ensuring that the draft is clear in its effect and immune from judicial reinterpretation, than to giving precise effect to the Minister's intentions. Counsel, by contrast, may feel that administrators are more concerned to get the Bill on the statute book to demonstrate that the Government has achieved its political goals, than with the needs of those who will have to work with the legislation. The relationship can be creative and can improve the quality of legislation without distorting its objectives; but too often it is beset by friction, exacerbated by the unduly compressed timetable, and can leave administrators feeling that the bill as drafted no longer achieves quite what was planned because priority has been given to form over substance, and Counsel that it falls short of the quality of drafting that he or she would aspire to and that users have a right to expect.

17. Frequently, the drafting timetable slips, because Counsel is overloaded or because agreement cannot be reached in time on whether Counsel's proposed draft achieves the desired policy objectives. It is also true on occasion that policy is still being formulated, and that "goal posts" are moved on a fairly regular basis. The target date for introducing the bill, however, comes to be seen as an absolute, either because of pressure from the Parliamentary business managers or because the Minister fears that delay will be perceived as indecision. Bills are therefore commonly introduced with significant parts missing, which it has been planned throughout to include. These provisions then have to be introduced by Government amendment, at a later Parliamentary stage, making it harder for those responsible to satisfy themselves that the bill fulfils its intended purpose, risking unnecessary complications in drafting because it is harder to deal with all the interactions between a new clause and

existing clauses, and indeed other Acts after the bill has been introduced, and limiting the scope for proper Parliamentary scrutiny because the bill is not seen as a whole until too late a stage.

18. It is during the drafting process that decisions are taken as to how far the details of the policy are to be given effect on the fact of the Bill, and how far in secondary legislation. By convention, instructions to Counsel may suggest, but not require, that Counsel adopts one course or the other. Ministers and administrators tend to favour maximum use of delegated powers, not so much to avoid full Parliamentary scrutiny as is sometimes alleged, but in order to retain flexibility to adapt the policy in the light of events or experience without having to promote further main legislation (which in turn reflects the problem of finding space in the Parliamentary timetable). Sometimes use of secondary legislation is proposed simply because the detail of policy has not been thought through in sufficient detail to permit precise instructions to be given. Counsel, by contract, is likely to stress the need for clarity as to the objectives of delegated legislation if the enabling power is to be drafted accurately and comprehensively and if subsequent use of the power is not to be struck down as ultra vires; this can result in the power being drafted in terms so precise that the benefit of flexibility is lost.

19. The outcome of the drafting process is, all too often, the introduction of what is no more than a first or second draft of the bill, with all those responsible conscious that they will have to spend the next few months refining it to ensure that it achieves its original intentions, besides the work arising from the Parliamentary process.

Consideration of legislation by Parliament

20. Much of the Parliamentary process is essentially political, concerned with considering the broad merits of the bill. The functional stages, when amendments are considered, are committee stage in the Commons, and committee and report stages in the Lords. During these stages, those responsible for a bill work under intense pressure. In the Commons, for example, t'.e standing committee may sit mornings and evenings on two days a week. Many amendments are tabled on a couple of days before they are taken. After a Tuesday session finishing at midnight, the administrator responsible may have to write perhaps fifteen speaking notes for the Minister for amendments to be taken on the Thursday, and agree these with the Minister. Lawyers and Counsel work under similar pressures in preparing further Government amendments, sometimes in response to concessions in debate, sometimes because technical defects in the original draft come to light.

21. The large majority of amendments, especially in the Commons, are political in intent, designed more to score points or to elucidate the Government's intentions than to improve the working of the bill. The Government can commonly rely, at least in the Commons, on a whipped majority to defeat most amendments, and to see the bill through. Some amendments of a more technical nature may command bipartisan support, and occasionally defections from the

government side will result in an opposition amendment being passed. Officials need to assess not only the merits of each amendment but also the prospective effect on the working of the bill if it is carried or accepted.

22. A defeat or prospective defeat for the government can, in conjunction with the constrained timetable, having damaging effects on the technical quality of Bills. Backbench and opposition amendments, drafted without access to the services of Parliamentary Counsel, rarely achieve precisely the desired effect, and in particular rarely provide for the necessary cross-references and consequentials. When a defeat is foreseen, therefore, the Minister will commonly offer to bring forward Government amendments with some or all of the effect desired by the movers. Drafting such amendments, at very short notice, puts further pressure on Counsel, who may still be working on Government amendments to achieve the initial purpose of the Bill. Occasionally, where a backbench or opposition amendment is carried or accepted, a Bill may become law without the implications of an amendment for other parts of the Bill having been considered or consequential amendments prepared. Once enacted, defects arising from this or other causes can go unremedied for many years, because of lack of Parliamentary time, and because the doctrine of "scope" means that, if the government expands another bill to carry an unrelated amendment, it risks attracting other unwelcome amendments which would not otherwise be in order.

23. After a major bill is enacted, there remains a great deal of work to be done, by way of drafting statutory instruments to give effect to the enabling powers in the Act, including consultation with interested parties. It is common experience, however, that Bill teams are scaled down very quickly after enactment, because of other pressures on the Department's staffing, and that work on implementation has to compete with other pressing business and that statutory instruments may not be laid until much closer to the date of coming into operation than would be desirable for users who may have to rearrange their business in the light of the Act.

Recommendations

24. The Association makes recommendations with hesitation, recognising that is it for the legislature to decide how it wishes to legislate. Nevertheless, it seems to us that there is scope for substantial improvement in the procedure, without tilting the balance of influence between legislature and executive.

25. It is sometimes said that the prime objective of legislation is that it should be clear and certain in meaning. In practice, that is not one objective but two, which can conflict. What appears clear to the layman may not be certain in meaning to the courts; and much of the detail in legislation, which can appear obfuscatory, is there to make the effect of the provisions certain and resistant to legal challenge. This in turn derives from the English legal tradition that the courts derive their interpretation of legislation from the text alone, and will not look beyond the text to construe statutory provisions. The intention of the legislation is generally irrelevant.

26. In reality, there is a choice to be made between clarity and certainty. The present system encourages administrators and in particular Counsel to err always on the side of certainty: the worst possible outcome, from a Minister's standpoint, is for legislation to be reinterpreted by the courts in a manner contrary to their intentions. It is far from clear that this bias towards certainty is in the best interests of users, or indeed in the public interest if it reduces clarity.

27. Whatever view is taken on the issue in the two previous paragraphs, there can be no dispute that legislation should be thoroughly prepared and should have been subject to full consultation with those affected. The present system fails to achieve this.

28. One principal remedy is in the hands of the Government. Enough staff should be dedicated to the preparation of legislation, and, crucially, at an earlier stage in the process, for a bill to be thoroughly prepared technically before it is introduced, and, unless there is genuine operational urgency, to have been published in draft and comments invited before introduction. This requires, for major bills, that preparation should begin before it has secured a place in the programme for the following session, permitting a more considered pace of drafting and further consultation.

29. Other remedies go wider. The Association offers only some tentative suggestions.

30. First, that bills should be permitted to be carried over from one Parliamentary session to the next. This would enable each bill to proceed at its own pace, and, for example, for a longer interval between stages when a need for extensive redressing arose, rather than being absolutely constrained by an external timetable. It is usually said that this reform would derive the Opposition of its only power, that of delay; but in practice that power is unusable when the Government's majority is sufficient, and the Opposition and Parliament generally would benefit both from better prepared Bills and less frequent use of the guillotine.

31. Second, there should be a process of post-enactment review of legislation, both immediately after its passage and intermittently thereafter. This would provide scope to respond to the problems resulting from the combination of the infrequency of opportunities for substantive legislation, and the pressures of the timetable itself, which commonly means that defects in an Act are identified soon after enactment, but no chance to redress them may arise for some years thereafter. The body best equipped to take on this role might be the Law Commission, though it would need to work closely with the promoting Department. A procedure would be required whereby amendments certified to be purely technical could secure accelerated Parliamentary passage; certification might be the responsibility of Speaker's Counsel advised by the Commission.

32. Three other suggestions are put forward even more tentatively for the Commission's consideration:
    - that there should be a source of independent drafting expertise available to the Opposition and backbenchers;

- That case law restricting reference by the courts to Parliamentary debates to construe the purpose of an Act should be repealed (a recent judicial decision has moved a small step in this direction), thereby reducing the need for excess verbiage designed only to bind the courts;
- that there should be a review of statutory instruments procedure, designed to improve Parliamentary scrutiny of delegated legislation and thereby reduce the suspicion with which enabling powers are regarded;
- we understand there is an exercise going on to look at the possibility of a House of Lords delegated legislation scrutiny Commission. Clearly this demands further consideration.

33. Some of the failings of the legislative process are the unavoidable result of the volume of public business combined with the strict constraints on the creation and scope of executive powers inherent in the UK tradition of government. It appears to the Association, however, that a combination of these reforms and others proposed by other bodies submitting evidence, together with an acceptance on the part of Government of the need to resource the preparation of legislation more thoroughly, offers the prospect of providing users with a better quality of legislation, without jeopardising the reasonable expectation on the part of Ministers that they will be able to put their policies into effect without undue delay, while furthering the overriding need for full Parliamentary and public scrutiny of the substantive effect of the legislation.

27 July 1992

M6   Bank of England

You will appreciate that the Bank's position is a somewhat special one, given its close relationship with government, and our experience will probably not be mirrored exactly by many of your respondents. Most of our practical experience in this area stems from the discussions we have with various government departments on draft legislation sponsored by them and affecting the financial system. Generally speaking, we have found that the consultation process works very well and due weight is given to any concerns we have expressed. We have occasionally found that difficulties are caused by each government department having its own lawyers and there being no centralised legal view, as well as by the convention that communication with Parliamentary Counsel is only through the sponsoring department. This can sometimes result in pieces of legislation which have the same intent adopting different definitions of the same concept – the numerical cut-off between professional and retail investors in the Financial Services Act and the EC Prospectus Directive would be an example.

There is really only one general problem which we would want to draw to your attention. This concerns the difficulties we sometimes experience in finding the opportunity to have small, technical and non-controversial changes in the financial area passed into law. At the moment, the obvious home for most of such items is in the Finance Bill but the Government will naturally always give priority in this to major budget changes which have political appeal. The result on occasions is that some desirable changes in technical areas are pushed out at the last minute and have to wait until next year; or they are poorly drafted as the draftsmen are concentrating on the more politically important items. It would in our view mark a distinct improvement to the current system if it were possible to take such technical changes outside the budget process altogether and perhaps incorporate them in a Finance Bill (Technical) at another time of the year. This approach to technical changes would, of course, only work effectively if an annual slot could be found for such a Bill.

Apart from that, the only other suggestion we have is that it might sometimes be sensible to involve UK lawyers at an earlier stage in the drafting of legislation in Brussels. We have on occasions found that, when amending domestic legislation to reflect EC Directives, our own lawyers' desire to be more precise than the (generally vague) wording of the Directive has led to unintended or illogical results.

Finally, it may be worth saying that the Bank itself actively seeks to improve consultation with interested parties in the markets. As an example of a consultation procedure which works well and which might perhaps be replicated elsewhere, we would cite the work of the Stock Borrowing and Lending Committee. This Committee, chaired by the Government Broker, exists to provide a forum in which the full range of issues of interest to the securities lending market as a whole can be discussed and resolved. The Inland Revenue take part as participating observers.

The SBLC's experience has been that in a forum of this type the technical merits, not only of the detailed implementation but also of the basic form and approach to taxing an activity, can be discussed effectively and fruitfully without in any way detracting from the ultimate rights of Ministers to reach their own views and Parliament to determine the end result in terms of statutory provisions. The input generated from technical discussions of this nature with market experts can lead both to a tax structure that works efficiently and also to acceptance of that structure as fair by market participants.

9 April 1992

M7   Mr George Bednar

As a victim of an ill-drafted, yet unavoidable statutory provision, I hope I may be allowed to share my thoughts with members of this Commission.

There is no doubt that by its very (increasingly pervasive) nature, statute law should be clear, intelligible and its legal consequences easily predictable. The reasons for this are many, although some are not as obvious as others:

(a)   The supremacy of Parliament precludes any claim for compensation arising out of ill-drafted legislation, either against the minister responsible or even through the Parliamentary ombudsman. The *innocent* citizen has no remedy.

(b)   In order to determine an alleged statutory right, a citizen may be *forced* into expensive and uncertain litigation. "The possibility of legal aid being made available automatically for all cases involving purely statutory interpretation...

(cannot) be regarded as a priority." (Private letter from Mr Michael Kron, Lord Chancellor's Department, 30 April 1992.)

(c) The interpretation of legislation should be uniform and should not benefit the more experienced or better skilled practitioner. Little publicity has been given to the findings of an American, Prof Robert Martineau, that only, "10–15% of appellate advocates were highly competent, 30–40% were competent and 50–60% were incompetent." (Prof Michael Zander, NLJ 12 April 1991). I shudder to think what a similar study would say of our county court advocates. And all are immune from action, by law!

(d) The statute itself should facilitate acquiescence and preclude any challenge. In its British Social Attitudes, 8th Annual Report 1991/2, Social and Community Planning Research posed the question, "The law should always be obeyed, even if a particular law is wrong." 10% agreed strongly, 36% agreed, 25% neither agreed nor disagreed, 26% disagreed, while 3% disagreed strongly.

As Mr Justice Stephen said of drafting some 100 years ago, "... it is necessary to attain if possible to a degree of precision which a person reading in bad faith cannot misunderstand. It is all the better if he cannot pretend to misunderstand it."

Because the so-called 1975 Renton Report with its 81 recommendations was government sponsored, it had, necessarily, to be a one-off enterprise. In a government answer to a Parliamentary question tabled on my behalf in November 1989, the government said that it had no plans for a green paper that would cover the same subjects.

But as there is obviously no other body that can undertake such a role, the Hansard Society Commission should feel no such constraints. The recommendations that will be made will need to be pursued and monitored, probably, over a number of Parliaments. My own suggestion is that the Commission prepare a few distinct series of related recommendations that can be phased into the legislative process, rather than one final, overwhelming list.

If such a gradual scheme would have the full support of the Hansard Society, the Law Society, the Bar Council, the Statute Law Society, the judges, the individuals who were invited to contribute and, when the Report is published, the support of the media, then I cannot see how Mr John Major, the prime minister, and Parliament cannot be persuaded. And if the deliberations can concentrate on what is "possible" in the early series, rather than what is ultimately "desirable", so much the better.

I do not know about all the changes that are being proposed, but it would seem that this year the Houses of Parliament will be getting used to the new sitting arrangements, with the inevitable knock-on effect on the legislative programme. Fortunately, this session continues until the Autumn of 1993. The deliberations of the Commission could thus not have been more timely.

I cannot pretend to have a detailed knowledge of the legislative process, but in his address to the Statute Law Society, Sir Henry de Vaal, QC, First Parliamentary Counsel said, "The principal pressures on the draftsman seem to flow from late instructions, short deadlines and sudden and quite elaborate policy changes..." [1989] Stat.L.R. 211.

Here are three, possibly crucial recommendations that surely need nothing more to their implementation than an application of a diligent and constructive attitude on the part of the officials concerned.

A. Policy

The concept should be as simple as possible. The policy which is to be given legislative effect should be signed as vetted by the minister responsible. Where practicable, rather than to try to provide for as many forseeable circumstances as possible, I feel that citizens would rather be obliged to satisfy one or two easily ascertainable statutory conditions in order to meet the objectives of the policy, thus precluding legal pitfalls. There may remain questions of fact for a court to decide, but how to comply with the law should be simple and beyond doubt.

B. Instructions

These should be as comprehensive as possible, and be signed as vetted by the secretary of state responsible for the policy-originating department.

Following the implementation of all these, say, six recommendations, it should be considered bad practice to bring forward new government amendments during the passage of a Bill, let alone to amend Acts by subsequent legislation.

C. Drafting

Parliamentary Counsel should be allowed all the time they need in relation to the legislation proposed, and the draft should be signed as vetted by the First Parliamentary Counsel.

It has often been said that the wording is directed at the judiciary, the last people to read the statute, and then only to decide random litigation. Would it not be possible to have the wording directed at high street solicitors? I am sure that if it is not the case already, appropriate interpretation courses for lawyers could be devised. I say this, because to my mind, if the rule of law is to mean anything to the citizen, it is that should two citizens be in dispute over their legal rights and duties, they should be able to consult their own solicitors in the confident knowledge that, as such, both will be given exactly the same answer. Only within such a system will the albeit disappointed citizen nevertheless have no grounds for a grievance; there can only be one predominant law, and statute law should be seen to be both impartial and universally binding.

D. Commencement dates

All enacted provisions should carry appropriate commencement dates, and there should be as little delay as possible in bringing the whole of the statute into force.

E. Bills

To facilitate the quality of the end product, it should be possible to carry over a Bill from one session to the next, but not beyond the life of one Parliament.

And certainly once the above have been implemented in, say, the first two sessions of this Parliament, it should be possible by the 1994–5 session to establish:

F. Pre-legislative scrutiny.

Although reflective comment must be allowed, the settled policy of a measure would necessarily need to be treated as sacrosanct. Otherwise, the committee scrutinizing (let us call it) the Text – eg Housing Text [1992] – would have unfettered powers of interview and amendment, to clarify the policy, ambiguities and obscurities. Parliamentary Counsel would draft the Text, and be responsible for any amendments to it. Only when the Text is returned to the sponsoring department, would a simplified procedure for preparing a Bill begin. If interested, citizens as well as bodies outside Parliament should be able to obtain a copy of the Text for their suggestions. At present, unless the government is prepared to adopt an amendment, one's efforts to seek independent consideration of an alleged anomaly are futile.

It is interesting to note that the Liberal Democrats made a commitment to such prelegislative scrutiny in their 1992 election manifesto, and that the Society of Labour Lawyers also endorsed such a proposal in their March 1992 pamphlet, "A Programme for Change."

Given the present appalling state of the legislative process, I do not think that Parliament would be able to absorb that many recommendations in any one Parliament. It is necessary to think in the long-term. Recommendations as to aspects of consolidation, delegated and European legislation might best be left for implementation in a second Parliament, particularly as it is likely to be under the same administration. It is a point worth considering.

I cannot end without expressing my gratitude to those who conceived this very laudable initiative. Perhaps, finally, some meaning will be given to the Act of Settlement 1700 phrase, "the laws of England are the birthright of the people."

7 May 1992

M8   The Public and the Legislative Process: Aide Memoire by Tony Benn

Types of Law

The involvement of citizens in the laws under which we are governed depends critically upon the nature of the laws themselves, and the source of their authority:

COMMON LAW based upon precedents laid down by the Courts cannot normally be altered save by Statute, and its reform therefore may require a public campaign, time, and a Parliamentary majority, which is hard to achieve, and should be made easier for the public – as for example in respect of the Blasphemy Laws.

STATUTE LAW may be very old and well established – as with the Justices of the Peace Act of 1361 – which is still in force, though it was passed long before Britain was a democracy. The revision of such a law is as difficult as for Common Law.

ENABLING ACTS, once regarded as very undemocratic, they are now widely used, and once enacted there may be no scope for Parliament to intervene, as with the 1972 European Communities Act.

ORDERS IN COUNCIL as made by the Privy Council may not require any Parliamentary approval – as with bodies operating under Royal Commissions, and here the public have no say whatever.

STATUTORY INSTRUMENTS requiring an affirmative resolution do go to Parliament for endorsement, though those that apply unless they are annulled are rarely debated for lack of Parliamentary time.

EUROPEAN COMMUNITY LAWS are made under the Crown Prerogative of Treaty Making, in the Council of Ministers, which is the real Legislative Assembly, and meets in secret. Because of the ease which which laws applying to the UK can be made through the Council, civil servants are tempted to use this mechanism rather than wait for a place in the Government's own legislative programme. Neither the public, nor Parliament itself has any formal role in the making of these laws.

THE SUPREMACY OF COMMUNITY LAW, which is provided for in the 1972 Act carries with it the effective repeal of all British statutes which are incompatible with the over-riding authority of Community Laws, and the British Courts will so interpret it, thus removing the authority of Parliament, and the public, in respect of such repeals.

JUDGE MADE LAW, which is the result of decisions reached by the Courts, may have the effect of changing the law as it was understood, or of drawing attention to the need for a new law to be passed by Parliament.

Why Laws are made
The main reasons why laws are made may be classified in this way:

STRUCTURAL CHANGE: To meet the need for structural change in some aspect of society – as with education, housing, health etc, and these may have been long discussed, after wide consultation, and with debates in both houses.

POLITICAL COMMITTMENT: To implement a Manifesto pledge which may have been fully debated within the party which wins the election and will then go to Parliament for consideration and enactment.

PUBLIC PRESSURE: Many bills are introduced to deal with a situation which has arisen at short notice (Safety at Football Grounds, Dog Control, Terrorism etc) and here public pressure for action may be strong.

ADMINISTRATIVE CONVENIENCE: Where a department decides that new arrangements would be desirable for internal reasons and the Minister can be persuaded to promote legislation.

THE ADVICE OF THE LAW OFFICERS which the Cabinet is required to accept, may lead to the abandonment of a government policy, or to the introduction of a new law to make that policy possible.

COMMUNITY LAW: This will usually be motivated by the drive to implement objectives agreed by ministers, or for administrative reasons.

How Laws are Planned
Most laws are conceived within a department, sometimes as a result of external pressure, sometimes on the initiative of officials, sometimes at the request of ministers and there may be consultations with interested bodies, followed by discussions on the guiding principles, and legal advice from within Whitehall. Later

the Legislation Committee of the Cabinet will meet to endorse or reject the proposal, and to decide whether or not it should have the priority it would need to get a place in the Queen's speech.

European Community Law may come, in draft, from the Commission who, under the the Treaty of Rome, have the sole power of initiation; or may be discussed at the inter-governmental level through COREPER, the Committee of Permanent representatives to canvass support for such a measure.

The Role of the Public
As is clear the role of the citizens or electors is very indirect, if it exists at all, unless the law stems from a public debate involving a political party, a pressure group or a powerful interest group.

Since most laws are developed internally long before they are ever mentioned publicly the scope for public pressure to influence them is very limited.

Possible Reforms
If it is intended that the public should have a larger role in the legislative process then a number of quite fundamental reforms would be required:

A FREEDOM OF INFORMATION ACT: By opening up the processes of government to greater public scrutiny, the citizens would have earlier notification of the intentions of the administration and could bring their influence to bear earlier.

GREATER USE OF SELECT COMMITTEES for legislation would offer those outside Parliament an opportunity to give evidence direct to the House of Commons before any bill was agreed by MPs.

ENDING THE PRIVILEGE OF SECRECY ENJOYED BY SELECT COMMITTEES: The present practice, under which the proceedings and papers of Select Committees are kept secret until presented to the House is both absurd and undemocratic because it excludes the public from having any influence.

AMENDABLE INSTRUMENTS: Instead of the present division between Bills which go through the whole Parliamentary process, and orders which are unamendable and may never be debated, it would be worth considering a new form of amendable order, which could go through an accelerated procedure allowing a vote, without debate, for second reading, a committee stage for amendments, and another vote without debate for third reading.

"EXTENSION OF REMARKS": If MPs, like US Congressmen, could circulate unspoken speeches in Hansard, the views of their constituents on legislation could be recorded and considered as legislation passed through.

MANDATING FOR COMMUNITY LEGISLATION: If ministers had to get Parliamentary approval before assenting to EC laws the role of MPs and their constituents would be safeguarded.

MORE PRIVATE MEMBER'S LEGISLATION: If more time was available for Private Members Bills, and if the choice of Bills was by vote rather than by Ballot, the prospects for relevant laws might increase.

REFERENDA ISSUES: If, as in some American States, it was possible for an issue to be placed on the ballot by a petition signed by a set percentage of the electorate this would give an initiative to the public that is now denied them.

EXPIRING LAWS: The greater use of the expiring laws procedure would have the effect of strengthening Parliamentary and hence public scrutiny, of controversial legislation.

19 December 1991

M9   Sir John Bourn KCB, Comptroller and Auditor General

I am not a key player in the legislative process, but I can perhaps offer one or two thoughts which you might find helpful.

I do have some concerns about the complexity of recent legislation. I come across the results of this in two ways. First, one of my functions as Comptroller and Auditor General is to ensure that expenditure by Departments and other public sector bodies complies with legislation once it gets on to the statute book. We find frequent examples of Departments failing to comply with legislation – not because they are seeking to act improperly but because they too have been confused by the complexities of legislation. For example, our report on the criminal legal aid appropriation account 1990–91 (HC 655-VII) shows the difficulties which arose because of unclear lines of accountability stemming from the Legal Aid Act 1988. Interpretation of complex legislation is even more of a problem when European directives are involved: for example, those concerned with agriculture. Our report on external trade measures for agricultural produce in 1988 (HC 275 1987–88) refers to the enormous number of directives and regulations imposed on various agricultural sectors in the UK in recent years.

If Departments and the National Audit Office find it difficult to interpret legislation, what chance has the man in the street? We have recently completed a number of studies which have touched on this question. In our examination of support for low income families (HC 153 1990–91) we found from our survey of potential claimants that there was a significant level of ignorance about the social security benefits system. Similar findings came from our examination of benefits for the elderly (HC 55 1990–91).

The National Audit Office does have some involvement in the legislative process. In order to discharge our Parliamentary responsibilities, we always try to ensure that legislation provides us with a proper degree of access to public sector bodies. This can only be done where Departments consult us at an early stage but despite the good contacts with central government which have been developed this does not always happen. I imagine it must be much harder for interested parties who do not enjoy close links with Departments to ensure that their concerns are taken into account at the right stage.

31 December 1991

M10 British and Irish Association of Law Librarians: Memorandum from Mr Stuart Cole, Chair, Standing Committee on Official Publications

The following are questions which have arisen within the last three or four years affecting members of the British and Irish Association of Law Librarians.

One important matter which has occurred within the last two years has been the problem of delays between the granting of Royal Assent for Acts of Parliament and their publication. It has been the experience of some of our members that while some Acts of Parliament are available within a few days of assent, a number do not appear until anything up to six weeks afterwards. These delays are particularly significant when Acts contain sections which come into force on Royal Assent, leaving at variance the law as it actually is and the law as it is published.

I understand that HMSO do not receive a final version of an Act for printing until Royal Assent has been given, and the work involved in preparing Acts for press means that they are unable to produce every one within a few days of them being passed through Parliament.

Unfortunately the Acts which suffer the greatest delays seem to be the larger, more complex ones – e.g. Companies Acts. These also tend to be the most important.

I believe that the LA SCOOP Committee suggested two solutions to this: i.e. delay of commencement until a reasonable time had elapsed from Royal Assent; *or* delay of Royal Assent until the Act is actually available. I do not know whether this situation has improved of late, but it has been of some concern to our members, particularly those in the private sector.

Also occasionally affected by this appear to be Statutory Instruments. It has been known for some secondary legislation to come into effect before copies have been available. This however does not seem to be as serious a problem for our members as that concerning primary legislation.

Another matter which has caused some of our members problems has been the relatively short print runs for some Statutory Instruments, which has led to delays in availability. This is possibly not a problem which would be under the scrutiny of the Commission, but it does seem to be relevant to the question of accessibility.

Also on the question of accessibility, Local Legislation appears to be another problem area. It seems that Local Statutory Instruments are not always easy to obtain – indeed some are not actually published in their entirety but are merely listed in the bound volumes which appear annually. Admittedly most of the members of the Association who have encountered problems appear to have done so with much older material, including Local Acts going back to the nineteenth and eighteenth centuries, but availability of current material is also a concern.

Finally there is the problem of an official source for updated statutory material. Many members find that Statutes in Force is not satisfactory as it is not current enough and unwieldy to use, and so go to commercial publications such as

Butterworth's Halsbury's Statutes. However there is a great deal of interest in a suitably up-to-date official version of the Statute Book, which is readily accessible to all.

15 June 1992

M11   British Broadcasting Corporation

Introduction

1. The Commission has a very important brief. Its terms of reference have never been properly considered before. The report on the Preparation of Legislation (Cmnd 6053) under the Chairmanship of the then Rt Hon Sir David Renton had terms of reference which excluded them from considering this important stage in the preparation of legislation.

2. It is accepted that the Commission is not concerned with the merits or demerits of particular Acts of Parliament or with government policies and that their concern is the processes by which legislation is made and not its political purposes. However the Commission would surely acknowledge that if the legislation is controversial then it is less likely that there will be a long consultation process and even less likely that any comments arising from whatever consultation takes place, will be adopted in the legislation – either as introduced or as enacted.

3. The observations set out below have been collated by the writer [Mr Gareth Roscoe, Legal Adviser] from the experiences of lawyers within the British Broadcasting Corporation of Bills and other legislation which has affected the Corporation in one way or another.

The Extent and Nature of Government Consultation

4. Our most recent Bill experience was the Broadcasting Bill now the Broadcasting Act 1990. There were few provisions which affected the BBC directly in this legislation because its principal objective was to make new provision with respect to the regulation of independent television and sound programme services. Nevertheless those provisions which did affect the BBC were extremely important.

5. Our general experience of the consultation process was one of considerable public debate prior to the preparation of the Bill but once the Bill had been introduced such consultation that took place was often too late, gave insufficient time for a considered response and many of the observations we made were ignored. It was another example of a Bill prepared in haste, policy not properly thought through and it became a question matter of getting the policy right during the passage of the Bill rather than improving and refining it. In some areas the Bill demonstrated little understanding of broadcasting and our impression was that little understanding was being sought. For example provisions relating to obscene publications (Part VII of the Act) were merely extended to programmes without much real thought of what was involved.

6. In theory the Committee stage of any legislation is supposed to involve a careful scrutiny of the drafting of the Bill in order to improve it and to ensure that powers are not being sought which are greater than those required to remedy the ill or the defect. It does not happen in practice. Ministers are reluctant to accede to amendments because most of their time is spent bringing forward government amendments to get the Bill in better shape.

7. The BBC's experiences over the Copyright Designs & Patents Act 1988 (C.D.P.A.) were in complete contrast. The CDPA had an unusually long gestation period. The Whitford Committee, which took extensive evidence was appointed in 1973 and reported in 1977. There were then 2 Green Papers (Reform of the Law relating to Copyright, Designs and Performer's Protection, Cmnd 8302, published in July 1981 and "The Recording and Rental of Audio and Video Copyright Material", Cmnd 9445, published in February 1985). The DTI made the draft bill available to interested parties before first reading and consultation continued virtually throughout the Bill's passage through Parliament. A significant number of the BBC's comments on the legislation were taken into account. There was, as far as the BBC could judge, little interest in the Bill at ministerial or Cabinet level.

8. *We would recommend* that Bills be published well in advance of introduction and that a special committee is set up to hear evidence from interested persons and experts in any technical area affected by the bill. This would have the advantage of ensuring that the bill in its draft form is properly considered prior to introduction.

9. Subordinate legislation is of course prepared by departmental lawyers. There is likely to be greater consultation on subordinate legislation than on the primary legislation which is perhaps ironic. Where the detail of the policy has not been set out in the primary legislation then, if it is to be implemented the subordinate legislation must contain the detail. It is often the case that departmental lawyers and administrators have to consult to ensure that what they are proposing is workable. The additional advantage is that they are not subject to the same pressures on the Parliamentary timetable as the legislation. In theory the subordinate legislation should be drafted before the enabling power is taken in the primary legislation to avoid problems of vires. *We would recommend* that the subordinate legislation be published and consulted on at the same time as the bill.

The Form and Drafting of Bills and Instruments

10. This topic was considered extensively by the Renton Committee and it is to be regretted perhaps that so few of that committee's recommendation have been implemented. There is in fact little more to be said on this subject. However our experiences do suggest that there is a tendency for bills to be drafted in a way which attempts to provide for every conceivable possibility rather than taking a broad and perhaps "continental" approach to drafting.

11. A detailed approach in legislation is understandable where it is desired to inhibit legal challenges to the exercise of Ministerial powers. Government departments

have been conscious since the early 1980's of the effectiveness of judicial review and the willingness of the courts to accept applications made for that purpose. This sort of detailed approach is also perhaps partly due to an unwillingness to trust to the courts the task of reaching sensible decisions. At the end of the day the courts will always strive to give effect to the intention of Parliament and therefore this approach seems somewhat misconceived.

The Accessibility to the Public of Legislation Passed by Parliament
12. The observations described in paragraphs 10 and 11 above are relevant here. The public would find simple language and textual amendment extremely useful.

Other Matters
13. For those affected by legislation it is often very difficult to persuade Ministers of the need for amendment particularly on "non-political" issues. The nature of the committee process is such that to move amendments requires a "friend" to put them down. It is difficult to brief a speaker during the debate in committee because of the physical layout of the rooms. It is difficult and expensive to obtain Bill papers, notes on clauses and copies of Hansard. These are perhaps small practical problems but they do inhibit effective consultation.

14 January 1992

M12   British Medical Association

Consultation with the Public
So far as major changes in legislation are concerned, we firmly believe that there should always be an early opportunity for interested parties to comment on Government plans before there is a firm commitment to the precise way in which those changes will be made.

There seems to have been an increasing reluctance on the part of Government to consult on matters which are seen as being of major significance to the Government. For example, the legislation introducing the recent NHS changes was based on a White Paper *Working for Patients* which was published in January 1989, bypassing the consultation procedure of a Green Paper. The proposals contained in the White Paper were made without consultation with any interested parties, and the then Secretary of State for Health made it clear that the only comments he was prepared to receive were those which would assist the Government in implementing the changes outlined.

Another example was the publication of plans for changing the Education System in 1987. The consultation process was over a period of 2 months during the Summer Holiday of 1987, with the Education Reform Bill being introduced in the Autumn. Within that timescale, it is very difficult to see that it would have been possible for any of the results of consultation to have had a significant effect on the drafting of the original Bill. In order to be effective, consultation should not be made subject so explicitly to the necessities of the Parliamentary timetable, but should be of a length, and conducted in such a way, as to enable real consideration of the issues which are the subject of consultation, both by the public and by the Department in preparing its draft legislation.

It is the responsibility of Government Departments to consult with representative bodies and independent experts on proposed legislation to ensure that the law can work in practice and is easy to comprehend. Consultative documents and Green Papers are essential procedures enabling consultation to take place. The BMA is usually sent documents of relevance to the medical profession for comment, but there are occasions when the deadline for comment does not provide sufficient time to enable comprehensive deliberations. Unless publicised widely, the public is often unaware that a consultation process is taking place.

Baroness Robson, speaking during the second reading debate on the Nurses, Midwives and Health Visitors' Bill on 12 November 1991, said – "It is not often that all professional bodies and noble Lords in all parts of the House welcome a Bill and are in general agreement with it. Perhaps the consultation that took place prior to its introduction is something from which we can learn".

Drafting of Legislation

Legislation is very often drafted quickly to meet the deadlines of the Parliamentary timetable. Draft Bills are rarely available for comment by interested parties. Even if comprehensive consultation takes place before the legislation stage, a draft of the Bill should be made available. This would enable interested parties to suggest changes, and technical inaccuracies could be amended before the Bill is presented to Parliament, thus saving Parliamentary time in committee and at later stages.

Obscurity of drafting often creates problems which ought to have been foreseen at an earlier stage. For example, there is at present widespread concern about a section of the Human Fertilisation and Embryology Act which restricts the disclosure of information concerning persons who have had treatment which is regulated by the Act. The effect of this section is to deprive an individual, in those circumstances, from seeking legal advice, since to do so would require the unlawful disclosure of information. This is clearly contrary to the normal principles of English law and, indeed, the European Convention on Human Rights.

Parliamentary Scrutiny of Legislation

The procedure of referring Bills to a special standing committee is very rarely used but, in some circumstances, could prove useful in extending the consultation process. The committee could take written and oral evidence from interested parties and independent experts, and considered judgements could then be taken by the Members of Parliament on the committee. It may be appropriate to consider whether the boundary between the select committee and the standing committee is appropriate, and whether the expertise of Members of Parliament resulting from service on select committees should be directly utilised in the scrutiny of legislation.

Public Accessibility

It is partly the responsibility of organisations to monitor legislation passing through Parliament but, when progressing quickly, it is often difficult for those outside

Parliament to obtain relevant documents in sufficient time. For example, at the committee stage in the House of Commons documents such as the marshalled list of amendments being debated that day, and the Order of Business, are not available to observers of the committee's proceedings. We understand that the availability of these documents was withdrawn on grounds of cost. Observers at these proceedings have to rely on MPs passing the documents to them. Purchasing the documents from HMSO in Holborn, or the new Parliament building, is not always a practicable alternative.

European Legislation
There is a parsity of information about planned European Community legislation which is to apply in the United Kingdom. The absence of a central reference point to obtain information about such legislation is a great disadvantage to all those who have a legitimate interest in the outcome. We often come across the situation of UK Members of Parliament being unaware of legislation being planned in Europe. Perhaps this particular problem could be addressed.

13 January 1992

M13   British Railways Board: Letter from the Secretary

The Board has been actively involved in the legislative process as a promoter of Private Bills although this activity will cease on passage of the Transport and Works Bill currently before Parliament. This response is concerned only with the Board's experience as a body affected by public legislation.

1.   Prior consultation on proposed legislation by Government Departments has been a problem in the past with Departments not involving affected bodies in sufficient time although in Board experience there has been some improvement recently. The Department of Trade and Industry has been one of the worst offenders.

2.   The drafting of legislation is always the subject of criticism, much of it ill-informed, because laymen tend not to appreciate just how vital it is to draft enactments as tightly as possible. Some of the criticism directed at Statutory Instruments, however, may be more justifiable, perhaps because they tend to be drafted by lawyers working in Government Departments rather than by Parliamentary Counsel.

3.   There is some evidence that even M.P.s have considerable difficulty obtaining up-to-date details of recent amendments to extant enactments. In the State of Victoria, it is believed that the entire corpus of legislation may be re-printed annually, incorporating all new enactments and amendments to existing enactments passed during the previous Parliamentary session. This is probably not practicable in the UK but the Treasury Solicitor needs to do much more to keep Statutes in Force up-to-date because, at the moment, that publication is years behind schedule. Unless one has access to a publication like Halsbury's Statutes of England, with its cumulative supplements and noter-up, it is virtually impossible to keep abreast of changes to statute law. Moreover, it is now in

vogue for Statutory Instruments to modify or repeal enactments and that merely adds to the general problem of inaccessibility.

4.   One proposal which has been canvassed for a number of years is that of pre-legislative select committees. The most obvious advantage is that they would give more weight to the consultation process which is invariably undertaken by Government at the last minute and under considerable constraints of time.

To be effective, the Government would probably have to publish a final draft of each bill and there would have to be some sort of timetable on the work of the Select Committee. However, one likely benefit of such select committees would be a reduction in the number of amendments to bills which the Government have to introduce, particularly at Report Stage in each House, in order to give effect to last minute changes of heart, etc. However, I doubt very much whether the idea will ever be adopted by the Government because of the risk of delay and a reluctance to have to justify proposals in public prior to a Second Reading debate when the Government of the day may see to it that its bills are whipped through.

16 January 1992

M14   The Campaign for Freedom of Information

Extract from a letter from Mr Maurice Frankel, Director of the Campaign, to Rt Hon William Waldegrave MP, Minister for Public Service and Science.

Consultation relating to legislation

Progress could be made by opening up the processes of consultation and lobbying surrounding new legislation. Some departments now encourage those responding to formal consultations to allow the department to make their comments public afterwards. However, these arrangements have a number of shortcomings.... These are (a) some departments don't bother with the approach at all (b) those that do allow respondents to veto disclosure of their comments (c) sometimes disclosure is so delayed that by the time comments are released they are of no practical use (d) existing arrangements apply only to formal consultation exercises, not to the often more important consultation and lobbying which takes place as legislation is drawn up and introduced.

We suggest that from the point at which government announces its intention to legislate, the process of consultation should be open to public scrutiny. Certain classes of information should be placed, as it arises, in a "Legislation File", open for public inspection in the department's own library and available in the libraries of the Houses of Parliament. There could be two main elements:

(i)   All inputs which the government receives from outside bodies should – subject to limited exemptions – be publicly available as they are received.

(ii)   The government's own assessments of the likely impact of the proposed legislation should be available as they are generated.

The first element would go substantially beyond existing practice. We suggest that (a) it should apply to all representations received about possible legislation, not just those relating to consultation documents; and (b) respondents should not, as at present, be free to insist on confidentiality. Instead, their inputs should automatically be available except where it was clear that disclosure would jeopardise a trade secret, invade personal privacy or damage national security. From the time the legislation is announced, until the bill completes its Parliamentary passage, all relevant correspondence to a minister or department from anyone outside government would become publicly available.

Such openness would not reduce the flow of information to government. Most of the comments come from representative bodies, such as trade and professional associations, whose explicit function it is to communicate their views to government, or from bodies who are seeking to ensure that their own interests are taken into account. They will continue to do so, regardless of possible public disclosure. They will be in the same position as those giving evidence to select committees, who know from the outset that their evidence will be public.

The information disclosed under the second element would include any internal assessment of the consequences of the proposed legislation and any assessment by the government's law officers of the scope and implications of the bill or amendments tabled to it. This type of information can be distinguished from the generality of policy advice which consists of the pre-decisional discussion of the merits of various options. The proposed disclosure refers to decisions which will have been taken and translated into draft legislation. Parliament is being asked to approve this and should be entitled to the best available information about its likely impact.

This approach would have many advantages. The public and MPs would have access to an unrivalled source of expertise about the implications of proposed legislation. The quality of public discussion and of Parliamentary scrutiny would be vastly improved. The intentions of the proposed legislation would be clearer, and the extent to which the government's proposals stood up to examination by those with relevant expertise could be seen. It would also provide greater balance in the information supplied to government. At present, each interest group argues its case to government in private. There may be little check on the quality of their information. Wider scrutiny will allow others to correct inaccuracies and help check the influence of vested interests.

22 June 1992

M15   Child Poverty Action Group

1. 'Skeleton Bills'

CPAG has become increasingly concerned about the trend towards "skeleton Bills", containing only a bare outline, with all the detail necessary to implement the legislative intent contained in statutory instruments. The most recent example was the Child Support Act 1991, which contained over 100 regulation-making powers.

Serious concern was expressed, in particular by Peers during debate in the House of Lords, about this. Although statutory instruments are subject to Parliamentary scrutiny, this is of a very limited nature. In particular, given our long experience of unsatisfactory drafting of regulations and the problems this can cause to benefit claimants, CPAG is concerned at the lack of opportunity for amendment in the Parliamentary scrutiny of regulations.

2. Directions

The bare outline of legislation described in 1. above can result in even less Parliamentary scrutiny when the Secretary of State is given the power to issue directions. One recent example is the social fund. In a letter to The Times of 4 July 1990 (The Times 9/7/90), Lord Molson repeated two Lords Justices' view that the Secretary of State's authority was exercisable without any Parliamentary letter of supervision in this example.

3. Consultation

a) CPAG is sometimes consulted by the government and frequently consulted by the Social Security Advisory Committee when SSAC has been consulted by the government. The Commission will be aware of the limitation on consultation with SSAC following new legislation. On other occasions, however, we believe that consultation with SSAC has been proved to be very useful from benefit claimant's perspective.

b) However, consultation with SSAC – or independently and directly with a wide range of orgnisations – is only effective if there is potential flexibility in the government's attitude to the proposed legislation. More recently the government has decided to modify several proposals after consulting SSAC. During the 1980's, however, this was in our experience a rare occurrence.

c) Consultation has different functions depending on the particular stage of the legislative process at which it is applied. From our experience, there are some particular dangers to be aware of:

- consulting at an early stage in terms so broad that very little guidance is given as to the government's intentions (as it could be argued happened during the social security review of the mid 1980s); or

- consulting only at White Paper stage, with no Green Paper in advance, and therefore consulting only on practicalities rather than policies and principles (as happened recently with the government's proposals on child support)

d) Following the concern expressed about the "skeleton" nature of the Child Support Bill (see a) above) the government promised wide consultation on the regulations etc. CPAG was pleased to be one of the organisations consulted on the outline of the contents of the regulations recently.

However, some areas in the outline are not clear and others have not yet been decided. Because of CPAG's long experience of the effects of badly drafted regulations, we have been pressing for the government to consult on the regulations themselves.

e) We believe that a useful purpose would be served by the government having to publish formally the results of a consultation exercise. Although some information is currently available via Parliamentary Questions, in most cases the government states that each organisation responding can publish its own response. When SSAC is consulted, the Secretary of State is of course obliged to publish SSAC's and his/her own response to it. This pattern could be a useful precedent for other consultation exercises, and would add to public knowledge about government decision-making.

4. Test cases

a) One of CPAG's areas of work is to pursue legal test cases on behalf of claimants, to clarify or challenge the interpretation of the law. We have on occasions had our costs underwritten by the government because of the shared interest in clear legislation. In the 1970s, when CPAG first began to take test cases, the government on occasions accepted the legal challenge.

b) However, in the 1980s the government has responded to test cases increasingly by changing the law to nullify their results, sometimes within a few days. It is also arguable that the government has attempted to reduce the impact of test cases (eg by the insertion of an amendment to the Social Security Act 1990 – which, it should be noted, was included in one of the schedules to the Act called "minor and consequential amendments").

January 1992

M16   Child Poverty Action Group: Supplementary Memorandum

Skeleton Bills and Acts

CPAG is very concerned about the increase in use of Skeleton Bills and Acts where all the substantial detail concerning complex issues, such as entitlement to income support, are left to regulations.

The advantage, as the government sees it, is that this allows a degree of flexibility. If something proves to be unworkable in practice it can be amended. The disadvantage, as CPAG sees it, is that Parliament does not have an opportunity to scrutinise and consider at any length the mass of detail contained in the regulations.

There is limited time available for debating regulations, especially where these are subject only to the negative resolution procedure. In addition, there is no opportunity for amendment so that even if one aspect of the regulations is criticised by Members it is unlikely in the extreme that the whole of the regulations would be voted down.

If the main body of the detailed proposals were contained in the Bill then proper consideration could be given to that detail when the Bill was in committee.

In addition, we are concerned that leaving so much detail to regulations leads to sloppy drafting, as the regulations can easily or quickly be amended when mistakes or inconsistencies come to light. This, however, is very unsatisfactory.

The Income Support (General) Regulations 1987, which contained all the main provisions concerning the operation of the income support scheme, were subject to affirmative resolution. They came into force in April 1988. Meanwhile, the first amending regulations came out on 31st March 1988 and between then and November 1988 there were eight sets of amending regulations.

During 1989, there were five sets of amending regulations, three during 1990 and six during 1991. 1992 has so far seen one set of amending regulations.

Income support is, of course, only one aspect of the means-tested benefits system introduced in April 1988. The detail of the family credit scheme, introduced at the same time, is also contained in regulations and that scheme also saw five sets of amending regulations during 1988.

We are also concerned about the lack of consultation on regulations. The Child Support Act, which received Royal Assent in July 1991, is another example of a skeleton Act, which contains over one hundred regulation-making powers.

We were consulted on the proposed content of the regulations which was a useful exercise. However, the Secretary of State has refused to consult on the actual regulations once they are drafted. We feel that this is unfortunate since consultation on draft regulations might help to ensure that the Department "got it right first time".

Directions

The Social Security Act 1986 established a system of discretionary loans and grants to be paid out of a fund called the social fund. (There is also a regulated social fund which deals with cold weather, funeral and maternity payments.) This replaced the old system of single payments to claimants for one-off items, such as a bed or a cooker.

The part of the Act dealing with discretionary loans and grants authorised payments to be made to meet needs in accordance with directions and guidance given by the Secretary of State. The Secretary of State used the power to give directions to limit the categories of need which could be met by the social fund.

The Act conferred a power to create a code of subdelegated legislation which the Secretary of State is under no duty to publish, and does not involve consideration by the specialist advisory committee, SSAC. Unlike regulations, directions are not subject to any Parliamentary control. They are not debated, but simply issued by the Secretary of State.

The use of this power was subject to legal challenge, in *R v Secretary of State for Social Security ex parte Stitt* (*Times*, 5th July 1990). The challenge was unsuccessful, but both the Divisional Court and the Court of Appeal expressed surprise (at the least) at the scope of the unsupervised power to give directions.

In his Judgment in the Court of Appeal (given on the 3rd July 1990), Lord Justice Purchase said:

"Mr Beloff was unable to direct our attention to any previous Act of Parliament under which such wholesale unregulated and unsupervised powers effectively to pass subordinate legislation had been granted to a Minister of State; but he submitted, with charm, that there had to be a 'first time for everything'. It is clear from the judgment of Woolf L.J. that he felt surprise and concern at such a

delegation by Parliament of its powers of supervision which, for my part, I also, with respect, share. It may be that in this case in the execution of the legislative process that 'Homer nodded' with the result that wholly exceptional and, it might be thought by some objectionable, powers without any Parliamentary fetter or supervision other than the annual report (section 32 (7B)) was achieved by the Secretary of State."

CPAG remains very concerned about the use of such power by the Secretary of State. The Courts concluded that the Secretary of State was acting perfectly lawfully in issuing such directions, since Parliament had conferred the power to do so on him. However, the use of such power is a worrying development and in our view an unnecessary circumvention of the legislative process. Regulations at the very least should be used when exercising such power, so that there is some, however limited, Parliamentary scrutiny.

May 1992

M17   Civil Aviation Authority

1. The Civil Aviation Authority (CAA) is responsible for the safety and economic regulation of the British civil aviation industry and for the provision of air traffic services in the United Kingdom.

2. The CAA was established by the Civil Aviation Act 1971 (now replaced by the Civil Aviation Act 1982, which was a consolidation measure). The Act sets out CAA's powers, duties and objectives. Although new primary legislation will shortly be needed to reflect the impact of the single European market on civil aviation and the fact that airspace has now become a scarce resource, the structure laid down in 1971 has proved sufficiently flexible and robust to accommodate and indeed facilitate the enormous developments which have occurred in civil aviation during the intervening 20 years.

3. This has in no small measure been due to the fact that the primary legislation gave wide powers for detailed matters to be dealt with in subordinate legislation. For example the nuts and bolts of safety regulation are contained in the Air Navigation Order 1989 (the ANO), which is made under powers granted by section 60 of the 1982 Act. The ANO includes provisions for the issue by CAA of air operators' certificates, certificates of airworthiness to aircraft, crew licences and aerodrome licences. It specifies in detail how aircraft are to be maintained, equipped and operated.

4. The ANO is regularly amended. Changes are usually initiated by CAA. Those parts of the industry likely to be affected by a proposed change are consulted by CAA. Consultation is relatively straightforward in that the civil aviation industry is well organised and sophisticated. It is therefore possible to reach those in the industry likely to be interested and they are in a position to respond even though the issue may be complex and technical.

5. The ANO is drafted by legal draftsmen. The aim of the draftsman is to achieve the precision required of a legislative instrument. Inevitably this means that the

ANO is not always as "reader friendly" as the CAA would like it to be. The ANO is of course scrutinised by the Joint Committee on Statutory Instruments and it is subject to the negative resolution procedure.

6. The ANO creates a large number of criminal offences and falls to be construed by the courts in the course of prosecutions of those who contravene its requirements. It may also fall to be construed by the courts either on a judicial review of a decision by CAA to refuse a licence or certificate required by the ANO or in an action for negligence brought against CAA for having, for example, granted a certificate of airworthiness to an aircraft which has subsequently proved not to be airworthy.

7. The existing legislation relating to civil aviation, whether primary or subordinate, is certainly not perfect, but it is generally workable and enforceable through the courts of the United Kingdom. There is a clear and well understood procedure for consultation and challenge of the subordinate legislation. However the UK domestic legislation is being overtaken by EC legislation and CAA does have concern about how this legislation, which is very different from UK domestic legislation, in style and content and in the method of preparation, is going to be absorbed into the domestic legal system. This is not of course a problem which is peculiar to civil aviation, but it can be illustrated by reference to the EC Regulation on the Harmonisation of Technical Requirements and Administration Procedures in the field of Civil Aviation, which came into force on 1 January 1992 and which, as technical requirements and procedures are developed, will replace all or much of the ANO. A copy of the final draft Regulation is attached for ease of reference.

8. The purpose of the Regulation is to ensure that there is a level playing field in aviation safety terms throughout the European Community. The CAA strongly endorses this principle. Airlines cannot compete on equal terms if some incur the costs of more onerous safety requirements than are imposed on their competitors. CAA's sole concern is with the legislative process by which the level playing field is to be achieved.

9. The Regulation provides that the requirements and procedures specified in annex II shall apply throughout the Community from 1 January 1992. Those standards and procedures (known as Joint Aviation Requirements – JARs) lay down the requirements against which the airworthiness of certain types of aircraft is to be assessed and the basis on which organisations maintaining such aircraft are to be approved. These JARs have been drawn up by a number of European Aviation Authorities, collectively known as the Joint Aviation Authorities (JAA) which are party to an informal Arrangements Document. JAA is preparing JARs on a whole range of airworthiness and operational matters.

The Regulation provides for further JARs to be adopted after they are submitted by the EC Commission to the Council and adopted by the Council. It is expected that the Commission will submit JARs as they are agreed through the JAA process, but the Commission cannot fetter its discretion to take its own initiatives and it may submit different JARs to the Council from those drawn up under the JAA process. Once adopted under the Regulation a JAR can be amended by the Commission with the assistance of a Committee composed of representatives of Member States. If in the JAA process an authority has identified a national variant which it wishes to retain in the interests of safety but it has been unable to persuade its fellow authorities of the value of the national variant, the Commission, through the Committee process, will determine whether that national variant should be included in the relevant JAR or abandoned by the authority which wishes to retain it. The Regulation provides for a Member State unilaterally to impose a safety requirement where a problem has become apparent as a result of an accident, incident or service experience. The Council or the Commission, with the assistance of the Committee, will then determine whether the requirement should be applied across the board or dropped by the State concerned.

10. As stated above the JARs will gradually replace much of the ANO. Under the JAA process, JARs will be drawn up by teams of technical experts, speaking a variety of languages. In any international gathering the difficulty of getting a consensus can result in a political compromise couched in woolly wording. (This problem is particularly acute in the case of the EC Regulations on the economic regulation of civil aviation where wording designed to obscure the precise meaning, in order to achieve compromise, is at times a negotiating objective rather than an undesirable by-product of the legislative process.) At no stage in the JAA or the EC process will a legal draftsman be instructed to give effect to proposals in clear and unambiguous "legal language". Thus in the future the instruments which will replace the ANO will not be drafted under the strict disciplines currently applicable to the drafting of domestic legislation. CAA therefore has some concern as to the effect this will have on the enforceability of safety regulation under domestic law.

11. The Technical Harmonisation Regulation has been under consideration by the Commission for many months. The civil aviation industry is well aware of it and of course strongly supports the principle of a level playing field. However there is little if any awareness of the contents of the Regulation among the general public. The Regulation removes the ability of Member States to determine safety standards for aircraft on its own register and operated by its own airlines. The effect this will have can be illustrated by actions taken following the accident to a B737 aircraft at Manchester Airport in 1985, when many passengers were killed by the fire which swept through the aircraft. Inevitably, aviation safety is often tightened up following an accident which has revealed a safety problem. The pressure to take such measures is most strongly felt by the aviation authority of the State of Registry of the aircraft concerned. The reason for the differences between aviation safety standards in various States can often be traced back to an accident which has led the aviation authorities of the State of Registry to act, but which has not been sufficiently persuasive to affect other authorities. After the Manchester accident, because passengers had difficulty in getting through the over wing exits to escape a fire, the CAA required UK operators to provide better access to the exits, either by

wider spacing between seat rows or by removal of individual seats next to the exits. Only the French authority was persuaded to follow suit at the time (though the US and some other authorities now intend to take a similar line). Therefore at present UK operators may not be able to carry as many passengers on a B737 and other aircraft with a similar exit as can most of their European competitors. Under the EC Regulation the CAA will not be able to maintain such a national variant unless it can carry the majority of its European partners with it. As stated above the CAA considers that this principle is a necessary pre-requisite of the single market. However the issue is an important one which will have a significant effect on CAA's ability to regulate aviation safety and on the extent to which public opinion will be able to influence safety regulation. One would have expected there to have been some public debate on such an issue, but because there is no mechanism to ensure that proposed EC legislation is brought into the public arena, there has been none.

12. It appears to CAA that the growing volume of EC legislation means that the legislative process is radically changing and that the assimilation of the new system may be painful and difficult. Indeed there is risk that during the transitional period serious mistakes will be made and that some of the legislation will prove to be both unworkable and unenforceable, and therefore incapable of achieving its objectives.

January 1992

M18   Clarity

Using plain English in statutes: A fundamental reappraisal of drafting approach?

A fundamental change?
At the outset of this submission we raise the question of whether there should be a fundamental change in the way in which legislation is drafted in the United Kingdom.

In 1974 Lord Denning spoke of Community law as an incoming tide flowing into our rivers and estuaries. It might now be regarded as a tsunami. But Community law is here to stay. It will have an increasingly pervasive effect on UK domestic law. We raise this question: instead of continuing to write law in a typical Anglo-saxon style should we not give careful thought to revolutionizing our style of writing to mould it along the best of continental lines? Can we afford not to do so?

Lord Diplock has pointed out that English judges, up to the last 20 years or so, may have been largely to blame for

the traditional and widely criticised style of legislative drafting ... familiar to English judges during the present century and for which their own narrow semantic approach to statutory interpretation ... may have been largely to blame.
Fothergill v Monarch Airlines (1981) AC at 280.

Purposive approach to drafting and interpreling legislation

Although the shift in statutory interpretation to a purposive approach is clear, there seems to be a reluctance by Parliament (or is it Parliamentary Counsel?) to enact or write law which facilitates that method of interpretation. The purposive approach to statutory interpretation is inhibited without legislation drafted in a way that takes account of and encourages that approach.

There is a considerable weight of authority in support of a purposive approach to drafting legislation. The Renton Committee encouraged the use of purpose sections in statutes, and Sir William Dale has been a leading proponent of that approach. Yet while the UK has moved towards increasingly closer ties with Europe it has seemingly not given considered attention to the interaction of domestic and Community law at the drafting level. That responsibility has remained with the Parliamentary Counsel Office; and that Office has traditionally opposed the continental drafting style.

There are good arguments for and against the continental style of drafting.[1] But the factor becoming more and more important, and the one that may in the end overwhelm the discussion, is that the UK *is* a member of the European Community governed by laws drafted in a style that is not solely English. In the face of that reality we may be forced to rethink our legislative drafting style. In short it means Parliament must trust its judges. It means also that the link between drafting and interpretation – and interpretation and drafting – must be given greater recognition. In a sense it means a new form of partnership between Parliament and the judiciary.

UK membership in the European Community

The UK cannot ignore the fact that Community law, drafted in a dramatically different fashion and with quite different rules of interpretation, will play an increasing role in our lives. We face a great danger that our domestic law, and the way we write it, may have less and less of an impact if we do not change. UK domestic law may well become relegated to the status of local government bylaws – treated as a curious quirk of the Anglo-Saxon. The judiciary have sent out some clear messages in the past decade – if drafters do not respond (or if the Government does not direct them to do so) the judiciary may hasten the relegation of UK domestic law to antiquity. The fact that the judiciary must apply continental methods of interpretation in cases involving international and community law may well cement judicial thinking.

Clarity's suggestion

Are these over-stated concerns? Perhaps. But it is worth considering a comprehensive re-examination of UK drafting style in light of our membership in the European Community.[2] The UK is undoubtedly able to contribute to the

---

1   Francis Bennion sets out the more common arguments in favour of the UK style starting on page 23 of *Bennion on Statute Law*, Longman (3ed) 1990.
2   This might be undertaken by a joint body composed of Law Commissioners, members of both Houses of Parliament, representatives of the European Community, and others.

expression of the law in the Community – but if we maintain our present drafting style we may never be able to do so fully.

From time to time we return to elements of the theme of continental drafting but the remainder of our comments are focused on present drafting style and practice and what might be done to improve it without making fundamental changes.

Part 1   Attitude and Education – and How to Get Them

The Renton Committee[1] said that little could be done to improve the quality of legislation

> *unless those concerned in the process are willing to modify some of their most cherished habits*

A habit comes from an attitude. The single most important element in using plain English in statutes is the attitude of the drafter.

The drafter's attitude

If drafters have an attitude to drafting that puts the ultimate readers' interests ahead of all others, an immense problem is overcome. The issue then becomes not whether to use plain English, but what steps can be taken to make difficult concepts, or complex sections, easier to understand. Energies are concentrated in that direction rather than endless and wasteful discussions about whether "plain English" should or should not be used.

How to get or encourage the right attitude

Creating and maintaining the right attitude to drafting needs attention at three levels:

The institutional level

A Government wide commitment is needed to use plain English in all forms of legislation[2] This not only gives an overall policy direction to drafters, but also

- encourages drafters to use innovative drafting ideas when instructing departments may oppose them. Drafters can rely on the Government wide policy to justify innovations that otherwise might be rejected
- a Government wide policy guides and directs drafters to that goal
- a Government wide policy is also something that can be used as an audit or check by others to see whether the product, the legislation, is in fact written clearly. The policy gives a measuring stick for commentators.

Reinforcement at the Ministerial level

There are many government policies which, if not reinforced by an active Minister, have only lip service paid to them. Ministers of the Crown should actively encourage, support, and audit plain English efforts within their respective Departments. This would be seen as a further refinement and support for a Government-wide initiative.

---

1   Report of a Committee appointed by the Lord President of the Council, chaired by the Right Honourable Sir David Renton: The Preparation of Legislation, Comnd 6053, 1975.
2   This need only be an extension of the Government's existing commitment to plain English forms and government communication (first instituted by Prime Minister Thatcher).

It should go without saying that controversial provisions should not be concealed by obscure drafting to ease their passage.

Parliamentary Counsel Office

As a unique office within Government and with unique responsibilities, the Parliamentary Counsel Office should have its own plain English drafting policies.

The plain English policy for the Parliamentary Counsel Office could include a drafting manual to give specific guidance and encouragement to drafters when considering different drafting approaches to problems. There are many drafting manuals around – one that is particularly directed to clear communication was described by Ian Turnbull, the Chief Parliamentary Counsel for the Australian Federal Government, in a recent article in the Statute Law Review.

We see a drafting manual as both a guide and incentive to Parliamentary Counsel, with its prime focus – clear communication. Improvement in drafting is a continuing process and we see some advantage to a permanent committee of both Houses of Parliament having some role in both raising issues about and commenting on drafting style, and in learning from Parliamentary Counsel some of their difficulties. The independence of the Office might then be better tailored to meet the needs of the user.

Education

Most Parliamentary Counsel, both in the United Kingdom and overseas, learn on the job. There are very few drafting courses for Parliamentary Counsel and those that do exist have no particular focus on clear communication. At present, knowledge of drafting techniques and approaches tends to be handed down from one senior Parliamentary Counsel to a more junior one. The training, such as it is, is incestuous. Unless a drafter is particularly innovative, it is difficult for new ideas to emerge and to develop.

Any kind of drafting course which encourages clear communication, and shows techniques to achieve it, is worthwhile for Parliamentary Counsel. But courses should be designed to help Parliamentary Counsel with specific legislative drafting problems. Developing a drafting course is a project that should be a co-operative one, combining the skills of Parliamentary Counsel with communicators and writers. Once focused on a non-threatening project, like developing a drafting course, significant progress would be made in creating useful course material and content for a drafting manual for all law writers.[1]

But much more needs to be done. Parliamentary Counsel should be aware of research that has been conducted about what helps people understand written text and what hinders comprehension. With that knowledge new ideas and techniques can be developed both internally and with the aid of outside experts. Links between the Parliamentary Counsel Office and universities having an interest in the area

---

1   There is a lot of existing material in courses from the University of Ottawa and Edinburgh, but for the most part, they deal poorly with the interests of readers.

could provide a valuable exchange of information resulting in an improvement in the quality and drafting of legislation.[1]

Parliamentary Counsel should become more aware of the difficulties people have in understanding legislation. Not just an awareness of general complaints, but the particular reasons *why* legislation is often difficult to understand. Once the difficulties are understood, drafters may take more active steps to improve the product of their work. There are often many ways to achieve a particular result – if the drafter gives priority to the way which will be best understood by the ultimate reader, a significant improvement in drafting would result.

Some awareness of difficulties can be shown by testing readers' comprehension of legislation and the difficulties they encounter. Video taping lawyers and layreaders as they struggle through a particular section of legislation would be a fascinating peek into how much time is wasted (and how much time can be saved) by clear writing.

Concepts of good organization of texts that help the reader from one point to another will put a new perspective on organizing legislation (both the overall organization of an Act and the internal organization of sections).

There has been considerable debate in legislative drafting circles in the last few years over what is commonly called the "common-law style" and the "civil-law style" of drafting. Unfortunately, the debate comes down to which is "best". Instead of asking that question, for which there can never be a complete answer, it would be more helpful if the debate focused on when it is more appropriate to use one style rather than the other; then to learn the techniques appropriate for each style and the difficulties and advantages associated with each.

All this should be built into drafting courses and seminars for those involved in drafting legislation.

Other thoughts on stimulating ideas about writing legislation

(1) Improving legal writing generally
The key to improving legal writing is:
- to turn ideas about communication into suggestions lawyers can use when they write; and
- to teach lawyers and those entering the profession how to write (especially that legal writing does not have to be turgid, complex and dull).

(2) Specific suggestions
With the aim of improving legal writing in mind, we should:
(i)   encourage more drafting courses and support initiatives to create them;
(ii) use other professions and disciplines in the design and teaching of drafting courses;
(iii) encourage and support research into how readers try to understand legislation and adopt practices which help readers;
(iv) distribute information about writing – whether by a newsletter; regular

---

1   The work of the University of Reading in information communication could be a worthwhile contact.

seminars or a network of contacts – "Clarity" is now internationally welcomed as providing a useful forum for doing this;

(v) establish exchanges of people and information about writing (for example, between Commonwealth legislative counsel offices, law reform Commissions, universities and the practising bar);

(vi) give opportunities to lawyers on sabbaticals to undertake writing or writing research projects, including legislation;

(vii) establish joint projects between university faculties, and with universities and others relating to teaching writing or writing research, and engaging in comparative studies of drafting techniques and related matters;

(viii) encourage the establishment of bursaries and scholarships related to drafting;

(ix) encourage a multidisciplinary approach to improving the expression of the law;

(x) write to a lay audience, not the judiciary, without losing legal certainty.

Quality control

How can quality control be maintained over legislative drafting? Here are some suggestions:

(a) a style guide

Particularly in an office of more than 2 or 3 people it is helpful to have a consistent style. It helps if drafters can agree on certain conventions and develop a style guide which drafters follow in day to day writing. Many legislative counsel offices have drafting style guides but not, as we understand it, in the Parliamentary Counsel Office.

(b) editors

Several legislative counsel offices overseas use editors to check on grammar and consistency of drafting. An increasing use is being made of them and English and linguistics experts. Is there room for such expertise in the Parliamentary Counsel Office?

(c) readability tests

Computer software will give drafts a "score" which gives some indication of how easy, or difficult, drafts are to read.

(d) peer review

The comments of colleagues are invaluable. One suggestion made in a Working Group Study to the Law Reform Commission of Canada called Drafting Laws in French (1979) could establish a consistent review process and direct the writer and reviewer to important issues in reviewing drafts. The Study suggested a "review control sheet" containing a checklist of issues of substance and drafting designed to maintain drafting quality.

Part 2   Solving Information Anxiety

Information anxiety

People read legislation looking for answers to questions. More often than not they find what Richard Saul Wurman calls "information anxiety";[1] the black hole between data and knowledge. It happens when "information" doesn't tell us what we want or need to know.

The starting point to fill that black hole is to accept that what we write is not for ourselves but for others.

The moment we accept that fact our minds start to reorient themselves. We start to think not only of getting what we write technically correct – but of getting the message across to those for whom we write. It means we become interested in clarity as well as precision. That leads us to ask:

● what helps people understand texts (and then to use those things in our writing); and

● what impedes understanding (and so avoid those things in our writing).

Writing for others means we are constantly on the look-out for ideas. Ideas that help communication. Ideas we can then use for particular drafting jobs. What we should be about is to reverse the extraordinarily strange situation that free societies have arrived at where their members enter binding obligations they do not understand and are governed from cradle to grave by legislative texts they cannot comprehend.[2,3]

Each advance of knowledge about how readers read and understand texts should be complemented by a shift in style, organization, word order, thinking, or document design by drafters.

Social and economic reasons for improving the language of the law

If laws cannot be readily understood by those most affected by them the social cost is an increasing ignorance of the law and growing disrespect for the law and those who administer it. Ignorance of and disrespect for the law damage the fabric of society.[4]

Unnecessarily complex language, redundant words, and language which fails to communicate, impose an enormous financial burden on all levels of society. Even minor improvements to the language of the law can bring substantial savings of time; time which can then be put to more productive use.

Communicating to an audience

Improved drafting techniques and ideas stem from accepting that legislation is intended to be read.

Understanding *by whom particular legal language will be read* and *how readers will use a document* gives writers ideas for writing documents so that they can be more easily understood.

1   Richard Saul Wurman: Information Anxiety, Doubleday.

2   A modification of Francis Bennion's comment:" It is strange that free societies should thus arrive at a situation where their membes are governed from cradle to grave by texts they cannot comprehend. The democratic origins are impeccable the result far from satisfactory... "
    F Bennion: Bennion on Statute Law, Longman (3ed) p10.

3   The admirable comment of a witness in the Wandsworth County Court comes to mind " I know that ignorance is no excuse for the law." Recorded in a footnote to A Russell: Legislative Drafting and Forms, Butterworths 4th ed p17.

4   See Sir John Donaldson's comment in Markur Island Shipping Co. v Laughton (1983) 1 A11 ER p334.

(1) Stating a purpose

Research shows that readers are better able to understand and interpret texts when they have a context for reading them. Purpose sections can create a context.

What are purpose sections?

Purpose sections are sections in an Act stating the basis of the legislation and which are themselves law making or intended to have legal effect. Sir William Dale has described the reason for including purpose sections in legislation this way[1]:

An enunciation of principle gives to a statute a firm and intelligible structure. It helps to clear the mind of the legislator, provides guidance to the Executive, explains the legislation to the public, and assists the courts when in doubt about the application of some specific provision.

Why purpose sections are becoming more popular

Every Act is passed for a reason. Those reasons may be, in the mind of the reader, of lesser or greater importance, valid or not. But there is, in the collective "mind" of Parliament, a reason for every Act it passes.

On that basis, if there is a reason, a purpose, for passing an Act, it is only common sense to say what that purpose is. In the absence of a statement of purpose, the reader is left to search for his or her understanding of the purpose.

If the reader has to come to a conclusion about the purpose of an Act, even if that conclusion is a mental exercise, why not help the reader by stating the purpose explicitly?

So the reason for a "purpose section" is to aid in understanding the text of the Act and an aid to interpreting it when questions arise. A purpose section is an aid to every reader – from the recipient of some benefit or obligation under the Act to the interpreter, whether that interpreter acts to administer the Act or to judge legal issues arising from it.

The problem with purpose sections

The major objection (raised by writers *not* readers) about including purpose sections in legislation is that they will be used! But used to obscure what the writer thinks would otherwise be clear.

Another typical objection to purpose sections is that they restate in different words what is said more specifically in later provisions of the Act.

A third objection is that purpose sections tend to lose their purpose and become merely statements descriptive of what follows (eg "this Act regulates the sale of liquor"), or much worse, a political manifesto.[2] This can be a real problem for legislative counsel.

---

1 Statute Law Review, Spring 1988, p15.
2 Francis Bennion probably sums up the drafter's objections best: "Draftsmen dislike the purpose clause. They take the view that often the aims of legislation cannot usefully or safely be summarised or condensed by such means. A political purpose clause is no more than a political manifesto, which may obscure what otherwise may be precise and exact... The draftsman's view is that his Act should be allowed to speak for itself."
F Bennion: Statutory Interpretation, Butterworths, London 1984 p580.

Aiding interpretation

The bottom line is surely that the proprietary interest a drafter has in the legislation he or she writes is fleeting. After the writing is complete the document gains a life of its own. New issues, different situations, new technology, human ingenuity all create situations the original writer may not have contemplated or have dealt with imperfectly. These issues most often arise years after the document leaves the writer. It is then that purpose sections can be particularly helpful in aiding interpretation.

Writing purpose sections is not easy, nor are they always helpful or desirable, but most readers *do* find them helpful. Drafters should think about including them in legislation more often than they do.[1] We urge the Commission to recommend their use.

(2) Document organization

Documents should be organised to help the most likely readers. Legislation is not read for pleasure but to get information. So, from a readers' point of view, good writing is writing that structures information in a way that enables readers to get the information they seek as easily as possible.

How will the document be used?

Organizing a document well means that we must know who the most likely readers of it will be. The writer is often not the best person to make decisions about the organization of a document. Clients can help here because they should know who the likely readers are and the questions they commonly ask and mistakes most often made by the readers they serve.

Research into how people read and react to documents can be a guide to internal organization. If we can foresee how readers are likely to use a particular document we can organize it so that it is as efficient as possible for their use. For legislation we have barely entertained the notion that testing, or reader considerations, should affect our writing.

Organizing for readers

The usual drafting practice is to impose the writer's thinking process and organization on readers. A process and organization that is entirely logical to the *writer* but not necessarily helpful for the reader.

We can look at organization of statutes on several levels:

(a) overall organization[2]

(b) organization within Parts and divisions

(c) sentence word order.

---

1 Using purpose sections is not an argument for a civil law drafting style instead of a common law style. It is intended as a plea to keep an open mind and to use whatever tools are appropriate to do the job. The Renton Committee supported their use.

2 It is entirely correct for a writer to start a drafting project making sure the foundations are properly established. Creating an administrative agency and providing for its operation for example - and then building on that structure. But when the writer is satisfied that all the pieces are correct he or she should think of organization from the reader's point of view. Is it helpful for the administrative agency to come first? Would it be more helpful if the important substance of the legislation came first - with the administrative agency coming much later?

For example: a typical legislative section will start a clause "Subject to ..." For the writer this is entirely logical. He or she knows that what is about to be written is qualified by something coming later. The writer wants the reader to be warned, so the automatic "subject to" pops into mind.

Now think of this from the readers' point of view. Before they read anything they are told to refer to somewhere else in the document. They look there, not knowing how the qualification relates to what they are about to read. They go back to the clause and read the rest of it. Inevitably they must then go back to the qualifying clause.

The reader is bounced about the document trying to understand the writer's logic. A different approach will often help readers. If readers first understood the basic content of the section they would then be much better able to fit qualifications into it. This could be done in a number of ways:

- putting the "subject to" at the end of the section
- briefly describing what the "subject to" is about, followed by the section reference
- structuring the whole document so that the basic thrust of sections comes in subsection (1) and exemptions or limitations in later subsections
- using a footnote to indicate there is a qualification to the statement[1]
- using typographical aids to highlight exceptions and qualifications to a statement.

What works best? Whatever works best for the readers for whom drafters are writing. Don't know? Do some testing ...,[2] ask some questions, take advice from others.

A specific example

Here is an example of what happens when surplus words are removed from a section and it is reorganized. It is taken from New Zealand legislation but the points apply to legislation in all jurisdictions. Section 4 of the *Disputes Tribunals Act 1988* reads:

> *4. Establishment of Tribunals - (1) The Minister may from time to time, by notice in the Gazette, establish such number of tribunals as the Minister thinks fit to exercise the jurisdiction created by this Act.*
>
> *(2) The tribunals established under subsection (1) of this section shall be known as Disputes Tribunals.*
>
> *(3) Each Disputes Tribunal shall be a division of a District Court.*
>
> *(4) A notice under subsection (1) of this section establishing a Disputes Tribunal shall specify the District Court of which the Tribunal is to be a division.*

---

1   Footnotes and typographical aids are not used in legislation but there is no reason that this should be so.
2   The Law Reform Commission of Victoria, Australia, commented on the practice of stating conditions before a rule in these words: "Linguists have discovered that that style of writing is only suitable for those who read or write in Japanese or Turkish. It runs directly contrary to the way in which ideas are presented in other languages, including English."
    Access to the Law: the structure and format of legislation (1990)

(5) *The Minister may at any time, by notice in the Gazette,*
  (a) *Disestablish a Disputes Tribunal; and*
  (b) *Direct how the records of that Tribunal shall be dealt with.*

Not including the heading, but counting the cross-references to "subsection (1)" as 2 words, the section contains 109 words. The number of words in the section can be reduced by more than 30% by:

  (1) deleting unnecessary words (reduces the text by 19%)
  (2) reorganizing the text (reduces the text by a further 11%), and
  (3) using the present tense.

(1) deleting unnecessary words
The underlined words can all be deleted without affecting the meaning of the section or its legal certainty:

  4. *Establishment of Tribunals - (1) The Minister may <u>from time to time</u>, by notice in the Gazette, establish <u>such number of</u> tribunals <u>as the Minister thinks fit</u> to exercise the jurisdiction created by this Act.*
  (2) The tribunals established under subsection (1) <u>of this section</u> shall be known as Disputes Tribunals.
  (3) Each Disputes Tribunal shall be a division of a District Court.
  (4) A notice under subsection (1) <u>of this section</u> establishing a Disputes Tribunal shall specify the District Court of which the Tribunal is to be a division.
  (5) The Minister may at any time, by notice in the Gazette,
    (a) Disestablish a Disputes Tribunal; and
    (b) Direct how the records of that Tribunal shall be dealt with.

21 words were deleted; a 19% reduction in the number of words used in the section. *The words deleted in subsection (1)* "from time to time", "such number of" and "as the Minister thinks fit" are superfluous. The words "from time to time" are not necessary because power given to make an appointment or to do an act or thing is capable of being exercised from time to time, as occasion may require (s.25(g) *Acts Interpretation Act 1924* New Zealand). The other words are unnecessary because the Minister has power to establish tribunals to exercise the jurisdiction created by the Act. It is implicit that in doing so the Minister will decide on the number to be established.
The words deleted in subsection (2) "of this section" are unnecessary. There is no other section to which subsection (1) could refer.

The reasons for deleting the words underlined in subsections (4) and (5) will be apparent from the preceding explanation.

(2) re-organizing the text
More words can be saved by a better organization of the section. At present section 4 breaks up the various elements of the section in the following way:

- establishment issues appear in subsections (1), (2) and (4)
- creating tribunals as divisions of the District Court is dealt with in subsections (3) and (4)

- the notice establishing a tribunal is dealt with in subsections (1) and (4)
- disestablishment is dealt with in subsection (5).

One way to reorganize the section is

- to deal with the establishment of a tribunal as a division of the District Court by notice in subsection (1)
- to establish the name and jurisdiction in subsection (2)
- to deal with disestablishment in subsection (3).

For example, a minimum of rewriting results in this:

4. Establishment of tribunals -

(1) The Minister may establish tribunals as divisions of a District Court by

(a) publishing a notice in the Gazette; and

(b) specifying in the notice the District Court of which each tribunal is to be a division.

(2) Each tribunal shall be known as a Disputes Tribunal, and may exercise the jurisdiction created by this Act.

(3) The Minister may by publishing a notice in the Gazette

(a) disestablish a Disputes Tribunal, and

(b) direct how its records are to be dealt with.

This reorganization results in a further reduction of 9 words, or 8% of the total number of words in the section.

The elimination of words is largely achieved by omitting words which connect one subsection to another; words like "established under subsection (1)" and "under subsection (1)". Well organized sections rarely need to connect one subsection to another by specific reference. A section must be read as a whole and meaning should flow from one subsection to the next, leading the reader logically through the section.

The object of the rewrite is to treat each subsection as one complete unit of thought within the section as a whole.

(3) using the present tense

Another word can be saved if the present tense is used in subsection (3). Instead of:

(3) Each Disputes Tribunal shall be a division of a District Court.

subsection (3) should read:

(3) Each Disputes Tribunal is a division of a District Court.

In this section, use of the present tense saves only one word. Clarity is imperceptibly improved.

The principle to be drawn from the research on organizing documents is this: *"writers should structure information around people performing actions or asking questions in particular situations"*. This principle has been called the scenario principle.[1]

---

1   PV Anderson, RJ Brockmann, CR Miller: New Essays in Technical and Scientific Communication: Research Theory and Practice (1983), essay by Linda Flower, John Hayes and Heidi Swarts called Revising Functional Documents: The Scenario Principle p41.

(3) The scenario principle

Here are some examples of the scenario principle:

(i) using questions

Most readers come to legislation with questions: can I do this? what happens if I do that? how can I get this or that?

How helpful it would be if readers coming to a document with a question not only found the same question in the document – but the answer. It is a simple matter for documents to be given appropriate headings stated as questions; and suddenly the document becomes alive, meaningful, useful – it becomes functional.

For example, instead of a heading "Eligibility" why not try "Who is eligible?"; instead of "Coverage" try "What happens if there is a fire?" Some commercial documents have started to use this technique but rarely is it found in legislation. It could and should be, either as a side note or as a section heading, particularly for legislation designed for consumers.

(ii) using diagrams

Some provisions are tough to write.[1] Despite efforts they may not be easy to understand. How can the reader be helped in these circumstances?

If there are a series of complex provisions in which it is easy to get lost an explanatory line diagram can help paint the big picture so that readers can find a road map out of the confusion. A line diagram was included in Alberta's 1973 Labour Relations Bill (although not enacted as part of the legislation) to explain how parties in collective bargaining could move to a strike or lock out position through a complex process. Australian drafters have gone further and included line diagrams as part of the Act.

(iii) using examples

Examples have been used occasionally in legislation.[2] They have been welcomed by a wide variety of readers and more use should be made of them. United Kingdom Parliamentary Counsel have been leaders in this field.

Examples illustrate ideas. The texts we write have ideas behind them – our ideas. If those ideas are not, or are inadequately, conveyed to the readers of the text there is a lack of communication. One way of making sure the ideas we have get across to readers is to help readers with examples. Examples then can be seen as some of the thoughts that the writer has for interpreting the text.

The use of examples, or ideas, embedded in a text can take many forms but the

---

1   In a great response to a question about why the Canadian Income Tax Act could not be drafted using a ten commandments style, Don Thorson, former deputy Minister of Justice and principal drafter of the Act said, " the fact is that Moses is not available for employment by the Department of Justice, and even if he were available it would be interesting to see what Moses could hope to do with concepts such as "tax paid undistributed surplus on hand" "control period earnings" and "foreign accrual property income...""

   (ML Friedland: Access to the Law, Carswell-Methuen, (1975) p65.

2   Section 14AD of the Australian Interpretation Act says how examples are to be treated if they are used in legislation.

fundamental reason for them is to help readers better understand the information presented in the text. Examples can be designed in various ways:

a simple illustration like this

(x) "writing" includes printing, typewriting, or any other intentional reduction of language into legible form, or to a form which can be converted into legible form by a machine or a device, such as language

   (i) on microfilm,

   (ii) in electronic, mechanical or magnetic storage, or

   (iii) in electronic data transmission signals;

(Extract from a Model Land Recording and Registration Act prepared by a Joint Land Titles Committee representing all Canadian Provinces and Territories, except Quebec, July, 1990.)

This simple kind of illustration is similar to the typical formulation of regulation making sections in Acts which start with a general statement followed by a list (of examples) of specific regulation making powers.

an illustration of how a complicated section works

This technique has been used to good effect. An outstanding example is the *Consumer Credit Act 1974.*

a way of helping to change long held attitudes and approaches

The traditional way of drafting local government bylaw making powers is to list in considerable detail what local government can make bylaws about. If as a matter of policy instructions are to draft bylaw powers as general statements, how can this be done while ensuring administrators know what they can advise their councils to do; councils have some reasonable assurance that they are not losing bylaw making powers; and the courts take a different approach to interpreting bylaw making powers?

One answer is to include in the Act a list of examples illustrating and indicating what bylaws a council can pass – all the questions listed above are then conveniently answered.[1]

(iv) using formulae

Quite often now used in legislation, the use of formula instead of words is a very helpful drafting technique. United Kingdom Parliamentary Counsel are to be congratulated for their frequent use of formulae in legislation.

(v) other techniques

Pictures, maps, graphs, algorithms, and logic trees are other techniques that could be used to good effect in some of our laws.

(4) Drafting in the present tense

Advice from experts

Everyone who writes about legal writing advocates use of the present tense. Yet

---

1   A separate paper expanding on the argument for using examples and encouraging their use is appended to this paper.
   [not published]

lawyers persist in complicating their writing by the use (and often misuse) of the word "shall" in various forms.

The advice to use the present tense in drafting legal documents is consistently given but persistently ignored by most lawyers, including Parliamentary Counsel. J.K. Aitken says:[1]

> *"The way is therefore open for draftsmen to restrict their use of shall to the expression of the will of the parties as to actions in the future in pursuance of the document. If this is a draftsman's practice, he will find that his language seems to be less cumbersome and is easier to follow. He may also avoid positive errors ..."*

J.K. Aitken then goes on to recount errors that can arise by using the future tense in drafting.[2]

Robert Dick, the Canadian author of Legal Drafting, concurs with the advice to use the present tense. He also goes on to point to the dangers of not using the present tense. He concludes with a quotation from Pigeon J. formerly of the Supreme Court of Canada who said (in translation):[3]

> *An error to be avoided is the unnecessary use of a tense other than the present tense ... the use of future tense is therefore to be avoided.*

Legislative drafting practice

In Australia, the United Kingdom, and New Zealand some legislation is in the present tense but there seems to be no uniform drafting practice. (Although in the 1991 UK statute book the improper use (in our view) of "shall" was consistent.) In Canada, legislation has long been written in the simple present tense.

The reason Acts were originally written in the future tense was best summed up by former Parliamentary Counsel Sir Harold Kent in his book, "In on the Act". In describing his first few days in the Office of Parliamentary Counsel he said he read Lord Thring's book, Practical Legislation:

> *The heart of the little book is Thring's analysis of legislative language, the form of an enactment. He says that in its simplest form it is a declaration of the legislature directing or empowering the doing or abstention from doing of a particular act or thing. He goes on to say that "if the law is imperative, the proper auxiliary verb is 'shall' or 'shall not', if permissive, 'may'." Later on in the Office I heard people speak of the "imperative shall" as a key feature of the legislative form. Indeed, even when an enactment is permissive, such phrases as "shall have power" or "it shall be lawful" are often used instead of "may". The truth is that a statute creates a new legal situation, and it is appropriate for a sovereign Parliament to command that it shall be so. (p 25)*

Later in his book Sir Harold notes:

> *from time to time I note that even the old imperative "shall" is yielding to the present indicative (p 106)*

On this analysis the use of "shall" is the command of Parliament rather than a

---

1 JK Aitken: Piesse The Elements of Drafting, The Law Book Company (6 Ed) p 81.
2 See also *Attorney-General v. Craig* [1958] VR 34 in which the Victorian Full Court commented on the practice of present tense drafting.
3 Redaction et Interpretation des Lois (Quebec: University of Laval, 1965) p 9

direction to exercise a power or duty at some future time. Whatever the historical reasons for its use its time has surely passed.[1]

The practice of drafting in the present tense has long been followed by legislative counsel in Canada, in part bolstered by Interpretation Acts which require legislation to be regarded as "always speaking".

All these views are little more than a restatement of the view expressed by George Coode, an English barrister, when he wrote in 1842:

> *The attempt to express every action referred to in a statute in a future tense renders the language complicate, anomalous, and difficult to understand ...*
>
> *If the law be regarded while it remains in force as constantly speaking, we get a clear and simple rule of expression, which will, whenever a case occurs for its application, accurately correspond with the then state of facts. The law will express in the present tense facts and conditions required to be concurrent with the operation of the legal action ...*

But still the imperative "shall" continues in UK legislation. Contrast this with the best in private drafting which has abandoned "shall" – for example:

(a) forms in Trevor Aldridge's *Practical Lease Precedents* (Longman)

(b) the Standard Conditions of Sale (first and second editions)

(c) the Rosscastle Letting Conditions in Murray Ross *Drafting and Negotiating Commercial Leases* 3rd edition (Butterworths)

(d) the Law Society's business leases.

We do not necessarily suggest that UK Acts use "must" for "shall" where "shall" is imposing an obligation as does New South Wales and several Canadian jurisdictions, but we do say:

(a) where Parliamentary Counsel feels the urge to use "shall", Counsel should consider whether or not it could be left out, or some other word or expression used; and

(b) the drafting must make clear what follows from a failure to do what an Act says "shall" (or "must", "will", "is to", or "has to") be done.

The objection to "shall" is not only that its use is now often used in an archaic way (though that would be enough to condemn it) but that the word is used for so many purposes that its effect is often unclear. A glance at the "shall" section in *Stroud's Judicial Dictionary* will confirm this.

Part 3   Structure and Format of Legislation

Development of the structure and format

Henry Thring is usually credited with developing the structure and layout of legislation. He first used a new format in the 1854 Merchant Shipping Bill which he was retained to draft. Thring continued to develop the numbering system used in statutes after the Office of the Parliamentary Counsel to the Treasury was

---

1   Even Lord Thring went on to say in Practical Legislation p 63, " An Act of Parliament should be deemed to be always speaking, and therefore the present or past tense should be adopted and "shall" should be used as an imperative only ..."

established in the United Kingdom in 1869. He was appointed the first Parliamentary Counsel.

Although Thring was the first to use a new format and numbering system, the idea of breaking up the text of Acts and legal documents had been promoted by Bentham over 50 years earlier. Bentham suggested[1]

> *Denominate, enumerate and tabulate principles. It facilitates reference, and thereby contributes to conciseness ...*
>
> *After the verb governing, interpose between it and the list of substantives governed, the words "as follows" with a punctum; – then give to each item a separate line, preceded by a numerical figure.*

Is there something better?

Our numbering system for statutes has served us well. But is there something better? – something that would work more conveniently with a computer? The Victorian Law Reform Commission of Australia thinks so. They suggest that a modification of the international standard for numbering (a decimal system) would

- reflect an international trend towards the adoption of decimal numbering systems
- help provide access to legislation in electronic form
- make data retrieval more convenient (brackets and letters would not be used)
- leave less room for ambiguity when retrieving a section
- make reading easier from a screen (numbers replacing letters).[2]

It is time for a thorough review of the way in which the page of the statute book is designed. The results would surely be worthwhile. What efficiencies and economies can be introduced? What changes would improve ease of reading and improve understanding? Is the typeface, line length, page colour, numbering system, margin line and margin note placement the best it can be? We need that research to be conducted not in isolation but in cooperation with other professionals who design texts to help readers.

If just one or two changes could be made to improve the design of the statute book think of the tremendous savings of time that could be achieved throughout the statute book on an ongoing basis. And those improvements could be used for statutory instruments, local government bylaws, company bylaws, collective agreements and club rules as well as other documents.[3]

---

1 Jeremy Bentham: Of Nomography, p 265.

2 Law Reform Commission of Victoria: Access to the Law, the structure and format of legislation (May 1990). But even so the Commission thinks letters are needed in some cases where Canadian jurisdictions would use ".1 or .2". The jury is out on the Commission's suggestion - but it is worth studying.

3 Say for example that comprehensive tests showed that readers were able to locate information a second faster if marginal notes were placed as true headings to sections - or that the placement of section numbers alongside section headings speeded section location - (or vice versa) think of the cost savings that could be achieved by everyone reading the statute book each time it is read.

Typography[1]
Another aspect to improving the readability of texts is by the use of typographical devices. With the range of typographic tools now available is there any reason why we should not use them much more in legislation? Why not emphasize critical provisions or those that might be misread, for example, by underlining or italicising or otherwise emphasising a word or phrase? Typographical devices are one more tool drafters can use.

The point we want to make here about numbering systems, page design and typographical devices is that drafters should at least be aware of them and have an open mind about their use. If new techniques, devices, or ideas will help communication, assist in aspects of computerization, help amendments, make consolidations easier, or help readers – then drafters should at least consider them.

Some observations on the 1991 statutes
We have already suggested that a drafting manual be adopted by the Parliamentary Counsel Office. Some of the following suggestions might be included in it.

In making the following suggestions we appreciate that a number of them have other ramifications. For example, one consideration Parliamentary Counsel apparently have in drafting Acts is to reduce the number of clauses so that the opportunity for debate in Parliament is reduced. The more clauses the more possibility for debate, the fewer clauses the less possibility. In our view, that approach to drafting should be disregarded. The number of clauses in a bill should be whatever number the drafter considers necessary to achieve the object with a view to making the legislation as understandable as possible. If a rule change is needed to make this happen then obviously we would urge a rule change. Many of the following suggestions are not new.

(a) Long title
We would eliminate them. They give legislation an unhealthy look and serve no useful purpose that cannot be achieved in other ways.

We appreciate that one purpose for long titles in the United Kingdom is to limit the amendments that can be introduced to a Bill. To eliminate long titles may require other rule changes. The point is that the rule about amendments to a Bill should not limit needed improvements to the legislative product. The rule should be designed to facilitate improvements in the product not impede them.

(b) Sentence length
Sentence length for legislation should be short. Where it is not possible to be short the clauses should be tabulated.

There is a division of opinion in legislative drafting circles on this point. Documents must be read in the context of the whole document. In most cases it can be assumed that one thought leads to another, and various techniques can be used to indicate that. The use of the long sentence without tabulation is not a technique that should continue. Having said this we must also say that we found no gross examples

---

1   J Hartley: Designing instructional text (2ed) (1985) Nichols Publishing.

of the long unbroken sections in the 1991 UK statutes – so perhaps the problem is no longer prevalent.

(c) Cross-references

Although we have pointed to some useful Canadian drafting practices cross-referencing in Canadian legislation is overdone and often unnecessary. Rarely are the cross-references helpful.

For the most part there is a different problem in the 1991 UK statutes. In an attempt to explain the cross-reference the text tends to give too much information. By the time the explanation about the cross-reference is absorbed, the sense of the text is lost. For example, in the *Statutory Sick Pay Act, 1991* (1991 c.3) section 1 reads:

> 1(1) In section 9 of the *Social Security and Housing Benefits Act 1982* (recovery by employers of amounts paid by way of statutory sick pay) in subsection (1)
>
> (a) in paragraph (a) (which requires regulations to make provision entitling an employer who has made a payment of statutory sick pay to recover the amount so paid by making deductions from his contributions payments) for the words "from payment" to "by making" there shall be substituted ...

In Canada, the actual amendment would be quite separate from the explanation. The equivalent amendment in Bill form in most Canadian jurisdictions would read:

> (1) The *Social Security and Housing Benefits Act 1982* is amended
>
> (a) in section 9(a), by striking out ... and substituting:
>
> NOTE: *Section 9(a) presently reads: ...*

The extract of the legislation would be included. An explanation of the amendment might then follow. When the Act is passed the explanatory notes are dropped from the printed Act.

While the UK approach appears to give more information at first sight it in fact gives less because it does not explain the *effect* of the amendment. More helpful would be an explanation of what the amendment does.

The other advantage to the Canadian approach is that amending Acts are, for the most part, purely a means of making a change to the principal Act. Once the amending Act is passed its job is done, it merges with the principal Act, it does not continue to have a life of its own (there are some exceptions to this but they are limited).

Several Canadian jurisdictions are working on computer systems to trigger automatic amendments to principal Acts once the amending Act comes into force – so having an up to date statement of the statute law available as soon as possible.

(d) Formulae

The 1991 UK Statute Book shows extensive use of formulae and Parliamentary Counsel should be congratulated.

(e) Archaic words

Needless to say, archaic words should be eliminated. On the whole we did not find this to be a major problem in modern UK statutes.

(f) Unnecessary words

In the 1991 UK Statute Book more words are used than are necessary.

For example, when an internal cross-reference is made in an Act it is usually followed by the word "above" or "below". But this is not consistent and we see no need for it. (This practice is better than saying "of this section" or "of this Act" after every section reference.)

The drafter of the *Registered Homes (Amendment) Act 1991* gave precise one word amending instructions, for example: "substitute", "add", "omit". Contrast that style with most of the other amending Acts in the 1991 statute book which say: "there shall be inserted", "there shall be substituted", "there shall be added", and so on. (See the *Crofter Forestry (Scotland) Act 1991* for example.)

To summarize – we think useful work could be done to standardize amending instructions – using the precise model of the *Registered Homes (Amendment) Act.*

As mentioned earlier the UK drafting style still clings to the outmoded "shall". For example:

(i) "This Act shall come into force on"
     (Why not this Act *comes* into force on ...?)

(ii) Paragraph (b) of subsection (2) above shall not apply where ... (s3 1991 c25)
     (Why not "Subsection (2)(b) does not apply when ...?) Yet earlier in the same section the following words were used: "This section *applies*" not *"shall* apply".

(iii) ... a person shall be entitled to the care component of a disability living allowance (s37ZB 1991 c21)
     (Why not "a person *is* entitled to the care component ..."?)

There are many other examples. Drafting in the present tense would not be a difficult change of drafting style to make but would improve the tone of the Acts considerably (as well as saving words!).

(g) Using examples

The United Kingdom has been the leader in using examples in legislation. The technique is not often used, but has been applauded by academics and the judiciary alike. More use could be made of them.

(h) Tone

A more conversational tone could be used in statutes.

For example:
     "A person who is under 18 years old"
instead of
     "a person who has not attained the age of 18 years".

(i) Definitions

Tend to be scattered all over the place, and difficult to follow and find.

(j) To summarize

Many of these suggestions may seem "picky", but combined they would lead to improvement in drafting.

The *real* test of course is to take a complete recent Act and try to redraft it in a plainer style *and* get the same legal effect in the rewrite. That would be a challenging project but probably the only way of proving what can be done. Unfortunately, time did not permit us to attempt that.

Computers and the drafter

No doubt the Commission will be familiar with what "the computer" can do to help drafters. But too many drafters either don't know, or worse, don't seem to care. Because the computer can be so helpful to legislative drafters in a variety of ways we touch on some of them here.

It goes without saying that the sooner legislation in all its forms is on a readily accessible database, and in its most up to date form, the better. We assume that the Parliamentary Counsel Office has computerized facilities which allows them to search the statute book to help with consequential amendments to other Acts, and to store and retrieve up-to-date versions of legislation.

The typical functions of a word processing system are well known: the capacity to move text around, to search and replace words and phrases, to spellcheck, to check the occurrence of words and of their use in defined senses, are all particularly helpful to legislative drafters.

But there are a number of facilities that are not as well known and not used as much as they might be in drafting. These include:

- automatic numbering and renumbering systems
- creation of tables of contents
- a program that will automatically mark all additions and deletions to a previous draft (extremely helpful for readers who just want to check the changes made from one draft to another)
- programmable programs which can be designed to automatically point out errors or inconsistencies, overlong sentences, overuse of the passive voice, and so on
- other editing functions.

Helping to design a precedent bank of questions and clauses

But a computer can do more than this. It can help drafters significantly improve the quality of their work.

(i) drafting the law

Not only must legislation be legally sound but possible alternative approaches, solutions or options to a given problem or issue need to be considered. The traditional precedent only gives a standard form answer – it does not exercise the mind. If the drafter does not think of an alternative a precedent will not help.

(ii) knowledge of the facts

Knowledge of the facts is based on asking the right questions. Again the traditional precedent does not help – it gives answers without necessarily knowing all the relevant facts.

(iii) integrating the law and the facts

The aim of drafting legislation is to achieve a client's purpose in the best way without unforseen consequences. Computer software programs are now available to help with the task. Computer programs can be developed to help draft the simplest to the most complicated legislation – but the program would take some time to develop.

(iv) the program

The program builds on what Parliamentary Counsel already have in a written questionnaire form (standard questions to ask) or what they have learned to ask clients through years of experience. Typically asked questions are redesigned and loaded into the computer program.

Any particular answer to a question will initiate a whole new series of questions. All the variations, options and alternatives Parliamentary Counsel would normally ask a client are put into the program. Each Counsel in the office would be asked to participate in the questions, variations, options and alternatives. The result is a very comprehensive program containing the collective knowledge and experience of the Office. It can, of course, be modified from time to time as necessary.

Because the questionnaire is computerized it can be structured in the form of a logic tree. This means the answers to certain questions automatically cause the system to move into specifically selected lines of other questions – questions that might not have been raised without the help of the computer. Alternatively, the computer will automatically eliminate other questions which are not relevant (a bit like the typical passport form which allows you to skip several questions if, for example, you are not married or have no children).

By this sophisticated branching system the Parliamentary Counsel is lead through all the questions necessary to get a detailed description of the law to be created. For many questions the computer provides a suggested answer – if the answer is accepted the return key is tapped – variations to the answer are also given if requested and problems highlighted.

The system can be seen as the collective wisdom of the Office in asking the questions to get the facts which can then be turned into clauses, reflecting the office drafting style.[1]

The advantages of this kind of program to lawyers in private practice are obvious. Even the most junior of lawyers has the benefit of the program when asking questions and thinking of the kinds of questions to ask. A similarly structured program to develop legislation seems to be equally advantageous. Parliamentary Counsel do not use precedents – certainly not in the same way or to the same extent as lawyers in private practice. The drafter is often left to his or her own devices. The dangers of the drafter not asking all the right questions, or of not thinking of all the options, are very real. With programs designed to ask the right questions the drafter has a helpful support system.

---

1   This description is based on a 11 November 1985 National Law Journal article called Help in drafting complex documents. The article described a program called "Workform" available at that time in the United States.

There are other programs similar to this on the market and some word processing systems allow this form of program to be developed. (See the Lawyer's PC, 1 October 1987 issue describing Wordperfect as a legal systems engine.) We do *not* know of any legislative drafting office that has experimented with this program. It is being used in some private law firms.

Over time it should be comparatively easy for the Parliamentary Counsel Office to pool its collective knowledge about the questions that should be commonly asked and the things that should be considered when designing particular pieces of legislation or elements of them.

Drafting precedents

Obviously computer programs that develop questions can also propose precedent clauses. Whether for law firms or Parliamentary Counsel Office standard clauses[1] can provide consistent style and quality. If a drafter proposes a variation to the standard, justification for the change could be required, or approval from a senior member of the office.

There seems to be a considerable opportunity to improve substance, style and consistency of legislation with this kind of project.[2] We suggest the Commission recommend it.

Part 4   Other Remarks

General

The best statutory drafting is now very good. See for example, the *Local Government Act, 1988* and the draft bill attached to the latest Law Commission report on land registration. Some legislative drafting is bad: see the notorious *Leasehold Reform Act, 1967*. Many problems remain with statutory amendments.

To the extent that they are not now the practice in the Parliamentary Counsel Office, Clarity endorses the recommendations of the Statute Law Society Memorandum of October, 1973 to the Renton Committee. Virtually all of those recommendations are part of normal practice in Canadian jurisdictions and have been the practice for many years.

Accessible statute law

The accessibility of statutes, that is, being able to get a copy of the law in its most up to date form, is obviously an integral part of having accessible and understandable law. This is not a new issue. In 1835, the Statute Law Commissioners said in their first Report,

The statutes have been framed extemporaneously, not part of a system, but to answer particular exigencies as they occurred.

The Statute Law Society made the same point in its memorandum to the Renton Committee in 1973. Although improvements have been made in recent years much more remains to be done. For example, a system of statute revision along Canadian

---

1   The great fear of precedent clauses is that once a precedent is established it stagnates. Parliamentary Counsel can avoid this by periodic review.

2   A project of this nature could be Commonwealth in scope – perhaps in one sense picking up on the suggestion made by Francis Bennion in 1980 in Statute Law (p24): "Standardization is an area where cooperation between Commonwealth countries would be fruitful. Model clauses on topics like strict liability or powers of entry could be drawn up in uniform terms applicable to any common law country."

lines should be considered in association with computerization of statutes and an automated amending system.

Vetting of drafting style

There have from time to time been suggestions that some form of vetting procedure be put in place to ensure consistency with other legislation and adequacy of drafting style. Some have suggested the House of Lords might perform that function, others that a special committee be established for vetting by experts. This proposal was made by Lord O'Hagan in 1877:

A department by which bills, after they have passed Committee, might be supervised and put into intelligible and working order, and then submitted for final revision to Parliament before they are passed into law.

The French have a system by which the Conseil d'Etat have oversight of style and this system of audit is supported by some.

The question of auditing bills has some intrinsic difficulties but in concept has some points to recommend it. This cannot replace the attempt at the earlier stages of drafting for clarity. An audit committee might be linked to the general concern about lack of proper consultation with those most effected by new law. Once again quoting the Statute Law Society,

We think it essential that ways are found whereby users can so far as possible be properly consulted:

(a) before a bill is drafted,

(b) when it is being drafted, and

(c) at all stages of its passage through Parliament.

That consultation and consideration could well include issues of clarity.

As Francis Bennion has said,

It is time for heads to go down and for close attention to be paid ... to statute law.

Earlier we suggested that a Committee of both Houses of Parliament might be involved in authenticating a drafting manual for guidance of Parliamentary Counsel Office. The same Committee might also be given oversight of Bills from a drafting perspective.

Other odds and ends

There are a multitude of other things that could be said; a new *Interpretation Act*; further support for recommendations of the Renton Committee that have not been implemented; support for Bennion's "Keeper of the Statute Book"; the uses of computerization of statutes; and so on.

The present statute law system has grown up to serve the legislators not the legislated. The whole movement for reform should be based on the principle that the legislative process should be concerned with the end product, and the ultimate users of it. While this may be over simplistic, we believe that goal must be kept in mind by reformers or else there will be a real danger of getting bogged down in apparently mind boggling, if not mindless, detail. Readers may note that we have not defined "plain English". We do not need to – we are confident that readers will give the term a purposive interpretation.

Last words

Parliamentary Counsel and other writers of law don't write for themselves; they write for others. The essence of writing law is communication.

There is no special language – grammar, syntax or composition for statutes.[1] The form of statutes over the centuries and in different countries attests to the correctness of that view. Each in their own way create law. Each in their own way must be interpreted by those who must administer them, the public affected by them, the parties bound by them, and by judges who must make decisions about them.

We can all improve our communication if we adopt the late Dr Elmer Driedger's philosophy which is valid for all legal writing,[2]

a writer of laws must have the freedom of an artist, freedom to use to the fullest extent everything that language permits, and (the writer) must not be shackled by artificial rules or forms; and further, laws should be written in modern language and not in ancient, archaic or obsolete terms or forms.

June 1992

M19   Commission for Racial Equality

The Commission for Racial Equality was established under the Race Relations Act 1976 with three statutory duties:

(a) to work towards the elimination of discrimination;

(b) to promote equality of opportunity, and good relations, between persons of different racial groups generally; and

(c) to keep under review the working of this Act and, when they are so required by the Secretary of State or otherwise think it necessary, draw up and submit to the Secretary of State proposals for amending it.

There are many legislative proposals which, while they do not refer specifically to race relations, nevertheless have implications for them. In some cases, like the Education Reform Act, we are consulted together with other interested groups, before the proposals are put forward in the form of a Bill. In others, like the Criminal Justice Act and the recent Asyium Bill, we are not, and if we think that the Bill should be amended in any way, either to avoid discriminatory effect or to enhance equal opportunity, we have to try to persuade the Government to make the necessary change or else operate like an outside pressure group, getting Committee members, for example, to put forward the required amendments.

There is a Government instruction that, before any Bill is put forward Parliament, it is subject to "equality proofing" by the originating Department in respect of both race and sex. To what extent this instruction is followed we do not know, but regardless of this we believe that it should be strengthened. In particular we recommend that in the case of all proposed legislation that could possibly have some

1   So wrote Dr. Elmer Driedger in "A Manual of Instructions for Legislative and Legal Writing", Canadian Government Publishing Centre, Ottawa.

2   Driedger's manual p4.

impact on equal opportunity and good race relations the Department concerned should be required to draw up and to convey to the CRE an equality proofing statement, and that the CRE should be given the opportunity to comment on this, before a Bill is presented to Parliament.

We appreciate that it will not always be easy for the Departments concerned to identify what may or may not have a significant impact on race relations. If they were required to send a report on every piece of proposed legislation, that would involve a lot of unnecessary work, both for the Departments and the Commission. On balance we believe that it would be best to leave this to the Departments' discretion, but that clear guidelines should be given about the way in which this discretion should be exercised.

More generally, we recommend that all major legislation, wherever possible, should be preceded by a process of public consultation before it is formulated in a Bill.

We are rarely consulted in advance on statutory instruments or Orders in Council, even where these have serious consequences for our work. This applies in particular to the area of immigration control.

14 January 1992

M20 Community Council for Somerset: Letter from the Director, Mr P W Lacey

I was a Chartered Accountant employed in practice until about 2 years ago when I moved into the Community Council. We are an independent Charity working for the people who live and work in rural areas. We meet regularly with Parish/Town Councils, Village Hall Committees etc.

I have followed a number of proposals from the initial political speech to the Act (and Regulations) and must report that I feel that substantial parts of the legislation could be published in draft form well in advance of the formal procedures in Parliament. Obviously some figures, limits etc would have to be left blank but the practitioners within this subject would be able to address the principles and the detail with more time at their disposal. This means that a better form of legislation should result. For instance:

a)   Finance Bill: So much of this annual exercise is gibberish to the average politician but is meat and drink to those working with such language every day. Publication of draft technical clauses in say, December, would lead to a better final Bill in April with fewer mistakes needing correction in the following year's Bill.

b)   Charities Bill: The present Bill is generally welcome but contains a few howling errors for those of us on the ground. As drafted it requires an "Auditor's Certificate" – a beast that disappeared long ago (now Auditor's Report). It also requires (as first published) every separate jumble sale to be separately registered with the local authority!

c) Poll Tax Legislation: So many regulations that Parliament could not keep pace. In the old rating system the Rating Authority collected a rate in the pound on all properties in an area which for the Parish/Town Council share was then placed in a Parochial Account. The precept of the Parish/Town Council (a lump sum rather than the product of the rate) was then paid out, leaving a balance which might be "over" or "under". These "overs" and "unders" remained at the end of the Rates: there is no legal power given to the Rating Authority to enable them to pay out any "over", nor to the Parish/Town Council to enable them to pay back any "under". I would have hoped that with more time the draft legislation would have been scrutinised well enough for this anomaly to have been spotted. Local government law is notorious for such errors.

Recently the Village Halls' Forum has been lobbying for change in VAT legislation to put UK Village Halls on the same footing as Continental Halls. This has followed the usual route of letters to the Minister and local MPs. We note that it takes up to 3 years for the point to be understood and sometimes accepted. A practice of publishing draft legislation early would leave MPs with less correspondence than at present and would enable them to concentrate on the policy matters that were really important rather than detail.

7 January 1992

M21 Community Council of Humberside: Letter from the Director, Ms Charlotte Hursey

Further to our correspondence at the beginning of the year, I hope the following comments are of interest to the enquiry. Similar comments have been submitted to the National Council for Voluntary Organisations.

First, as a generalist voluntary organisation it is extremely difficult to obtain or comment on all the aspects of legislation which impinge on CCH or its clients. We do not have the resources locally, not is it possible to discriminate from the mountain of material we receive from colleague organisations nationally. We look to bodies such as NCVO or Action with Communities in Rural England to provide us with intelligence, as we are probably one of the few local organisations which has a holistic view of the impact of legislation on communities, especially in the rural areas.

Second, there is a problem in obtaining the relevant documents. Even we cannot afford every Bill or Act, and we do not have easy access to large public or university libraries. Should we order them through a local bookseller, it can take many days for them to arrive, assuming they have not been sent for reprint. Most rural organisations will have this disadvantage.

Third, voluntary bodies often do not meet regularly enough to fit in with consultative timetables. This was the case with our own Committee and the impossibly short time scale for responses to the Department of Environment Consultation on the Local Government Commission.

Fourth, not all the relevant papers are properly publicised or circulated. Using the example above, the most important papers for us were the Consultation Papers and Guidance Notes. These had to be chased up, and even then only single copies made available. This was despite the fact that we provide the advisory service to parish councils in the county, who have a primary interest in the implications. We are not in a financial position to photocopy 250 copies and mail them first class, even though we feel they should have been sent.

Fifth, more papers could have a summary extract which is geared to the general public and is suitable for onward distribution or use in newsletters. This should contain clear information on the availability of further information and the contact person(s) concerned.

Sixth, the language used is virtually impossible to understand. A good example is the recent Charities Bill/Act. This was of primary concern to thousands of local groups and needed NCVO to act as an "interpreter", issuing its own summary documents. In addition, the Bill was inadequate on its own: reference also had to be made to previous Acts, which is itself prohibitive in terms of time, cost and energy.

Seventh, the impact of legislation on voluntary organisations is tremendous. Examples we could quote are the regulations affecting use of community buildings arising from the Food Act or Children Act. More effort should be made to consult on the implications at local level, using case studies, before decisions are taken which often go against the public interest. In the above example many groups are having to fundraise to meet new regulations, and facing possible closure if they do not. This could have a knock-on effect in other areas of social provision which legislators did not anticipate. Financial provision to help such groups meet new legislation should be considered.

31 July 1992

M22   Confederation of British Industry

The CBI represents a quarter of a million businesses. Its mission is to promote the international competitiveness of British business. Part of its role is therefore to help with the formulation of an appropriate legislative framework for economic success. We welcome the opportunity to contribute to the Commission's review of the process, in particular the three identified aspects:
i)   Consultation
ii)   Drafting
iii) Parliamentary scrutiny.
The CBI is able to address all three points from direct past and current experience. That experience encompasses a broad range of issues but paramount, on a regular basis, is the annual Finance Bill. As long ago as 1977, the CBI's Taxation Committee urged the Government to recognise the need for reform of the UK legislative procedure on fiscal matters.

A copy of the Report (E 244 81) of the Taxation Committee, entitled "A Technical Taxation Bill – the CBI's Proposals", has been passed to the Secretary of the Hansard Commission and the particularly relevant pages (2,3,16-20) covering proposed changes, which are still outstanding, are attached to this paper as Appendix A, together with extracts from pre-Budget memoranda since 1982.[1]

Whilst this Memorandum will mention other examples of the legislative process, the CBI's experience in the field of taxation offers a good opportunity to examine methods to improve the way the United Kingdom enacts its legislation.

An increasingly important feature of UK legislation is of course the European dimension, both the EC Regulations, which take direct effect in the UK without reference to Parliament, and the Directives, which mostly require Westminster legislation to give them effect – although these too can be put into effect without that action in certain cases. These elements need careful scrutiny.

Members of the Commission will be aware too of the concern about the volume of present day legislation: such quantity may well adversely affect quality: and the sheer task of assimilating it puts a burden on even the largest companies.

Although the three elements of the current review are closely interdependent, the points the CBI would like to make are organised under the separate headings.

1. Consultation

CBI representations have frequently emphasised the fundamental importance of consultation before legislation is introduced. In theory at least, this is recognised by both the executive and the legislature – not just as part of the democratic process, but in order to arrive at the most effective solutions, avoiding as far as possible bad law and expensive ambiguities. They will also reduce the time needed for consideration by Parliament (enabling it to dwell on substantive issues rather than technical points) and the courts' involvement in the subsequent interpretation of legislation.

It is clear that the level of consultation varies substantially, with the urgency – and sometimes the political sensitivity – of some legislation curtailing opportunities, but effective and timely consultation should be the norm.

For a representative organisation, such as the CBI, it is important that consultation periods should be as long as possible (and certainly not under two months for a major piece of new or complex legislation) to allow proper consultation of members.

Experience in the tax field suggests that consultation has become more widespread, though by no means universal. The role that it can play in such technically difficult areas of legislation is explained in our Appendix A and in two further papers – "Tax Law After Furniss v. Dawson", a report in 1988 by the Special Committee of Tax Law Consultative Bodies (of which the CBI is a member), and "Recommendations on the Enactment and Amendment of Tax Legislation", a further report in 1990 of The Special Committee. Copies of both have been supplied to the Commission's Secretary.

The desirability of early consultation in tax matters applies equally to European legislation, as we have made clear in our paper "Agenda Europe – Completing the Single Market".

---

1 Not published

On other fronts, we have been happy to note improvement in the lead times allowed in such areas as company and consumer law (under the Department of Trade and Industry), especially on EC Directives either under negotiation or being enacted into UK law. Particularly during the rush of 1992 Single Market legislation, the European Commission has sometimes not given enough time. Though it too has improved, by issuing Green Papers and early drafts of proposed Directives, especially on technically difficult and contentious issues such as intellectual property, performance is still patchy and the Commission has further to go.

The Commission's version of a White Paper – a Communication to the Council – does offer some prospect of consultation (referred to as "green edges") but in fact experience has shown that the central propositions are rarely changed materially.

Both the Commission and HMG are expected to produce compliance cost assessments of planned legislation which might affect business. These should be published as a matter of course. Whilst quantitative estimates are difficult in all cases, parties affected would find it useful to know factors impacting on costs. Indeed, proposers are helped by the requirement to think through the practical implications of their legislation. The EC draft Data Protection Directive, for instance, is deemed inoperable in its present form due to a failure to assess beforehand the implications for companies.

On a similar note, both Commission and Member Governments, when transposing Directives into national law, could usefully issue an assessment of enforcement (fiches d'application): an exchange between the Commission and Member States in Council would be salutary in ensuring that proposals were workable and that governments had thought through how they were to be policed.

CBI Members have long recognised the importance of practical advice to lawmakers from companies affected. As well as the channels through UK Departments of State, we therefore keep in touch with Community developments through UNICE (The Union des Confederations de l'Industrie et des Employeurs d'Europe) and Commission Directorates-General, with the help of a CBI office in Brussels.

Secondary legislation

Consultation should not of course be confined to primary legislation. Secondary legislation is of great concern to businesses as it often contains the detailed rules with which they have to comply. The CBI opposes the increasing use of legislating by means of Statutory Instruments. Inevitably the Statutory Instrument is debated less fully than if it were included in primary legislation and there is always the risk that it passes through the House unnoticed by those who would otherwise wish to be heard on it. Also the detail is not always available in advance. It is a fair question to ask how Parliament and other interested parties can properly evaluate a particular piece of proposed legislation if they do not have the total package of primary and secondary legislation available for consideration together. The CBI objected to the substantial use of Statutory Instruments under the Companies Act 1989. We consider that at the very least there should be full, detailed and measured consultation on Statutory Instruments. The extensive consultation on the TAURUS

Regulations is an illustration of the proper way to handle this type of legislative instrument.

2. Drafting

The implication of remarks already made about the value of pre-legislative consultation must be that drafting of legislation could indeed be improved. The material we have supplied on taxation matters makes the case abundantly clear. We observe that this very point was again recently referred to in the House of Lords Debate on the Taxation of Chargeable Gains Bill (see Appendix B[1]).

Some of the worst cases of Parliamentary log-jams and failures of scrutiny could be mitigated by the publication of draft versions before they are promulgated at First Reading. This is done in the case of technical legislation from time to time, when it is not contentious in a party political sense. It could be done more. The main constraint will be the sponsoring Department's time, when Ministers have set a tight timetable. The interplay between the officials of the Department who issue the drafting instructions and the Parliamentary draftsman can be a time-consuming process. But expert comment from practitioners on a draft Bill can save Parliamentary time, especially at Report Stage when technical points still often arise. Unclear legislation can also put a heavy cost on business, which may not be able to plan its affairs without an unnecessary element of risk, or have to consider a test case to inject greater certainty.

That laws are unintelligible to the layman is a well-worn theme. There would be greater clarity if the principles were stated first and there were less detail (in France the sponsoring Ministry drafts the legislation without the intermediary of a Parliamentary draftsman), but to change the UK system would run counter to a whole culture: a literal interpretation of statute law by the courts and an insistence by lawyers and laymen alike (seen, for instance, in CBI Committees) on certainty and detail which cater for every conceivable eventuality. Brave and learned men have pressed for plain English and statement of principle before detail in Bills, but is there any improvement?

Drafting skills are particularly strained when a Bill sets out to encompass a wide range of issues, perhaps demanding considerable detail and yet constrained by the Parliamentary timetable. There have been instances when, perhaps partly due to this and partly due to a wish for future flexibility (sometimes justifiable), the primary legislation has provided for the subsequent Regulations to lay down the detail or left considerable discretion to the responsible Minister. This device can be a serious impediment to business being able to identify the likely effect of the legislation before Parliament and also reduce Parliament's democratic control of the Executive.

One point which might be borne in mind as regards drafting is the difference in approach between Continental EC Member States and the UK.

It is also worth noting at this juncture the value of and need for consolidating legislation of which the Capital Gains Bill referred to above is but one example. Although it is not perhaps in the mainstream of the Commission's enquiry, the

---

1   not published

Commission will be aware that, largely because of the pressures of the Parliamentary timetable, Governments rarely update, reform or codify or even consolidate legislation with sufficient regularity.

The Law Commissioners, who do not have jurisdiction in tax matters, review the less politically contentious areas of law (often where judgements of the courts have accumulated to leave uncertainty and confusion), but their timetable is leisurely and there is no guarantee that their recommendations will be acted upon by Government, even when there is a wide consensus in favour among those directly affected. Recent examples of unwelcome delay (although stemming from the DTI) are in trademarks, where the UK Act goes back to 1936 and badly needs updating, and in restrictive trade practices where the Government consulted through Green and White Papers but has not in two years brought in the much needed Bill. The Law Commission proposals in 1986 for an overdue reform of the law relating to tenants' continuing liability for rents after assignment of the lease have not been implemented; the problem has now been exacerbated by the recession.

Another example would be insolvency law. The Cork Committee took four years to review a patchwork quilt of legislation, some of which dated back a hundred years or more, and the Government then enacted reform that only took on board the more important recommendations. If it becomes apparent from the experience of this recession that the law needs further reform, a large head of steam will have to be developed to find time within the next Parliament.

Equally, from time to time a particular area of law which has been amended frequently needs consolidation (codifying would be better, but that is a more radical and time-consuming step) to enable practitioners and lay users to find all the legislation in one place and presented in a coherent fashion. The Companies Act 1985 is a good but rare example of what could be done more widely. The DTI initiated the exercise which took a year of the time of a retired Parliamentary draftsman. The 1985 Act has been overtaken by a 1989 amending one. We need another consolidating measure. The Law Society's suggestion last year of a separate Company Law Commission to consider and develop proposals for amending company law has merit.

It sometimes happens that Departments are well aware of the need for reform but hold back, because they know that the European Commission has it in mind to introduce proposals in the same area. The Commission may be tardy and thus compound the UK's own delays. Sometimes it is better for the UK to go ahead and risk having to change the law twice in a brief period.

Perhaps Departments should formally be charged with reviewing areas of law for which they are responsible and the Law Commission should be the place where the project is carried out. There is no reason why additional qualified people should not be brought in to do the job and, if need be, the Law Commission, together with the Department covered, could set up a committee of the learned and interested to advise and report. As it is, a variety of means is used, the process is ad hoc, and there is no assignment of continuing responsibility.

It would clearly help if the convention could be developed that each Administration would set aside time for the non-contentious (in a party political sense) reform of areas of law in the life of a Parliament. Perhaps that should be initiated by the Lord Chancellor, taking the advice of the Law Commission. It is inevitable that professional bodies would play a key role in presenting the case for change, but lay people could become engaged if the process were formal and known.

3. Parliamentary Scrutiny of Legislation

In the context of Parliamentary scrutiny, it is worth mentioning that CBI Members and staff are in touch with MPs and Peers on a wide range of business issues and general information by correspondence (including briefs) and personal contact. The latter includes exchanges with specialist committees and CBI members' direct links with their constituency MPs. It is believed that this flow of exchange and information is of some help to Parliamentarians' understanding of business concerns, especially to those who have no personal business experience, and therefore to the appreciation during scrutiny of how legislation might affect business.

In the tax field the question of Parliamentary scrutiny was fully explored in the papers to which we have referred. It may be that Members of Parliament themselves would wish to have better descriptive briefs on the legislation before them and there seems to be no good reason why such material should not be available to the public at large. The quality of scrutiny would be enhanced by special standing committees, able to take evidence in the same way as Select Committees.

The ability to table amendments to legislation in Committee is a useful and important aspect of Parliamentary scrutiny and control. However, given the adversarial nature of the British political scene, legislation is improved less by this means than by proper early consultation, especially when Government enjoys a large majority. For this reason, too, the work of the House of Lords has assumed greater importance in non-financial legislation.

A particular weakness in the Parliamentary system, again noted in the "Furniss v. Dawson" booklet chapter on reforms, is in the lack of Parliamentary control over secondary legislation (as mentioned earlier). This category of legislation should always be subject to appropriate consultation and committee scrutiny in detail.

Scrutiny of European legislation is not sufficient, especially the "fine points". The House of Lords European Communities Committee and its sub-committees perform a valuable role in the scrutiny of European legislation, since they look at Directives while they are still in draft form. They often question Commission officials responsible for them, testing the need for the legislation and assessing its compatibility with existing UK legislation. The Lords are thus a preparing, as well as a revising, Chamber. As EC integration proceeds, the importance of full and timely consideration of draft EC legislation will increase. Now is a good time to review the present procedures in both Houses to ensure they are as effective as all concerned would wish.

Private Members' Bills

We consider that the procedure for Private Members' Bills is a useful and often effective one. For example, the Computer Misuse Act was a much needed measure brought in by a Private Member. Waste of Parliamentary time can arise however if such measures are not successful. One example of this was the Consumer Guarantees Bill, which was widely supported by back benchers from both sides of the House, and proceeded through detailed consideration in Committee to Third Reading – at which stage it was defeated on a technicality. It could be argued that, if the Bill was defective, the technicality should have been brought out at a much earlier stage and we think this illustrates a weakness in the way in which Private Members' Bills are handled.

Private Bills
As the whole area of planning legislation and regulation is the subject of CBI Task Force work at the moment, no comments are made at this stage.

Summary
Business is concerned that it may operate in the best legal framework. To achieve this, a proper partnership is required to balance the experience of parties affected, knowledge of experts in the particular field and the objectives of lawmakers. The growing extra dimension of European Community law has to be recognised. The key to this partnership is communication, with the objectives clearly set out and a thorough consultation as early as possible in the legislative process. The more thorough the consultation the better the drafting that results, the less Parliamentary time wasted and the better the law enacted.

Parliamentary scrutiny would also be more effective as the issues and concerns would be better known. The use of special standing committees, taking evidence, would enhance this, notably in the field of taxation.

Mention has also been made of the need for more consolidating legislation, to simplify and to update laws that have become complex through quantity or confusing judgments.

February 1992

M23 Consumers' Association

Consumers' Association welcomes the opportunity to make a submission to the Hansard Society's Commission on the Legislative Process. We have an interest in all aspects of legislation, but have decided to focus on the issue of consultation since this is an area in which we have extensive and direct experience.

1 The Role of Consultation in the Legislative Process
1.1 **Consultation** is crucial to the modern legislative process. The bulk, complexity and technicality of modern legislation necessitates additional specialised consultations of experts and groups closely interested or affected by each proposed measure. It is through this process that organisations such as ourselves, who represent the consumer interest, are given a say in the shaping of legislation. Extensive consultation is taking place at any given time and we are currently preparing responses to thirty consultative documents. Potentially, consultation should perform several valuable functions.

1.2 **Improve the efficacy of legislation** First, and most obviously, consultation should enhance the efficacy of statute law. It enables Government, at a relatively small cost, to confirm in each case whether legislation is the right approach to adopt, whether the proposed measure is technically adequate for its purposes, and to ensure that it will not have unforeseen and unacceptable side-effects.

1.3 **Lightening Parliament's load** Secondly, by ironing out technical problems in Bills and draft Orders, consultation should ease the passage of legislation through Parliament. It should enable MPs and peers to concentrate on the underlying merits of legislation, and, in considering matters of technical detail in Committee, to function as a final "court of appeal", rather than as a court of first instance. It also allows them to have a clear picture of how it will affect different interest groups.

1.4 **Implementing the principles of "Open Government"** Thirdly, it is consistent with the ideas of open government and freedom of information that the government consult all interested parties. Consultees need to be able to see the arguments put forward by other bodies and the Government should explain why they have decided to take a particular course of action.

1.5 **Identifying the views of all interested parties** Finally, consultation is indispensable as a method of establishing the viewpoints of all competing interests and pressure groups. If there is not full and fair consultation there is a danger that those preparing legislation will only hear the views of those organisations which are in the best position to lobby; namely the richer and more powerful organisations.

2 Shortcomings in Current Consultation Practice

2.1 The current consultation process is, in our experience, characterised by diversity. It can occur once only, or several times before the legislation is finally put before Parliament, or not at all. It can vary from a request for general ideas and information on which a Bill or Order might be based, to one asking for detailed consideration of fully-formed proposals. It may have all the formality of a Green or White Paper presented to Parliament, or may consist of a few "soundings" conducted over the telephone. It can be a genuine request for help, or merely an attempt to legitimise proposals that the Government has already made up its mind to pass into law.

2.2 Our experience suggests that much of the variation in the practice of consultation is not simply due to the diversity of legislation itself, but by the absence of a coherent policy regarding the role consultation should play in the legislative process. Although we are aware that there are Civil Service guidelines laid down for the consultation process, it is not apparent that these are followed in practice. There are inconsistencies in approach between, and even within, Government departments and agencies and other statutory bodies. This results in a mixture of good and bad consultation practice, and, more fundamentally, in a distortion of the whole consultation process.

2.3 Overt failure to consult

2.3.1 In our experience, this is rare and occurs mainly where proposals are strongly party-political. Whilst it is understandable that Government is unwilling to consult on *whether* to implement manifesto commitments, there is a need for consulting on *how* such measures can best be achieved. It would seem, however, that Departments are sometimes unwilling to consult on such measures at all.

2.3.2 Examples of this were the Community Charge legislation and the National Health Service reforms. The principle of these reforms had been determined in advance by the Government's party line and both proceeded immediately to a White Paper without any attempt to seek the views of those most affected. The principle of these reforms had been determined in advance by the Government's party line. Some interested parties made comments nevertheless, but the resulting legislation afforded little evidence these comments had had any effect. The question of how these reforms should have been implemented – for example whether there should have been pilot schemes – should have been a subject for consultation. There is no justification for refusing to consult *at all* on the grounds that proposals contain some party political elements and the Government wishes to circumvent awkward pressure groups completely.

2.3.3 Similarly, in our view, the preparation of the Budget is subject to a quite unnecessary degree of secrecy. Relatively few tax and public expenditure proposals are market-sensitive, and these could be dealt with separately. The ill-effects of failure to consult on tax issues was illustrated by the fate of the attempted withdrawal of exemption from capital taxes liability in connection with post-death variations of wills. The withdrawal was itself withdrawn after strenuous representations from organisations representing those affected. Had they been consulted in advance, this confusing and wasteful demarche could have been avoided.

2.4 Covert failure to consult

2.4.1 Government and other public agencies sometimes go through the motions of consultation but pay no attention to the results. This is difficult to prove, but our experience, that of other organisations with which we are in touch and an obvious lack of changes of any kind to certain proposals consulted upon, leaves us in no doubt that it is correct. This assertion is supported by academic research which found civil servants "quite prepared to identify cases of 'sham consultation' where the policy was not really amenable to change"[1].

2.4.2 A recent example was the proposed extension to Compulsory Competitive Tendering contained in the Local Government Act 1992. We received the consultation document at the same time the Bill was being debated in the House of Lords and it was passed by the Lords before the end of the consultation period. Not only does this make it difficult for consultees to respond, as the proposals on which comments are based are at the risk of constantly being amended, but it also undermines confidence that responses to the document will

---

1   Jordan and Richardson *Government and Pressure Groups in Britain* (OUP 1987), pp 154f.

be given proper consideration. It suggests that the consultation is being undertaken mainly or wholly as a matter of mere routine.

2.5 Lack of transparency

2.5.1 Lack of information can also suggest that the consultation process is simply spurious and we consider there should be more feedback on the process from Government departments. Clearly freedom of information legislation would resolve this problem, but we think some steps could be taken now to improve the openness of the consultation process. It is increasingly common for Government departments to seek the consultees' permission for publication of their comments. MAFF in particular have started doing this. Responses are not necessarily published, but are available on request from departmental libraries. We consider that this should be extended so that responses to *all* consultations should have to be made public. The only grounds for confidentiality should be limited to those areas involving commercial secrets, personal privacy, defence/security and interference with law enforcement.

2.5.2 There is often no "feedback" indicating the reasons why consultees' comments have or have not affected the legislative outcome. This, together with the lack of information on the comments of others, leaves consultees uncertain as to the effect and value of their participation in the consultation process. It also deprives them of the guidance they need to shape and direct their future responses in order to be more effective. This feedback should occur before the final conclusion of the consultation process, since the object of consultation would be lost if draft legislation is based on proposals which differ substantially from those that were the subject of the original consultation. Government obviously cannot consult repeatedly but it could provide consultees with at least one summary of what submissions have been received and how proposals have been reshaped in response to them. This could also deter "sham" consultations.

2.5.3 One current example of good practice is the feedback we are receiving from the Home Office on the progress of the EC Directive on Data Protection. In January 1992 we received a letter from them in order to "keep you in touch with the progress of negotiations on the draft Data Protection Directive". The letter clearly set out the results of recent meetings, the issues discussed and the areas of agreement and disagreement between Member States. We consider that this could be standard for all departments dealing with similar issues.

2.5.4 The form of consultation is also important. Whilst we appreciate that some issues are complex, it is helpful if the documents are clear, concise and easy to read. It is also useful if the document highlights the specific questions that it wishes consultees to address. Two recent examples where this applied were the Motorway Service Area Deregulation proposals from the Department of Transport and the Changes to the State Pension Age from the Department of Social Security. The latter is a good example of how a relatively complex subject area can be produced in a simple, lucid way. We were also impressed by the Department of Health's "The Health of the Nation". This consultation document clearly explained the Government's objectives and the strategies proposed for meeting them. Consultees were given a series of specific questions to address. Also very useful was a summary of the proposals produced as a separate document.

2.5.5 It is possible for Government departments to provide simple guidelines to Parliamentary Bills. This is already done on the day a Bill is first scheduled to be discussed in Parliament. The Government publishes a Press Release which gives the background, aims and objectives of the Bill and also provides a brief, comprehensive explanation clause by clause or section by section. Some departments also do this when they are consulting on EC Directives. It would be of assistance if Government could also do this for all consultations on draft Directives, Regulations and Bills.

2.6 Consultation too late in the day

2.6.1 If consultation takes place, as it sometimes does, only towards the end of the preparation of legislation, the scope for implementing consultees' suggestions is inevitably much diminished. Consultation on legislative proposals that are more or less fully-formed may result in improvements to details and consequently assist their passage through Parliament without damaging amendments. Yet it is often more important to have full consultation before drafting so that comment may be made on the general principles and objectives of the legislation.

2.6.2 One good example where these issues were addressed was the consultation on Orders made last year under the Estate Agents Act 1979. General reviews of estate agency and the the working of the 1979 Act were undertaken by the OFT in 1988 and the DTI in 1989. In September 1989, the OFT issued a consultation document reporting in March 1990. The draft Orders were based on this report and were circulated twice more for consultation in June 1990 and March 1991 before being laid.

2.6.3 The point also needs to be made that consultation should not be terminated too early, just as it should not be begun too late. Our experience does not suggest this is a common problem, but where it happens, potential objections to the detail of legislation (particularly details which arise from changes to proposals made in response to the early consultation) cannot be raised. It places an unnecessary burden on Parliament, and imperils the drafting of legislation. It is highly undesirable that complex legislation should be, as for instance in the case of the Companies Act 1989, the subject of heavy amendment during its passage through Parliament.

2.7 Too little time for consultation

2.7.1 Associated with the problems arising from lateness of consultation are the difficulties which arise if there are short deadlines. Our experience suggests there can be a lack of sensible regard for consultees in the setting of deadlines. Most of the 100 government and quasi-governmental[1] documents sent to us in the first five months of 1991 set a deadline for replies. In about 10% of cases this was within three weeks or less (in four cases a week or less) of the date the

---

1 Including consultations by executive agencies and statutory regulatory authorities. Strictures upon Whitehall generally do not necessarily apply to all of these, as, indeed, they do not apply to all consultations carried out by all government departments.

document was received. A further 20% of documents had a four week deadline. The full range varied from under a week to over eight months.

2.7.2 Many consultation documents are highly technical, and an adequate written response to consultation often requires research. A significant amount of work must therefore be undertaken by one or more person with a relevant specialism. Their work schedule may not be readily alterable at short notice. In our case all draft responses are circulated to senior and other relevant members of staff and amended in the light of their comments. The final draft has to be carefully checked for accuracy before the response is completed. In our experience, 6 weeks is a reasonable time to allow for responses to be made. Smaller and less well resourced organisations may have even less flexibility and need an even longer period.

2.7.3 Longer deadlines or prior notification of consultations would enable us to undertake research necessary to support our responses. The Lord Chancellor's Department allowed a 3 month consultation period for its proposals on Commonhold (admittedly a complex area). This gave us sufficient time to Commission research and surveys which improved the quality of our response.

2.8 Unbalanced consultation

2.8.1 Certain major "producer" interests have close relationships with "their" government Departments (for example, airlines and the Department of Transport). On issues that affect them they are closely involved at all stages of the legislative process and are likely to be informally consulted prior to any formal consultation. Other groups and interests, including consumer representatives, tend to be brought into the process at a much later stage and usually in the general trawl of "all interested parties". This often takes place once most of the policy has been all but finalised and any effect is likely to be minimal.

2.8.2 The situation is exacerbated in the European legislative process. Major "producers" have the ability to influence the formulation of EC proposals since they can afford to have representatives in Brussels. The national government encourages such involvement to protect British interests. Due to the costs involved, representation of the consumer interest is comparatively weak, and, in some cases is not even invited.

2.8.3 The Directive on food packaging regulations was one example of this. A framework Directive was agreed in 1986 without any input being sought from Consumers' Association. Although we are now being consulted on the implementation of the Directive, it is too late to alter the general policy lines. The issues require considerable expertise and it is doubtful if the cost of mastering the subject can now be justified given the limited chance to influence the basic proposals. The Directive on food additives is another case in point. The DTI has expressed its disappointment to us that consumer representatives were given no chance to participate in the preliminary discussions leading to policy formulation by DG III, although the food industry was represented at most meetings.

2.8.4 This may not be a general conspiracy to privilege some interest groups at the expense of others, but it does show a lack of understanding on the part of Government (EC and UK) of the need to compensate for the ability of some groups to advance their interests more effectively than others. There is usually no recognition in the consultation process of the dangers of bias created by inequality of resources and access to influence. This defeats one of the main objects of consultation, which is to give Government a clear and undistorted picture of the considerations which need to be taken into account.

2.9 Unrepresentative advisory bodies

2.9.1 Inadequate consultation can also result from unbalanced representation on advisory bodies. These have in recent years come to play an influential role in the early stages of the legislative process. They often exist specifically to be consulted by government on specialised policy matters. They not only comment on legislative proposals, but can initiate them, and are thus involved in the very early stages of the legislative process. Again, there is a tendency for the "producer" interests to be over-represented and consumer groups to be in a correspondingly weak position. This is often the case even where members of the committee are there in an individual rather than a representative capacity. For example, in 1989, financial interests with the pharmaceutical industry were declared by 18 of the 21 members of the Committee for the Safety of Medicines, 16 of the 24 members of the Medicines Commission, 12 of the 18 members of the Veterinary Products Committee and 12 of the 17 members of the Committee on the Review of Medicines[1]. Not one of these committees has representatives from consumer organisations.

2.9.2 In order to compete on equal terms with producer interests on committees advising on highly technical subjects, consumer representation could also be strengthened by having experts who are clearly charged with representing the consumer interest. Some Government departments MAFF for example invite consumer organisations to make nominations. However, there is often a difficulty for consumer groups in finding experts who are independent of producer interests in addition to the money needed to pay for their time and expenses.

2.9.3 This problem also exists in Europe, exacerbated by the difficulty non-producer organisations face in meeting the high cost of playing a role in Brussels. More funding is needed via the Consumer Protection Service for consumer representation. The influence of consumers in Europe is further undermined by a historical tendency to regard the trade union and co-operative movement as representatives of the consumer interest – the Consumers Consultative Committee includes such representatives despite the fact that they have vested interests which will often conflict with those of consumers.

---

1 See Campaign for Freedom of Information's *Secrets* No 22, article on conflicts of interests on
 Advisory Committees.

3 Conclusion

3.1 General approach

3.1.1 We consider improvements are possible by the standardisation and promotion of good practice rather than a need to introduce radical changes. We would not recommend the introduction of a rigid multi-staged consultation procedure to be used in all cases. Given the diversity of legislation and its preparation, there is a need for flexibility in the practice of consultation. However, variations should not be accidental but related to the desired outcome. We suggest the exercise of discretion as to when and how to consult should be subject to carefully considered guidelines, and the whole process of the preparation of legislation made more open to public scrutiny so that compliance with such guidelines can be monitored.

3.1.2 The Commission may care to consider which body could be given the task of drawing up consultation guidelines, how they should be implemented and how their effectiveness should be monitored. We consider that these guidelines should apply to *all* regulatory bodies established by statute as well as to Government departments. They should encompass all National and European legislation, including non market-sensitive tax legislation.

Below we put forward some of our own ideas as to what guidelines for consulting bodies should cover:

3.2 Consultation guidelines

3.2.1 **Two-stage consultation**. Consultation should not be restricted either to a preliminary "policy search" where "the Government has no very clear idea" as to what to do, or to a final "insurance policy" check on the acceptability of a fully-developed proposals[1]. As a general rule, where a measure is being prepared ab initio it should normally take place in at least two stages, broadly corresponding to the preliminary and final stages of preparation. A model for this framework two-stage consultation process can be found in the practice of successively publishing Green and White Papers, or (in the case of regulations) policy papers followed by draft Orders.

3.2.2 **The rough draft stage**. The first part of such a two-stage consultation should ideally take place as soon as those preparing legislation have developed ideas which can be put into the form of "rough draft" proposals, but before they have actually made up their minds. If there is to be a preliminary "policy search", asking for suggestions, it should not replace this first stage of consultation.

3.2.3 **The final draft stage**. The second-stage consultation document should be as close to a "final draft" as possible, to ensure that detailed points and drafting considerations can be dealt with. We do not consider that draft Bills themselves should normally be exposed for consultation – not because such a practice would breach Parliamentary custom but rather because too many consultees are legally unqualified and might find difficulty in interpreting draft Bills. The objective of ensuring that the details of a Bill are subject to expert scrutiny

---

1   These terms are borrowed from Jordan and Richardson's *Government and Pressure Groups*, p 143.

could generally be achieved by consulting on a detailed account of its proposed contents, based on draft instructions to Parliamentary Counsel. (It is, of course, common practice to consult on draft Orders, but these are generally less complex than Bills).

3.2.4 **Draft Bills**. Possibly consultation should take place on draft Bills when they embody mainly "lawyers' law" – for example company law, insolvency, property law etc – where most consultees are lawyers and the details of drafting are of critical importance. The Commonhold consultation paper in November 1990 (CM 1345) usefully included a draft Bill. However, we recognise that pressure on the drafting resources available to Government must limit the usefulness of a practice that will necessarily entail draft Bills being returned to Parliamentary Counsel for redrafting.

3.2.5 **Feedback**. It is important that a document is circulated after the consultation period has ended. It should give an account of the responses received, indicate the points at which suggestions have been adopted and give adequate reasons for the rejection of other comments, [particularly when the same views have been expressed by a number of consultees.] This would provide the "feedback" that is usually missing from the present consultation process. In addition all responses should be made publicly available.

3.2.6 **Notification of consultation**. Wherever possible, prior notification and an indication of the scope of the consultation should be given to those who are likely to wish to comment. When the documents are circulated, consultees should be given an adequate response time. Time must be suffient for all consultees, not merely those with plentiful research resources.

3.2.7 **Balanced consultation**. *All* potentially interested parties should be given the opportunity to comment on proposed legislation at both stages of preparation. In addition all those consulted should be given a list of the other parties that are being asked.

3.2.8 **Advisory committees**. Where consultation takes place through an advisory committee, every effort must be made to ensure that the membership has a balanced representation of interests. Potentially interested parties should be made aware of the existence and membership of such committees, and if excluded should be able to raise this with the Government department concerned. Where it is not possible for full and fair representation to be achieved, for instance because the spread of interests is too wide, the advisory committee itself should engage in a consultation exercise before making its recommendations.

3.2.9 **Informal consultations**. Where informal consultation takes place in private meetings this should not normally be a substitute for any stage of the consultation process, since such meetings will obviously not be capable of providing a balanced picture of views on proposed legislation. The incidence and effect of such meetings should be reported in the account of responses received as outlined in 5.2.5.

3.2.10 **Programmes of legislative work**. All Government departments, executive agencies, and publicly-funded bodies involved in the process of recommending and preparing legislation or statute-based regulations should (as some already do) publish programmes of their intended legislative work in advance of undertaking it. MAFF has recently done this by publishing (albeit late in the year) its 1992 programme for safety and consumer protection. These should:-
  (i) give a brief account of the area of policy under consideration, and the likely scope of legislation, to alert potentially interested parties;
  (ii) name a contact and give a telephone number and address to enable interested parties to request that they be consulted;
  (iii) include timetables indicating the approximate dates at which consultation exercises will be carried out, to provide additional advance notification.
Work programmes with at least some of these characteristics are already produced by, for instance, the Law Commission and the Accounting Standards Board. In the case of government departments, a main bulletin would presumably be published at the time of the Queens' Speech, with regular updates.

3.2.11 **Publication of lists of consultees**. The lists of organisations and individuals to be consulted on particular subjects that are maintained by consulting Departments and other organisations should be open to public scrutiny, so that potential interested parties can check whether they are included or not.

3.2.12 **Advisory committees**. The details of advisory committees, including the names of their members and the organisations they represent (if any), should similarly be made easily accessible to public scrutiny, so that those not represented can make the case for their inclusion. Members should declare any connection they have with an interest group affected by the proposals if they are not explicitly acting as its representative.

March 1992

M24 English Heritage: Letter from Mr Michael Brainsby, Director of Legal Services

1. The pressure on Parliamentary time caused by the growth in the quantity of legislation and, possibly, the increasing politicisation of legislation, means that, in my view, more and more primary and secondary legislation is hurried and consequently insufficiently considered.

2. The recent Local Government Finance Bill is a good example, where, because of the necessity to complete the legislative process before the end of this Parliament, it has been necessary to impose a guillotine. Experience of the community charge legislation suggests that the lack of opportunity for detailed consideration will almost certainly lead to anomalies and errors in the eventual Act, which will have to be ironed out later.

3. The pressure to hurry legislation through also leads to lack of clarity. Whatever the purpose of particular legislation may be, the clarity of drafting should be

given the highest priority. If anything, recent examples tend to suggest that the trend is the other way. The new Education (Schools) Bill contains some extraordinarily vague terminology, for instance "where the Secretary of State determines that there are special circumstances which make it right".

4. Whilst on the subject of clarity, I would also mention the problem of negative drafting in secondary legislation. It has become common practice nowadays for Ministers to take powers in primary legislation which they can exempt by statutory instrument or direction. An example is section 15(1) of the Listed Buildings Act 1990:-

    The Secretary of State may direct that in the case of such descriptions of aplications for listed building consent as he may specify, sections 13 and 14 shall not apply.

    This can lead to some very complicated negative drafting in the secondary legislation, for example in the direction contained in paragraph 86 of Circular 8/87 made under what is now section 15(1) of the 1990 Act. This direction contains a triple negative which has to be applied in order to decide whether the Secretary of State must be notified of an application.

5. Another consequence of haste is that too little thought is given to implementation after enactment. Nowadays, legislation is usually brought into effect in bits over a period of time by various commencement orders. This makes it difficult to be certain whether a particular provision is in force or not and one must check each time.

6. Often, too, the follow-up guidance is slow to appear. We are still awaiting the revised version of Circular 8/87, some 18 months after the consolidated 1990 Listed Buildings Act was enacted. This is important because the Circular contains statutory directions and procedural guidance which is now out of date so far as the enabling legislation is concerned. It will eventually appear as a new PPG but not, I suspect, until nearly two years after the legislation was passed.

7. In the above comments I have concentrated on drafting and implementation. So far as consultation is concerned I do not think we have any particular difficulty here. English Heritage is generally consulted fairly well on legislation which concerns us and I do not think we therefore have anything to say about the consultative process.

9. One final, more general point is that there are often resource difficulties in using legislation to the intended effect. While recognising that this may not be within the remit of your Commission, it is worth pointing out that hard-pressed public bodies often find it hard to make good use of even the best drafted legislation where there are costs involved. Perhaps more thought should be given, even before drafting, to the difficulties and cost implications of conscientious implementation.

10 December 1991

M25   Equal Opportunities Commission

The Equal Opportunities Commission is pleased to comment on the process by which legislation is made in England and Wales (including the application of EC legislation).

By s.53 of the Sex Discrimination Act 1975 the EOC has the statutory duties of working towards the elimination of sex discrimination, promoting equality of opportunity between men and women generally and monitoring the Sex Discrimination Act 1975 and the Equal Pay Act 1970. Both the 1975 and 1970 Acts have been extensively modified and overlayed by EC legislation.

The EOC is concerned with the operation of legislation which affects fundamental rights of individual men and women. At the present time legal aid is not available for representation at industrial tribunals to which the majority of complaints of unlawful sex discrimination and equal pay proceed. Whilst the EOC has the power to assist individuals in relation to proceedings where special grounds exist, the operation of its power is inevitably constrained by financial considerations and the need to be strategic.

The legislation with which the EOC is principally concerned contains difficult concepts such as indirect discrimination, and as regards the Equal Pay Act the notion of equal pay for work of equal value. The latter concept was grafted on the Equal Pay Act following the judgment of the European Court as a result of Article 169 proceedings brought by the European Commission against the United Kingdom (Commission of the European Communities v. United Kingdom of Great Britain and Northern Ireland (1984) IRLR 29).

The equal value and accompanying procedural regulations were described by Lord Denning during the House of Lords debate on them as "beyond compare". He said that "no ordinary lawyer would be able to understand them", and that "the industrial tribunal would have the greatest of difficulty and the Court of Appeal would probably be divided in opinion".

In the circumstances the EOC believes that consideration should be given to involving strictly lay groups in addition to others in the scrutiny of draft legislation. If the final form of the legislation is such that individuals cannot even form a basic understanding of the scope of legislation which affects their fundamental rights and which they are expected to utilise unaided, then the whole legislative process has been in vain.

Apart from the identity of those who might be consulted there is also the issue of timing. Consultation usually takes place once a Bill or Instrument has been drafted by which time Government will generally have committed itself to the main provisions, leaving scope for fine adjustments only. In appropriate cases we feel that consultation prior to the drafting of a Bill or Instrument would be advantageous.

A particular feature of equal treatment legislation is the operation of "equality proofing" whereby Government departments scrutinise proposed legislation to identify whether it is likely to result in discrimination between men and women. Equality proofing is a step from which the EOC is excluded notwithstanding its statutory duties and its extensive experience and expertise built up over some fifteen years. It seems unfortunate and inefficient for Government Departments not to take advantage of the EOC's availability and willingness to contribute in this area which could assist them to head off possible future difficulties for citizen and Government alike.

14 January 1992

M26 General Council of the Bar Law: Working Party of Law Reform Committee

Access to the law
Report of Working Party (Chairman James Goudie Q.C. with Mr. Registrar Adams and William Blackburne Q.C.) Approved by Law Reform Committee 21st May 1991.

Introduction
The inaccessibility of statutory law to the public at large and even to legal practitioners, especially legal practitioners outside major urban centres, has increased, is increasing and ought to be diminished.
Statutory law is inaccessible in two major respects.
First, it is hard to find.
Second, once found, it is hard to understand.

Hard to Find
A combination of factors make statutory law (which is increasingly bulky and prolix) hard to find to a scandalous extent. These include the following:-
1. A major new statute may have been enacted but be unavailable for some weeks thereafter at HMSO. Example: the Local Government and Housing Act 1989. Meanwhile one has to make do with the Bill. The latest print will not, however, include the latest amendments; and clause numbers and section numbers will not correspond.
2. No sooner has a statute been enacted than it may be subject to massive amendment, as in the case of the Criminal Justice Act 1987 by the Criminal Justice Act 1988. The former is then misleading without the latter; and the latter is incomprehensible without the former.
3. Even when legislation is consolidated this may then be subject to immediate change. Example: the consolidating Town and Country Planning Act 1990 is already being followed by the biggest changes in planning law for twenty years in the Planning and Compensation Bill.
4. Primary legislation may be changed by statutory instrument made under other primary legislation: the so-called Henry VIII clause, of which there has been a flurry in recent years; but despite this, not even the initial regulations under a statute are scheduled to the statute itself.
5. Legislation almost never now comes in to force on a single date. Different sections, and even subsections, are brought in to effect (by a succession of commencement orders) on a series of different dates over a period that may run

to years; and some provisions may never be brought into effect at all. Example: the Consumer Credit Act 1974, in respect of which the final commencement order was made in 1989, and a table included in a textbook as an outline guide to the commencement situation occupies 11 pages.

6. Notwithstanding that we are in the age of word processing, and despite experience elsewhere, e.g. Canada, how a statute currently stands can be discovered only by an elaborate and time consuming paperchase or by resort (in some areas) to the expensive updates in private enterprise encyclopedias, which are tedious to maintain, or by resort to Lexis.

7. Although the legislation itself is rarely skeletal, a mass of flesh is often added by statutory instruments, subject in practice to a minimum of Parliamentary scrutiny, with the negative resolution procedure being preferred to the more effective affirmative procedure. Moreover, statutes and statutory instruments thereunder are drafted in different offices.

8. Even when it is possible to gain access to all the relevant and most up to date legislation on a particular subject, this will often not be enough to provide a complete picture of the law: one commonly has then to attempt the difficult task of completing and understanding the jigsaw created by the combination of legislation which covers certain aspects of an area of the law, and cases which continue to cover the remainder.

9. Many other areas of the law which could now readily be codified are still to be found only from cases decided over many years and scattered across a number of different series of reports.

Hard to Understand

If the searcher after enlightment has not already been defeated in the quest to discover what statutes and statutory instruments are currently in force he or she is then confronted with the task of divining what they mean. If a judge (encouraged by the Court of Appeal, Criminal Division) incants the words of the statute (e.g. the Theft Act) then he or she is liable to be met by looks of blank incomprehension from the jury. If he or she is able to paraphrase the statute in a way that is simple and suited to a lay audience then one must ask whether this could not usefully have been done by Parliament in the first place.

Bewildering complexity is by no means confined to revenue statutes. Although, as the Renton Committee on the Preparation of Legislation (Cmnd. 6053) suggested, in paragraph 11–20, there is scope for mathematical formulae, those in Schedule 1 to the Child Support Bill (calculation of child support maintenance) are a glaring case of misuse of such formulae. Is it not time for a return to the style of say the Sale of Goods Act 1893?

Very often the vices identified above are found in combination. For example, the draft Commonhold Bill is very long, very involved and very complicated, and yet very important provisions are to be left to regulations.

Moreover, often three (or more) sets of provisions have to be considered: old law which has been repealed but is still relevant for some purposes; new law which is not yet fully effective; and extremely complex transitional provisions, which will remain part of the statute long after they have ceased to be applicable.

What Should be Done

The main problems are the attitude of Government (which promotes and drafts virtually all the legislation that Parliament enacts) and the need to consider the legislative process, democratic and often thorough though it is capable of being. The Bar should identify and promote a series of proposals for making the content of the law more accessible and comprehensible to the public at large. The focus of these proposals should be the needs of the user and they should combine both detailed recommendations as to the presentation of statute law with general recommendations as to the formulation and future role of legislation in our legal system. Examples of such proposals would be as follows:

Presentation

All legislation, including statutory instruments, on a particular subject should be contained in its latest form and comprehensively in one place. The user should be able to find all the statute law on that subject quickly and conveniently, without having to make reference to exterior amending Acts, or sections of other Acts which primarily relate to a different subject-matter.

To this end:

1. The arrangement of statutes should, as with "Statutes in Force", be on the basis of subject; and "miscellaneous provisions" legislation should be avoided.
2. All statutory instruments enacted under a statute should be appended to a republication of the Statute.
3. New provisions relating to a subject covered by an existing Act should be incorporated by textual amendment into that existing Act rather than forming a separate statute.
4. Publication of new and amending legislation should be in a form which allows quick and easy updating (possibly on the basis of a loose-leaf system with the issue of individual replacement pages).
5. It is extremely important that publication should always be before the date upon which the legislation takes effect.
6. The date upon which legislation comes into effect should be readily apparent on the face of the legislation itself, subject only to unavoidable exceptions.
7. The titles of new legislation should be in accordance with a clear subject index already established for existing legislation.
8. Unavoidable detail should not appear in sections of the Act, but should be put in schedules, save for details of a changing or technical character, for which statutory instruments are appropriate.

Formulation

Legislation inevitably originates in government departments yet it is at this early stage when improvements could most satisfactorily be made that our present legislative process lacks any machinery capable of carrying out the necessary consultation with outside interests. This function may well merit having a body with responsibility specifically to scrutinise the form, arrangement and language of proposed legislation so as to ensure that it meets the requirements of clarity and comprehensiveness before the legislation is submitted to Parliament and so as to ensure that it continues to meet these requirements subsequently. One problem is that no person or body is now effectively responsible for scrutinising legislation as a whole before it is introduced, the Legislation Committee of the Cabinet having largely abdicated this function.

In particular:

1. Legislation must be expressed in clear and simple language, avoiding the confusing legalistic style of drafting which predominates in most existing statutes. The Maintenance Enforcement Bill is an outrageous but typical example both of extraordinary complicated provisions for the most part incomprehensible to the persons affected by them, and of numerous earlier statutes being amended. Unintelligible legislation is the negation of the rule of law and of Parliamentary democracy.

2. Legislation should expressly state whether it is intended to be retrospective or is intended to reverse the effect of some rule of law.

3. The structure of statutes should follow a logical, sequential pattern that allows for most convenient reference by the user; statutes should be annotated; and there should be a wider use of definitions.

4. The substantial content of legislation should be contained within the statute itself rather than added later in the form of statutory instruments.

5. One Act should cover only one subject, a practice introduced by Britain in many Commonwealth territories.

6. The structure and language of statutes should be kept under constant review, by a body responsible for scrutiny, such as we have suggested.

7. Legislation should (in the European tradition) state its purpose, and lay down general principles. It should avoid whenever possible trying to cover every envisageable situation, and then both having to be amended at every available Parliamentary occasion and, once enacted, and new situations are thought of, having to be further amended.

Any body established to carry out these functions could also have responsibility for increasing consolidation and codification.

Consolidation

Consolidation on a comprehensive and ongoing basis of the variety of statutes covering a particular area of the law provides an answer to many of the problems of access to legislation outlined above. The user then only needs turn to one statute in which all the legislation relating to one subject, or one aspect of a subject could be both structured and clarified.

Codification

A logical extension to both revision and consolidation of legislation as a means of improving the accessibility of the law is codification whereby the existing law both enacted and judge-made is reduced into comprehensive and comprehensible statutory form. The user need look only to one unified source for all the law in a particular area.

Arguments against codification are powerful. They stress the undoubted advantages of authoritative judge-made law, namely its flexibility, certainty and capacity to develop in response to the pressure of changing social conditions conveyed through the channel of litigation. However the flexibility of case law is a gradual process limited by the constraints imposed by the unstructured pattern of cases falling to be decided. Codification should be able both to retain the flexibility of case law whilst at the same time allowing for the reform and clarification of the law. Its gradual development should be encouraged, provided that:

1. There is allowance for adequate study, research, consultation and planning, which should include the opportunity for the layman's voice to be heard in the process of law-making and which should result in a commentary to accompany any code to aid interpretation.
2. Codification must be both comprehensive and sufficiently detailed so that a code on a particular area of the law is, not only in theory, but also in practice, the effectual source of the law for the user.
3. Codes should be kept under continuous review, the initial code being the first rather than the last stage in the process; and the advantages and disadvantages of codifying a particular area of law and of codification generally should be kept under review.
4. The need to focus on the requirements of the user in the formulation and presentation of statutes should similarly apply to the formulation and presentation of any codes.

Conclusion

Although the Renton Committee which reported in 1975, made 81 recommendations for improving our statute law, only 39 of them have been fully or mainly implemented. Several of the most important ones have not been implemented. Since then the situation has become worse: legislation has become more voluminous, more detailed and more difficult to find and to understand. The next Parliament should reverse this trend as a matter of urgency.

November 1991

M27   Independent Television Commission

A. Background

1. The Independent Broadcasting Authority and Cable Authority were closely involved in the passage of the Broadcasting Act 1990. This memorandum reflects that experience.
2. The declaration of Government's intentions to introduce major new legislation on broadcasting was made in a White Paper in November 1988 (Broadcasting in the 1990s: Competition, Choice and Quality – Cm 517). The White Paper had been preceded by an enquiry by the Peacock Committee into the Financing of the BBC, published in July 1986; and by a report on the Future of Broadcasting by the Home Affairs Select Committee, published in June 1988. The

Broadcasting Bill was introduced and had its First Reading in December 1989. It received the Royal Assent in December 1990. Among its main provisions were the abolition of the IBA and the Cable Authority, and the replacement of these bodies by the Independent Television Commission as the body responsible for regulating independent – ie commercially funded – television broadcasting.

3. The previous experience of the IBA (and its predecessor the ITA) went back to the Television Act 1954, with subsequent major legislation in 1963, 1972, 1980 and 1984. Senior staff as well as Members of the respective bodies had experience of the legislative process from within government and elsewhere. There was therefore considerable knowledge to build on in addressing the new legislation.

4. In its request for comments on the process by which legislation is made in England and Wales, the Commission refers to four main issues: consultation before legislation is drafted; the way in which legislation is drafted; Parliamentary scrutiny of legislation and accessibility of the public to legislation passed by Parliament. The comments in our memorandum are confined largely to the last two of these. However it may be helpful to refer briefly, after stating the IBA and Cable Authority interest, to our experience particularly on the first of the points.

B. IBA and Cable Authority Interest

5. Major broadcasting legislation had been presented to Parliament at roughly 10 year intervals in the past, and it was evident at the outset that much hung for the future of the broadcasting system on the outcome of the new legislation. Both regulatory bodies were directly interested as the publicly appointed custodians of a system which was to be fundamentally changed by the Act. But they were also the focal point for expressions of concern by many interests, both among viewers and in the broadcasting industry, who sought endorsement for views they wished to express to the Home Office which was responsible for the Bill and to Parliament.

6. In addition to representations made to government at Chairman level, the IBA therefore established its own small unit of staff to monitor the development of progress of the legislation in order to influence the process by providing information to others and arguing for a particular outcome as necessary. Thirty "Briefing Notes" covering a wide range of broadcasting topics were provided to MPs and Peers in time for important debates at the Committee and Report stages in both Houses. The information provided was declared useful in debate from both sides of the House. On occasions amendments were put down through sympathetic MPs and Peers. Political advisers were retained to assess opinion among members of both Houses and to report on the key features of all debates. Members of the Authority were kept informed of progress as the Bill went through its stages. The Cable Authority undertook similar activities, employing political advisers, disseminating information, following the Bill and proposing amendments to it.

C. Preparation of Legislation

7. The tendency of the past thirty years has been for Broadcasting legislation to be preceded by a Committee of Enquiry appointed by government with terms of reference to investigate the specific areas on which it was proposed to legislate. This did not happen with the latest legislation. Although ideas considered by the Peacock Committee (see above) were incorporated into the legislation, the foundations of the Broadcasting Bill were not based on a thorough and considered examination of the evidence for inadequacies in the existing statutory provision and of the case for change. The 1988 Report of the Home Affairs Select Committee on "The Future of Broadcasting" was a helpful summary of prevailing views on some of the major topics. But the Committee had neither time nor resources to pursue investigations into the detailed consequences of its broader lines of enquiry.

8. No doubt partly in consequence of this, many details remained to be worked out in the Bill as it was introduced in December 1989. As initially published, it contained only 167 clauses, as compared with 204 in the Bill when it had completed the Parliamentary process, with eleven schedules to begin with, as compared with 22 at the end. In our experience, the bodies most likely to be concerned are often consulted informally and in confidence by the relevant government departments on the drafting of legislation; but the consultation is necessarily largely on points of detail. The Bill as it was eventually presented to Parliament would undoubtedly have benefited from a period of prior exposure to scrutiny as a totality, with the opportunity for informed opinion to comment on it.

9. The substantial new Broadcasting Service Bill in Australia, which covers much of the same ground as the Broadcasting Act 1990, is now going through just this process. It was issued in the form of an "exposure draft" on 9 October last year, and is likely to be debated in its final form in the Autumn of this year.

D. Process of Legislation

10. Against this background, we offer a few specific comments under three headings:
    (i) Guidance
    (ii) Accessibility
    (iii) Facilities

(i) Guidance

11. Despite the considerable accumulated experience referred to above, understanding the details of the process of legislation still proved difficult. "Fact Sheets" which were available from the House authorities on the stages in the passage of an Act of Parliament and on the vote bundle quickly proved inadequate as a guide to the intricacies of the process. Even after a full year, we were still occasionally left to catch up with sudden and unexpected turns of events.

12. It may be that, as a prior step, the public and the lobbyist need to be accorded recognition *as direct participants with their own legitimate role in the*

Parliamentary process. It would then follow naturally that proper guidance should be given by the authorities in the performance of this role. It is undoubtedly true that the cost of acquisition of the necessary information is sufficient to provide a living for numbers of professional consultants. Better provision of basic information would help to reduce the costs of access to the Parliamentary process.

13. However we would like to set on record the helpful and professional assistance we were always given on specific points by the *public information office in the House of Commons library.* Our experience is that the services of this office are not as widely known about as they deserve to be.

(ii) Documents

14. Coming to grips with a piece of legislation which is as long and as complicated as the Broadcasting Bill also proved difficult. The Minister responsible for the Bill gave an overall view in his statements moving introduction and second reading, but these were necessarily brief. It was only when the Bill had reached the end of its Committee stage in the Commons some months after its introduction that certain aspects of the way the legislation fitted together and the full implications of certain key clauses were finally made explicit. We would have welcomed *publication with the Bill of an explanatory memorandum,* by the Home Office as the relevant department in this case, stating, at the outset and clause by clause, the purposes of the legislation.

15. This document would not, of course, be identical to the "Notes on Clauses" provided for the Minister's own use. But it would be a by-product that could be provided without substantial additional effort.

16. The financial and manpower implications of the legislation are of course published with the Bill. But as part of any further "explanatory papers" on the lines set out above, we would see particular merit in *government being required to state at the outset its provisional timetable for all the activities which are to be set in motion by the Act.* This is to avoid undue emphasis – entirely understandable amid the pressure of events once the Parliamentary process starts – on the legislation as an end in itself, and will help to focus attention throughout the passage of a bill on its consequences once the Parliamentary process is completed.

17. A significant barrier to access to the process proved to be *the way amendments to the legislation were published and dealt with in debate.* The "Notices of amendments" were often available only immediately before the Standing Committee sat, leaving virtually no time for consideration or possible action/response. Often copies were obtained only as a result of an "ad hoc" arrangement between a member of the Committee and our political adviser. The present practices seem to allow amendments to be tabled even in handwriting up to the very moment when the debate starts. This gives no opportunity for scrutiny by public or interested parties.

18. Attempting to follow the progress of an amendment from the published documents is also no easy matter. Amendments are numbered in the order in which they are tabled and then re-arranged into clause order. This makes it

difficult to trace a specific numbered amendment, particularly where the amendment is referred to in debate only by its given number. Consolidated lists of amendments are periodically published, which means that preceding Notices can be dispensed with. However, no clear reference is given in the new list as to when the consolidation was made.

19. Although it is helpful to distinguish between the Notices of Amendments given on the previous day which are printed on *blue paper*, and those consolidated for the current day's business on *white paper*, the colour coding identification is lost by photocopying. Considerable confusion occurred at the start before it became clear by trial and error that blank sides in the published lists counted as numbered pages.

20. A practical test for whether any alternative system was more effective would be whether it was possible:

    (i) to know, at least for a reasonable period in advance, *the amendments which were to be called for debate*; and

    (ii) to cross-refer after the event from the text of the amendment, in whatever list it appears, to the record of the Committee proceedings to establish *how it was debated and what had been the outcome.*

(iii) Facilities

21. The *embargo on note-taking* in the strangers' galleries often complicated the work of following the debates. Unless a person has access to the Press Gallery (and press passes are formally only available to accredited members of the lobby), observers of the debates are not allowed to make notes (or even to draw) in either of the Commons or Lords Strangers' Galleries. This rule does not appear to extend to Standing or Select Committees. Where one needs to brief quickly and in depth after a debate, this rule appears particularly unhelpful. It is also surely of questionable value as a matter of principle now that Parliament is being televised. Although the text of Hansard is generally available the following day, if the debate continued after about 10.30–11.00 pm, the Hansard text was not available until the second day after the debate.

22. A further difficulty also arose out of the *size of the rooms* in which Committee sessions were held. Although it varied, the rooms generally used in the case of the Broadcasting Bill only seated about 20 people. To ensure a seat for the start of the debate, it was often necessary to queue for at least an hour beforehand. People with a direct interest in the debate could sometimes not get a seat. This may be preferable to reserving seats for "important" people. But it introduced an arbitrary element in following the debates which resulted both in wasted time and occasional lost opportunities.

16 January 1992

M28 Industry and Parliament Trust: Letter from Mr Fredrick Hyde Chambers, Director

We were asked to give evidence to the Select Committee on Parliamentary hours. The basis on which we produce recommendations is relevant to the Commission. We drew on 75 industrialists who have undertaken the Parliamentary Study Programme, a copy of which is enclosed,[1] so that they did have an appreciation of the problems of Westminster. As you will see, they made specific recommendations relating to legislation, having gone through the process in some detail.

Additional points which may be of interest and which constantly arise in discussion with our corporate members are:

1. The problem of timescales. Invariably a company learns about a piece of legislation when it is well down the drafting stage. Consultation periods are often too short for trade associations to make an adequate impact on the individual companies who could be drastically affected.

2. Some trade associations and companies who are working in Brussels have a very good feel for EC legislation, but for the most part business finds the timescales, I think, too rapid or too slow. For instance, a decision can be pending for some years and yet have major implications as regards investing in plant.

3. The current approach of any government towards the revision of legislation within Standing Committees does little for the standing of Members in the public's perception and is felt to be detrimental for legislative effectiveness. The point is often made that this could be improved once the principle of the legislation had been the subject of rigorous political debate, the detailed legislation could be approached in a more pragmatic way. It is appreciated that there will be some legislation which will be political through and through.

4. There is some concern at the growth of statutory instruments.

5. The shop in Parliament Street making available Parliamentary papers over the counter is an enormous advance, as previously there could be long delays in being able to get hold of these papers.

18 August 1992

M29 Institute of Chartered Accountants in England and Wales

Introduction

1. The Institute of Chartered Accountants in England and Wales welcomes the opportunity to comment to the Commission on the Legislative Process appointed by the Hansard Society for Parliamentary Government. As comments on the legislative process have been made by us and others over the last

---

1 Not published

twenty-five years, especially on tax legislation, we will refer only briefly to some of these past comments throughout our memorandum rather than make the same points again in detail.

2. A seminal study of this subject was the Report of the Committee on the Preparation of Legislation chaired by the Rt Hon Sir David Renton published in May 1975 (Cmnd 6053). The six accountancy bodies made a joint submission to the Renton Committee in November 1973, using tax legislation as an example. That submission referred to the report of the Statute Law Society, "Statute Law Deficiencies" (known as the Heap Report) published by Sweet and Maxwell in 1970 and the report of the committee appointed to propose solutions to the deficiencies identified in the Heap Report, "Statute Law: the Key to Clarity" (known as the Stow Hill Report), published by Sweet and Maxwell in 1972. The Renton Committee was appointed in response to the Stow Hill Report. More recently the Special Committee of Tax Law Consultative Bodies (comprising representatives of some 22 professional and other bodies, including this Institute) has published two reports on the process of forming tax legislation, "Tax Law after Furniss and Dawson" (1988) and "Recommendations on the Enactment and Amendment of Tax Legislation" (March 1990). Both were published by the Law Society on behalf of the Special Committee.

3. If the volume of reports can be taken as an indication of concern, there are problems with the legislative process and with the ultimate form legislation takes. The various reports also propose similar solutions which would indicate that there are possible solutions which may help ameliorate the problems.

Problems

4. Accountants are mainly concerned with legislation on tax, insolvency, company and financial sector law. They are important as the legislation affecting the conduct of business and the tax regime can have economic consequences for the country as a whole and its citizens. Uncertainty in the law in these areas or unclear drafting which may have results which were not intended by Parliament can affect many. An example of this is the damage that may have been done to the City of London as an innovative and leading financial centre because of the uncertainty in the law regarding interest rate swap options.

5. The smooth operations of business require law that is certain, fair and understandable. Businesses need to know the consequences of different courses of action so that they can plan properly. They should also not need to spend an unreasonable amount of time or money on determining whether they comply with the law.

Inaction

6. The report of the Renton Committee was probably the most authoritative of the reports on the legislative process. Most of its recommendations are still valid today. The Commission may wish to consider why so few of the recommendations in that report have been implemented despite it having been well received – frequent references to its recommendations are still made today.

It may also be worthwhile to analyse why even where there has been acceptance in principle, so many of the recommendations have made little progress. Close analysis of the difficulties or barriers which prevent implementation of the recommendations proposed may suggest what action is necessary to achieve progress.

7. Our comments are structured to follow the four topics outlined in the invitation. We will also seek to identify possible barriers to implementing past recommendations.

Extent and Nature of Government consultation on proposed legislation

8. Since the submissions to the Renton Committee there have been advances in consultation on company and tax law. The Department of Trade and Industry and the Inland Revenue now consult on many matters. However, for complex legislation, such as tax legislation, the consultation period is still too short (see paragraph 12). The increase in consultation has appeared to reduce the length of time given for consultation. This can create difficulties for representative organisations whose members have the experience and expertise and need to be consulted before response.

9. An example of a difficult timetable is the consultation process on the present Friendly Societies Bill. One draft of the Bill was sent out by H M Treasury on 19 December 1991 for comment by 13 January 1992. We had commented on a previous draft with both substantive and detailed comments but most of the substantive points were not reflected in the later draft. The Treasury's promised reply to our previous letter was not received until 3 February 1992. Until that reply was received, it was difficult to make a meaningful comment on the latest draft.

10. Special considerations apply in considering tax legislation. The annual Budget followed by the Finance Bill provides a guaranteed slot in the Parliamentary timetable for Treasury Ministers which is not available to others. However, the legislation is subject to inadequate effective scrutiny because of the speed at which it passes through Parliament (without the benefit of scrutiny by the House of Lords).

11. Furthermore, the Parliamentary process for tax measures is governed by the Provisional Collection of Taxes Act 1968 which gives statutory effect to the Ways and Means Resolutions. If passed in March or April these resolutions expire on 5 August; if passed in any other month they expire after four months.

12. The timetables for 1990 and 1991 were as follows:

	1990	1991
Budget statement	20 March	19 March
Publication of Finance Bill	19 April	17 April
Royal Assent	26 July	25 July
Days available between publication and Royal Assent	98 days	99 days

We doubt if any other major free-enterprise economy introduces substantial and complex fiscal legislation in a discussion period of under 100 days.

13. In 1991 the Standing Committee met on nine occasions between its first and last meetings on 14 May and 20 June 1991 respectively. Part of the legislation ultimately enacted arose from clauses introduced at Committee and Report stages, for which there was clearly inadequate time for consideration by Parliament, let alone by outsiders. The original Bill had 100 clauses and 17 Schedules, the one amended by the Standing Committee had 117 clauses and 19 Schedules, while that finally enacted had 124 clauses and 19 Schedules. Similar problems of substantial enlargement while under Parliamentary scrutiny have usually arisen in earlier years, and in other measures (for example the 1981, 1985 and 1989 Companies Bills).

14. Additions are often made to proposed legislation after consultation has taken place: not as a result of consultation but because a matter has recently arisen, been overlooked or has been put forward opportunistically in Committee or in Parliament. Sometimes these additions are not subject to consultation and unforeseen problems may arise with them.

15. An improvement which has occurred is the advance publication of draft clauses, though this is still relatively rare. The great advantage of publication before a Bill is tabled in Parliament is that the draft clauses can be revised without Parliamentary formality.

16. The Law Society has suggested that a standing Company Law Commission should be established. We support this and also believe that the principle should be extended to cover all commercial law such as contract law, banking law, commercial credit, sale of goods etc, rather than company law alone, even if not on a continuous basis. The same principle should be extended to tax legislation.

17. The DTI had an advisory panel on company law which was abandoned in 1983 on cost grounds. This should be reintroduced as it served a useful purpose in consulting interested parties. Its terms of reference could be broadened so that it was more in the nature of a permanent body of experts available for consultation in the preparation of legislation. This procedure would have a much narrower function than a Law Commission but would provide expert input at the drafting stage. We recommend that consideration should be given to adopting such a system.

18. Possible barriers to these recommendations are:
    a. lack of resources in the sponsoring departments so that proper consultation cannot be made;
    b. inadequate time available for consultation due to Parliamentary timetables;
    c. lack of time for consultation when amendments are made in Committee or in Parliament. A panel of experts may be particularly useful, when there is not time available for a wider consultation;
    d. a common view that some forms of legislation, particularly tax, should be kept secret until introduced formally in Parliament.

These barriers are all surmountable though changes in timetabling would require a change in the way that Parliament arranges its affairs.

The form and drafting of Bills and instruments

19. The report of the Renton Committee and earlier reports such as the Heap Report emphasised the utility of using textual amendments and also consolidation. "Textual amendment" is the process of making changes by adding to or deleting from the wording of the original Act. This is contrasted with "non-textual amendment" where additional provisions are made in a later Act without altering the text of the earlier Act. To ascertain the present state of the law under a non-textual amendment system, it is necessary to consult both the original Act and the amending Act, or frequently Acts. Sometimes amending legislation may appear in an Act apparently unconnected with the legislation being amended. For example, the Financial Services Act 1986 was amended by the Companies Act 1989.

20. Consolidation is the process of rewriting the scattered provisions on a given topic in the form of a single Act. Ideally, the consolidating Act should be continually amended by textual amendment. Unfortunately it is affected by non-textual amendment with the result that consolidation is needed afresh. Consolidation is now more frequent. The Companies Act 1985, a consolidating Act, was very welcome. However, extensive changes and alterations have been made by the Insolvency Act 1986 and the Companies Act 1989 with no further consolidating Act. It has proved difficult to follow through the effect of changes. As regards tax legislation, there should be a once and for all consolidation of the legislation, and continuous consolidation thereafter. In other words, the tax system should be codified along the lines of the US system.

21. We would welcome the use of textual amendment, more consolidation and the maintenance of consolidation. A meeting was held in December 1989 between Parliamentary Counsel and representatives of the accountancy and legal professions, at the request of the professional bodies, to recommend these approaches. Subsequently, the professional bodies made representations to the Statute Law Committee of which the Lord Chancellor is chairman and which includes Ministers, Members of Parliament and officials who have an interest in the legislative process. A copy of the letter dated 4 May 1990 is attached.[1] It outlines ways of consolidating fiscal legislation which we believe are practicable and sensible.

22. Another problem with the form and drafting of Bills and instruments, stems from what we describe as the "tree" approach to drafting legislation. This arises where a complex piece of legislation needs to address separate issues which are placed in separate sections of the measure but all of which relate to the same topic. The following illustration explains the principle:

Section 1: Certain people cannot perform a certain action.
  (a) The class of people who cannot perform the action is set out in subsection (b).
  (b) These people cannot perform the matters laid out in subsection (c)
  (c) The matters are as follows:

---

1 not published

(i)

(ii)

Section 2: Certain matters are exempted from section 1(c)(i) as follows:

A user who wishes to ascertain whether a particular matter is permitted has to work his way back and forth along the branches to understand the position.

23. Bills and instruments are often drafted in a form that eases the task of the draftsman and may assist the legislator but does not necessarily help the user. They may be drafted in a way that makes the change in the law clear and enables Parliament to see the effects. However, a user is not primarily interested in the change, other than for a transitional period. The user needs to know the current state of the law as it affects a particular action.

24. There are several solutions to these problems of accessibility and comprehensibility. Textual amendment and consolidation have already been mentioned. Renton also suggests greater use of explanatory notes and memoranda. Making available to users the notes that are prepared for Standing Committees would be helpful. An attractive approach is to provide explanatory notes opposite draft clauses. However, this assistance is normally only provided at the consultation stage and not in the Bill presented to Parliament. If it were, this would enable explanations to be given to Parliament while using the textual amendment system.

25. An added problem arises from the effort to create certainty in the law. This often has the effect of making the law convoluted and the original purpose may be obscured. Seeking undue certainty can ultimately lead to such opaque drafting that the objective is lost.

26. We also consider that greater use of information technology (IT) should be explored, particularly by applying database technology to the Acts and associated instruments. This would facilitate the relevant cross-referencing between the provisions within different Acts and associated instruments, the cross-referencing of definitions within one Act or instrument to similar or associated definitions in others and the cross-referencing of the database through word-searching. These advances would facilitate the processes of drafting and of reviewing legislation and reduce the number of conflicts between different laws and regulations. It seems possible that IT techniques could further improve the process of reporting changes made to proposed legislation during its progress through the Committee and Report stages in both Houses of Parliament.

27. Possible barriers to these recommendations are:
   a. lack of resources both in the office of Parliamentary Counsel and in the Law Commissions;
   b. the fact that legislation is actually prepared for Parliament rather than for the ultimate user;
   c. the need for greater resources in information technology;
   d. a view that legislation has to be drafted using conventions rather than in "plain English."

These barriers are all surmountable provided sufficient resources are allocated to the legislative process.

Parliamentary scrutiny of legislation

28. As previously noted, on complex legislation such as the Finance Bill there is often insufficient Parliamentary time for proper scrutiny of or debate on the draft legislation. We suggest that research and support facilities to MPs should be increased. A greater use of explanatory material could be explored. Timetabling should be realistic and allow reasonable time for consultation. We suggest there may be merit in having separate Bills for technical matters (such as a technical Finance Bill) which could be subject to longer and more informed scrutiny than the Finance Bill as a whole.

29. We draw attention to the adjournment debate in the House of Commons on 7 March 1990 (Hansard, cols 977–984) on the administration of the tax system. The debate was initiated by Mr Tim Smith MP, the member for Beaconsfield and a member of the Committee of Public Accounts. In his reply, the Financial Secretary to the Treasury acknowledged the need for simplification and to make legislation "user friendly", but said that there is always a need to have tax avoidance measures, which are necessarily complex. He was not in favour of a technical Finance Bill, which has been advocated from several sources in the past, including a former Chancellor of the Exchequer (Sir Geoffrey Howe). The Minister concluded by undertaking to consider Mr Smith's suggestion for an enquiry or Commission to study the subject matter of the debate.

Accessibility to the public

30. The general public finds a good deal of legislation impenetrable. To a certain extent the same can be said of professional users of the law. Many accountants, even those working in the specialist areas of company and tax law, have great difficulty in certain areas ascertaining the current state of the law let alone interpreting it. This is because it is difficult to ensure that all the latest amendments have been identified with their effective dates and to follow the language; because different Acts relate to the same topic; because legislation on one topic is in several different places; and because statutory instruments also need to be considered.

31. The barriers that have been described in the previous sections all contribute to the lack of accessibility of legislation to the public. If these barriers cannot be removed, further solutions need to be found. One approach might be to introduce a system for editing legislation after preliminary approval by Parliament.

32. A quasi-official person or body would have the task of ensuring that legislation was in a logical, coherent form that was reasonably comprehensible to the non-specialist. He would act as a drafting interpreter. This would involve converting legislation into a more easily understood and usable form. Every opportunity should be taken to make use of consolidation, textual amendment, explanatory memoranda, and to convert "tree" legislation into tables. The difficulty is that the resulting text would undoubtedly need to be approved

afresh by Parliament. This would make further demands on scarce Parliamentary time and give rise to considerable extra cost. Such costs would have to be balanced against the current cost to users created by complexity, obscurity and uncertainty.

33. Legislation would be more accessible if Acts were published in their textually amended form. This has been done commercially in certain areas of the law. For example the amended Companies Acts were published commercially in consolidated form after the enactment of the Companies Act 1989. The publication incorporates the 1989 Act into the 1985 Act and has a separate comprehensive index. It is a widely used publication, but it is not a substitute for formal consolidation.

34. We advocate the increased use of IT to help accessibility. HMSO sells a disc containing pension rules and superannuation rules as these are continually being changed and it is necessary to have up-to-date, consolidated information (Occupational Pension Schemes: Practice Notes: IR12 (1991)). It would be attractive to extend this approach to other areas of law. Once the basic data has been input, it should be relatively easy to keep them updated. A further illustration of the possibilities is provided by the availability of computer-assisted legal information retrieval services which retrieve all relevant data on a topic.

35. The Inland Revenue produces simple explanatory leaflets on various aspects of tax legislation. The Department of Social Security and H M Customs and Excise also produce leaflets for the general public. This approach could be extended to parts of company law. The 900,000 companies in the UK represent many potential users. Leaflets would be of great help to the commercial sector and make legislation more accessible.

Conclusion

36. Our main recommendations to improve the legislative process are:
   1. more consultation on all matters, with enough time for a reasoned response to be given;
   2. use wherever possible of textual amendment when existing provisions are being changed;
   3. more frequent consolidation, or where possible a once and for all consolidation of Acts and of instruments, subsequent changes in legislation being made to the consolidating Act or instrument;
   4. directing attention to the user when legislation is produced rather than the legislator, or the enforcer;
   5. the exploration of wider use of information technology;
   6. the provision of more explanatory material to Parliament, commentators and the general public;
   7. the creation of an advisory body with authority to advise and recommend on all matters relating to the development, preparation and introduction of new commercial legislation as regards style, presentation and publication

(but not content) so as to ensure maximum comprehensibility and ease of use.

37. We believe that most of the recommendations of the 1975 Renton Committee are as valid today as they were when issued.

March 1992

M30   Institute of Directors

1. The Institute of Directors is a representative business organisation with 38,000 members in the United Kingdom.

2. In order to represent its members' interests the IOD consults them through sample surveys of the membership, Branch discussion groups and through a network of Policy Committees. The IOD concentrates on broad issues which impinge upon the legal duties and responsibilities of Company Directors and which affect the general economic climate in which their companies operate.

3. Over the past three years the IOD has become increasingly aware that much of the legislation affecting companies, or with potential effects on companies, originates in Brussels. It therefore has to ensure that it monitors the legislative process at all stages from the Commission services to Westminster and the European Court of Justice.

4. The gradual change of emphasis has affected the way in which the IOD organises its work on legislation. It is no longer primarily focused on the Westminster Parliament and on the details of UK Bills, but the degree to which the focus has shifted varies from subject to subject depending upon whether the primary legislation originates in Brussels or Westminster.

5. The experience of the *IOD's Taxation Committee* is instructive. It has made its reputation as a focus for tax expertise through well drafted annual **Budget Representations**. These are prepared during the Autumn and sent to Ministers before Christmas. After Christmas a meeting is held with the Chancellor of the Exchequer – a sort of "oral examination" on the written text. Representations of a more *technical* nature are the subject of an earlier submission, which is discussed at a meeting with the Deputy Chairman of the Inland Revenue in November/December. In 1991, the Chancellor in his speech to the IOD Convention listed seven recommendations from the IOD's Budget Representations which he had implemented in the Budget, saying, *"This was our [the Government's] reply to the representations from business"*.

   Following the Budget Speech, the IOD begins work on details of the Finance Bill, making representations to Ministers, briefing MPs, drafting amendments and new clauses, etc. In the case of the Finance Bill, therefore, the focus remains firmly on Westminster.

6. In 1991, however, the IOD worked on the details of the expected clauses of the 1992 Finance Bill which will give effect to EC legislation on VAT post 1992 (at the time of writing – December 1991 – we still did not have an agreed Council

text). This work was pro-active, with IOD experts working closely with Customs and Excise Officials and Treasury Ministers.

7. On the day [21 October 1991] that the Chancellor announced in Parliamentary Answers the new system of monthly payments of VAT to be brought in for large traders at the same time as the EC changes, the IOD and CBI met to discuss details with the Treasury Minister in charge and also Customs and Excise officials.

8. A European Standing Committee Debate was held on 2 December on VAT and Excise duties. The IOD provided a brief to Members and was quoted – particularly by the Minister, with whom the IOD had had several meetings. The debate was, however, dominated by the issue of Excise duties, particularly duty-free sales, on which subject a massive campaign had been waged by the Scotch Whisky Association. The irony of this is that there is no agreed text on Excise duties either, and not likely to be one in time for the Finance Bill 1992.

9. The issues involved in post-1992 VAT are complex and highly technical. Few people understand these (including the EC Commission!). The special expertise provided by those with practical business experience of the actual operation of VAT systems is invaluable to the legislators (ie. the Treasury and Customs and Excise), as in the British system the law must be practical and workable.

10. This example shows how even the IOD's Taxation Committee, generally quite "homebased", has had to invest a considerable effort in European inspired legislation, not least at the early, pre-legislative stage.

11. We expect draft clauses on post-1992 VAT to be published as soon as the text has been agreed and will then examine them very closely. For the Finance Bill, the IOD will be in close contact with Officials, Treasury Ministers, and MPs.

12. This experience also reveals that influence in the legislative process does not start in the lobbies of the House of Commons. In the case of tax legislation, it logically starts with officials, Ministers and, in some cases, a network of advisory Committees on which bodies such as the IOD are represented.

13. The *IOD's Law Committee's* work has been considerably affected by European legislation. Over the past three years it has spent a considerable amount of time on the *Proposal for a European Company Statute*, as well as on issues such as *Liability for Suppliers of Services*, etc.

14. At an early stage this IOD committee decided that it should examine in detail the proposals for a European Company Statute, clause by clause. Having undertaken this exercise, the IOD worked closely with members of the EC Economic and Social Committee to ensure that many of its points appeared in the ESC "Opinion", and Mr Peterson, its rapporteur, gave evidence to the House of Lords European Committee [reference HL.71, 1990, pp. 196–209], as did the IOD [ibid. pp. 45–50]. The IOD's expert was invited by the Socialist Group of the European Parliament to brief it on the technical details of the proposal.

15. The revised Commission Proposal [COM(91)174 Final] is currently being examined by the IOD's Law Committee, once again in detail, clause by clause. Many of the changes reflect the IOD's detailed work.

16. By the time the European Company Statute comes to be debated by the House of Commons (if ever), the IOD's work may largely have been done. This experience reveals clearly how little the House of Commons is engaged in the legislative process where the power of initiative lies with the European Commission.

17. The fact that the House of Commons, or its Select Committees, fails to examine European legislative proposals in detail at early stages renders the House particularly without influence (let alone power) over EC legislation – and thus, ultimately, over UK legislation.

18. The *IOD's Employment Committee* has, over the past two years, had a mixed focus – both Westminster and European. On the Westminster front, further industrial relations legislation was proposed in July 1991 [Green Paper *Industrial Relations in the 1990s*]. The IOD issued a discussion paper on this subject to its branches at that time, and thus it was able to take an active part in feeding its members' opinions directly into the pre-legislative stages by responding to the Department of Employment's consultative document.

19. The IOD gave evidence to the House of Commons' Select Committee on Employment in March 1991 on the future prospects for employment. This enabled the IOD to promote its views on the way in which an efficient labour market should operate.

20. The *IOD's Employment Committee* has spent a considerable amount of time examining proposals emanating from the European Social Action Programme. In 1990, it lobbied in Brussels against the three draft directives on part-time and temporary work, and it has worked closely with other organisations representing small businesses in campaigning against EC legislation in the field of employment.

21. In general, the IOD finds the British Government very open. Its approach to pre-legislative consultation with interested organisations is a model – the exceptions (eg. changes to Statutory Sick Pay in 1990/91 and piecemeal changes to income tax and National Insurance contribution rules affecting expenses and benefits) merely prove the rule. Representative bodies feel that relations are soured if they are not consulted.

22. Government, for its part, needs the feel for the practical effect of legislation that representative bodies can provide.

23. The European legislative process, often characterised by its openness, is far from ideal. Distance, truly dreadful drafting (proposals are often admitted to be mere try-ons), poor timetables and, ultimately, a secret (in the Council of Ministers) legislative process have turned representation into a nightmare. The next stage, post-Maastricht, should be further to refine the limits of the EC legislative competence.

24. This Memorandum gives merely a flavour of the Institute of Directors' views on the legislative process and it would be happy to explore the issues raised in a meeting with the Hansard Society. The point which should be emphasised is that the Institute sees the legislative process as much wider than Parliament. It is a long drawn out process involving interactions at many levels and that today,

particularly with the growing scope of the competence of the European Community, the Westminster Parliament (Ministers apart) is a residual, last-stage focus of pressure. This conclusion must have very serious implications for our traditional views of Parliament as a legislator.

10 January 1992

M31   Institute of Public Relations: Government Affairs Group

1. Introduction

Following a meeting of the IPR Government Affairs Group on 18 March 1992 addressed by Michael Ryle, the Government Affairs Group agreed to submit a Memorandum of Evidence to the Commission. This is set out as follows:

2. Areas of Concern

a) Consultative Process

The Group believes that there are serious weaknesses in the present consultative process as embodied in Green Papers and White Papers.

While it accepts that the process for making representations on Green and White Papers is reasonably adequate, it is what happens thereafter that is of concern, namely how the representations are incorporated into any resulting Bill. Often the way Green and White Papers, as amended, are converted into draft legislation does not fully or accurately reflect the points that have been made. While it is perfectly possible to make representations to Members of Parliament, once a Bill has been published, this is not always satisfactory and can result in poor legislation being placed on the Statute Book. This may often mean time being wasted at a later stage with amendments, the contents of which would have best been dealt with before a Bill became law.

The IPR Government Affairs Group, therefore, proposes that consideration be given to an additional stage for major pieces of legislation, namely the publication of a "Green Bill". This would comprise the legislation in draft form, which would then be put through a similar consultative process as the Green and/or White Paper which preceded it.

b) Clarity of Intention for Legislation

Because of the legal language in which a Bill is drafted, the intentions of the Government of the day in proposing the legislation are often not as clear as they might be. This can lead to confusion once it is passed into law, particularly if aspects of the Bill have to be interpreted later by the Courts.

As at present, the judiciary is prevented from reading the Hansard coverage of the legislative stages of the original Bill, the IPR Government Affairs Group proposes that a non-legal document should be prepared simultaneously with the Bill for non-legal audiences setting out in clear and unambiguous language the Governments's intentions and objectives in proposing the legislation. This document should then be available to the legal profession and the judiciary should any aspects of the legislation later be challenged in Court.

c) The Scrutiny of Legislation

A major weakness in the present legislative process is the manner in which Bills are considered in detail, and the timetable for such consideration.

House of Commons Standing Orders provide for a Bill to be referred to a Special Standing Committee, and for evidence to be heard from outside bodies in four sessions of not more than three hours each. The Committee may then go through the Bill clause by clause as does an orthodox Standing Committee.

The Government Affairs Group regrets that this procedure has been little used since 1980, and urges that it should be established for major Bills such as the Shops Bill. This would enable both witnesses to be summoned to give evidence as required, and a proper timetable for the Bill's consideration to be set from the outset.

It is recognised that the political parties would not particularly like this proposal, but as some compensation, the Opposition would be given the right as well as the Government, under the Rules of Procedure, to call witnesses.

An alternative suggestion would be to let the relevant Select Committee look at the "Papers" relevant to the particular Bill, call witnesses as usual and then prepare a Report for Parliament setting out its comments and conclusions.

An important criterion for both proposals is that either the Special Standing Committee or the appropriate Select Committee would be able to test the proposed legislation properly.

It is further proposed that, when Bills are going through the legislative process, Government amendments should be tabled with, say, four days notice having to elapse before such amendments are considered.

d) European Legislation

The IPR Government Affairs Group is concerned about the present inadequate arrangements for the Scrutiny of European Legislation. As this is now of considerable importance, and will become increasingly so, these need to be reviewed as a matter of urgency. We make two proposals in this respect:

● first, that a strengthened Scrutiny Committee for European legislation be established, again whose rules of procedure and membership would be as for Select Committees

● second, that European legislative proposals are debated, at least once a month, on the floor of the House of Commons, thus allowing for wider participation by all those Members of Parliament who may be concerned about, or interested in, them.

e) Statutory Instruments

The IPR Government Affairs Group is concerned that the Government is resorting more and more to the use of Statutory Instruments and that these are not being as thoroughly scrutinised as they should be.

We believe that both the affirmative and the negative processes by which Statutory Instruments are introduced into Parliament and approved need a thorough overhaul.

As part of the revisions that are made, we would hope that consideration be given to the production of an Explanatory Memorandum, similar to that proposed earlier for Bills/Acts of Parliament, for all Statutory Instruments. Furthermore, we believe that all Statutory Instruments outstanding at the Dissolution of a Parliament should lapse at that time and that the successor Government should be obliged to lay them afresh as appropriate at the commencement of a new Parliament.

f) House of Lords

We believe that the procedures for the scrutiny of legislation by the House of Lords are more open than those of the House of Commons. This is largely accounted for by the fact that Bills in Committee are considered on the floor of the House.

We accept that this is impractical for the House of Commons, thus our earlier proposal for a Special Bill Committee in that House.

However, we would suggest that the House of Lords could be used more for debates on Green and White Papers in order that the principles behind any resulting legislation could receive a full public testing in addition to the normal consultation process with interested parties.

We note, with concern, that the possibility of moving the Lords' Committee stages of Bills upstairs into a special committee has been mooted. We believe that this would not be in the best interests of the Lords' Scrutiny of Legislation and hope that this will not become a serious option.

g) Post-legislative Review

The IPR Government Affairs Group believes that little attention is paid to post-legislative review of major legislation. We advocate this, not so much to correct faults – for we have made a proposal earlier to avoid these as far as possible – but to ensure that such legislation continues to be relevant and to respond to changes in circumstances that have occurred since it was first introduced.

We propose, therefore, that, at the time legislation is first being considered, a timetable is set for its review by the appropriate Select Committee. To ensure the effectiveness of this Procedure, we further propose that, if it were to be implemented, Scrutinising Committees would need to be given greater powers to recommend any changes that may be necessary. This proposal would exclude all Finance Bills but it would apply to those pieces of legislation, which might also be subject to a departmental review by the appropriate Government department.

h) Interface between Government, Legislature and interested Parties to Legislation

The Institute of Public Relations has been concerned for sometime about relationships between Members of Parliament and interests outside Parliament. The Government Affairs Group recently reviewed the evidence given to the Select Committee on Members' Interests in the last Parliament and is of the view that there are still some serious problems in this whole area.

Our concerns were set out in a recent paper produced as part of the preparatory process for the Institute's evidence to the Select Committee on Members' Interests in 1991, a copy of which is attached to this Memorandum as Appendix I.[1] The

---

1 Not published.

Institute's response to the Report on the Select Committee, which was published in September 1991, is attached.[1] We believe that the key points at issue require serious consideration and should be commented on by the Hansard Society Commission.

3. Finally

This Memorandum of Evidence has assumed the existence of benign Government. We are aware that no such thing exists in the real world and that is the reason why the present imbalance between the devices of Government and often conflicting views of interested parties, such as industry, commerce and non-governmental organisations is often too firmly weighted in the Government's favour. We believe that the proposals we have made would go a long way to rectify that.

13 May 1992

M32 Mr Ralph Instone, QC

The most obvious candidate for reform is the process of enacting the annual Finance Bill.

The Budget speech is widely regarded (not least by Chancellors) as the principal Parliamentary occasion of the year, preceded by the ritual brandishing of an old tin box, and consisting as to the first 80% of the rapid reading of an economic review which to the audience and the media is largely an irrelevance for which oral delivery is quite unnecessary. MPs and the public are primarily if not exclusively interested in the tax changes announced in the final half-hour, kept to the end ostensibly until after the Stock Exchange has closed (which since Big Bang it doesn't), but more justifiably in order to keep MPs in the Chamber.

The elaborate secrecy in which Budget proposals are enshrouded is largely unnecessary and militates against adequate preparation of the Finance Bill. It is rare for any tax change to affect individual market prices, save for variations in VAT rates, which can be effected at any time by Treasury order. And the ever-lengthening Finance Bills of recent years are mostly concerned with technical changes in fiscal legislation for which pre-Budget confidentiality is counter-productive.

There is an urgent need for all such legislation to be published in provisional or Green Paper form at least four weeks before Budget Day. (Changes in tax rates could be embodied in a separate Bill.) This would allow time for informed comment to be reflected in the first edition of the Finance Bill, and would reduce the need for vast numbers of amendments to be tabled at later stages.

There are numerous highly-experienced lawyers and accountants in the House of Lords, who customarily display in Finance Bill debates a great deal more expertise than is possessed by the Government spokesmen, but whose amendments cannot be accepted unless the Government chooses to adopt them. This results in Finance Bills being bulldozed through the Upper House in unamended form, with or without an undertaking from Treasury spokesmen to consider the Lords' amendments on the

---

1 Not published

Bill's return to the Commons. This is an insult to the efforts of peers to improve the Bill.

It frequently happens that changes in fiscal legislation have an impact on other fields, notably in company law. One example is the "demerger" legislation in the Finance Act 1980. The method of taxing dividends has twice been changed since the war (in 1965 and 1973), and it was obvious on the second occasion that the Inland Revenue had not consulted anyone else, in particular the DTI, on how to do it. The result was a provision in the Finance Act 1973 which was so absurd that a High Court judge declined to believe that it had been intended by Parliament (see *Sime Derby London Ltd. v Sime Derby Holdings* Ltd., 1973 3 All E R 691 at p 695, per Brightman J), and avoided the absurdity by giving the provision a construction which was "at first sight grammatically illogical". To acquiesce in this construction apparently involved too much loss of face for Somerset House, and its original concept was reinstated in the Finance Act 1976.

The Department of Trade and Industry has long since recognised the advantages of widespread consultation on proposed legislation on company law before any Bill is published. It is high time that the same lesson was learnt in Somerset House, and the tradition of unnecessary secrecy for fiscal legislation abandoned.

November 1991

M33   The Hon Mr Justice Paul Kennedy

A.   This Judge's Perspective

Although I will be meeting the Commission as the representative of the Judges' Council, and I have taken the precaution of circulating your letter to the members of the Council, I have no "Council brief". The comments contained in this letter are largely my own, and they must be viewed against the background of my own experience. My knowledge of the Parliamentary process in this country is relatively slight as I have never been involved in it, my knowledge of Parliamentary process elsewhere is really non-existent, and neither in practice at the bar nor on the bench have I found interpretation of legislation to be a frequent problem. Prior to my appointment in 1983 I had a general common law practice, mainly on the North Eastern Circuit and since 1983 when not on circuit most of my time has been divided between criminal appeals and the Crown Office List. Occasionally a criminal case does throw up a problem of statutory interpretation, and rather more frequently such a problem arises in connection with an application for judicial review. So far as judges of the Queen's Bench and Family Divisions are concerned I suspect that my experience is typical. The perspective of judges who sit in the Chancery Division or the Court of Appeal may be slightly different.

B.   What does the Statute say?

With the assistance of competent counsel it is of course possible to discover how the statutory provision under consideration was worded at the relevant time, allowing for pre-existing and subsequent amendments, implementation dates, etc. but the tracing exercise can be difficult, and with modern technology that difficulty could be easily overcome. Apparently a database is now being completed, possibly by Butterworth, but should this be left to private enterprise?

C. Could it not be simpler?

No doubt everyone would agree that all legislation, particularly in fields which directly affect the "man in the street", should be in such a form that it can be read and understood by an intelligent layman. Most lawyers look back with nostalgia to the Sales of Goods Act 1893 and some other statutes of that period, but we recognise that it is not always possible to deal with a complex problem in a simple way.

On balance I believe that judges would take the view that if a problem cannot be dealt with in primary legislation in a simple and coherent way it would be better if the Act were to confine itself to statements of principle, leaving the detail to statutory instruments or interpretation by the courts. However that would tend to highlight two other problems which I mention in (D) and (E) below.

D. Interpretation

If the words of the statute are clear and unambiguous no problem arises, but if there is an ambiguity it is tempting to say that courts should not hesitate to look at ministerial statements, or at Hansard to get a better idea of the problem which Parliament was attempting to address. But having regard to what happened subsequently during the Parliamentary process the reference to a ministerial statement or a White Paper could be misleading, and Lord Donaldson has suggested to me that if Hansard could be referred to there would be a strong temptation to members of both Houses to make speeches giving their own (misleading) version of the mischief to which the statute was addressed. It seems to me that it is also desirable, if litigation is not to become ever longer and more expensive, to set reasonable limits to the material to which a court ought to have regard when attempting to interpret. What Lord Donaldson suggests is that after an Act has been enacted a neutral, in the form of Speaker's Counsel, should be required to prepare a memorandum of the purposes of the Act. The memorandum would have to be approved by Parliament but would not be capable of being amended, and thereafter it could be a valuable aid to construction, that document alone being recognised by the courts. I see the attractions of that suggestion, but not every statute would merit a memorandum, and at least in relation to non-contentious legislation, or legislation passed substantially as proposed, there might be a lot to be said for allowing judges to look at ministerial statements and notes to clauses. I know that Mr Justice Laws favours that approach, but no one has suggested to me that the constraints on resorting to Hansard should be completely relaxed.

E. Subordinate Legislation

An obvious danger which arises if detail is confined to subordinate legislation is that the legislation may not be properly scrutinised. At present enabling legislation followed by subordinate legislation is used to enable Parliament to enact more legislation than would otherwise be possible and Henry VIII clauses are used to enable legislation to be updated. I doubt if most judges have any strong reaction to that, but could subordinate legislation not be capable of amendment? It has been said to me that the present system whereby subordinate legislation is either approved or quashed gives the government of the day too much power and prevents either House and in particular the House of Lords, operating as a revising chamber. Judges sometimes suspect, maybe wrongly, that amendments made to a Bill at Committee stage distort the balance, create internal contradictions and may even not give full effect to the intentions of the person who proposed the amendment. It has been suggested to me that the problem might be overcome by such amendments, whether to primary or to subordinate legislation, taking the form of concepts rather than revised wording. If the concept is approved then Parliamentary Counsel acting independently of the government could do the drafting necessary to give effect to it.

F. Common Law

As Lord Simon has suggested it is probably better not to legislate where the law can develop satisfactorily without legislation. Judicial Review is a prime example of healthy Common Law growth and it might well be stultified by any attempt at codification. In due course confidentiality and privacy may be adequately protected by the Common Law, and even in the sphere of criminal law some development is possible (e.g. rape within marriage). It may be that judicial creativity should be enhanced by opening the door, at least in some cases, to advisory opinions or prospective rulings, but that is a topic which is perhaps outside the remit of the Commission.

G. Law Commission

However it is all too common for there to be changes which are widely recognised to be desirable, which do require legislation, which are not really politically contentious, and which cannot be enacted because of shortage of Parliamentary time. Often the Law Commission, after careful consideration of a problem, proposes legislation which would command wide support in the legal profession (e.g. codification of the criminal law) but nothing happens. This seems to many of us to be deplorable, and it seems futile to extend the role of the Law Commission until that problem is resolved. Could there be a separate procedure, perhaps a select committee system, for dealing with technical Bills with no serious party political content? This would incidentally increase the legislative capacity of Parliament.

H. Judicial Input at the Legislative or Revision Stage

Except through the medium of the Law Commission and judicial representation in the House of Lords I do not at the moment believe that the judges could usefully contribute to the drafting of legislation before it is finally enacted. We have no English equivalent of the Conseil d'Etat. Similarly I do not at the moment see how the judiciary could play a more systematic or formal role in revising the statute book in the light of what has been decided. If that is done by the Cour de Cassation I no longer recollect how the system operates.

J. European Law

So far the judicial experience of the impact of European Community Law is limited. Obviously there may be problems arising from the attempt to translate the directives into statute law or from differences in drafting styles, but that must be true of almost every member country.

K. Conclusion

I have attempted in the course of this letter to say something about each of the matters to which your letter referred. Obviously there is much more that could be said, but hopefully this letter can at least act as a basis for further discussion when we meet.

24 March 1992

M34 Dr David Kinley, Australian National University, Canberra.

The following is based on an argument more fully expounded in a forthcoming book of mine entitled *The European Convention on Human Rights: Compliance without Incorporation*, to be published by *Dartmouth* in autumn 1992. An *Outline of Chapter Contents* attached hereto[1] is intended (hopefully) to represent to the members of the Commission how the thesis in the book is developed.

Presently there exists considerable concern over the protection and advancement of human rights and civil liberties in the United Kingdom. More specifically, attention has been focused on the United Kingdom's poor record in complying with the rights enshrined in the European Convention on Human Rights. The European Court of Human Rights has decided against the United Kingdom on 26 occasions (see Appendix 1); considerably more than any other member nation of the Council of Europe. The rate at which decisions against the United Kingdom are being made, what is more, is increasing: whereas 11 of the above judgments were delivered between 1960 and 1984, 15 were handed down between 1985 and 1990. Evidently, this country's initial enthusiasm in respect of the Convention – not only was the United Kingdom instrumental in its creation, it was also the first member nation to ratify the Convention – has not been sustained in its implementation.

Though this issue is one central to the on-going Bill of Rights debate, its particular importance, in respect of the concerns of your Commission, lies in the fact that of the above mentioned 26 cases decided against the United Kingdom, no fewer than 20 have directly concerned legislative breaches of the European Convention. That is, legislation passed subsequent to the United Kingdom's ratification of the Convention in 1951 has been held to be inconsistent with the rights it protects. [Detailed analyses of these legislative breaches are provided in the book in order to demonstrate not only the inadequacy of Parliament's consideration of the compatibility of the relevant legislation with the European Convention, but also the enormous breadth of areas involved. The issues affected include: freedom of speech; corporal punishment; trades unionism; immigration; prison rules; prevention of

---

1 not published

Table 1: All UK cases found by the European Court of Human Rights to constitute violations of the European Convention on Human Rights, including an indication where caused by legislative provisions

	Reference	Name	Articles	Details	Legislation?
1	Series A No.18 21.2.75	Golder	6,8	Prisoner's access to Court	Yes
2	Series A No.25 18.1.78	Government of Ireland	3	Interrogation techniques (Northern Ireland)	No
3	Series A No.26 25.4.78	Tyrer	3	Judicial birching (Isle of Man)	Yes
4	Series A No.30 26.4.79	Sunday Times	10	Freedom of expression; contempt of court	No
5	Series A No.44 13.8.81	Young,James & Webster	11	Closed Shop	
6	Series A No.45 22.10.81	Dudgeon	8	Homosexuality (Northern Ireland)	Yes
7	Series A No.46 5.11.81	"X"	5	Mental patient; right to have detention reviewed	Yes
8	Series A No.48 25.2.82	Campbell & Cosans	Protocol 1 Article 2	Corporal punishment in schools (respect of parents' philosophical convictions)	No
9	Series A No.61 25.3.83	Silver & Others	6,8,13	Prisoners,correspondence	
10	Series A No.80 28.6.84	Campbell & Fell	6,8,13	Boards of Prison visitors: conduct of disciplinary proceedings	Yes
11	Series A No.82 2.8.84	Malone	8	Telephone tapping	No
12	Series A No.94 28.5.85	Abdulaziz,Cabales & Balkandali	8 with 14,13	Immigration – discrimination on grounds of sex	
13	Series A No.109 24.11.86	Gillow	8	Guernsey housing Law	No
14	Series A No.114 2.3.87	Weeks	5	Parole Conditions	Yes
15	Series A No.1208.7.87	"O"	6	Child Care Procedures	Yes
16	Series A No.120 8.7.87	"H"	6,8	Child Care Procedures	Yes
17	Series A No.121 8.7.87	"W"	6,8	Child Care Procedures	Yes
18	Series A No.1218.7.87	"B"	6,8	Child Care Procedures	Yes
19	Series A No.121 8.7.87	"R"	6,8	Child Care Procedures	Yes
20	Series A No.131 27.4.88	Boyle & Rice	8	Prisoners,Correspondence	
21	Series A No.145 29.11.88	Brogan *et al*	5	Pre-trial detention without charge	Yes
22	Series A No.160 7.7.89	Gaskin	8	Access to childhood personal records	Yes
23	Series A No.161 7.7.89	Soering	3	Extradiction to USA to face murder charges *	No

Reference	Name	Articles	Details	Legislation?
24 Series A No.174 23.3.90	Granger	6(1)8(3)& (4)	Refusal of legal aid to appeal against conviction	Yes
25 Series A No.182 30.8.90	Fox,Campbell & Hartley	5(1)&(5)	Arrest and detention under emergency powers in N.I.	
26 Series A No.183 30.8.90	McCallum	8	Prisoners,correspondence	
27 Series A No.190 25.10.90	Thynne,Wilson & Gunnell	5(4)	Opportunity for review of lawfulness of detention	

terrorism; homosexuality; child care; mental health; criminal justice, and legal aid – see Table 1, and Chapters 3 & 4 in *Outline*].

Parliamentary scrutiny of legislative proposals for compliance with the Convention in this country is almost non-existent; the Government maintains that it conducts such vetting, but the methods it employs are informal, inconsistent, and, most importantly, ineffective. It is suggested that there be established a scheme for the pre-legislative scrutiny of all prospective legislation to ensure compliance with the Convention's provisions. Inspiration and encouragement may be obtained from the experiences of legislative scrutiny schemes to ensure the constitutionality of legislation in other countries (see Chapter 5 in *Outline*) when considering the establishment of a similar scheme in the United Kingdom. Of particular relevance in this regard are the structure and procedures of the two scrutiny committees in the Australian Senate (one for bills and one for regulations and ordinances), which have yielded to them considerable authority in imposing a preventive effect on the Government (in respect of such broad matters as the "protection of personal rights and liberties against violation").

It is concluded that the most effective scheme for the United Kingdom would be one based on two Parliamentary committees – one for primary and the other for secondary legislation. Both would be joint committees and, thereby, both would possess the inquisitorial powers to examine witnesses and receive expert advice. Each, also, would be assisted by a permanent adviser – not unlike the current role played by the Speaker's Counsel in respect of the Joint Committee on Statutory Instruments in this country (see Chapter 6 in *Outline*), or the advisers to the two Australian Senate committees. The principal function of the proposed committees would be to detect *prima facie* breaches of the Convention by draft legislation at the earliest possible stage of its Parliamentary consideration (either immediately prior to, or after, introduction) and to report accordingly to both houses. Furnished with this information, it is argued, Parliament would be able, where appropriate, to bring considerable preventive pressure to bear on the Government to amend draft legislation so as to ensure its conformity to the Convention (see Chapters 7 & 8 in *Outline*).

In the light of the attitudes of apparent indifference to, or ignorance of, the demands of the Convention historically exhibited by members of both the Government and the legislature such a scheme would necessarily contribute significantly to the protection and improvement of civil liberties in the United Kingdom by requiring stricter observance of the provisions in the European

Convention. Thereby, in serving to heighten the awareness within Westminster and Whitehall of the importance of the Convention, the scrutiny scheme not only would provide a means whereby violations of the Convention could be anticipated and prevented rather than merely repaired, but also the greatest responsibility for the legal protection of human rights and civil liberties would lie, appropriately, with the elected legislators rather than (as would be the case with an entrenched bill of rights) the appointed judiciary.

January 1992

M35 Law Commission

1. The Law Commission (like the Scottish Law Commission in relation to Scottish law) occupies a unique position in originating and producing Bills ready to be introduced in Parliament. It is the independent body charged under the Law Commissions Act 1965 with promoting the reform of the law of England and Wales and is given the statutory duty of keeping under review all that law with a view to its systematic development and reform including in particular the codification of such Law, the elimination of anomalies, the repeal of obsolete and unnecessary enactments, the reduction of the number of separate enactments and generally the simplification and modernisation of the law. For that purpose it is required to submit to the Lord Chancellor for his approval programmes of law reform and, if such approval is obtained, to examine the relevant branch of the law and to formulate by means of draft Bills or otherwise proposals for reform. It is also required to provide advice and information to government departments and other bodies concerned with proposals for the reform or amendment of any branch of the law. From time to time on a reference from Government it will report on an area of the law not within a programme of law reform but will nevertheless usually, if recommending reform, submit a Bill to implement its recommendations. Similarly in pursuance of its duties of securing consolidation and statute law revision it will cause draft Bills to be prepared.

2. There is no statutory requirement governing the methods by which the Commission performs its duties, but once the subject of a law reform project has been chosen, the Commission's normal procedures involve several stages. First, after considerable research it will prepare a consultation paper. In such paper typically the existing law will be set out, its defects explained, the law (and any published recommendations for reform) of other countries relating to the same area summarised, the options for reform listed and discussed, and provisional recommendations and the reasons therefor given, and the Commission invites comments on the paper generally and its provisional conclusions in particular. The paper will be circulated widely among those thought likely to be interested and to respond (including not only the judiciary, practising lawyers and academics but also Government bodies and relevant professional and voluntary organisations and interest groups) and publicity is

sought to be given to the paper through legal correspondents of newspapers and television companies and legal journals being supplied with the paper. In addition further copies of the paper can be purchased from HMSO. Sometimes the consultation process is taken further by the holding of seminars to discuss the paper. Next, the responses to the consultation are analysed, and in the light of the views expressed the Commission will formulate its policy. It will then prepare its final report and if it decides that the law needs reform, in the report it will set out its proposals and explain in detail the reasons for those proposals. It will at the same time as preparing the report usually instruct Parliamentary Counsel to prepare a draft Bill to implement those proposals.

3. Between 4 and 6 Parliamentary Counsel are at any one time attached to the Commission. They are instructed in much the same way as they would be if at 36 Whitehall receiving instructions from a Government Department. But because they work in the Commission's premises, they may at times be more involved in the detailed elaboration of policy and have their drafting subjected to closer scrutiny than if they were drafting Government Bills. However the accepted convention is that while the Commission is ultimately responsible for the policy of the Bill, the wording of the Bill is ultimately for Counsel, and the Commission, even if it dislikes the style and language of the Bill, cannot compel Counsel to adopt any particular style or wording provided that his draft gives effect to the Commission's policy. But the Bill leaves the Commission in a form capable of immediate introduction.

4. The Commission's report, usually with Bill and explanatory notes included, is submitted to the Lord Chancellor who is required to lay it before Parliament. Again the report is widely circulated, and again the Commission gives publicity to the fact of publication, and sometimes, on a topic of wide interest, it will even hold a press conference. Again the report is available to be purchased by the public from HMSO. The detailed legislative proposals are thereby made available to anyone interested in them and frequently representations on them are made to the relevant Government Department by members of the public and interested groups. Invariably reports of the Commission will be analysed and discussed in legal journals.

5. Whilst there is a special Parliamentary procedure which ensures that consolidation Bills and statute law revision Bills are quickly introduced, examined by the Joint Committee and enjoy an expedited passage through Parliament, no special procedure has ever been instituted for law reform Bills produced by the Commission. There is not even an obligation to give any consideration in Parliament to the Law Commissions' reports. The absence of any special procedure was immaterial so long as Government was prepared to include such Bills regularly in its legislative programme. But the increasing pressure on Parliamentary time in recent years has led to Government preferring more political Bills for inclusion in that programme and the omission therefrom of Commission Bills. Of the 38 wholly unimplemented law reform reports of the Commission (out of 113 such reports) 28 (out of 41) were published since the end of 1984. Of the 38 unimplemented reports the Commission is only

aware of 2 having been specifically rejected by Government. Several are now too dated to have a realistic chance of implementation. Others have been publicly approved by Government but are said to await a suitable opportunity for their introduction. To others no indication has been given by Government of approval or disapproval.

6. The Commission has welcomed the suggestion made by the Lord Chancellor to the Committee on the Committee Work of the House of Lords that that House might use special standing committees to consider and take evidence on law reform Bills with a view to facilitating the passage of such Bills onto the statute book. As yet the House of Commons has not sought to reconsider its procedures. The Commission submits that it is proper that recognition should be given by Parliament in its procedures to the fact that law reform Bills of the two Law Commissions are produced by the independent law reform bodies specifically designated by Parliament, have been preceded by extensive consultation and explained in a detailed report, have been drafted by Parliamentary Counsel and have been published in a manner that gives full opportunity to the public to comment thereon before their introduction.

14 February 1992

M36   Law Society

1. Introduction

1.1 The Law Society welcomes the initiative of the Hansard Society in setting up a Commission on the Legislative Process and the opportunity to participate in the exercise by submitting both written and oral evidence.

1.2 This paper is submitted with the approval of two Committees of the Council of the Law Society – the Courts and Legal Services Committee and the Property and Commercial Services Committee who share responsibility for supervising the work of the Law Society's Specialist Committees which cover the following main areas of practice: Civil Litigation, Company Law, Consumer and Commercial Law, Criminal Law, Employment Law, Family Law, Immigration Law, Land Law and Succession, Mental Health and Disability, Planning Law and Revenue Law. It is through these various Committees that most of the Law Society's Law Reform and Parliamentary work is undertaken. These Committees are primarily concerned with the law, procedure and practice in particular specialist fields; with difficulties encountered by solicitors and their clients in relation to the current law and procedure and, thus, with the process of reform. The Committees' initiate proposals for reform and respond to those made by others; they comment in detail on Law Commission and other Government consultation papers concerning changes to primary legislation, rules, regulations etc and they also produce briefing papers and draft amendments to Bills where necessary.

1.3 The Society has, therefore, a considerable interest in the subject of the Commission's enquiry. The law and its subsidiary procedures are the main "tools" of a solicitor's trade and if they are seen as bad or obscure it is often the solicitor, as the frontline operator of the legal system, who will be blamed by dissatisfied clients. In commenting on the process of legislation, therefore, the Law Society is representing both a public and professional interest.

2. Law Society Objectives

2.1 The Society's main objective in proposing reforms to the current process of legislation is to ensure that both the legislative process and the final legislation are effective and accessible.

2.2 More specifically the Law Society would wish to see legislation that is "user friendly"; clearly drafted in plain English and intelligible both to the lawyer and layman.

2.3 Further, not only must individual measures be comprehensible but amendments to existing legislation, commencement dates, delegated powers, etc must all be easily identifiable, as should the effect of European legislation on domestic law. The law of the land must be easy to find, easy to read and easy to understand otherwise the law makers are guilty of a serious failure of communication.

2.4 As a matter of constitutional propriety there should be a controlled balance between the use of primary and secondary legislation: general principles should, so far as is possible, be embodied in primary legislation and not regulations. There must be an effective means of scrutinising all proposed legislation – both primary and secondary.

The mechanism of scrutiny should include duties to consult and restraints on the extent to which powers can be delegated to the executive.

2.5 Finally, the process of legislation must be open and follow clear, constructive and consistent Parliamentary and departmental procedures so that all interested parties can find out when changes to legislation are proposed; what the timetable for implementing those changes will be and what procedures are to be followed. Thus those with an interest in the subject matter can play an effective part in the process.

3. Constitutional and Political Factors

3.1 There is a widely held view that the British legislative process is unsuitable for current needs. It was devised at a time when there were many fewer Bills for Parliament to consider and those Bills were, in turn, much shorter than those currently put before Parliament. In 1991 there were 71 Public and General Acts (including 2 Church Measures) adding 2486 pages to the Statute Book; 39 Local Acts and 2945 Statutory Instruments. During previous decades the pages added by Public and General Acts have totalled, on average, as follows:

1980's	2540 a year
1970's	1874 a year
1960's	1500 a year
1950's	1000 + a year
1940's	1000 - a year

In making comparisons between the 1980's and 1991 it should be noted that the size of the Queen's Printer copy was increased (in 1987) from Royal Octavo to

A4. In the past two decades Statutory Instruments numbered just below and just above the 2000 mark, respectively. It is interesting to note, by way of comparison, that the whole Statute Book of Sweden is shorter (by several hundred pages) than the Official Index to the Statute Book of the United Kingdom. There are now over 3000 Acts in force in this country.

3.2 Many legislative measures now considered by Parliament are mainly or partly of a highly technical nature, particularly those dealing with tax, financial services and commercial matters, and few MPs or Peers have the necessary specialist knowledge or interest to contribute to a detailed debate on such issues. The traditional Parliamentary forum in which the Opposition opposes whatever the Government proposes is not well suited to the process of legislation which is increasingly specialist and/or technical: it is fine for debating motions but not for formulating complex statutory provisions on politically uncontroversial issues. Because of the deficiencies of the legislative process it can be argued that in some cases the quality of legislation is adversely affected and that the Government's intentions may not be carried out by that legislation. Frequently legislation needs amending very soon after it has been put onto the Statute Book and this in turn increases the complexity and uncertainty of legislation in any particular field. Where statutory provisions are unclear this may cause people to be put to the expense of seeking legal advice and where the law is particularly obscure such advice may prove costly as it is not always a quick and easy task even for lawyers to find out what is in force and what it means. It is not satisfactory to rely upon the courts to clarify the meaning or validity of legislation: not only is this unfair on those who have to litigate such matters, it could also be said to cause unnecessary work for the courts. Given the limited resources available for the court system Government money might be better spent on improving the process of legislation. Clearer legislation might also reduce the legal costs for businesses and others who need to understand the legal environment in which they operate. Further, it is particularly important that the law is accessible and intelligible in fields where those governed by it have no right to legal aid, for example tribunal claims. In extreme cases bad law could have a subversive effect on the rule of law.

3.3 Changing the legislative process, however, requires constitutional and political reform and it is not easy to see where the motivation for such a change is likely to come from. The Hansard Society is not the first to conduct the sort of exercise that they have undertaken. The last major attempt was undertaken by a Committee appointed by the Lord President of the Council under the chairmanship of the Rt. Hon. Sir David Renton whose report on "The Preparation of Legislation" (Cmnd.6053.) was published in May 1975. This was an extensive and detailed Report but very few of its recommendations have been implemented, although some have been superseded by events and developments. The dilemma seems to be that the legislative process is not generally perceived by the Government or MPs as being seriously deficient: it is the "end users" (particularly lawyers and other specialist advisors) who take a different view. It is only the politicians, however, who can effect change and the sort of changes that are generally regarded as necessary would require radical reforms to the constitution of Parliament and traditions that are centuries old.

3.4 One of the more fundamental questions for consideration is whether the detailed text of statutes, as opposed to policy objectives, should be a matter for politicians? To a large extent, and for the reasons indicated above, it might be thought that Parliament's role in relation to legislation has already been taken over by ministers and their officials. The detailed content of a Bill is settled within the relevant Department (or Departments) and by the time it reaches Parliament the objective is to get it through with the minimum of amendments. Except where MPs or Peers are briefed by lobby groups the specialist expertise in the subject matter of the Bill will be largely confined to the Minister (as briefed by his officials) and as a result they will usually be able to "shoot down" any opposition – at least on technical points.

3.5 It is a fact of political life that some laws are often changed in response to recent incidents and political (and media) pressure (e.g. dangerous dogs and joy riding). Legislation of this sort is likely to suffer from not being fully thought through. Some legislation may have only a limited shelf-life before it is superseded by yet further changes either in the shape of completely new pieces of legislation or complex amendments to existing legislation. From the end user's point of view legislation would frequently be much better for more advance planning and thought.

3.6 The difficulty is proposing a solution which would balance the needs of both the makers and users of the legislation: give legislation more durability and certainty but at the same time preserve the sovereignty of Parliament and the democratic process.

4. A Comparative Analysis

4.1 A brief analysis of how other countries deal with the process of legislation would seem to suggest that the element of the process which involves consultation, scrutiny of policy objectives and drafting and consequent revision is sadly lacking in this country.

4.2 In France the Conseil D'Etat, which was set up after the French Revolution "to resolve difficulties which might arise in the course of administration", provides a "Rapporteur" to scrutinize every draft law in detail; to submit recommendations to the Council's General Assembly and to return a revised text to the responsible ministry. In this way the Conseil D'Etat provides specialist drafting expertise. (In France there is no equivalent of Parliamentary Counsel and those who draft laws within ministries are not necessarily legally trained). The Rapporteur will, however, not just confine his or her comments to the technicalities of drafting but will also consider the likely effect of the measure in achieving the Government's objectives. In the event of a difference of opinion between the Conseil D'Etat and the responsible ministry, the Council of Ministers will decide.

4.3 When draft laws are submitted to Parliament they are further scrutinized by a Parliamentary Commission and by a second Rapporteur working to that

Commission. At this stage amendments may be put forward by the Commission and other members of Parliament and discussion will involve the Minister and his officials. Although not public, the Commission's deliberations are published and their report considerably assists the French Parliament's consideration of the draft law and forms part of the "Travaux Preparatoires" available to assist the courts in interpretation. After first reading a draft law may be sent back to the Commission for further consideration. Commissions are appointed in both Houses of Parliament.

4.4 In **Sweden** the Government will usually appoint a drafting Commission to investigate a particular matter and to prepare legislation. Such a Commission may consist of one person only but will usually include senior lawyers and often a judge along with politicians, if the subject matter requires. The Government can also nominate experts to be at the disposal of the Commission. The Commission will consult widely both at home and abroad and the Ministry responsible will also consult on the drafting Commission's report before drafting a Bill for Parliament. This Bill will, in turn, be circulated to Ministries for comment and also the Prime Minister's Legal Adviser – established to examine the drafts of proposed legislation and to offer general guidance on drafting. A further draft is then submitted to the Cabinet who may then refer it to the Law Council to discuss with the relevant Ministry. Although the Law Council's report is not binding the Government must give reasons for not following their advice. Once a Bill is before Parliament it is referred to a committee who may seek the further assistance of the Law Council, recommend amendments or return the Bill to the Government for further consideration. After all this consultation it is not surprising that it is rare for Parliamentary debate on a Bill to continue into a second day.

4.5 The **German** system is not dissimilar to the French, save that there is no independent central body, such as the Conseil D'Etat to scrutinize legislation. However, in Germany this function is performed by the Ministry of Justice which examines all draft legislation and has separate divisions to deal with each Ministry. Further scrutiny is undertaken by committees of the German Parliament.

4.6 In **Australia** a Senate Committee on Scrutiny of Bills was set up in the late 1970's to replicate an equivalent and successful committee which scrutinizes regulations and ordinances. The Committee's terms of reference are to report to the Senate whether a Bill "by express words or otherwise":

(i) trespasses unduly on personal rights and liberties;

(ii) makes rights, liberties and/or obligations unduly dependent upon insufficiently defined administrative powers;

(iii) makes such rights, liberties and/or obligations unduly dependent upon non-reviewable decisions;

(iv) inappropriately delegates legislative power; or

(v) insufficiently subjects the exercise of legislative power to Parliamentary scrutiny.

The Committee's reports are not necessarily considered by the Senate but individual Senators may rely on the report to support an amendment to the Bill. The Committee is assisted by a legal advisor and considers Bills within a matter of weeks. Concerns are communicated to departments who may, or may not, take notice of them. The Committee is generally thought to be a successful innovation, in terms of curbing abuse of delegated powers, and although it does not replace the Committee Stage of a Bill, it does save time.

5. Chronological Analysis of the Process of Legislation (primary)

A. Consultation

5.1 Most Parliamentary Bills emanate from Government Departments although other sources include the Law Commission and private members. The first main stage in the process of legislation, after the initial policy formulation, is consultation and this can occur at two points in the process:-
   a) on the policy or merits of the proposed legislation
   b) on a draft Bill or clauses.
In an ideal world consultation should take place at both stages but this is not always the case and there are many occasions when time does not allow because of the speed with which the Government wishes to act.

a) External consultation

5.2 Uncontroversial law reform legislation, which is the staple diet of the Law Commission, follows a classic consultative programme in that the Commission will invariably issue "green" consultation papers followed by "white" reports which take account of the views submitted in response to the consultation paper and which very often include an annexed draft Bill to implement the policy recommendations in the report. All Law Commission papers are widely disseminated and publicised and are available from HMSO and other booksellers. Government Departments will sometimes follow a similar process of issuing green and then white papers before introducing legislation, with various amounts of time allowed in between for comments to be submitted. Sometimes the green or white paper might be issued by or be in response to a Royal Commission Report or the findings of some other body. The practice is not, however, consistent as between Departments or subject matter and some "green" papers may have quite a lot of "white" in them. This may not always be disclosed and may mean that the consultation is accordingly limited.

5.3 It is recommended that in all but exceptional cases there should be full consultation with all interested organisations and bodies on the policy of proposed legislation before a Bill is drafted. This consultation should allow adequate time for response (and take account of holiday periods).

5.4 Full consultation on a draft Bill or clauses is "said not to be possible" because of the constitutional impropriety of disclosing the precise contents of a Bill before it has been announced in the Queen's Speech and before MPs have had the opportunity to see it. However, this rule is more often honoured in the breach than the observance. Law Commission Bills are, for example, available in advance of being introduced into Parliament although the Queen's Speech rule remains to the extent that officially, at least, there will be no advance announcement that a piece of legislation is going to be included in a particular legislative programme. Problems also arise in relation to the invariably detailed and complex legislation which follows a Budget. These Parliamentary rules severely restrict the opportunity to comment on a draft Bill or clauses which many would say is as important, if not more important, than the opportunity to comment on the proposed policy changes. It is, after all, not always until policy has been translated into statutory provisions that it is possible to determine how workable and intelligible it will be. Lawyers are invaluable in assessing whether or not draft legislation will work in practice: they will be the people called upon to advise on the final legislation and consequently have the experience to know what sort of provisions are likely to cause difficulty in practice.

5.5 It is particularly important for technical Bills in the tax and commercial field to be scrutinised by practitioners at this early stage and other Law Society Committees (Revenue and Company Law) have proposed (amongst other things) the setting up of Advisory Bodies, with terms of reference confined to a specific area, to assist the Government in producing legislation in their particular fields. Further, it is submitted that the proposed technical content of a Finance Bill can often be distinguished from the general economic announcements of changes in duties, rates and allowances made in the Budget. Politically sensitive provisions, containing information which cannot be disclosed in advance and which require immediate effect, could perhaps, be dealt with separately from those making longer term changes to the tax system (whether in different parts of the same Bill or by means of separate Bills).

5.6 Specific proposals in relation to specialist and technical legislation are contained in papers of the Special Committee of Tax Law Consultative Bodies on "Recommendations on the Enactment and Amendment of Tax Legislation" and "The Process of Tax Reform in the United Kingdom, A Discussion Paper" and the Law Society's Company Law Committee Memorandum on "The Reform of Company Law" which are set out at Annexes A, B and C respectively.[1] It must be remembered that commercial and tax legislation forms a vital part of the business environment (both domestic and foreign) and technical errors or uncertainties can, therefore, be expensive.

5.7 There is no reason why the benefits of the suggestion made above should be confined to tax and commercial legislation; there could, for example, be standing advisory bodies on family law, criminal justice, etc. Such bodies should include the expertise of practitioners who are, after all, the people who have to operate the legislation at the end of the day. These bodies must also be distinguished from existing groups, such as the Criminal Law Revision Committee, whose concern is more with policy changes than with the "nuts and bolts" of legislation.

5.8 Another suggestion might be to extend the remit of and resources of the Law Commission to enable them to take on a much wider responsibility for all areas of law reform and to co-ordinate the work of other Departments. (See Law

---

1   not published

Society Memorandum on Ministry of Justice, May 1991). In this way legislative reform could be undertaken as much more of a planned strategy. Others have suggested that a Law Council or Conseil D'Etat should be set up in this country, along the lines of the Swedish and French models referred to earlier. Such a body would be charged with the task of advising the Government on draft Bills from the point of view of clarity, style, legality and suitability for attaining the Government's objectives and would be made up of judges, practising and academic lawyers and consumer representatives. Given the similarity of composition it would seem sensible to use the existing Law Commission rather than set up a new body. The Commission could easily work with specialist bodies or advisory groups in certain fields. It is envisaged that this would be a more formal liaison than the consultation process used by the Commission in its law reform projects.

5.9 It is therefore recommended that the Law Commission, working with specialist bodies or advisory groups, should be equipped to provide independent advice to the Government on all draft Bills.

b) Internal consultation

5.10 Currently, there is very little scrutiny of legislation before it is introduced into Parliament, either inside or outside Whitehall, although all draft legislation must be approved by a Cabinet Committee and referred to the Attorney-General. In France the Government is required to submit all draft Bills to the Conseil D'Etat; in Germany this function is performed by the Ministry of Justice and in Sweden there is a special legal adviser to the Prime Minister and a Law Council to comment on draft legislation. (see above). If the Law Commission or some other body were to take on the function of a Law Council or Conseil D'Etat this could provide independent advice to the Government and co-ordinate the views of interested Departments as well as outside bodies – thus co-ordinating the internal and external processes of consultation along with the Commission's other work of recommending policy reforms, consolidation and statute law revision (repealing provisions no longer needed).

c) Parliamentary consultation

5.11 Once a Bill has been introduced into Parliament there is very little time for it to be considered as there is a fairly rigorous timetable to be followed in order to fit in all the necessary stages before the end of the session. This is particularly so in the case of the Finance Bill which is not introduced until April. Parliamentary rules prescribe a minimum number of weekends which must elapse between, for example, first and second reading, second reading and committee stage etc and increasingly the Government is not allowing more than the minimum time to elapse. Legislation must be completed by the end of the particular Parliamentary session in which it is introduced otherwise it falls. There is, therefore, pressure to get legislation through before the session finishes. There is also considerable pressure to deal with an increasing quantity of legislation and other Parliamentary business which means that very often individual Bills have to be time restricted in order to fit them into the programme.

5.12 Many think that this consideration is not sufficiently detailed and have suggested the setting up of some sort of select committee; perhaps a joint committee of the Lords and Commons. In Australia, for example, there is a Committee of the Senate to scrutinise all Bills before they go through the full Parliamentary process. It is noted that the Report of the Select Committee on the Committee Work of the House (February 1992) has recommended that such a Committee should be set up in this country on an experimental basis, specifically to monitor the use of delegated powers (just one of the Australian Committee's terms of reference). It is envisaged that the Committee should consider Bills within the week following introduction, collect views from officials and ministers (but not outside bodies) and report before the beginning of the committee stage, so as to avoid delaying the legislation programme. The Committee would not seek to submit amendments. It is recommended that such a Scrutiny of Bills Committee should be set up in this country and that it should also be assisted by standing advisory bodies and call evidence from interested organisations in the process of assessing all Bills submitted to Parliament both in terms of policy and drafting. Alternatively and/or in addition a joint select committee could seek advice from the Law Commission. It is also suggested that the Committee be a joint committee of both Houses, as was proposed in Australia.

d) Conclusions

5.13 It is suggested that the amount of Parliamentary time needed to scrutinise legislation in Parliament could be reduced by earlier consultation with interested bodies – co-ordinated by the Law Commission and a Joint Scrutiny of Bills Committee of Parliament. This latter part of the suggestion would perhaps go some way towards satisfying those who might be concerned by loss of Parliamentary control. By implication the current "Queen's Speech" rule would have to be amended.

5.14 Forward planning and published timetables would also help. In many cases such timetables would need to span a number of years. In this way those interested in a particular piece of legislation could make early contact with relevant MPs, Peers, and Government officials and in the absence of a green and/or white paper submit representations – as happens in advance of the budget.

5.15 The legislative programme is, however, determined on an annual basis with Government Departments submitting bids early in the year for the Parliamentary session beginning in November of that year. Departments may be reluctant to commit resources to the necessary preparatory work for a Bill that may or may not be included in the programme, particularly as further preparatory work may need to be done when time is made available. Very often Parliamentary Counsel are only instructed once a slot in the legislative programme has been secured although this is not always the case. The resource limitations of Parliamentary Counsel, however, are such that they rarely have capacity to draft anything other than the legislation that is most urgently needed. Thus, in order to produce a reliable timetable of legislation over, say, five years the current short term approach would necd to be revised. It is recommended that the Government should publish five year plans listing proposed changes to primary and secondary legislation and setting out a timetable for consultation, Parliamentary consideration and implementation. In this way Departmental resources and Parliamentary Counsel could be booked in advance and proper consultation time allowed for.

5.16 One of the main features of United Kingdom legislation is the haste in which it is processed and, although the final product may sometimes be of an extremely high quality, given the time allowed; the quality could be higher still if a more sensible timetable were set.

B. Style of drafting

a) Audiences for legislation

5.17 The current style and format of legislation appears to be more determined by the needs of the Government and the Parliamentary process than the ultimate users of legislation. It should be remembered, however, that the Parliamentarians' involvement with the legislation is fairly short term as compared with the many years during which practitioners are likely to have to struggle with it. Even if it is accepted that English legislation is, on the whole, more detailed than its European counterparts there is no reason why drafting should not be clear and intelligible. The draftsman of the Children Act has been particularly congratulated by the Lord Chancellor amongst others for achieving such clarity whilst at the same time ensuring that the Act deals fully and comprehensively with all of the situations which it was intended to provide for. Drafting style is not, however, just about choice of words, punctuation or layout and the draftsman should not always be blamed for unclear legislation. The quality of legislation can only be as good as the thinking of those involved in its preparation and there is no doubt that legislation is very often woolly or ambiguous because the policy it is intended to implement has not been sufficiently distilled to produce the necessary clarity of thought on which clear drafting can be based. A system which allows the draftsman to become involved in the development of policy at an early stage is to be preferred to one where the instructions are delivered so late as to restrict the draftsman's opportunity to clarify policy intentions.

5.18 Another factor in the style of drafting in this country is the Government's inevitable wish to make legislation "judge proof" to try to ensure that their policy intentions can not be mis-interpreted by the courts. This means that the draftsman is required to try to tie up every last loophole in the Bill which can make the drafting rather convoluted. This might suggest a lack of trust in the judges or, perhaps, point to the need to reform the current rules of statutory interpretation in this country which currently deny judges access to supporting papers that might explain the Government's intention or at least what was explained to Parliament when they passed the draft Bill.

b) Henry VIII clauses and delegated powers

5.19 A particular problem of drafting arises in relation to provision for delegated powers and the use of "Henry VIII" clauses. (A Henry VIII clause reserves to a minister the power to change primary legislation by means of secondary legislation and can be described as a direct subversion of Parliamentary sovereignty.) While it is accepted that there are legitimate needs for secondary legislation to deal with detail and enable certain provisions to be prescribed or amended fairly quickly it is nevertheless necessary to maintain a balance between primary and secondary legislation. In recent years there has been an increasing use by the Government of skeletal Bills containing, in some cases, hundreds of delegated powers, many in the form of Henry VIII clauses. This means that it is very difficult to criticise and amend the Bill because there is so little of substance in it. More significantly it means that the substance will be legislated by a process which does not allow very much scrutiny by either Parliamentarians or outsiders.

5.20 Examples of skeletal Bills include the Legal Aid Bill (1978/8) and the Child Support Bill (1990/1). The latter measure creates a new framework for the assessment and payment of child maintenance based on a statutory formula to be operated by an executive agency. Although the formula was set out in a schedule to the Bill it remains meaningless until regulations insert the relevant figures on which the calculations can be based. Further, as the Agency is a creature of pure regulation it was very difficult for those lobby groups opposed to the Agency to frame appropriate amendments to the Bill. If draft regulations could be made available before the Bill receives its final Parliamentary consideration it could greatly assist lobby groups to decide whether to oppose or amend the enabling powers.

5.21 It is submitted that the current balance between the scrutiny of primary and secondary legislation is wrong. Too much time is spent considering skeletal provisions and too little time is spent considering detailed matters of substance which are very often in rules and regulations. The Select Committee on Statutory Instruments is, on its own admission, inadequate to deal with the quantity and technicality of statutory instruments which are now made. It is, therefore, suggested that some primary legislation could be considered by a select committee and certain sorts of secondary legislation should be subjected to the more traditional and detailed Parliamentary scrutiny involving second reading, committee stage, etc (see below). It would, however, be necessary to identify a fast track procedure for secondary legislation required to make changes at speed but it does not seem to be unduly difficult to make a distinction between these sorts of regulations and those which contain substantive provisions.

5.22 It should be noted that a further reason for using delegated powers is often to allow Government officials time to work up the arrangements which need to be put in place to implement the new legislation. Again the need for delegated powers could be minimised if legislation was planned more in advance and consulted on fully before being submitted to Parliament for endorsement by the elected representatives.

5.23 It is recommended that the delegation of powers (and in particular, Henry VIII clauses) should be restricted and that their inclusion in drafts of primary legislation should be monitored by the Joint Scrutiny of Bills Committee and Law Commission (see recommendations at paras. 5.9, 5.10 and 5.12 above) and that the joint committee should have power to refer a Bill back to the department responsible if the number of delegated powers is considered excessive. It is noted that the Report from the Select Committee on the Committee Work of the House (February 1992), in recommending a Delegated Powers Committee, forbore to try and establish what should be reserved to primary legislation and what is appropriate for delegation, preferring to leave this for the new Committee to determine.

5.24 Delegated powers should be clearly identifiable along with the procedures to be followed to make them. It is noted that the Renton Committee (see para 3.3) called for delegating powers to be listed in the Explanatory Memorandum. This proposal is supported. It is, therefore, recommended that a list of all the delegated powers contained in a particular Bill, along with the necessary enactment procedure required, should be set out in the explanatory memorandum which prefaces a Bill when it is first published.

5.25 Further comments on the consultation and procedure for statutory instruments are set out below.

c) Process of amending legislation

5.26 Much of the criticism of the current legislative process turns on the way in which existing legislation is amended by subsequent legislation. There are various methods in which legislation can be amended and these methods require reference to increasing numbers of statutes in order to understand the current law on any particular matter. This means that practitioners need to have any number of different Acts of Parliament to hand at any one time and commercial publishers have a bonanza opportunity to produce annotated statutes showing all the different changes which have been made to any particular piece of legislation. Indeed without commercial publications of this kind some parts of the Statute Book, particularly those dealing with tax, would be virtually incomprehensible even to specialists.

5.27 Some statutes seek to resolve the difficulty of keeping track of amendments by the use of Keeling schedules in which a piece of legislation which has been heavily amended by the Act in question is restated as amended. The reproduction of the Guardianship of Minors Act 1971 in the Family Law Reform Act 1987 is an example of this. On other occasions it is thought appropriate to repeal the original section(s) or sub-sections(s), and where possible the whole statute, and to reinstate it requiring reference only to the latter piece of legislation. The Children Act 1989 is an example of the latter technique: it repealed at least 8 whole Acts and numerous other provisions to produce, along with many new provisions, a single piece of legislation which deals comprehensively with virtually all legal aspects of bringing up children. These techniques are to be encouraged particularly as computers have now made the task very much easier for those preparing the legislation.

5.28 Another cause of irritation is the fact that legislation is very often amended in the very next session after it has been enacted. It must be arguable that if the original legislation was more carefully thought through in advance this immediate corrective legislation would not be necessary, or at least not necessary with the same frequency as it currently seems to happen.

5.29 A valuable way of tidying up the Statute Book is by means of consolidation and codification. In this way vast numbers of provisions in a wide range of statutes, which may represent layers of amendments, can be brought together into one piece of legislation. The benefit of this to the "end user" of legislation is considerable and it might achieve an overall saving of time and money spent by litigants, lawyers and courts if more resources were made available to the Law Commission for this sort of work. Again it should be noted that computers have made this task very much easier. Consolidation Bills (with or without Law Commission amendments) also have the advantage of being able to use the "fast track" Parliamentary procedure provided by the Joint Committee on Consolidation Bills.

C. Parliamentary process

a) Timetable

5.30 As has already been noted the Parliamentary process is driven by the need to get Bills through to Royal Assent before the end of the session and also the political pressures to accommodate other Bills and Parliamentary business. The turnaround times between the different stages of Bills are invariably too short to allow very effective contribution from MPs, Peers and lobby groups. The timetable also requires Parliamentary Counsel and their printers to work unsocial hours to say nothing of late sittings of Parliament itself. It is, therefore, recommended that the rule which causes unfinished bills to fall at the end of the Parliamentary session should be reviewed to enable legislation to be allocated adequate Parliamentary time. It is not proposed that this should be a general rule as it is recognised that forcing the Government to make the best use of its timetable is one of the few pressures the Opposition can bring to bear. In any event it should not be possible to carry unfinished Bills over following a General Election.

5.31 It is also a matter for concern that the timetable is almost entirely in the control of the current administration to the extent that it can cut short discussion on any particular matter by use of the guillotine and other procedures. Government amendments are often not tabled until the last minute thus allowing very little time to consider them in advance of committee or report stage. Further, it is increasingly common for Government Departments to submit vast tranches of new provisions to Bills at fairly late stages in the Parliamentary process thus allowing next to no consideration of either the policy or the drafting. This happened in the case of the Children Act 1989 and a particularly vivid example of this occurred in relation to the Companies Act 1989 where a number of important clauses, including, for example, those on ultra vires, were added during the committee stage in the House of Lords (the Bill having been introduced in the Commons). There was no pre-Bill consultation on these provisions at all and they have produced a situation which is extremely complex and uncertain. They have largely failed to achieve what was intended (the abolition of the ultra vires rule as it affects those dealing with companies) and many advisers take the view that it is safer to ignore the protections which the sections were designed to provide.

5.32   It would have been much better to have delayed the Companies Act to allow for proper consideration of these issues. Government Departments are, however, very often under acute pressure to include provisions in a piece of current legislation as there may not be another suitable legislative vehicle for some while. This practice exacerbates the usual haste with which Bills are prepared and again more forward planning, consultation, and thinking through of provisions to be included in a Bill could avoid the need for this sort of last minute action.

5.33   It is recommended that there should be some Parliamentary control on the numbers of amendments which can be introduced after committee stage – particularly when they have not been subject of prior consultation.

b) Notes on clauses

5.34   These must be distinguished from the explanatory memorandum which is printed with the first copy of a Bill. Notes on clauses have been traditionally produced only for Government spokesmen but are now increasingly available to lobby groups although there is no regular or standard practice about this. It is difficult to see why the intended meaning of clauses in a Bill should be kept a mystery when presumably the Parliamentary process is intended, in part, to ensure that legislation does clearly convey the meaning intended. Indeed many have commented approvingly on the Law Commission's practice of printing notes on the page facing the clauses in the draft Bills annexed to their reports.

5.35   It might be said that notes on clauses should not be generally available because they cannot and should not be used by judges in the interpretation of legislation and that too heavy a reliance upon them at the formative stage of legislation might make it difficult to do without them at a later stage. In other words Parliament's intention should be clearly determinable without the need for interpretative aids. However, it might be said that the process of resolving any discrepancy between the meaning of the notes on clauses and the draft Bill may assist in producing clearer legislation. It is recommended that notes on clauses should be regularly available from the sponsoring Government Department, HMSO and Parliament or, alternatively, printed "Law Commission" style with the Bill.

c) Consideration of detailed provisions of a Bill

5.36   The stage of the Parliamentary process at which detailed consideration is given to each individual clause, sub-section and paragraph etc is the committee stage. However, committee arrangements vary: in the House of Lords, for example, the committee is regularly a committee of the whole House and thus anyone can participate and no other business can be conducted at the same time. The House of Commons routinely sends public Bills to a standing committee specifically set up for the purpose. The House of Lords has recently made use of a Public

Bill Committee, for the Charities Bill, due to pressure of time and the Select Committee on the Committee Work of the House (February 1992) has recommended that this be repeated, on an experimental basis, for one or two Bills a session. It is recommended that the House of Lords should make greater use of Committees to scrutinise legislation.

5.37 There has been some experimentation in the past with special Standing Committees. These committees can take written and oral evidence from interested organisations and bodies and then consider the Bill, clause by clause. They have been described by the House of Commons Practice and Procedure Committee (1977) as the "best way to harness the positive attributes of select committees to the scrutiny of legislation" and were successfully used in relation to a number of Bills in the 1980's, for example the Matrimonial and Family Proceedings Bill 1984. The Select Committee on the Committee Work of the House (February 1992) has recommended that use of special standing committees be resumed particularly for legal and technical Bills such as those prepared by the Law Commission or Bills on Company Law. This recommendation is welcomed. Select committees can also consider current Bills. For example the Social Services Select Committee considered some of the implications and provisions of the Child Support Bill whilst it was being considered by Parliament in the 1990/1991 session. In both cases the Committees took evidence from a number of interested organisations and bodies (including the Law Society's Family Law Committee). In the latter case the Select Committee took the unusual step of publishing an interim report before the committee stage of the Bill was completed, so appalled were they about some of the possible consequences of the Bill. The main report, however, was not published until long after it was possible to amend the Bill.

5.38 It is submitted that the practice of committees hearing detailed evidence in relation to Bills being considered by Parliament is a very effective means of collecting the views of interested bodies and it is recommended that such committees should form a regular part of the Parliamentary scrutiny of the Bill and be capable of calling for specific amendments and produce reports to assist Parliament with the remaining stages of the Bill. Most lobby groups are not well qualified to submit properly drafted amendments to legislation although they are often more than well able to put forward the substance of the amendment. This is often acknowledged when the Government accept the spirit of an amendment but reserve the right to refer it to their own draftsman so that it can be properly incorporated into the Bill. Given the accepted need to have highly skilled Parliamentary draftsmen it is bizarre to allow legislation to be amended by amateurs as part of the democratic process. A committee to take evidence from interested bodies would at the same time allow MPs, Peers and lobby groups to put forward their views and allow drafting of the legislation to be left in professional hands. This sort of approach could also mean that it would not be necessary to look individually at each clause, sub-section, paragraph etc but to look at sections or groups of sections as a whole. This might be less tedious and slow than the current procedure and it might also avoid the inevitable practice of nodding through provisions which come at the end of a Bill and those which are contained in schedules because time does not allow any alternative. Inevitably committees tend to take more time analysing the first few clauses and thus those preparing the legislation can be tempted to put controversial provisions at the end where they will get less attention!

5.39 To pick up on a point made elsewhere in this paper (see para. 5.21) it is also recommended that Bills which are in effect mainly collections of enabling powers should be considered by means of committee arrangements similar to those provided for Statutory Instruments and Consolidated and Statute Law Repeal Bills. Such Committees could also call for evidence, as suggested above. It is not intended that this proposal should deny Parliamentarians a proper opportunity to consider the basic elements of a new statutory scheme – merely that the mechanism of scrutiny would be different.

5.40 In considering the Parliamentary process of scrutinising and amending legislation it is worth noting that one of the more successful means of securing an amendment to a Bill involves making representations to the relevant Government officials with a view to persuading them to put forward a Government amendment. Obtaining access to the relevant officials is, however, not easy and it is even less easy to have contact direct with the draftsman. Again, if the process of legislation allowed for early consultation on drafting the need for this might be minimised.

6. The Process of Secondary Legislation

6.1 Secondary or delegated legislation is not defined either judicially or by statute, although the Statutory Instruments Act 1946 defines a "Statutory instrument." It can take a number of different forms (for example, regulations, rules, Orders in Council etc) and is promulgated in ever increasing quantities. The different forms of secondary legislation vary in terms of status, enactment procedures and formality of language giving rise to uncertainties about validity, commencement, interpretation etc. There are a variety of different ways of remedying these deficiencies which may involve legal proceedings, either statutorily prescribed or in the form of judicial review, or reference to an Ombudsman. As with primary legislation the cost of providing the remedy might be reduced if the process could be improved so as to minimise the uncertainties.

A. Consultation

6.2 Consultation on the content of regulations before they are drafted is not common practice although it has recently been conducted in relation to some of the 90 odd pieces of secondary legislation which are required to implement the Child Support Act 1991 and for the Probate Complaints Regulations to be issued under the Courts and Legal Services Act 1990. It also occurs quite regularly in relation to company, tax and securities market regulations, perhaps because they are politically neutral and also very technical. Consultation on the form of draft regulations is not quite so uncommon but it is not standard practice and the time limits allowed for making comments are often very short.

Further, this sort of consultation tends to be done selectively by Government Departments rather than making consultation papers publicly and generally available. The lack of full consultation on draft regulations is compounded by the fact that there is very little Parliamentary opportunity to scrutinise such secondary legislation: indeed it is not always easy to find out when regulations are presented and laid before Parliament let alone find an opportunity to make representations or to resist the instrument. It should be noted that once introduced statutory instruments are not susceptible to amendment; are rarely debated and can only be "affirmed" or "negatived".

6.3 It is recommended that early consultation on the policy content of secondary legislation should become a more regular practice and that draft rules and regulations should be circulated to interested bodies in every case (allowing adequate time for comment). In an ideal world draft rules and regulations should be made available before the Bill receives its final Parliamentary consideration so that the legislators and lobby groups could see more clearly what the final legislative produce might look like.

B. Style of drafting

6.4 The style of drafting used for secondary legislation is, if anything, on the whole worse than that for primary legislation and this can perhaps be explained by the fact that secondary legislation is not prepared by specialist Parliamentary draftsmen but by departmental lawyers who despite best efforts and training perhaps do not have the opportunity to build up the necessary skill and expertise. Given the quantity and importance of this legislation it is recommended, therefore, that secondary legislation should also be drafted by Parliamentary Counsel (See Law Society Memorandum on Ministry of Justice, May 1991).

6.5 As with primary legislation there is a need for full explanatory notes to be made available with draft statutory instruments. Also the same suggestions as have been made for amending pre-existing primary legislation apply to statutory instruments. If anything the tangled web of cross-references between different statutory instruments is even worse than it is with primary legislation and it is next to impossible sometimes to ascertain which particular provisions of any given statutory instrument have or have not been repealed, amended or otherwise affected by a subsequent instrument. Even a complex and sophisticated index and the assistance of a computer cannot completely remove this uncertainty.

C. Parliamentary Process

6.6 As is clear from comments above, the Parliamentary procedures used for statutory instruments are obscure and the presentation of such instruments to Parliament is not much publicised, which makes it difficult to take part in the procedures at all. Very little assistance can effectively be given by the Joint Committee on Statutory Instruments because of the sheer quantity and technicality of instruments requiring consideration. It is not adequate to rely ultimately upon the courts to determine questions of vires and interpretation.

6.7 It is submitted, therefore, that much can be done to improve the Parliamentary scrutiny of secondary legislation – mainly by recognising that it is not "secondary" in importance but is as important, if not more important in some cases, than primary legislation, and therefore should be accorded the necessary time for full and detailed scrutiny.

6.8 It is, therefore, recommended that certain sorts of secondary legislation should be subject to something akin to the procedure currently followed for primary legislation. This recommendation mirrors the earlier recommendation (see para 5.39) to the effect that skeletal Bills, composed mainly of enabling powers, should be considered by Committee. The two recommendations are intended to achieve a reversal of the current arrangements for scrutinizing primary and secondary legislation. There will inevitably be a need for guidance on which Bills/statutory instruments follow which procedure. The test will be, as far as Bills are concerned, the extent to which they are "enabling" only; and in relation to statutory instruments, in effect the reverse – the extent to which they contain substantive provisions. It is suggested that the Joint Select Committee on Bills (proposed at para 5.12) and the existing Joint Select Committee on Statutory Instruments could determine the procedure in cases of doubt or argument. It should be noted that under the proposed new procedure for secondary legislation it would become possible to amend an instrument during the Parliamentary process; a facility which is not currently available.

D.   Rules of Court

6.9 Rules of court are another form of secondary legislation. They are at the moment made by statutory rules committees and are, in effect, not considered by Parliament at all. Rules committees do not always meet and consideration of drafts is, therefore, confined to individual written comments from members – who do not necessarily see the comments of others. Access to rules committee members or officials who serve them is limited and consultation on draft rules is similarly limited in most cases. Some statutes contain a specific requirement to consult certain organisations such as the Bar and the Law Society or to include their representatives on a rule committee. Such arrangements are not a standard practice and thus, yet again, the practitioners who have to operate the rules of court often do not have a real opportunity to comment upon how they might work in practice until it is too late for such comments to be taken into account.

6.10 It is questionable whether the procedure for making rules of court should be any different to that for any other secondary legislation. In any event consultation at an early stage should be standard practice.

E.   Codes of practice, leaflets etc

6.11 To an increasing extent codes of practice, leaflets, guidance and circulars are used to supplement the wording of legislation and they constitute, in effect, a tertiary layer of legislation. The status of many such measures is less than certain and the fact that in some cases, such as the Highway Code and Codes of Practice in the employment field, this sort of measure can have evidential value, makes uncertainty about status all the more serious. In other cases, such as under the Police and Criminal Evidence Act 1984, the Codes of Practice are, in effect, secondary legislation and have been consulted on and laid before Parliament. Status is also not necessarily consistent as between guidance notes and circulars issued by different Government Departments for different purposes. In relation to tertiary legislation issued in respect of the Children Act 1989 the Department of Health felt it necessary to produce an explanation of principles and practice in relation to regulations and guidance which sought to explain the status of different documents. It is accepted that as with other types of secondary legislation uncertainty in guidance and circulars etc can be a ground of invalidity but, as Mrs Gillick found, it is difficult to prove that a particular piece of guidance is sufficiently obscure or confusing.

6.12 Further problems with this sort of "legislation" arise out of the fact that there is very often little or no consultation before they are issued and they are drafted in language more akin to that used by advertising agencies than a Parliamentary draftsman because of the perceived need to make them intelligible. This does not necessarily mean, however, that the leaflets and codes etc are drafted in plain English and very often the absence of statutory language makes them even more ambiguous.

6.13 The increasing number of citizen's charters might also be classified as tertiary legislation – particularly as they appear to confer rights on patients, parents, travellers etc albeit by means of setting standards to be met by those providing public services.

6.14 It is recommended, therefore, that the existence of such tertiary legislation should be discouraged but, where unavoidable, acknowledged and that processes should be introduced to regulate it; to ensure that there is proper consultation and an opportunity to scrutinize not only the policy content, but also the drafting, by organisations and bodies who are likely to have to work with the end product. It might also be considered whether such legislation should be subject to any form of Parliamentary scrutiny.

F. European Community Legislation

6.15 This paper does not attempt to deal fully with the issues raised by the legislative process of the European Community, except to the extent that an increasing proportion of domestic legislation (both primary and secondary) is the result of EC legislation. The EC legislative process presents a distinct set of problems which require to be addressed separately and to some extent have been by the Select Committee on the Committee Work of the House (February 1992).

6.16 One of the main problems with EC legislation involves distinguishing between different types of legislation: regulations, directives and decisions; working out when they are effective in this country (i.e. is it automatic or is an implementing Act needed) and to what extent they override domestic law. To an extent knowledge of EC legislation can be improved by training but it is submitted that the Government has a vital role to play in ensuring that adequate information on EC law is disseminated and ensuring that it is implemented in the correct manner at the correct time. As far as dissemination is concerned it is further suggested that where domestic law is affected by EC legislation the relevant statutory provisions could be annotated in the official publications.

6.17 Problems of implementation and interpretation are well illustrated by reference to the Transfer of Undertakings Regulations 1981. These regulations were made under some pressure from the EEC to implement a 1977 Directive that was already overdue for implementation. The regulations received little or no scrutiny; they make no attempt to clarify the relationship between the Directive and parallel domestic provisions, and, in addition, do not conform with the Directive in a number of respects. Much of the consequent uncertainty was resolved by the House of Lords decision in Forth Estuary Engineering Ltd v. Litster but this decision came seven years after the regulations came into force. Numerous other decisions, including some from the European Court of Justice, have been necessary to clarify other points of uncertainty or ambiguity. This cannot be regarded as satisfactory. It is acknowledged, however, that some of the difficulties of implementing EEC provisions might be overcome if primary and secondary legislation in this country was subjected to the sort of increased scrutiny that has been recommended earlier in this paper.

7. State of the Statute Book

7.1 A number of comments have already been made about the current state of the Statute Book in connection with the process of amending existing legislation: it might however be worth repeating here the need to encourage the process of consolidation and codification of statutes which is currently undertaken by the Law Commission and also the process of going through the Statute Book repealing those provisions which are no longer required, which is also undertaken by the Law Commission. The Law Commission's resources, even when supplemented by Parliamentary Counsel on secondment, are, however, not large and thus candidates for consolidation, codification and repeal can wait a long time before being attended to. In the interests of having a more user friendly Statute Book it is, therefore, suggested that more resources should be allocated to this work.

7.2 It is also **recommended** that the Government improve the availability of up to date statutory texts, both in printed and electronic form – thus making it possible to get an official version of any Act, as amended. It would be helpful if Acts could be annotated not only to refer to overriding European legislation but also to list the exercise of delegated powers. In addition it is vital that information about commencement is readily available as many lawyers, and doubtless others, spend hours trying to find out if and when particular statutory provisions came into force. This applies to both primary and secondary legislation and the problem is compounded by the fact that commencement powers are now almost invariably delegated to Ministers and their exercise is often relatively unpublicised.

7.3 It is noted that there is a current Government project to set up a Statute Law Database but that this is, at least initially, intended for Government use only. If such a database is established it would seem odd not to allow access to others – outside Government.

7.4 The fact that the Lord Chancellor established a new Advisory Committee on Statute Law in 1991 is welcomed as is the Lord Chancellor's acknowledgment (on announcing the new Committee) that he has a responsibility "to ensure that satisfactory arrangements are made for the publication of the Statute Book, in order that the citizen may know by what laws he is bound". It is hoped that in the exercise of their responsibilities the Lord Chancellor and his Committee will take note of some of the suggestions for improving the state of the Statute Book which are contained in this paper and other proposals which may be made by the Commission.

8. Summary of Recommendations

8.1 In all but exceptional cases there should be full consultation with all interested organisations and bodies on the policy of proposed legislation before a Bill is drafted.(para 5.3).

8.2 The Law Commission, working with specialist bodies or advisory groups, should be equipped to provide independent advice to the Government on all draft Bills and to coordinate the views of interested departments as well as outside bodies. (para 5.9 and 5.10).

8.3 A joint committee of both Houses of Parliament should be set up (to be assisted by Standing Advisory Bodies and able to call for evidence from interested organisations) to scrutinize all Bills submitted to Parliament both in terms of policy and drafting. (para 5.12)

8.4 The Government should publish 5 year plans listing proposed changes in both primary and secondary legislation and setting out a timetable for consultation, Parliamentary consideration and implementation. (paras 5.14 and 5.15).

8.5 The delegation of powers (and in particular, Henry VIII clauses) should be restricted and their inclusion in drafts of primary legislation should be monitored by the Joint Committee and the Law Commission (see recommendations at paras 8.2 and 8.3 above). The Joint Committee should have power to refer a Bill back to the Department responsible if the number of delegated powers is considered excessive. (para 5.23)

8.6 A list of all the delegated powers contained in a particular Bill along with the proposed enactment procedure should be set out in the explanatory memorandum which prefaces a Bill when it is first published. (para 5.24).

8.7 Wherever possible statutes, sections or sub-sections which have been heavily amended should be repealed and restated thus reducing the need for reference back to earlier provisions. (para 5.27).

8.8. More resources should be made available to the Law Commission for consolidation and codification work. (paras 5.29 and 7.1).

8.9 The rule which causes unfinished bills to fall at the end of the Parliamentary session should be reviewed to enable legislation to be allocated adequate Parliamentary time (para. 5.30).

8.10 There should be some Parliamentary control on the number of amendments which can be introduced after committee stage – particularly when they have not been the subject of prior consultation. (para 5.33).

8.11 Notes on clauses should be regularly available from the sponsoring Government Department, HMSO and Parliament or, alternatively, printed on the page facing the clause. (para 5.35).

8.12 The House of Lords should make greater use of committees to scrutinise legislation. (5.36).

8.13 Special standing committees should form a regular part of the Parliamentary scrutiny of a Bill and be capable of calling for evidence from interested bodies and of recommending specific amendments. (para 5.38).

8.14 Bills which are in effect mainly collections of enabling powers should be considered by means of committee arrangements similar to those provided for statutory instruments and consolidated statute law repeal Bills. (para 5.39).

8.15 Early consultation on the policy content of secondary legislation should become a more regular practice and draft rules and regulations should be circulated to all interested bodies (allowing adequate time for comment) in every case. (para 6.3).

8.16 Secondary legislation should be drafted by Parliamentary Counsel. (para 6.4).

8.17 Full explanatory notes should be made available with draft statutory instruments and where one instrument makes amendment to another the amended provision should, wherever possible, be repealed and restated in the later instrument. (para 6.5).

8.18 Certain sorts of secondary legislation should be subject to something akin to the procedure currently followed for primary legislation. This recommendation mirrors the earlier recommendation (see 8.13 above) to the effect that all skeletal Bills, composed mainly of enabling powers should be considered by a committee procedure. It is also recommended that the proposed new Joint Scrutiny of Bills Committee (see 8.3 above) and the existing Joint Select Committee on Statutory Instruments should have power to determine which procedure should be followed in cases of doubt or argument. (para 6.8).

8.19 The existence of tertiary legislation in the form of codes of practice, guidance, leaflets and citizen's charters, should be discouraged but, where unavoidable, acknowledged and processes should be introduced to regulate it; to ensure that there is proper consultation and an opportunity to scrutinize not only the policy content but also the drafting, by organisations and bodies who are likely to have to work with the end product. (para 6.14).

8.20 The state of the Statute Book should be improved by greater availability of up to date statutory texts, in both printed and electronic forms annotated with references to overriding European legislation, and the exercise of delegated powers – in particular commencement orders. (para 7.2).

March 1992

M37 Local Authority Associations: the Association of Metropolitan Authorities, the Association of County Councils and the Association of District Councils

Introduction

The Associations represent county, non-metropolitan district and metropolitan district councils in England and Wales. The Associations welcome the opportunity to contribute to the work of the Commission, believing it to be timely and directed to an issue of considerable importance and urgency.

Local government is well-placed to offer comments and suggestions on the legislative process, since the legislation concerning local government matters has dominated the political agenda for much of the last 13 years. A total of 143 Bills with a direct application to local government in England and Wales was enacted between 1979 and 1992, of which 58 were major provisions. Local authorities have been subject to probably the largest series of legislative proposals ever enacted in a comparable period which have represented a revolution in the organisation and activities of major democratic bodies.

The volume of legislation, and the scope of such reserve powers, have tested – perhaps more than ever before – the ability of Parliament properly to scrutinise legislation emanating from the Executive. It is against this background that the Associations present their evidence on the current state of the Parliamentary law-making process.

The Commission invites evidence in four main areas:

A: the extent and nature of Government consultation on proposed legislation (including statutory instruments and the implementation of European Community Directives);

B: the formal drafting of Bills and statutory instruments;

C: Parliamentary scrutiny of legislation;

D: Accessibility to the public of legislation.

Our evidence is arranged in response to these issues. A summary of proposals follows.

Summary of Proposals

A: Consultation

1. Representative bodies of local authorities and similar organisations should be included within an agreed process and timescale of consultation with central government on all policy proposals which will become the subject of legislation.

2. Major changes of policy should be preceded by an open debate, based on a Green and White Paper wherever practicable.

3. Green Papers should invite consultation responses over a realistic timescale, and a paper analysing the response should be published before a White Paper is produced.

4. Local authorities should be given early copies of Bills affecting their powers by the relevant Department.
5. Draft legislation should refer in the Explanatory Memorandum to the consultative document(s) from which it arises.
6. Green and White Papers, with a summary of responses and of any further Government response, should be routinely made available with copies of bills.
7. All major statutory instruments relevant to local government should be subject to consultation at both pre-draft and draft stages.
8. SIs laid before Parliament should carry a statement of the major bodies consulted, for the information of Parliamentarians.
9. The UK Government should review its processes of consultation on EC policies, draft EC legislation and UK legislation arising from EC requirements, with the objective of involving representative bodies in policy formulation at a meaningful stage.
10. The UK Government should take full opportunity of the enhanced consultative arrangements embodied in the Maastricht decision to create a Committee of Regions, by nominating local authority representatives to the 24 UK places.

B: Form and drafting of legislation
11. The clarity and precision of drafting of legislation should be improved.
12. The trend towards "framework" legislation should be resisted; the policy of a bill should be deducible from its drafting.
13. The Executive should be urged to reduce the rapid creation of change upon change by legislative means.
14. Each bill should include in its Explanatory Memorandum a statement of the number and type of Ministerial powers contained in it (on the basis of a typology developed as proposed in 16 below).
15. Parliament should publish sessional reports on the number and type of Ministerial powers granted.
16. Principles relevant to the granting of Ministerial powers to serve as a reference point of Parliamentarians should be considered (possibly by an ad hoc select committee of the Lords on Central/Local relations, if created).
17. A Parliamentary Committee should develop an official typology of the various powers available under statute, including those for which no Parliamentary scrutiny is available.
18. A Parliamentary Select Committee (perhaps jointly between both Houses) for the scrutiny of statutory instruments should have a remit going beyond vires, including powers to reject on grounds of obscure or unsound drafting. It should operate with the backing of guaranteed period of notice before SIs come into effect (unless abrogated by agreement).
19. Draft SIs should include a statement of related secondary legislation and, where relevant, a consolidated form of wording.
20. A pre-publication scrutiny committee on bills should be established, to meet in private, to look at the technical quality of drafting and to approve the Explanatory and Financial Memorandum.

C: Effectiveness of Scrutiny

21 The Explanatory and Financial Memorandum to each bill should include a detailed statement for the policy of the bill, and detailed staffing and financial estimates. The latter could be certified by the National Audit Office (or the Audit Commission, in the case of local government implications), and the whole Memorandum submitted to the pre-publication scrutiny committee for approval (as to whether its contents matched the bill). The Memorandum should be available two weeks before Second Reading.

22. More detailed Notes on Clauses should be published (also 2 weeks before Second Reading) for the information of the whole of each House.

23. A pre-Committee Stage scrutiny of civil servants should be established, to enable members of the Committee (or selected peers in the Lords) to put factual questions. More use should be made of Commons Special Standing Committees and Lords Public Bill Committees, especially on technical bills.

24. The principle should be adopted that it is the obligation of the Executive to make available sufficient material to Parliamentarians and interested bodies to produce an informed debate.

25. Timetabling of legislation in the Commons should not weaken the position of non-government supporters. Timetabling should only proceed on any bill by agreement. A "points system" could be examined as one means of enabling the Opposition parties to design the layout of the legislative business, while a minimum tariff related to length and maximum periods between stages would prevent Governments from rushing legislation through with inappropriate haste.

D: Accessibility of Legislation

26. Visitors to Parliamentary debates should be offered copies of relevant documents where these relate to legislation.

27. Acts of Parliament should carry an adapted version of the Explanatory and Financial Memorandum (without legal force), including some of the detailed explanation from Notes on Clauses.

28. Acts should carry a table (also without legal force) summarising the repeals and consequential amendments, schedules and cross-referencing to other statutes.

29. Local authorities should receive copies from the relevant Department of all SIs, EC directives and EC regulations.

30. The Government should review facilities available to public bodies and to the public for the inspection and obtaining of EC documents.

31. Consolidation of primary legislation should be given higher priority.

32. The Government should undertake the more regular production of local government Miscellaneous Provisions bills.

A: Consultation

Parliamentary Bills

In recent years there has been a serious decline in the extent and nature of consultation and inquiry undertaken before legislation is proposed in Parliament. The Associations have viewed this development with concern, and have pressed repeatedly, both in general and on specific occasions for improved consultative arrangements.

Proper consultation is of great value (not least to Government) in producing policy proposals whose implications have been properly considered, and in engendering consensus between policy-makers and those charged with implementation and interpretation. Perhaps the best statement of the meaning of proper consultation is that given by Webster J. in *R v Secretary of State for Social Services, ex parte AMA*:

> "...the essence of consultation is the communication of a genuine invitation to give advice and a genuine consideration of the advice...it must go without saying that to achieve consultation sufficient information must be supplied by the consulting to the consulted party to enable it to tender helpful advice. Sufficient time must be given by the consulting to the consulted party to do that, and sufficient time must be allowed for such advice to be considered by the consulting party. Sufficient, in that context, does not mean ample, but at least enough to allow the relevant purpose to be fulfilled.
>
> By helpful advice in this context I mean sufficiently informed and considered information or advice about aspects of the form or substance of the proposal as to which the Secretary of State might not be fully informed or advised and as to which the party concerned might have relevant information or advice to offer."

The deterioration has taken several forms. The traditional pattern of the establishment of the Royal Commission, or at least a Committee of Inquiry, before the introduction of major changes of policy has been abandoned. Structural reforms in London in 1964 and in the metropolitan areas in 1972 were preceded, for example, by Royal Commissions. The reform of local government finance was the subject of a Royal Commission which reported in 1976. No government of the day would have considered legislation in either area without the benefit of a detailed and independent external of this type. Yet in 1985 and in 1987 fundamental legislation was approved by Parliament in both of these areas. It is perhaps no coincidence that the legislation to abolish the Community Charge was announced within the first year of its application in England and Wales, and that in the General Election held six years after the abolition of the GLC all parties put forward proposals to amend local government arrangements in the capital.

One of the defining features of recent policy-making has been the increased pace of change, as new developments are superimposed on others which have barely been implemented. Under the Education Reform Act, serial change was built into the legislation as the introduction of local financial management in schools was followed within a year by the introduction of grant-maintained status while competitive tendering for school cleaning, catering and grounds maintenance was also under way, in addition to the application of the National Curriculum.

The abandonment of Royal Commissions has been mirrored by decline in the Green Paper/White Paper system. The publication of consultative proposals by Government could be expected in a major policy area to be followed by a White Paper setting out a firm policy. Legislation would then follow after extensive consultation between civil servants and interested parties such as the Associations as to the details of practical implementation. There was a perceived need for orderly public policy-making, and for balance and consensus in the process.

The recent pattern has seen fewer White Papers, the severe compression of consultative deadlines, the dropping of formal Green Papers in favour of looser "consultative documents" and the frequent exclusion of interested parties altogether from consultation even on implementation.

The timing of consultation has been of long-standing concern to the local authority Associations and their member authorities. It is often the case that Government allows inadequate time to enable an Association properly to ascertain the views of its member authorities and advisers, or for the authorities to seek the views of elected members. There is an allied concern that consultation can be undertaken at inappropriate times of the year. A number of consultation papers were issued, for example, last year on the implementation of various provisions of the Planning and Compensation Act 1991. Several of these were issued in late July with a deadline for comments in the early autumn. It was very difficult for affected local authorities to obtain the views of elected members on major policy questions with substantial resource implications (e.g. the publicity to be given to planning applications) at a time of year when many councillors would be away and committees in recess. There has also been some unwillingness in Associations to act as a "post office" for central government, by being compelled to send consultation documents to authorities where the department concerned does not do so itself. The following examples serve to illustrate some recent developments:

Education Reform Act 1988: A major measure which introduced the National Curriculum, grant-maintained schools, devolved school budgets and the abolition of the ILEA. There was no White Paper on any of these school-related proposals. Short consultative documents were published in haste in July and August 1987, allowing from 5 to 11 weeks for replies over the period of the school holidays. No analysis of the response was published. On ILEA, the proposals were radically amended during the Bill's passage to provide for complete abolition. There was, therefore, no reasoned statement of the Government's eventual policy in this area. Local education authorities were, other than on the subject of school charges which proved less controversial, at no stage involved in consultative discussions. The Bill was published a few weeks from the end of the consultative period, and differences between it and the consultative proposals were mostly on minor points.

Housing Act 1988: The legislation introduced the right for tenants on council estates to vote as a bloc to "opt out" to a private landlord, created powers to transfer estates to Housing Action Trust and amended the Right to Buy rules. The normal process was reversed: a White Paper ("Housing – The Government Proposals") was published first, followed within days by a series of consultative documents inviting responses over about four weeks. Second Reading in the Commons, however, had taken place before the end of the consultation period.

Local Government Act 1992: Sections 7–11 of this Act, deal with the extension of Compulsory Competitive Tendering to white collar local authority services. The Bill was published in November 1991 and a consultative document, albeit a detailed one ("Competing for Quality: Competition in the Provision of Local Services") was published the same month, inviting responses by 31 January 1992. By the expiry of the consultation process, the Lords had completed their consideration of the Bill and the Commons had reached Committee Stage. Detailed debate on the CCT provisions was effectively frustrated, since Ministers responded to all questions with the formula that the matter was subject to consultation. By the dissolution of Parliament, the Government had yet to announce its final plans.

Reduction in the number of White Papers has been matched by a significant alteration of their content and style of presentation. The traditional white A5-sized Command document has become a larger, multi-coloured glossy booklet, with photographs, graphics, departmental logos and occasionally a signed Foreword by the Prime Minister. More significantly, the content has moved from a discussion of the issues – albeit from a declared policy standpoint – to a broad promotion of the policy concerned without reference to alternatives. It is instructive to compare the White Paper which preceded rate-capping ("Rates", Cmnd 9008, August 1983) with the White Paper proposing the removal of Further Education colleges from local government ("Education and Training for the 21st Century", Cmnd 1536, volumes 1 and 2, May 1991). No-one would have regarded "Rates" at the time of its publication as a paradigm of reasoned argument. The contrast between the two documents is, however, striking. The case set out in the 1983 White Paper includes: background statistics on local finance; an analysis of responses to an earlier Green Paper on forms of local taxation; a detailed description of the proposed operation of rate capping; and the Government's conclusions on options for other reform of the rating system. In summary, the case is argued and the pros and cons of other options considered. The 1991 paper relies largely on assertion. It opens with "Aims" and "Achievements", including unverified claims such as: "the National Curriculum is already setting new and higher standards in schools". Headlines employed such as "Higher Achievement"; "A Stronger Education Base"; and "A Revolution in Learning" indicate the style of the text. The proposal to remove FE colleges from local authority control is justified in a single sentence, as follows:

> *"Colleges lack the freedom which we gave to the polytechnic and higher education colleges in 1989 to respond to the demands of students and of the labour market." (Volume 1, para 9.2, page 58).*

No further reasons or statistics are given. On this basis, a reorganisation of the public sector accounting for £2 billion per annum of public expenditure was proposed to Parliament.

There appeared at the end of 1990 to be a prospect of a return to closer consultation, with the establishment by DoE Ministers of a Review of Local Government, to which the Associations were initially invited to contribute. Results were, however, disappointing. The papers produced were superficial and there has been no real interchange of views between central and local government. Forty one internal "Questions" produced (after consultation) at the outset of the Review as a foundation for its work remain unaddressed eighteen months later.

A more hopeful development has been the recent involvement of the local authority Associations in implementation discussions on the Regulations to introduce the Council Tax. Technical experts nominated by the Associations have been directly involved with DoE officials at a near formative stage, with draft Regulations being assembled while the primary legislation was still being debated in Parliament. The timescale for the introduction of the tax is still very tight. Although final regulations had largely been issued by May 1992, there are acknowledged errors in drafting which will need correction and inevitably complicate the development of software for introduction of the tax on 1 April 1993. On the general issue, such discussions are no substitute for proper consultation on the determination of initial policy.

The provision of a copy of all bills affecting them direct to local authorities would greatly assist both the Associations as representative bodies involved in consultation, and authorities themselves in preparations for implementation. Consultation would still be channelled to Departments through the Associations, but the proposal would do much to assist knowledge of Government plans at an early stage and the quality of consultation. The Associations would be assisted in discussing issues with their membership in being relieved of the expensive and often complicated burden of either circulating or interpreting draft legislation, while authorities – as well as participating more fully in the policy process – could begin several months earlier their consideration of implementation.

The reduced role of consultation has had a direct effect on the Parliamentary process. Outside organisations have increasingly in recent years used the legislative process to clarify issues of policy and implementation. Policy debates have served in part to remedy the deficiencies of consultation, but have frequently been criticised by government spokesmen as "Second Reading debates" on the principles of the legislation. On matters of detail, bodies such as the Associations now devote resources to Parliamentary work – to the extent of employing full-time staff – which were unnecessary ten years ago. Parliamentarians have with greater frequency been approached to move "probing amendments" to establish points which relate not to policy alternatives but to the practical effect of the legislation. The efficiency of these debates as a means of determining policy implementation issues can seriously be questioned. The process of devising in amendment form alternative proposals to those in a Bill for the purpose of testing points is artificial and can produce obscure debate. Much of the detail is too small for full-scale debate and appropriate to that format, consisting of questions on timescales, notifications, administrative processes etc. Many Parliamentarians, however, notably in the Lords, regard it as their duty to meet a need which officials have been prevented from addressing in consultative discussions.

The consultative process, even where it occurs, is poorly integrated with the Parliamentary one. Consultative documents are, as a matter of course, available to MPs and peers, but no serious effort is made to spread awareness of their contents; the function which necessarily falls to interested outside organisations. Lack of information in the House as a whole, combined with the constraints of the debating format, frequently create difficulties for peers or MPs seeking to advance the debate. As a partial remedy, consultative documents, together with analyses of responses to them from the Department concerned, could usefully be made routinely available to

Parliamentarians with copies of Bills as a small step towards closer scrutiny o Government proposals.

Statutory Instruments

The Associations are routinely consulted on certain important Statutory Instruments although it is by no means the case that all major Statutory Instruments are subject to consultation in this way. Full consultation at a proper stage is increasingly important in this area in view of the trend examined below for the creation of wide Ministeria powers, including the power to amend primary legislation by statutory instrument.

Consultation will frequently take place on the basis of a near-finished draft rathe than at the formative stage. Consultation at this stage means that timing is very tigh and that there is less likelihood of comments being incorporated: a recent example was of the regulations governing Members' interests under the Local Governmen and Housing Act 1989. In this case, at least one authority which contacted the relevant Department over practical difficulties with the draft was told that no changes could be made in any event. Where discussion does take place on the basi of a pre-draft policy paper, the actual draft may not be seen by the Associations unti publication. Neither system is wholly satisfactory from the viewpoint of loca authorities charged with implementation. It would be desirable if Government were to adopt the principle that all major Statutory Instruments relevant to loca government should be subject to consultation at both predraft and draft stages. Thi could be backed by the publication alongside the draft Statutory Instrument of statement of the major bodies consulted at each stage of its drafting, for th information of Parliamentarians.

Statutory instruments, which are produced by Departmental Lawyers rather tha Parliamentary draughtsman, frequently contain obscure drafting. This can place a even greater strain than the wording of primary legislation on officers charged witl implementation in local authorities as elsewhere. The meaning of significan provisions in primary legislation, while possibly unclear at the outset of th Parliamentary process, will usually at least in substance have been established by th end of that process.

As well as the need for proper consultation on statutory instruments, th Associations would also be concerned to establish consistent consultative procedure on circulars and guidance. This is of particular importance in view of the growth o "government by circular" – legislation requiring authorities to "have regard" t guidance issued by Ministers.

European Legislation

The level and process of consultation with local government in the Europea policy-making process is becoming a matter of increasing concern to th Associations. Local Authority Associations will be consulted in a few instances b the lead government departments, but such discussions often take place towards th end of the long European policy-making process, either at the stage when th Council of Ministers is due to consider the proposal, or more usually when the UI Government itself is considering its own process of implementing Europea legislation. Where consultation takes place, local authorities are thus cast in the rol of bodies offering "advice" to Ministers representing a UK viewpoint, or are involved merely at the implementation stage. The consultation is a "paper based" exercise conducted at a distance. Discussions are rarely held directly with departmental officials, and no indication is given of the view subsequently advanced by the Department. The involvement of authorities through this route is often too late to represent effective consultation, and this criticism applies as much to Regulations which have direct effect as to consultation on Directives which will then either lead to domestic legislation or have direct effect themselves.

The local authority Associations have established the Local Government International Bureau to promote their interests in international, and particularly European Community, affairs. The Bureau acts as a channel for information to and from central government, the European Commission and other Community institutions. The Bureau provides an established mechanism through which central government could involve the local authority Associations at a formative stage in its European policy-making.

More productive discussions have been held with some professional bodies, and there are certain mechanisms of consultation in which local government is formally involved – e.g. on trading standards. Given the fact, however, that European legislation may in the medium term account for the majority of new initiatives and standards of public regulation, much of it directly binding on local authorities, the present arrangements are inadequate. The impression is gained that Whitehall may itself have problems in coordinating its input to European legislation. There appears to be little willingness to draw local authorities closer towards deliberations in Brussels.

There are four problems with the consultative process through the British Government:

(a) consultation is formal and amounts to "information gathering" by central government departments;

(b) the UK Government is only one actor amongst twelve, and even if it wished to do so could only to a limited extent enable outside organisations to have a more direct and formative involvement;

(c) consultation is conducted at a late stage in the process; and

(d) consultation is partial, covering only certain matters of interest to local authorities.

The UK Government could seek views from domestic organisations at an earlier stage and could draw on the technical expertise of local authorities amongst others to a considerably greater extent to inform its own policies.

One consequence of this situation is that the local authority Associations are having to become "lobbyists" on the Brussels/Strasbourg stage, to get nearer to the seat of decision-making (and in particular to the Commission). UK local government is, for example, currently fighting a rearguard action to safeguard British procedures for the disposal of waste in the context of European harmonisation. Local authority officers were instrumental in persuading the Commission that the British system, which differs from its continental counterparts in disposing of most types of waste jointly rather than separately, carries sufficient advantages to warrant its continuation. Local government is now lobbying in the European Parliament against counter-moves in favour of the continental system. The UK Government has yet to become involved in this debate, since the matter is yet to be referred to the Council of Ministers, and this example may serve to illustrate the inadequacy for local government of relying on that route.

Difficulties have also arisen for local authorities in that UK regulations on occasion differ from the terms of Directives, and represent only a partial implementation of the UK's obligations. Recent examples have included regulations on Equal Pay and Transfer of Undertakings. Case-law in the European Court of Justice has clearly established that public authorities are bound in certain circumstances by the terms of Directives, even where those requirements have not been translated into national law. (Freight Transport Association v London Boroughs Transport Committee, Court of Appeal, 1990, 1 Common Market Law Reports, 720). One of the Associations has given evidence on this issue to the House of Lords Select Committee on the European Communities ("Implementation and Enforcement of Environmental Legislation" – HL Paper 53 – I March 1992). It is of critical importance to all parties concerned to establish points of concern over implementation – and the likely costs thereof – at the earliest practicable stage. The issue underlines the importance of proper consultation between the government and bodies charged with implementation before the production of draft legislation.

The European Community has agreed proposals in the Treaty of European Union at Maastricht for the creation of a "Committee of Regions" which is intended to provide an avenue of consultation between the Commission/Council of Ministers and elected representatives of regional and local authorities in Europe. At the time of writing, the composition of the UK delegation to the new Committee from 1993 is a matter of dispute, and may not comprise elected local authority members from this country. UK Ministers have announced their intention to consider nominating representatives of central government, and the wording in English of the Treaty has been amended after Maastricht so that the committee is expressed as comprising "regional and local bodies" rather than "regional and local authorities". There has been no change of wording in any other Community language, and the Commission has expressed its concern that the Treaty may not be implemented in the intended manner in the UK. It is the firm policy of the local authority Associations that all the UK representatives on the new Committee should be elected members of local authorities. On this assumption, it will be critical to ensure that the new Committee provides a vehicle for detailed scrutiny and consultation between local authority bodies and the Community's institutions. The local authority representative body in Europe, the Council of European Municipalities and Regions, is developing a series of Committees served by a Secretariat which could provide an important new avenue for detailed consultation at the formative stage. The success or otherwise of this new initiative, however, will depend in large measure on the willingness of the European Commission and of the Council of Ministers to facilitate detailed consultation at a sufficiently early stage in the policy-making process to affect outcomes.

Conclusions: Consultation

Bodies such as local authorities should be included within an agreed process and timescale of consultation with central government on all policy proposals which will become the subject of legislation.

Major policy changes should be preceded by genuine and open public debate, on the basis of Green Papers and White Papers wherever practicable. Green Papers should invite consultative responses and a paper analyzing responses should be published by the relevant department before a White Paper is produced before proceeding to legislation. Draft legislation should refer to the document or documents from which it arises, and the Green or White Papers, plus the response document or a summary thereof should routinely be available with copies of Bills in an attempt to produce more informed debate.

The British Government should be urged to improve its process for consultation with local authorities and their Associations on European Community legislation, and should be encouraged to take full advantage of the opportunities for early consultation offered by the Committee of Regions.

B: Form and drafting of Bills/Instruments

Bills are greatly increasing in length, if not in number. In 1989 2,581 pages of legislation were enacted. In 1978 the total was only 830 pages (Lord Rippon, House of Lords, 31 January 1990, Col 386). There has been no equivalent reorganisation of the priorities of either House over this period, and the rise in sitting hours has been considerably more limited, with the effect that scrutiny must in at least a literal sense now be less detailed. One possible disincentive to lengthy drafting would be for the House to adopt rules linking the Parliamentary timetabling of a bill to its length, variable perhaps in relation to its importance (see below).

Scrutiny has been affected not merely by quantity. The Government has found it increasingly necessary to revise its legislation as it has gone along. A Lords working group on the Workings of the House identified what it called a tendency to "legislate as you go" and concluded that "legislation may have been introduced without adequate consideration". The number (for example) of Government amendments in the Lords – the great majority of the total passed – has risen very rapidly in the 1980s, notably on local government bills. In 1946/47, at the height of the Attlee Government's legislative programme, 1,027 amendments were passed to twenty-three bills. In 1966/67, a similar number (978) was agreed to thirty-nine bills. In 1985/86, 2,651 amendments were made to twenty-nine bills. The preponderance of changes made to local government bills was as seen in the 1987/88 session, when 1,259 amendments were agreed to three local government bills alone (the Education Reform Act 1988 – 569 amendments; the Housing Act 1988 – 273 amendments; the Local Government Finance Act 1988 – 417 amendments). In the 1988/89 session, 606 of the 2,401 amendments made in the Lords were to the Local Government & Housing Act 1989. In the decade from 1979 to 1989, there was a 57% increase in the average annual number of Lords amendments. Something is clearly amiss within the process of Government policy making, or in the drafting procedure, for so many amendments to be brought forward during the passage of bills.

Many government amendments, furthermore, are brought forward in large numbers at short notice. In the Commons Committee Stage of the Local Government Finance Act 1988, for example, 88 Government amendments were brought forward in one day. During the Lords' consideration of the Housing Act 1988, 100 were tabled in one day. Many of these amendments are technical, and it is extremely difficult for organisations with limited resources, such as the Associations, to deal sensibly with this volume of amendments.

The complexity of draft legislation frequently seriously hampers both proper Parliamentary scrutiny and effective implementation. A recent example is provided by Part V of the Local Government and Housing Act 1989, regulating local authorities' involvement in companies. The Act has proved so complicated that few observers really understand it. Regulations have not been produced in nearly three years – the drafting appears so far to have defeated the draughtsmen.

To these problems for Parliamentarians should be added the rapid changes of direction to which Government has become prone, at least on local government issues. This has involved the frequent redrafting or repeal of legislation, occasionally even from session to session. An example is provided in the organisation of local government finance, where local authorities have had to set budgets in an era of restricted financial resources amidst a series of almost annual changes to the rules. Legislation in 1980 introduced new capital and revenue grant systems, producing an annual process of the fixing of targets, penalties and expenditure limits. In 1982, legislation set up the Audit Commission, abolished supplementary rate making powers in the course of a financial year, and altered the rules on grant allocation to "protect" low spending authorities. In 1984 an education provision introduced a new specific grant, which was subsequently amended in 1986. Also in 1984, rate limitation was introduced for the first time in England and Wales, following its effective adoption from 1981 in Scotland. Other provisions in the same year introduced a new Urban Regeneration Grant, required rates to be set by a certain date and retrospectively legalised the then current round of rate limitation and grant calculations. Three Local Government Finance Acts followed in 1987, dealing with the further validation of block grant and rate limitation in that year, unclaimed grant rules and so-called "deferred purchase" schemes. Another Act in that year removed a major area of budgetary discretion by transferring the setting of teachers' salaries to national government. In 1988, legislation for the Community Charge and the National Non-Domestic Rate was enacted, together with a new form of revenue grant. A separate bill closed down the old grant system. In 1989, the capital financing regime was again reformed, subsidies to housing revenue accounts from general authority revenue banned, and transitional relief introduced for the Community Charge. In 1991, four further bills amended or clarified capping and Community Charge rules, and established the valuation process for Council Tax. These were followed in 1992 by a major bill abolishing the Community Charge and establishing the Council Tax. In the period 1984–89, twelve bills were enacted on local government finance.

The form and drafting of legislation gives rise to increasing concern. There is an urgent need to improve both the clarity and precision of draft legislation. There appears to be a determination on the part of the draughtsman to cover every eventuality, causing both defects in drafting and the creation of wide powers for Ministers. A more limited approach might make for better law-making.

Most bills are now presented as "framework" legislation, conferring powers exercisable by Ministers either outside Parliamentary scrutiny or by secondary legislation. Legislation is thus increasingly a vehicle for Executive action rather than a statement of law arising from a policy purpose. As McAuslan has argued (Political Quarterly, October-December 1989) the "policy" or principles of legislation are frequently wholly absent: Parliamentarians are asked to agree that the Government needs powers to act in a given area, but that the form such action will take cannot be predicted in advance. Ministers have begun to argue that "framework" legislation confers the advantage of "flexibility". This argument owes everything to attractiveness to the Executive and nothing to Parliamentary scrutiny. The pace with which legislation is presented in response to inchoate needs has played a significant part in this development, obliging Departments and draughtsmen to seek general powers on issues where little groundwork has been done. The use of powers made under secondary legislation to determine principles rather than details of implementation is now a matter of serious concern, and itself has major implications for the adequacy of the consultation then undertaken on Statutory Instruments.

Several examples of this trend can be found in recent local government legislation (e.g. the Local Government Act 1992). One particularly serious feature is the narrow scope of judicial review available in relation to the legality of activities undertaken under these powers.

Structure of Waste Management: After pressure on the Government on the future of waste management during the passage of legislation abolishing the GLC and metropolitan counties, Section 10 of the Local Government Act 1985 provided powers by order to substitute joint arrangements for the devolution to boroughs and districts proposed in the Bill for the four month period after Royal Assent. The only constraint was that the Secretary of State needed to consider that such arrangements "could with advantage" be made. Further powers were given at any time thereafter to create or dissolve single authorities where "satisfactory arrangements" would not continue. The only constraint was a requirement to have particular regard to the need for "satisfactory arrangements" for hazardous wastes. The powers remain on the statute book and further reorganisation is expected.

Revenue Support Grant: The distribution of local authority Revenue Support Grant is made annually under powers in Section 78A of the Local Government Finance Act 1988. This requires the Secretary of State of the Environment to produce an annual report, specifying the basis of distribution, whose general nature is notified to local authorities and which is placed before the Commons. The distribution of RSG is thus made under statute, but the Secretary of State operates under no legislative constraints (eg. as to equity within classes of authority) and in relation to no criteria specified in the statute as to the precise allocation. The starting point for the calculation – the Standard Spending Assessment – is not specified, and these are in any case revised annually.

Council Tax Capping: Designation for capping is made under powers conferred by Section 54 of the Local Government Finance Act 1992. The Secretary of State may designate an authority "if in his opinion" its budget is "excessive" or if there is an "excessive increase" over the previous year. The decision to designate is made "in accordance with principles determined by the Secretary of State", although those principles must either be common across classes of authority or the same as between authorities which were or were not capped in the previous year. The scope for a judicial challenge is effectively limited to the application of the principles across classes of authority.

City Challenge and Housing Investment Programme: The introduction in 1991 of competitive bidding by eligible authorities for resources for urban regeneration has effectively received no scrutiny in Parliament, despite the constitutional implications of enabling the Secretary of State to make detailed determination between schemes where local discretion formerly remained with authorities. The introduction of a competitive element into the allocation of Housing Investment Programme resources raises similar issues.

School Inspections: The Education (Schools) Act 1992 creates new national schools inspectorates in England and Wales. Sections 2(5) and 6(6) require the Chief Inspectors to "have regard to such aspects of Government policy as the Secretary of State may direct". The term "Government policy" is not defined and is thought to appear for the first time in legislation. For the courts, the normal test of the terms of the statute or instrument is replaced by the probably non-justiciable criterion of the mind of the Secretary of State.

Parliament has very few yardsticks by which to measure the volume or type of Ministerial powers granted in primary legislation. Statistics for the numbers of statutory instruments made take no account of the vast range of decisions made under powers to "determine", "specify", "prescribe", or "direct". Nor do these differentiate between different types of activity undertaken through delegated powers. The practical effect of this absence of information is that Parliament, in debating any particular provision to which members may object, has no objective basis against which to generalise the argument and to place it into a wider constitutional context.

One suggestion would be for Parliament itself to publish a sessional report on the number and type of Ministerial powers granted in primary legislation, in order to inform Parliamentary and public debate. This could be based on a further proposal that the Explanatory Memorandum should carry a statement of the number and type of Ministerial powers contained in the bill. By these means, both the overall trend and the contribution to it or otherwise of a particular bill could be made subject to debate. The development of an objective measure of powers would also remove the current trend for the Government to ignore "powers counts" produced in debate by the Opposition.

An official typology of powers would need to identify at least the following different varieties:

(i)   powers to make orders or regulations in statutory instruments which then receive Parliamentary scrutiny (by negative or affirmative procedures) on administrative matters of implementation;

(ii) powers following the process in (i) above but which cover policy decisions;

(iii) powers to make statutory instruments, covering policy or administration, which are not capable of Parliamentary scrutiny;

(iv) powers to amend primary legislation by order (whether or not subject to Parliamentary scrutiny); "Henry VIII" clauses. Examples would include powers to amend Council Tax bands under Section 5(4) of the Local Government Finance Act 1992 and powers to amend compulsory competitive tendering legislation in connection with the extension of CCT to white collar services under Section 8 of the Local Government Act 1992.

(v) powers to make determinations, specifications, notifications, directions, calculations and payments – none of which is subject to Parliamentary scrutiny;

(vi) powers to issue guidance, where "contravention" carries some penalty or disadvantage (eg. Section 9(3)(f) of the Local Government Act 1992).

The determination of such a typology could be an important function of an ad hoc Select Committee of the House of Lords on Central/Local Relations, if one were to be created following the report of the Select Committee on the Committee Work of the House due to be debated in mid-May 1992. It could be helpful to consider principles which could serve as a reference point for Parliamentarians in granting delegated powers. The first objective would be to limit the number of statutory instruments; the second would be to enable Parliamentarians to gauge in relation to a given statutory instrument the scale of power being granted. One possible principle would be that no power would be acceptable unless either:

(i) its purposes, and the circumstances of its use, could be specified on the face of the legislation; or

(ii) examples of its purpose and the circumstances of its use could be set out in an expanded Explanatory Memorandum.

One specific issue which could be examined is whether there has been a decline in the use of affirmative instruments, and whether a mechanism is needed for their consideration in the Lords in a committee. An affirmative resolution was required, for example, to vary the expenditure heads of the Education (Grants and Awards) Act 1984 as amended but the whole of the National Curriculum (Education Reform Act 1988) was introduced by negative instrument (although amendments to the list of Curriculum subjects require an affirmative instrument).

Awareness among the public (and to some degree Parliamentarians) of the importance of delegated legislation is hampered by the inadequacy of its scrutiny. The practical effect of this is that there is little incentive on the draughtsman to ensure proper preparation. The inability of Parliament to consider amendments to statutory instruments – by their nature detailed – gives debate where it takes place an often unreal atmosphere in which the text may not be under discussion. The creation of a committee to scrutinise instruments, with a remit going beyond vires, and guaranteed notice periods before instruments came into effect would assist more detailed and constructive consideration. Such changes would also doubtless provide the necessary spur to better consultation and drafting. To underline this need, more advanced scrutiny should also include power to reject on grounds of clarity a statutory instrument whose drafting is obscure. Interpretation of secondary legislation by bodies such as local authorities often requires considerable research by them where it is unconsolidated. The presentation of draft instruments should thus also include a statement of related secondary legislation and, where relevant, of a consolidated wording incorporating the new drafts.

In relation to standards of drafting, one proposal could be for Parliament to establish a pre-publication scrutiny committee, meeting privately, which could look at the technical quality of drafting (and also approve the Explanatory and Financial Memoranda). Such a committee is no substitute, however, for improving the basic quality of drafting. The Education (Schools) Act 1992 for example, contains (aside from the novel powers noted above), such non-legal terminology as "special circumstances which make it right that", and tendering "at arm's length", neither of which is defined. (Schedule 1, para 3(3) and Schedule 2(2)(a) respectively.) The normal process of Parliamentary scrutiny proved inadequate in either of these cases to improve these drafting weaknesses.

Conclusion: Form and Drafting of Legislation

The trend for framework legislation should be resisted and Parliament should take steps to ensure that the granting of powers by itself to the Executive is transparent and debated in an informed constitutional context on each significant occasion. It should require the publication in an Explanatory Memorandum for each bill of analyses of the provisions giving rise to delegated powers and secondary legislation, and establish a typology of such powers which would enable the publication of an annual report. The establishing of objective yardsticks on this issue would allow a proper analysis to take place of the trend, which is currently only subjectively identified, whereby principles are being removed from primary to secondary legislation. A separate pre-publication committee should be instituted to screen the technical quality of the drafting of primary and secondary legislation. Parliament should be urged to establish wider mechanisms for the scrutiny of statutory instruments, with explicit powers to reject SIs on grounds of obscure or unsound drafting.

C: Effectiveness of Scrutiny

The scrutiny of legislation under the Parliamentary system is currently determined by a culture of oral debate rather than written presentation. From a local authority viewpoint, Parliament compares unfavourably with other public bodies in the degree to which discussion of the Executive's proposals, and of their cost and practical implementation, is conducted in debate rather than on paper. The practical effect is that Government proposals receive less detailed scrutiny than those presented to bodies such as local authorities.

Parliamentarians are hampered by a lack of written detailed information and have no opportunity – routinely available in any local authority – to question paid officials direct. Even in Commons or Lords Committees, where the most detailed scrutiny of legislation can be expected, the mediation of the process through formal speeches and Ministerial replies limits the degree to which detailed questions can be pursued. A Commons Committee will normally have in front of it no more documentation than the bill (including its Explanatory and Financial Memoranda), amendments proposed and their selection list, and increasingly the Notes on Clauses formerly available to the Minister. Copies of relevant consultative documents, White Papers, etc, will be available to Committee members but not formally placed in front of them. Other documents to which they have access may be Commons Library research papers on the bill, materials from outside bodies and any relevant Parliamentary Questions printed in previous Hansards. No detailed statement of the Government's policy will be presented to the Committee. There will be no financial or staffing estimates beyond those already in the Financial Memorandum, and no document relating any public spending proposals to the totality of public expenditure. There will be no assessment in writing of alternatives to the Government's proposals, beyond any which may have appeared in previous consultative documents.

The Explanatory and Financial Memorandum should be developed as a fuller document, setting out the bill's policy, assessing alternatives and including a detailed breakdown of the financial and staffing estimates. Validation of these estimates as reasonable could be a function allocated to the National Audit Office, to provide an objective basis for debate. In the case of financial and staffing estimates relating to local government, the Audit Commission would be the appropriate body to undertake this scrutiny.

The practice of Ministers releasing "Notes on Clauses" to Committee members is welcome, but the nature of the documents themselves means that they rarely impart more than a bare summary of the purpose of a clause. Notes on Clauses have occasionally been found to provide a slightly partisan analysis of the bill's provisions, and this is hardly surprising given their provenance as a briefing aid for Ministers. They are, furthermore, now routinely made available at the start of Commons Committee sittings, when a detailed analysis of the bill would have been helpful to the House as whole in reaching decisions on its principles at the earlier Second Reading stage.

The practice should be developed so that a written statement of the policy of a bill, together with the meaning of each important clause, is issued with the bill when it is published. In practice, such publication should take place not less than two weeks before the date of Second Readings. The issuing of such a statement would raise the level of debate by concentrating attention on a document rather than on the Minister's speech, and enable questions on the policy to emerge in public discussion before the debate itself. The present situation would be avoided, whereby the Minister's speech at Second Reading is in formal and actual terms the only point at which the policy of a bill is presented and opened for debate in each House. The present conventions, whereby the House is deemed to have approved the principles behind all the major proposals in a bill through a single vote at Second Reading works enormously to the advantage of the Executive and frequently requires the sponsoring Minister to do no more than read a short summary of the Explanatory Memorandum.

The deficiencies of the Second Reading debate are carried into the Committee Stage through its continuing reliance on a debating format. The longstanding call by academic observers for a pre-Committee Stage at which civil servants could be interrogated by Committee members would greatly assist and probably shorten the ensuing Committee debate. Professor John Griffiths' proposals for reforms, first put forward in 1971 to the Select Committee on Procedure and advanced in a revised form in his book "Parliamentary Scrutiny of Government Bills" (1974), were designed to enable Parliament to establish greater information about the policy of a bill and the purpose of its drafting. Such a proposal would greatly advance the work done by bodies such as the Associations in Parliament, since questions could be posed directly rather than in amendment form, and much groundwork could be cleared without involving professional politicians in lengthy debates. Greater use of existing provisions for the creation of Commons Special Standing Committees and for Public Bill Committees in the Lords would also assist scrutiny of bills, especially those of a technical nature. (The Public Bill Committee on the Charities Bill in the last session, for example, was particularly effective). It is unsatisfactory that the burden of securing from Government an explanation for its proposals rests largely on the activities of organisations such as the Associations in briefing non-Government and dissident Government MPs and Peers. It is not going too far to say that in this respect the effectiveness of the Parliamentary process currently depends on outside bodies, themselves frequently operating on the basis of very little information as to the Government's proposals. Underlying the call for a pre-Committee interrogation stage, and for the publication of a statement of policy alongside a bill, is the principle that there should be a basic obligation on the Executive to make available sufficient explanatory and documentary material to Parliamentarians and interested bodies to produced an informed debate.

The Commons is currently considering proposals for the timetabling of all bills. From the viewpoint of outside organisations such as the Associations, it would be important to ensure that timetabling did not simply become another means for the Executive to streamline consideration of its bills. The interest of the Associations is in using the legislative process, for want of better means, to establish the maximum information on behalf of their member authorities, and in appropriate cases to press for changes. The cardinal requirement, therefore, of any reform would be that it did not significantly weaken the hand of non-Government supporters in the Commons. Timetabling of any bill should proceed only by agreement through the whips, with the opportunity for at least the major Opposition party to withhold agreement. One possibility would be to adopt a variant of the "de Honte" system used in the European Parliament, which enables the party groups to "spend" a certain number of "points" in bidding for the lead role on certain legislation. In the same way, the Opposition parties (possibly including the Liberal Democrats) could enjoy an allocation of points (representing time or prime debates) which could be deployed across all the bills in a session. This would prevent open-ended opposition where no timetable was agreed, but would enable the non-Government parties effectively to design the layout of the legislative business. A simpler variant would be to enable the Government to determine the end point of a bill, but for the main or all the

Opposition parties to have free reign in the timetabling of debates. If this proposal were adopted, however, it would be important to establish a minimum tariff related to the length of bills which would prevent the Government from rushing legislation through other than by agreement. As part of the same exercise, the House could be urged to adopt fixed deadlines between legislative stages, and a fixed maximum number of days or hours in a week which could be allocated to a given stage. This would prevent the process which was applied to the Local Government Finance Act 1992, which was guillotined after Commons Second Reading, and put into Committee Stage on three days in the week, instead of the normal two, after only a one week gap. A bill of 118 Clauses and 14 Schedules passed through Commons Committee in three weeks. The creation of a minimum tariff linked to the length of bills would on the Government side encourage concise drafting.

Conclusion: Effectiveness of Scrutiny
Publication should be required in advance of the Second Reading of detailed staffing and financial estimates, and these could be certified as reasonable by the National Audit Office. More detailed Notes on Clauses should also be published before the Second Reading, together with a statement at the time of the bill's publication of its policy. Second Reading should be followed by a pre-Committee Stage scrutiny of civil servants by members of the Standing Committee. These requirements should be adapted to provide more information on Government amendments tabled during debate in the course of a bill's passage. Agreed timetabling of legislation in the Commons should be examined, without diminishing the rights of the Opposition, with a minimum tariff of time for consideration linked to the length of a bill. The Commons should adopt fixed deadlines between the stages of bills, which could only be abrogated by agreement between the main parties.

D: Accessibility of legislation
At the legislative stage there is a relative lack of effort made to encourage public and press understanding of Parliamentary proceedings. Visitors to Commons or Lords Committees receive no copies of amendments or other documents relevant to the Bill, without which the proceedings are almost literally incomprehensible. Interested persons and outside organisations often experience considerable difficulty, or incur noticeable cost, in obtaining copies of such documents to enable them to contribute briefing or draft amendments to Parliamentarians involved in the debate. The Palace of Westminster itself is normally the only source of printed amendments at a sufficiently early stage to be useful, which inevitably leads to reliance on access through Parliamentarians or their research assistants. The process is exclusive and leads to reliance on personal contacts and access. The House could be asked to consider the establishment of a retail outlet at Westminster through which printed materials were made available to the public, in the same way as to MPs and their researchers, and the scale of charges for such materials should be reviewed.

There is a corresponding – and surprising – lack of effort to ensure effective implementation. It is a fact often overlooked that Acts of Parliament carry no explanatory material. A simple aid to public understanding and the effective implementation of legislation would be for Acts to include (without legal force) an adapted version of the original Explanatory and Financial Memorandum. This could be accompanied by a table summarising the consequences of the schedules in the legislation dealing with repeals and consequential amendments (the summary also being without legal force). This summary could cross-refer to other extant statutes, and show for each previous relevant provision the subsequent provision introduced by the Act concerned. From this it would be possible to see listed without reference to handbooks the relevant current statutory provisions on a given topic contained in the legislation.

Local authorities have had to absorb and adapt to more legislation than ever before over the past decade. In the course of legislative discussion, teams of lawyers and specialists have had to be mobilised by the Associations on major bills to provide effective advice to Parliamentarians and to local government as a whole. At the implementation stage, authorities have coped with the demands made on them, but with considerable difficulty and at no little cost. The first problem for bodies such as local authorities seeking to implement legislation is the delay in the publication of Acts and lack of publicity for their contents. (A recent example of delay was the Education (Schools) Act, a short provision, which remained unavailable well into the recess period after the end of the 1991/2 session and went out of print). Local authorities currently receive one copy of each Act, undifferentiated by topic, but no copies of statutory instruments, EC directives, EC regulations, or of bills in draft form. Authorities are inevitably involved in the task of identifying legislation which applies to them, and the absence of statutory instruments requires them to undertake time-consuming perusal of publications such as the HMSO Daily List, the Weekly Information Bulletin published by the House of Commons and the EC Journal. The Associations obviously play a role in alerting authorities to the practical implications of new legislation, although this cannot be an effective substitute for official information made available through the resources of Government. Once identified, authorities incur considerable cost in purchasing statutory instruments and EC legislation, whose prices have risen substantially faster than the rate of inflation in recent years.

In relation to EC legislation, a small number of academic libraries exists which retain complete sets of statutory provisions. Too little has been done by the UK Government to make available to public bodies EC facilities such as those contained in Documentation Centres.

The essential difficulty, therefore, for authorities is that central government does not see itself as having a responsibility for ensuring that all authorities are sent all relevant legislation and circulars affecting them. Although a number of the proposals put forward in this document, such as greater explanatory documentation and pre-Committee enquiries, would assist implementing bodies by providing greater detail and advance warning of legislation, there can be no substitute for a formal responsibility on the part of the Executive to facilitate so far as possible the implementation of its legislation by bodies charged with that function.

A further difficulty is that very low priority appears to be accorded to the consolidation of legislation (including legislation arising from statutory instruments). The law of Parks, for example, is still operated under an Act dating from 1875. The regular consolidation of primary and subordinate legislation would greatly assist authorities in "auditing" the current state of legal requirements.

A linked proposal would be that Government should undertake the more regular production of local government Miscellaneous Provisions Bills. Such Bills were produced in 1976 and 1982, and performed a very useful function in clarifying and delineating areas of doubt as to legal powers, which could otherwise have given rise to costly litigation. The Associations would welcome the more regular bringing forward of such tidying up legislation.

Conclusion: Accessibility of Legislation
The Parliamentary process remains impenetrable to most members of the public, and little attempt is made to remedy this situation. Greater information needs to be made available both by Government Departments and by the House authorities to make legislation accessible, and to ameliorate the growing gulf between ever more law making and its effective implementation. Particular steps need to be taken to improve information to major public bodies with statutory duties, including the routine circulation of statutory instruments and EC legislation and placing a clear responsibility on Government Departments to ensure that relevant legislation and circulars are made available to them. Information in plain language alongside legislation could play a significant part in improving public understanding of the aims and purposes of legislation. Ultimately, an attempt better to explain the purpose of legislation may be more fruitful than attempts, however desirable, to simplify the drafting of legislation itself.

26 May 1992

M38   Magistrates' Association

We are invited by government departments to comment on a considerable number of green papers, white papers and bills. We have the following observations:

(a) This organisation is committee based with 58 Branches in England and Wales. We do not often consult direct with Branches as they have elected representatives on Council. However, we do need to consult with relevant standing committees which only meet three times a year. It is a common failing of government departments to allow insufficient time for consultation. They are aware of our structure, and the length of time required for a properly considered response, from an organisation such as this Association which is committee based.

(b) Being committee based it is necessary to circulate bills and papers to members. Often, government departments have difficulty in providing additional copies and they have to be purchased from the HMSO at considerable expense. Government departments should make provision to supply sufficient copies – particularly to charities – so that there can be proper consultation.

(c) Large organisations, such as The Law Society, have a senior employee who is solely responsible for Parliamentary relations and keeps a detailed track of bills. In small organisations (12 persons in our case) it is not possible to have a person solely, or even partly, responsible for Parliamentary relations. It would therefore be extremely helpful if there was a proper information desk for both Houses where well informed information on the passage of a bill could be obtained. For example, the time-table of the bill, when in committee, when likely to reach a particular clause or schedule and so on. The current arrangements are hit and miss. It is sometimes very time consuming to even find out basic information about legislation and its passage through Parliament.

(d) Bills/notes should be written in clear concise English so that they are easily understood by the lay person.

Consultation with the public would have to be carefully controlled. Unless all the facts are widely known and understood an inaccurate result may be reached.

18 December 1991

M39　Mr Edward Mercer

1. I am a solicitor in private practice. I have also during my career been a local authority chief officer and secretary to a statutory corporation established to regulate cable television in the United Kingdom. I have over the last few years been involved in commenting upon, lobbying and advising in respect of new legislation particularly in the fields of broadcasting, copyright and telecommunications. My present practice is almost exclusively in the field of cable television and the provision of telecommunication services in competition to British Telecom and Mercury. The industry which I serve has only arisen out of legislative changes that have occurred since the early 1980s. By and large my clients' affairs are governed by statute or regulations or licences made pursuant to Acts of Parliament. New and proposed legislation, both domestic and European, in the broadcasting and telecommunications fields is of great interest to my clients as, naturally, it can have a significant impact upon their businesses.

2. With the exception of the Copyright, Designs and Patents Act 1988 (of which more below), domestic legislation in the fields in which I am interested has been first published to Parliament and in some cases undergone radical amendment during particularly its Committee stages. In the case of the Broadcasting Act 1990 the Government amendments were put forward with such speed during the Committee and later stages that it was almost impossible either to keep abreast of them or to give them careful consideration before they were considered by the Committee. The complex nature of regulation affecting the newer broadcast technologies and telecommunications meant that it was often difficult to assess completely the impact of particular wording produced at short notice which will be in force (even given the quickening nature of legislative renewal) for around 10 years. I have no doubt that several areas of ambiguity within the Broadcasting Act 1990 which may result in expensive future litigation might have been resolved had greater time been given to consideration of the actual

words used by those with a direct concern in their implementation and daily usage.

3. In my experience I can only think of one Bill of which the major clauses have been published prior to their introduction into Parliament. They were the first 150 main clauses of which is now the Copyright, Designs and Patents Act 1988 which were published by the Department of Trade and Industry to a consultation list of around 100 persons prior to the Act being published to Parliament. As I recall, it was considered that for the most part provisions relating to copyright are not a party political subject but such a complex one that wide consideration of the form of words to be used was necessary in order to gain useful comments from those who are involved in or advise the industries concerned. The Cable Authority for whom I was working at the time was lucky enough to be one of the consultees in this process. The advanced warning of the legislation enabled me to set up an ad hoc committee of other practitioners who were interested particularly in that case of looking at the position of the new media and of new technologies. I am quite sure that other groups or interested parties in the same or other industries also took advantage of being able to peruse the clauses before they were put to Parliament and make useful suggestions. In particular I recall that the Department of Trade and Industry were grateful for assistance in dealing with areas covering new technologies where knowledge of the way in which they operate was not widely held. Suggestions made by practitioners in those areas may well have contributed to the shaping of various key definitions and clauses in the Bill. In particular significant amendments were made to the definition of "broadcast" so as to better take account of new technology. There was some disquiet in government circles about the prior consultation which was regarded by some as being in "contempt of Parliament" or a breach of privilege.

4. It is a truism to say that as society becomes more complex so its laws will naturally follow suit. I, for one, should not like to have to be a Parliamentary draftsman having to frame laws governing technologies about which I may know little more than is contained in my instructing department's brief. I think both the Parliamentary draftsman and their instructing departments could have their jobs made easier by a technical consideration of a first draft by a group of practitioners in the area. The object of such a review would not be to make particular points concerning the substance of the legislation or its aim but rather to examine its effect and efficiency in dealing with its subject matter. Such a review panel would be aiming at clarity rather than in influencing policy.

5. There exists throughout the legal and other professional bodies committees and panels made up of specialists in particular fields. It should not be too difficult for departments or Parliament to establish lists of those who are experienced practitioners in the areas concerned and whose view on the technical drafting characteristics of a Bill would, I think, be of considerable assistance both to the sponsoring department and to Parliament itself.

6. It is my view that though most public Bills receive, where appropriate, considerable public attention as to the policy behind them and to the proposed

affect of the legislation, too little thought is permitted or practicable concerning the actual words used to effect the policy. Given the complex nature of modern legislation, more time needs to be spent in considering the fine print before it is enacted. I therefore would address the second question in the News Release of the 8th November by saying "yes" – the drafting of legislation could be improved by its preliminary consideration by a panel of lawyers or other professionals experienced in the area concerned and this panel could also examine amendments as they were suggested in the same way.

7. My concern is for Parliament to enact statutes that may be interpreted without recourse to the Courts as far as is possible and which take account of the particular circumstances of their subject matter. With the exception of emergency legislation and perhaps some other limited categories, I think there would be some merit in drafts being distributed for comment to experienced legal practitioners in the areas concerned for review, not as to their policy but as to drafting.

8. As far as European legislation is concerned, it is often difficult despite the mountain of paperwork distributed by the European Commission to readily identify draft proposals in a particular area. All too often it seems to me that the European Commission will preview, say, draft directives only to certain unidentifiable groups and that it may be difficult for others to keep up-to-date with constantly changing proposals. It is my suggestion that the European Commission should be obliged to send all proposals including draft directives and other regulations to all those who register with an interest in that particular area with them.

9. In both domestic and European legislation there is much to be said for allowing much more comment, in my opinion, on the technical drafting than is at present allowed.

17 March 1992

M40　National Association of Health Authorities and Trusts

The one comment the Association would like to make, relates to the passage of Bills through the Committee Stage in the House of Commons.

We are somewhat concerned that the amount of time given to some clauses of Bills is insufficient. This is often due to protracted debate on early clauses within a Bill, and then the consequent imposition of a time-table.

We think that in order to ensure that legislation is as good as possible, we need to ensure that every part of a Bill receives equal and considered attention.

6 December 1991

M41   National Consumer Council

1. Introduction

The NCC was set up by government in 1975 to give a vigorous and independent voice to consumers in the United Kingdom. We aim to ensure that the interests of all consumers are taken into account by decision-makers. We consider the interests of consumers of goods and a wide range of services, from healthcare to housing. In addition we have special briefs to promote the interests of consumers in international trade matters and to promote independent local advice and information services.

This submission is based on the experience and views of staff at NCC. Annexes are attached from Consumers in the European Community Group (Annex I and IA[1]) and the General Consumer Council for Northern Ireland (Annex II[2]). The Scottish Consumer Council is sending in a separate submission. (M49)

We have focused on the consultation procedure, access to information in or about legislation (including the need for Plain Language) and procedures for lobbying on delegated legislation and EC directives.

2. Consultation

2.1 Groups consulted

We are consulted on a wide range of issues. Experience of different UK government departments varied. For example, the Ministry of Agriculture, Fisheries and Food (MAFF) has consulted a large number of groups on recent proposals and improved its record in this area considerably.

NCC is frequently asked to contribute to Department of the Environment consultations on housing issues. However we have often been in the embarrassing situation, when liaising with the many other housing groups we work closely with, of finding that they have not been consulted at all. For example, the Campaign for Bedsit Rights, a specialist group with considerable expertise and experience, was not consulted about Houses in Multiple Occupancy when we were.

In order that practices across all government departments become more consistent and rigorous, we recommend that:

- consultors, whether government departments or other public authorities, invite appropriate organisations (including smaller ones and those outside London) to give them details of their specialisms and the subjects they would like to be consulted on;
- any organisations missed should be able to ask to be put on the list;
- this list would then be used as a resource when the consultors compile the mailing list for each consultation document;
- efforts should be made to keep the list up-to date;
- where appropriate, consultors should publicise the fact that they are consulting and invite anyone with an interest to request the consultation document and to

---

1   Not published
2   Not published

comment on it. For example, on a social housing issue consultors could publish a notice in an appropriate housing journal like Inside Housing.

2.2 Form of consultation documents

There was agreement that some consultation documents were not presented clearly and precisely. Some did not allow for easy cross referencing to the relevant draft regulations and orders. We recommend that:

- the consultation documents should be in plain language and clearly presented;
- consultors should ask for comments on specific issues but also give the option of more general comments.

2.3 Timing of consultations

During the passage of the Education Schools Bill 1991/2 we were disturbed by the fact that consultation (of a rather limited number of groups) on the information to be included in the proposed School League Tables took place after the primary legislation specifying what information should be included had been published.

A lot of consultation documents on related topics are often issued in quick succession after a piece of primary legislation has been passed. This can make responding in adequate detail difficult.

There are great variations in the amount of time given for responses, and some evidence that the time allowed is getting shorter. For example, a recent DTI consultation on tying in services to mortgage loans was published on 6 March 1992 with a deadline of 24 April 1992. NCC responses sometimes need to be approved by our Council committees and this kind of time limit is too short to allow for that.

There are particular difficulties with responses to some consultations on EC directives being expected too quickly. We recommend that:

- if it is at all practicable, consultors stagger the publication of related consultation documents;
- consultors should always allow as much time as possible for a response;
- if a consultation document is long or complex consultors should allow for this in the time given for response;
- efforts are made to send out consultation documents on EC directives as soon as possible.

2.4 Feedback

We commend the Department of Health for its commitment in a recent consultation on the EC directive on the Hygiene of Foodstuffs to publish responses unless those consulted asked otherwise. Generally, we do not get enough feedback about what other groups consulted have said, the consultor's view of our response, or the extent to which the responses affected the consultor's final decision. We recommend that:

- where appropriate consultors make responses available to the public (having gained the permission of the consultees first).

2.5 Statutory commitments to consult

Increasingly primary legislation is enabling legislation giving the government or other authority the power to make important decisions on the detail in subsequent regulations.

In the 1991/2 session the Competition and Service (Utilities) Bill and Local Government Bill both required the relevant authorities to consult consumers and their representatives, or "people likely to be affected" before making regulations. During the Bills' passages through parliament ministers clarified that they interpreted the range of people and groups to be consulted quite widely and we welcomed this approach.

In contrast, there was no mention at all of consultation on the face of the Education (Schools) Bill. NCC lobbied the government (without success) to amend the Bill to require the Secretary of State to consult before making regulations about the information to be included in School League Tables. We recommend that:

- primary legislation enabling the government or other authority to make subsequent regulations includes a commitment to consult people likely to be affected by such regulations.

2.6 Consumer representation on consultative committees

We welcome the fact that more consumers are being invited onto consultative committees such as MAFF's Food Advisory Committee. However it is still the case that such committees advising government on key consumer issues are too often dominated by people representing the producer interest. We recommend that:

- where appropriate, consumer representation is increased on all relevant advisory committees.

3. Consumers' access to information about legislation

3.1 The need for plain language in legislation

For some time now, the National Consumer Council has been campaigning against the use of legalese and bureaucratic jargon in official forms, leaflets and standard letters. Too often, when challenged, those responsible for producing the offending material claimed they were obliged to meet the absolute requirements under the "law". Clearly, they felt it was too risky and/or difficult to attempt to interpret the "law" in layman's terms. A surprising number of standard letters contain direct quotes from secondary legislation or attach copies of circulars etc.

Our special concern is for social legislation which places a duty on, or provides opportunities to, the majority of citizens, e.g. traffic laws or council tax. From time to time a law is targetted at a significant minority group who are in some way disadvantaged, e.g disabled persons, the elderly, or claimants. In this case, special care should be taken to ensure the "law" can be understood *and* acted on by its intended audience.

- We feel there is a very strong case for all primary legislation to be in plain language.
- Where it is clear that standard letters, forms and leaflets will be generated around new legislation, government should provide "models" in plain language. It should seek professional help and guidance from such bodies as the Plain English Campaign, etc.
- Organisations such as the citizens' advice bureaux and law centres are often in a position to comment in a most constructive and helpful way on official forms

and leaflets. They should be commissioned to help and advise when appropriate.

3.2 The case for a plain language law

For some time now, we have felt that the standard of comprehension used in many contract and legal documents requires a major overhaul. We have been giving some thought to the possibility of developing a plain language law which would provide consumers with protection in law where a contract could be demonstrated to be unclear, confusing or difficult to understand. Such a defence is available in the USA and Canada.

An EC directive "Unfair Contract Terms" is currently being considered. It would have the effect of banning gobbledegook in consumer contracts. This may help to extend good plain language practice into legislation.

3.3 Consideration of consumers' need for information about new legislation

Some new legislation has an immediate and major impact on all, or part, of the population. It can provoke a sharp increase in the need for information and advice. Too often, the strategies to respond to these predictable demands are poorly conceived and under resourced. At present, an "Explanatory and Financial Memorandum" is required as an introduction to a Bill.

- We believe the "Explanatory and Financial Memorandum" should include a description of the information and advice strategies needed to ensure that most, if not all, members of the public affected by the changes know about them, and know how to respond appropriately. Clearly, such strategies will have cost implications, and not necessarily only over the short-term.

Another concern we have is the impact legislative change can have on independent advice services such as CABx, law centres and neighbourhood advice centres. In the case of the introduction of the community charge, citizens' advice bureaux experienced an increase in "taxation" enquiries of 89% between 1988/89 and 1989/90. The government subsequently acknowledged this by giving the National Association of Citizens Advice Bureaux and the Federation of Independent Advice Centres grants to help them train and inform their local advice workers to deal with the avalanche of new enquiries. Regrettably no grant aid was available to ease the burden on the local advice services. We recommend that:

- advice services should be consulted about the "information and advice" implications of new legislation;
- financial help should be available to the national networks of local advice centres to help them prepare for enquiries provoked by the legislative changes and when it is clear there will be a large increase in enquiries at the local level, extra funding should be available.

You may be interested to see the attached letter (Annex III[1]) to Tim Kirkhope MP, from Sir Geoffrey Howe (dated 23 March 1990) responding to the questions we raised on the role of the "Explanatory and Financial Memorandum". Attached for

---

1 Not published

your information is a background note (Annex IV[1]) prepared for the Advice Services Alliance by NCC's Parliamentary Research Officer. It raises some interesting questions on the problems associated with secondary legislation and makes the case for the use of Regulatory Impact Assessment (RIAs) to examine secondary legislation.

4. Scrutiny of delegated legislation

NCC notes the government's increased use of delegated legislation. Opportunity for debate, amendment and proper scrutiny are severely limited as the submissions particularly from the Scottish Consumer Council, General Consumer Council of Northern Ireland and CECG show.

17 June 1992

M42   National Trust

1. During the course of 1991 the Trust will have responded to or made submissions in respect of more than 50 consultation exercises by Government Departments. We have in addition made just under 20 submissions to public agencies such as the Countryside Commission and the National Audit Office and to Parliamentary Select Committees in the form of written evidence. A handful of our responses, including some of those made directly to Government departments (mainly the Ministry of Agriculture), have been in respect of European Commission consultation documents.

2. In each of the last three years the Trust has also been closely involved in legislation before Parliament to the extent of promoting amendments to the Bills concerned. These have included the Water Act 1989, the Environmental Protection Act 1990, and the Ports Act 1991. We would therefore like to make the following observations.

Consultation

3. The Trust is, on balance, content with the degree of consultation afforded by Government departments on the matters with which it is concerned. If anything, we sometimes feel overwhelmed by the volume of consultation documents published by departments (though the Trust would obviously not wish to see less consultation), and it is mainly in this respect that we have a few reservations.

4. We feel that the departments involved in drafting documents could allow more time for consultation. The deadlines for responses to draft legislation especially often allow no more than two or three weeks. If the subject matter is sufficiently important, the responses will need to be drafted following extensive internal consultation and may occasionally require reference to relevant committees of the Trust. Very short timetables will, of course, preclude such mechanisms for response. In such circumstances, we may be forced to send an inadequately

---

1   Not published

considered response or delay it until after the deadline has passed at the risk of the response not being taken into account by the department involved.

5. The Trust also feels that sections within Government departments could coordinate their consultation exercises better. Proposals for changes to planning legislation, for example, are often published in separate documents but at similar times according to subject matter. In our view the scope exists in such circumstances for more consolidated proposals to be published thus reducing the number of responses required.

6. We also have the impression that consultation is seasonal – that proposals will be published in greater numbers at certain times of the year, usually in order to meet institutional holiday arrangements. The period immediately prior to the prorogation of Parliament in July is, in our experience, an especially busy one in terms of the publication of documents. Given the greater manpower resources at the disposal of the civil service compared to those available to bodies like the Trust, we feel that more effort should be put into ironing out such troughs and peaks.

Responsiveness

7. The Trust is also reasonably content with the degree to which the Government responds to recommendations for change made in response to consultation exercises especially bearing in mind the number of conflicting opinions which must be received by the departments concerned. This is particularly so with more detailed and technical changes to legislation which tend to be less controversial or prone to ideological designs.

8. By contrast, proposals which are the result of major policy decisions or which stem from ideological presumptions present the greatest difficulties for bodies like the Trust to get their views accepted. The considerations which underlie this problem are beyond the Trust's remit but we do feel, in such circumstances, that the processes of Parliamentary legislation could be placed on a more systematic footing and greater allowance made for the views of relevant outside interests. Improvements in this vein would greatly facilitate the discussion of matters of importance within Parliament and, at the very least, prevent their implementation without adequate consideration of the issues.

Legislation

9. In attempting to get its views discussed and received favourably on those few occasions when we have found it necessary to do, the Trust has been more impressed by the legislative arrangements in the House of Lords than in the Commons. Largely because of the relative lack of party politics and the greater depth of understanding of the issues concerning us which exists in the Lords, business appears to be conducted much more efficiently and more attention is devoted to central concerns than is true of the "other place".

10. It is this degree of efficiency from which we feel the Commons could most benefit. Especially in the Committee Stages of a Bill, the Trust believes that business should be conducted as much as possible to stricter timetables. This

would both ensure adequate discussion of issues and allow outside bodies to learn more precisely when their specific interests are most likely to be debated.

11. In this context, the Trust would also favour much more warning in advance of when Bills or their relevant clauses are to be debated so that it can make representations as necessary. The Trust receives the Commons Weekly Bulletin, usually on a Monday, but it is of limited value in that it only describes business for the week ahead. Despite the views expressed in the previous paragraph, we feel that this is a fault of the House of Lords as well.

12. If the practices recommended above are to have effect, however, it is important that the information concerning the new timetabling arrangements should be made more readily available than is presently the case. As stated, we receive the Commons Weekly Bulletin and the Lords Weekly Agenda but it is often difficult to obtain more precise details of, for example, proposed timetables for discussion of the contents of a Bill in its Committee stages. Such details are, anyway, subject to change under the present arrangements.

12 December, 1991

M43 National Trust: Supplementary Letter from Mr D U Pullen, Solicitor and Secretary

I thought it might be helpful if I supplemented the general note (see above) with two current examples relating to draft legislation. The first bill started off life as the Rights of Access to Neighbouring Land Bill but this has now been shortened to the Access to Neighbouring Land Bill and it received its second reading in the House of Lords on 11 December. The original bill had an extraordinarily swift passage through the House of Commons and may well have been adequate to deal with the particular problems identified by Mr John Ward but it failed to recognise the position of owners such as the Trust and those represented by the Country Landowners Association. I am glad to say that as a result of our representations the bill is now much improved but this could have been avoided by better consultation. I can elaborate if necessary.

The second bill is the Charities Bill which, again, is requiring a good deal of amendment either as a result of inadequate consultation, or poor drafting, or both. I will give just one example and that concerns the definition of public place in clause 63. I am sure it was never the Home Office's intention that this clause should extend beyond street and house-to-house collections but the way in which the clause was drafted covered charity shops, coffee mornings etc. Again, I should be happy to elaborate if this would be helpful.

18 December 1991

M44 National Union of Mineworkers

1. Clearly the legislative making process needs to be based on a network of communication so that those affected by legislation are consulted and we welcome the opportunity to comment and maybe contribute in some small way to making the process more responsive to the needs of a modern democratic society.

2. It is the view of the NUM that the communication process can be improved on. We consider that it is not only at the initiating stage of legislation that changes are important, although this is a most important stage. It is, in our opinion, vital that at the administration stage complex legislation should be continuously under review. Without a mechanism for review, citizens may suffer because an aspect of legislation is administered in an altogether different way to that intended by Parliament. We shall give an example of this below, drawn from a recent experience.

3. A Select Committee for Legislative Review, quite apart from the Commissioner for Parliamentary Affairs, to deal with complaints from MPs specific to the administration of legislation would, we feel, be a help in ensuring that aspects of legislation were administered in a way that Parliament intended. This is all the more important with legislation or directives originating from the European Community (EC) that affect and can modify domestic legislation.

4. At the proposed legislative stage, it is important that the government of the day should obtain the views and opinions of those affected by EC directives etc. This is a point that the Select Committee on the European Community needs to address. Unless this issue is positively dealt with, there is a likelihood of cynical manoeuvres being made. This is precisely how the current government's attempt to use the EC Directive on Working Time to repeal the Coal Mines (Regulations) Act 1908, was perceived by the public.

5. The 1991 Coal Industry Bill, which was put on the Statute Book on 14th November, contains powers to repeal the Coal Mines (Regulations) Act 1908. This Act currently regulates the length of an underground shift to seven and a half hours. It also underpins the provision of the Five Day Week Agreement which sets down a negotiated shift length of seven and a quarter hours plus one winding time for underground workers and eights hours for surface workers.

6. The repeal of the 1908 Act, according to the Department of Energy, would not commence until and unless the EC Directive on Working Time was implemented. They justified their proposed abolition of the 1908 Act on grounds that the EC Directive would regulate the working hours of industry throughout the entire European Community and that it would, therefore, necessitate the agreement of new working practices for British Coal's workforce. The repeal of the 1908 Act was seen to be an essential part of that process.

7. The decision of the British government in this respect was inconsistent with their general attitude towards directives originating from the EC Social Chapter. In our view, it was a back door method of supporting British Coal Corporation's

campaign to deregulate hours of work in the deep coalmining industry in preparation for privatisation.

8. It is well known that since 1986, British Coal Corporation had been trying to get the 1908 Act repealed. When the Technical Director gave evidence before the Energy Select Committee in 1986, he admitted that in order to introduce their strategy for the coalmining industry they required the repeal of the 1908 Act.

9. Had we been consulted about the likely impact of the EC Directive on Working Time on the coal industry, we could have pointed out that the Directive did not nullify the 1908 Act as the Department of Energy was suggesting. Indeed, Article 16 of the Directive states it is not intended to overrule any national legislation or collective agreement which provides workers in member countries with a greater degree of protection. Article 16 states:

"This directive shall not affect Member States' rights to introduce laws, regulations or administrative provisions more favourable to the protection of the safety and health of workers or to facilitate or permit the application of collective agreements concluded between the two sides of industry which are more favourable to the protection of the safety and health of workers."

10. In no way was the Directive meant to be introduced as an all embracing piece of legislation decreeing working time throughout the Community. It was designed to provide a minimum standard of protection in those areas where none had previously existed.

11. A further recent experience concerning the administration of legislation causing us to suggest a Select Committee to review legislation relates to an interpretation of Schedule 14 under the Employment Protection (Consolidation) Act 1978, and concerns the formula which the Department of Employment had advised British Coal Corporation to use when calculating redundancy payments.

12. It was drawn to the Union's attention that it was believed paragraph 5.2 of the Schedule was being incorrectly interpreted by British Coal Corporation. They had been advised by the Department of Employment as it is assumed had other employers. Paragraph 5.2 of the aforementioned Schedule states:

"Where in arriving at the said hourly rate of remuneration, account has to be taken of remuneration payable for, or appertainable to, work done in hours other than normal working hours, and the amount of that remuneration was greater than it would have been if the work had been done in normal hours, account shall be taken of that remuneration as if:
(a) the work had been done in normal work hours, and
(b) the amount of that remuneration had been reduced accordingly."

13. The construction put on that paragraph by the Department of Employment was that overtime hours stripped of their premium rate enter the divisor. This has the effect where a bonus payment is made on normal hours but not on overtime hours of diluting the average hourly rate of remuneration. We contended that Parliament could not have intended that a man who works overtime and receives the kind of payment outlined above, should be worse off for the purpose of redundancy calculation than a man who works no overtime.

14. It was our contention that the correct construction is that overtime hours should be stripped down to the level of the average hourly rate of remuneration. If the overtime rate of pay is greater than the average hourly rate of remuneration then it is untouched because paragraph 5.2 says it is only reduced if it is "greater than it would have been if the work had been done in normal hours".

15. There is currently no Select Committee mechanism to refer such issues by way of a complaint to an MP to obtain Parliament's view on what they intended. We were forced to go to law. The case proceeded from an Industrial Tribunal which found in the appellant's favour, to the Employment Appeal Tribunal who dismissed the appeal but gave leave to go to the Appeal Court. At great expense, the case next moved to the Appeal Court where it was allowed but refused leave to appeal further. Therefore, the appellant had to petition the House of Lords who agreed to hear the case. The case was finally heard in the House of Lords in January 1990, judgement was given by a majority decision in favour of the defendants.

16. At the Employment Appeal Tribunal and in the Court of Appeal the Secretary of State supported our submission. But at the end of the day we had to accept, at great expense, a judge's interpretation of what Parliament intended. This despite the fact that those who devised the forumula supported the appellant at least as far as the door of the House of Lords. The mechanism we have suggested above, would be more satisfactory in these kind of situations and it would relieve pressure from the House of Lords.

January 1992

M45   Professor Philip Norton, Professor of Government, University of Hull

There are four principal stages in the legislative "process": those of gestation, preparation, deliberation, and implementation (see Figure 1). My purpose in this memorandum is not to offer comment on all four stages but rather to focus on that stage – deliberation – in which the House of Commons is the principal actor. However, as no stage in the process can be totally disaggregated from the others, my comments will not be exclusive to that stage.

The House of Commons is at the heart of the legislative process. It is a powerful body. It is powerful because there is popular acceptance, at both elite and mass level, that measures of public policy are not legitimate unless approved by Parliament.[1] Legitimisation is the oldest function of the House of Commons and its legitimising authority has been strengthened by virtue of longevity and, since the 19th Century, by election by a mass electorate.

The House of Commons thus stands in a unique position in relation to government. Government requires the assent of the House to legislation and supply.

1   See P. Norton, "Parliament in the United Kingdom: Balancing Effectiveness and Consent?" in P. Norton (ed), *Parliaments in Western Europe*, London: Frank Cass, 1990, pp. 11–12.

Figure 1: Legislative Process in the UK

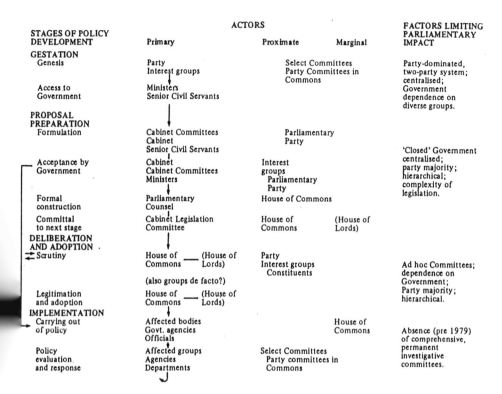

STAGES OF POLICY DEVELOPMENT	ACTORS Primary	ACTORS Proximate	ACTORS Marginal	FACTORS LIMITING PARLIAMENTARY IMPACT
GESTATION Genesis	Party Interest groups ↓	Select Committees Party Committees in Commons		Party-dominated, two-party system; centralised;
Access to Government	Ministers Senior Civil Servants ↓			Government dependence on diverse groups.
PROPOSAL PREPARATION Formulation	Cabinet Committees Cabinet Senior Civil Servants ↓	Parliamentary Party		
Acceptance by Government	Cabinet Cabinet Committees Ministers ↓	Interest groups Parliamentary Party		'Closed' Government centralised; party majority; hierarchical; complexity of legislation.
Formal construction	Parliamentary Counsel ↓	House of Commons		
Committal to next stage	Cabinet Legislation Committee ↓	House of Commons	(House of Lords)	
DELIBERATION AND ADOPTION Scrutiny	House of ___ (House of Commons Lords) (also groups de facto?)	Party Interest groups Constituents		Ad hoc Committees; dependence on Government; Party majority; hierarchical.
Legitimation and adoption	House of ___ (House of Commons Lords) ↓			
IMPLEMENTATION Carrying out of policy	Affected bodies Govt. agencies Officials		House of Commons	Absence (pre 1979) of comprehensive, permanent investigative committees.
Policy evaluation and response	Affected groups Agencies Departments	Select Committees Party committees in Commons		

Source: P. Norton, "Parliament and Policy in Britain: The House of Commons as a Policy Influencer", *Teaching Politics*, 13 (2), 1984.

The House is thus placed in a powerful position to force government to justify its actions and explain its measures. It has adopted procedures – developed over centuries – to consider in detail the legislative proposals placed before it.

Parliament itself is not a law "making" body. It never has been for any continuous period in its history: it has looked instead to the executive to initiate policy. The growth of party in the 19th Century ensured that policy making was confirmed as essentially the preserve of the executive. Parliament thus does not constitute a "policy-making legislature", with the capacity to generate and substitute policy of its own for executive-sponsored measures, but rather a "policy influencing legislature", with the capacity to amend, even reject, measures brought forward by the executive but not to formulate and substitute policy of its own.[1]

---

1 The typology is drawn from P. Norton, "Parliaments and Policy in Britain: The House of Commons as a Policy Influencer", *Teaching Politics*, 13 (2), 1984, pp. 198–221.

It is as a policy-influencing body that the House of Commons should be evaluated. The government is responsible for generating a coherent programme of public policy and can be held responsible for that programme by the electorate. Parliament's task is to deliberate on behalf of the citizenry, to place measures alongside their electoral promises, their conception of the national interest, and the demands made by citizens individually and collectively to judge whether those measures should be modified or even rejected. It is a vital task and the capacity of MPs to fulfil it underpins the political authority of Parliament.

The Problem Of Parliament
The capacity of the House of Commons to subject bills to sustained and informed scrutiny is limited. This is apparent from a range of hard data[1] and constitutes the basis on which submissions to the Commission dealing with the deliberative stage are made. The House is constrained by a lack of time, information, specialisation and resources from submitting bills to effective scrutiny.

The roots of the problem are to be found in 19th Century attitudes towards what constituted a "good" House of Commons: a deliberative body of men of independent means and thought, coming together from other pursuits as a public duty to discuss in plenary session the merits of public policy. The public domain was then not extensive and issues were not difficult to grasp. The emphasis was very much on the amateur and on the floor of the House. Those emphases lingered into the era of party government and it suited the party in government that they remained. There was a reluctance to contemplate a more professional and a more specialised House capable of subjecting the measures of government to critical scrutiny.

This attitude thus militated against the use of committees. As party dominance increased in the 19th Century so the use of committees declined. In the 20th Century, the only extensive use of committees has been of standing committees. They have been crafted to favour government. Several can sit at the same time, allowing a number of government bills to be considered simultaneously, avoiding a log-jam on the floor of the House. Their appointment on an ad hoc basis – they are anything but "standing" – militates against developing any form of specialisation or corporate spirit. The absence of the power to send for papers, persons and records limits what they can consider. The replication not just of party strength on the floor of the House but more especially the party structure (with ministers and – especially since 1945 – whips appointed) has meant that committee deliberation has tended to be a continuation of the partisan debate at second reading. Consequently, deliberation – in both debate and vote – has tended to be predictable.

It is only relatively recently that select committees have been employed on a systematic and extensive basis. Though not quite repeating some of the powerful investigations of some of their early predecessors they have constituted a useful step

---

1 As, for example, the number of government amendments accepted, and the number of Opposition and government backbench amendments rejected, in committee. See J. A. G. Griffith, *Parliamentary Scrutiny of Government Bills*, London: George Allen & Unwin, 1974.

forward, differing significantly in powers, composition and permanence from standing committees.[1] They could be strengthened considerably – and, in my view, need to be strengthened considerably[2] – but nonetheless fulfil their functions more effectively than standing committees fulfil theirs.

Standing committees probably reached their nadir in the period from 1945 to 1970, when party cohesion was at its strongest and extended, via the whips, to standing committees. Significant changes since then have had some modest effect on standing committee deliberation. On the whole, the changes have been beneficial to deliberation in standing committee but, nonetheless, have not achieved a paradigmatic change and, in combination, contribute to a growing pressure on the House that could overwhelm MPs and, hence, the work of committees.

The years since 1970 have witnessed a relative weakening of party cohesion. This has been reflected in the division lobbies and, to some extent, in standing committee.[3] Government members of a committee cannot always be taken for granted and on occasion have been persuaded of the case for an amendment and helped carry it against government advice. Government defeats were pronounced in the 1970s, facilitated by a small or (after 1976) non-existent overall government majority. Defeats were fewer but not unknown in the 1980s, facilitated not by a small government majority – some defeats took place in the 1983–87 Parliament when the government enjoyed the largest Conservative majority since 1935 – but rather by greater links developed between committee members and outside groups. Lobbying of MPs by outside groups was a major phenomenon of the 1980s,[4] resulting in Members receiving a wider range of information and advice than was previously the case. Government backbenchers worried by a particular part of a bill were not necessarily more numerous than before but they were better armed. This pressure appears to have influenced backbench behaviour and government willingness to accept amendments. The 1986 survey of organised interests by the Study of Parliament Group found that most groups surveyed not only lobbied MPs but deemed their efforts to be "very" or "quite" successful.[5] To these developments may now be added the entry of the television cameras. Coverage of committees –

---

1   See G. Drewry (ed), *The New Select Committees*, 2nd ed., Oxford: Oxford University Press, 1989, and *The Working of the Select Committee System: Second Report from the Select Committee on Procedure*, Session 1989–90, HC 19-I.

2   See my memorandum to the Procedure Committee, *The Working of the Select Committee System*, Vol. II: Minutes of Evidence, 1989–90, HC 19-II, pp. 139–46; and P. Norton, "Committee Under Scrutiny", *The House Magazine*, 12 November 1990, p. 22.

3   P. Norton, *Dissension in the House of Commons 1945–74*, London: Macmillan, 1975; *Conservative Dissidents*, London: Temple Smith, 1978; *Dissension in the House of Commons 1974–1979*, Oxford: Oxford University Press, 1980; "The House of Commons: Behavioural Changes", in P. Norton (ed), *Parliament in the 1980s*, Oxford: Basil Blackwell, 1985; J. Schwarz, "Exploring a New Role in Policy Making: The British House of Commons in the 1970s", *American Political Science Review*, 74 (1), 1980, pp. 23–37.

4   P. Norton, "The Changing Face of Parliament: Lobbying and its Consequences" in P. Norton (ed), *New Directions in British Politics?* Aldershot: Edward Elgar, 1990, pp. 58–82.

5   M. Rush (ed), *Parliament and Pressure Politics*, Oxford: Oxford University Press, 1990, Q7, p. 285.

standing and select – has been more extensive than Members anticipated[1] and has apparently encouraged a somewhat greater willingness of government backbenchers to neglect reading and writing letters in favour of actually contributing to discussion. The use of televised footage has also increased media attention, qualitatively as well as quantitatively: items concerning the Commons now come higher in the running order in news programmes.

The combined effect of these developments is to render standing committees more open and informed. That is, relative to the closed and uninformed position they occupied previously.[2] There is still much more that can – and should be done – to take this process further. However, problems abound, not least because of a countervailing pressure to the developments just outlined; indeed, some of the developments contribute to this pressure.

MPs – collectively and individually – are in danger of being overloaded with work. The pressure comes from several sources: from the sheer volume of public business, from constituents, from pressure groups, from European Community business, and from Members themselves.[3] The demands on MPs time are now extensive and Members do not have the resources to cope. The result is that some activity has to be limited or discarded. In the last Parliament, for example, attendance at Conservative party committees appeared to be badly hit. The greater the demands on MPs' time, the greater the threat to their being able to give time and attention to standing committees. What flows from this is that any consideration of the legislative process in the House of Commons cannot be confined to procedures alone. It must extend to the resources available to Members: resources in terms of time, information, and support staff. There is no point crafting new processes if the MPs that have to make them work lack the wherewithal to do so.

Recommendations

Given the nature of the problem, various remedies would seem necessary. From the foregoing, it is clear that I consider committee stage constitutes the part of the parliamentary deliberation that requires most attention. Most of my recommendations will thus focus on that stage.

Special Standing Committees

Special standing committees – with power to take evidence in three public sessions prior to reverting to traditional standing committee format – were introduced on an experimental basis in 1980/81 and provision for their appointment subsequently embodied in standing orders. In 1986 the House voted, against government advice, to allow any Member to move for a bill to be referred to such a committee.

In practice, only five bills have been considered by SSCs and those in the first half of the 1980s. However, the committees proved popular with those Members

---

1   See A. Hetherington, K. Weaver and M. Ryle, *Cameras in the Commons*, London: Hansard Society, 1990, p. 1.
2   See, generally, P. Norton, "Parliament Since 1945: A More Open Institution?" *Contemporary Record*, 5 (2), 1991, pp. 217–34.
3   P. Norton, "The House of Commons: From Overlooked to Overworked", in B. Jones and L. Robins (eds), *Two Decades in British Politics*, Manchester: Manchester University Press, 1992, pp. 139–54.

who served on them.[1] The first SSC, on the Criminal Attempts Bill, was a particularly good example of what such committees can achieve. As a result of the evidence given to the committee, the first clause had to be withdrawn by the government and a new clause substituted.[2].

Special standing committees offer a means of subjecting bills to more informed scrutiny than exists under normal standing committee procedure. By examining witnesses and receiving evidence, the committees are better able to test government claims about the merits and, more especially, the practicalities of a bill. By listening to interested and informed opinion, the committees are more likely to render a bill "more generally acceptance", their principal task according to *Erskine May*. Taking evidence may also serve to increase the critical faculties of Members – faced with evidence that challenges particular provisions – and concomitantly facilitate some degree of bi-partisanship.

But SSCs have further advantages that are both psychological and symbolic. By taking evidence, they fulfil a valuable safety-valve function. However extensive and thorough the consultation between government and interested bodies at pre-parliamentary stages, there is always the danger of particular groups feeling excluded from the process. There is the danger that the public perception may be one of deals being made in the privacy of Whitehall departments. Public hearings in Parliament allow potentially disaffected groups to make their case in a public, authoritative forum – and to be seen to be so doing. Parliament allows for a degree of openness not possible at earlier stages of the legislative process.[3] It also offers a second-stage scrutiny, subjecting measures to scrutiny on behalf of a wider constituency than that solely of organised interest.

I would therefore recommend the more extensive use of such committees. Indeed, I would tend to the view that their use should be the norm rather than the exception. In other words, they should cease to be "special" standing committees. The name suggested by the Procedure Committee in 1978 – public bill committees – would seem appropriate. Standing orders could be amended to stipulate that each bill will stand referred to such a standing committee unless the House directs otherwise. This

---

1 A survey of MPs who served on the first three SSCs found that, of 37 respondents, 28 felt that the experiment had been "very worthwhile" and only one said that it made no difference. B. George MP and B. Evans, "Parliamentary Reform: The Internal View", in D. Judge (ed), *The Politics of Parliamentary Reform*, London: Heinemann, 1983, p. 89.

2 See ibid. pp. 88–89.

3 I am conscious that pre-legislative Swedish-style commissions might also allow for some openness, but such commissions – if involved in the gestation and preparation of legislation – endanger the principle of government responsibility. Public general bills laid before Parliament should, in the main, form part of the government's programme for a Parliament, a programme for which it can be held responsible by the electorate at the next election. Bills generated by commissions would be "irresponsible" measures – similar to Private Members' Bills – in that there would no single body that the electorate could penalise or reward at the next election. The concept of the mandate has no formal status in the UK, but parties in government have a strong track record in implementing policies promised in election manifestos. See R. I. Hofferbert and I. Budge, "The Party Mandate and the Westminster Model: Election Programmes and Government Spending in Britain, 1945–85", *British Journal of Political Science*, 22 (2), April 1992, pp. 151–82.

move would be a major departure from existing practice, comparable to the chan in standing orders of 1907.

The obvious objection to such a move, apart from the practical problems, is th many or most bills do not lend themselves to such a process. The empirical eviden suggests otherwise. Only a small minority of bills introduced each session could I categorised as "partisan" bills – that is, analogous to the definition of money bil bills that contain solely provisions that are contested between the parties. One stud of the 87 bills introduced in the two years of 1970 and 1985 found that only twel fell into the category of being "controversial". The rest were either "maj reforming", "significant reforming" or "minor": the largest single number (34) fe into the last category.[1] There is thus considerable scope for most bills to I considered, wholly or in part, by such evidence-taking committees.

I thus concur with successive Procedure Committees that the use of SSCs shou be more widespread, though I would go further in advocating their use as standa practice. However, the greater of use of such committees has significant implicatio for both the procedures and the workload of MPs and cannot therefore be consider in isolation. It has to be linked with changes in the sessional cut-off for legislatio in timetabling, in the appointment of members, and in the resources made availab to committees *qua* committees and to committee members.

Sessional cut-off

The use of SSCs, to be effective, requires allowing them the opportunity to ho more evidence-taking sessions than presently allowed by standing orders. Th means that some bills will be in committee for some considerable time. Timetablir will permit a balanced consideration and prevent filibustering. However, there little justification for allowing consideration of a major piece of legislation to I rushed in order to prevent it being lost because it has not completed all its stages t the end of the session.

The justification used for the present sessional cut-off is that it imposes a usef discipline on government. That argument cannot be sustained against the dama done to legislative scrutiny by the haste that it necessitates. Discipline could I maintained by restricting carry-over of a bill from one session to the next but n beyond. That, coupled with timetabling, would avoid a bill lingering in committe Carry-over is used for private bills and, in effect, consolidation bills. As the Clerk the Parliaments told the House of Lords Select Committee on Practice ar Procedure in 1976–77: "It would only be an extension of existing practice if son government bills were to be treated in a similar way".[2]

Allowing a carry-over would allow more sustained consideration by a committe It would also prevent the problems, not least in terms of time, that presently aris

---

1 Research undertaken by Dr E. C. Page of the Politics Department at Hull University, cited in P. Norton, "Public Legislation", in M. Rush (ed), *Parliament and Pressure Politics*, Oxford: Oxford University Press, 1990, p. 210, n. 11. Note also the discussion on the distribution between "policy" and "administration" bills in I. Burton and G. Drewry, *Legislation and Public Policy*, London: Macmillan, 1981.

2 *First Report from the Select Committee of the House of Lords on Practice and Procedure*, 1977, HL 141, p. 79.

when a bill is lost because of the sessional cut-off and has to be introduced afresh in the next session. It would also have the advantage of helping get rid of the legislative "hump" that develops, in the Commons at the start of a session, with bills having to be introduced early in a session, and in the House of Lords towards the end of a session, the House variously having to sit longer in the summer or return early in the autumn to deal with the measures that have to complete their final stages in the Upper House.

Timetabling

The timetabling of bills has been considered by successive Procedure Committees. In 1985 the committee recommended that a timetabling procedure be introduced. The House narrowly defeated this recommendation in 1986, largely because of a solid turn-out to vote against it by the pay-roll vote. The opposition is sometimes described as acting as the "alternative government". This was a rare occasion when the government acted as the "alternative opposition", opposing the recommendation on the ground that it would destroy the opposition's power to delay a bill. In practice, the defence of the existing arrangement was based on Commons' mythology.

At present, timetabling is variously employed. Allocation of time motions (guillotines) could be moved for every bill. In practice, they are used for bills that are contentious and are introduced after lengthy debate on the early clauses. As a consequence, they are seen as partisan weapons at the disposal of government.

Introducing timetabling for bills likely to spend considerable time in committee would allow for more balanced scrutiny of a bill, preventing undigested legislation flowing down the corridor from the Commons to the Lords. It would discourage opposition members from talking for the sake of it and may encourage more participation from government supporters, since the need for vows of silence would no longer be needed in order to get the bill through by a particular date. It would dove-tail with the use of evidence-taking sessions, encouraging informed scrutiny of the various provisions of a bill.

The change would be to the benefit of the House – what is now seen as a partisan device would be replaced with a procedure employed by the House and encourage scrutiny. If combined with evidence-taking sessions, opposition members would have greater opportunities than now to indulge in critical scrutiny. The losses to the opposition would be non-existent. The claim that it would lose the power of delay has no empirical basis. There are very few, if any, instances in recent history of an opposition achieving substantial concessions by means of delay alone.[1] Far from being a "power", attempts at delay tend to be counter-productive, annoying ministers and making them less reluctant to concede anything. Introducing a regular system of timetabling would be neither a great constitutional departure nor a threat to the powers of the of the opposition; if anything, the reverse.

See the memorandum of evidence submitted by the Study of Parliament Group's study group on legislative procedure, *Public Bill Procedure: Select Committee on Procedure, Session 1984–85*, HC 49-iv, p. 74.

Appointment of members

There is little point in reforming the committee structure without considering membership and resources. Sustained scrutiny is presently discouraged by the fact that committee members are appointed solely for the lifetime of a committee established to consider a bill and are essentially recruited to serve by the whips. Some independent-minded Members, sometimes by the device of speaking during second reading debate, get appointed but the bulk of Members are present because they have been cajoled into service. None of this encourages informed and critical scrutiny. There is no possibility of specialisation, except perhaps for those appointed each year to consider the Finance Bill, and no corporate spirit.

The use of SSC procedure and timetabling in combination will encourage more informed and critical scrutiny. So would allowing for some degree of permanent or core membership, allowing Members to specialise in particular areas of legislative scrutiny. There are practical problems in trying to create a permanent set of committees. Emulating the select committees in number would make great demands on backbenchers. There would be problems if more than one bill sponsored by a particular department was introduced in a session. There are various options. One would be to move toward the system employed for select committee membership, allowing the Committee of Selection greater freedom in selecting members, possibly on the basis of self-nomination. (That, though, as present practice with selection of members of select committees shows, is not problem free.) Another would be to create a small pool of permanent members, those with particular knowledge in the subject, including one who would chair evidence-taking sessions, with other members added when bills are introduced. That would allow for some flexibility.

The most radical option of all would be to give responsibility for committee stage to the departmental select committees. That is an option worth further consideration. However, to be feasible, it would require a dramatic increase in the resources of the committees, not least in terms of support staff and in the resources of members individually. Even with increased resources, the demands on the time and attention of the existing members would be substantial. One could address this problem by solving another. Combining select and standing committees would run the danger of MPs excluded from committee service resenting what may appear to be a two-tier Commons membership. The answer would appear to be enlarging the size of the committees. This would allow the committees to absorb the energies of MPs keen to be involved and provide extra manpower resources. The committees, for example, if enlarged to a membership of twenty each (thus occupying the commitment of almost half the membership of the House) could then operate through sub-committees.

Resources

There is no point in setting up committees if those committees, collectively and individual, cannot fulfil the responsibilities given them. To be effective, committees require sufficient support staff not only to provide advice (clerks) and clerical back-up but also to undertake various research tasks. This is especially likely to be the case in the event of SSCs – public bill committees – becoming standard. It would be even more so in the event of select and standing committees being combined. In that event, there would be an even stronger case for committees to have dedicated rooms and a small team of researchers.[1] There is also a powerful case for them to have budgets that would allow them to commission particular pieces of research.

The pressures on individual Members are growing and increased committee responsibilities would add to those pressures. I would therefore recommend that members of committees be provided with an additional office cost allowance so that they may hire additional research support (or, perhaps more appropriately, buy in independent research on a particular bill, especially when a large or complex bill) or office support to relieve them of some of the mundane administrative tasks which Members still carry out themselves. Even under the present arrangements, committee members – receiving submissions from outside groups that sometimes pile up more than two feet high – are having difficulty coping. Even assistance with sorting submissions would help reduce the burden.

On grounds of equity and merit, I am also inclined to the view that committee members should receive an additional salary for their service. Members are able, should they wish, to pursue paid activities outside the Palace of Westminster. Their experiences can enrich debate and the knowledge of the House. However, those who devote themselves to the committee work of the House receive no recompense for their additional services. I would therefore regard payment for committee service as justified.

If the SSC, or public bill, format becomes standard, a particular burden will fall on those Members who chair the committees, especially if present practice is employed of the relevant select committee chairman chairing the evidence-taking sessions. In 1978, the Procedure Committee raised the possibility of select committee chairmen receiving some payment for their service. I pursued this recommendation in my evidence to the Procedure Committee in 1990 and I would repeat it here. Given the burdens that would be placed on chairmen in the event of the foregoing proposals being implemented, the case for payment is stronger than ever before.

Payment, in addition to the higher profile and more rewarding experiences – via evidence-taking – that committees would have, may also act as an incentive to serve on committees. If a core membership was to be formed, or standing and select committees merged, then committee work could achieve greater significance in the eyes of Members, as well as those outside the House, and create more of an alternative career route than presently exists to front bench careers.

Additional and necessary resources are those of time for considering a bill's provision and more information about a bill's contents. These can, in part, be met by longer intervals between stages and more information provided with the printed bill.

Intervals between stages
There is a strong case for a standard interval between the stages of a bill being taken in the House and a particularly strong case for longer intervals than at present exist. There is often too little time between second reading and, equally if not more importantly, between publication of the names of committee members and

---

1   On this, see my memorandum of evidence to the Procedure Committee, *The Working of the Select Committee System*, referred to in n. 5 above.

committee stage for the purposes of outside groups to marshal their comments and get them in to committee members. The gap between appointment and the committee proceedings getting under way also places pressure on those committee members determined to undertake a thorough scrutiny of the bill's provisions. Given the recommendations for timetabling and carry-over, the present case for rushing as quickly as possible from second reading to committee stage disappears.

Information

Information is a vital resource. At present, standing committees have too little, having to rely too much on official sources, limited opposition research and generally volunteered information from interested groups outside the House. Such information varies considerably in quality and is, by its nature, self-serving.

Some of the foregoing recommendations – principally providing committees with research staff or a budget to buy-in specialist research, and providing members individually with a research allowance – would allow for committee members to receive information independently of the vested interests that presently supply the bulk of the explanation and comment on a bill's provisions.

However, it would also aid committee members – as well as members generally and those outside the House likely to be affected by its provisions – if the contents of each bill were explained in fairly straightforward terms. The explanatory memorandum is useful but limited. One possibility, as the Commission knows from previous evidence, would be for the notes prepared by the sponsoring department to be more widely available. Another, I think more attractive, proposal is for explanatory notes to be appended to the printed bill. (They would not form part of the bill and would be discarded when the bill has completed all its stages.) The provisions of a bill could be printed on one side of a page and the explanatory detail on the other. I recognise there may be problems with this proposal: the legal status of the explanatory detail for example and the fact that discussion in committee may focus on the explanatory detail rather than the formal provisions ("But it says here …"). However, I believe that the advantages would be considerable, facilitating greater and quicker understanding of a bill. This would be to the benefit of committee members and outside groups. On balance, it is also likely to benefit government, reducing the need (potentially at least) to have to deal with exploratory amendments. A government confident in the case for a particular measure should not be worried about explaining the provisions designed to achieve the desired goal.

A Wider Package

The foregoing proposals are designed as a package. Each links with the others. Together they can help ensure a more effective parliamentary scrutiny of the bills brought forward by government. However, this package should not and cannot be seen in isolation. Improving resources for committee members needs to be linked with an improvement for all Members – improvements in physical conditions, working hours, information, communications, and support staff. That could be characterised as looking at the situation horizontally – across the parliamentary dimension. It also has to be looked at vertically that is, as one part of the legislative process. Parliament, as I mentioned in my opening paragraph, links with that process substantially only at one stage.

Within the parliamentary process, there are other areas that I have not addressed but need careful attention. The most obvious is that of *delegated legislation*. My own view is that a separate, very thorough review needs to be undertaken of scrutiny of SIs. As the House of Lords Committee on the Committee Work of the House has recognised, there needs to be more rigorous criteria for determining which delegated legislation is to be subject to affirmative, negative or no resolution procedure and for a more extensive use of committee scrutiny.[1] The present procedure deters interest by Members. Given the subject matter, this is likely to remain a problem. However, allowing for delegated legislation to be amendable would give Members greater influence and would be likely to increase representations from outside bodies.

There is also the dimension of the other chamber, *the House of Lords*. The recommendations I have made focus not just on committee stage but committee stage in the Commons. Any proposals for evidence-taking committees in one House have implications for the other. If both have such committees, there is the obvious danger of overlap and unnecessary duplication of effort. The Lords' Committee on the Committee Work of the House has already recommended the experimental use of special standing committee procedure.[2] One means to avoid overlap would be for the Lords to use the SSC procedure for particular categories of bills, as suggested by the Lord Chancellor.[3] There would, in any event, need to be consistent contact and co-operation.

There is also, still within the parliamentary process, but looking at a different stage of the legislative process, the capacity for select committees to engage in some measure of *programme evaluation*. Government has no systematic procedures for evaluating public policies once implemented. Members of Parliament serve as a valuable barometer of public reaction. Complaints from constituents affected adversely by a particular programme are taken up by their MPs. Multiple letters from MPs alert departments to the fact there is a problem. This procedure for redressing constituents' grievances is well-established and extensive. It serves a very valuable safety-valve function.[4] It is essential that it be retained and strengthened, not least through an increase in the resources of the hard-pressed Member. The increase in constituency correspondence in recent years has been dramatic and Members have difficulty now in keeping up with it.[5] However, there is a case also for a more systematic evaluation of programmes, extending beyond present

---

1 The Committee has recommended the appointment in the Lords of a Delegated Powers Scrutiny Committee. *Report from the Select Committee on the Committee Work of the House*, Session 1991–92, HL 35-I, para. 133.

2 Ibid, para. 132.

3 Ibid., paras. 57 and 132 and appendix 8. He suggested Law Commission bills and bills, for example, dealing with company law.

4 P. Norton, "'Dear Minister...' The Influence of MP-to-Minister Correspondence", *Parliamentary Affairs*, 35 (1), Winter 1982, pp. 59–72.

5 See, for example, P, Norton, "The House of Commons: From Overlooked to Overworked", op. cit., pp. 144–46.

value-for-money evaluations carried out by the National Audit Office and Public Accounts Committee. Select committees could usefully devote a greater proportion of their time to programme evaluation as well as (following the excellent example set by the House of Lords Committee on Science & Technology) holding more follow-up sessions to find out what has happened to their earlier recommendations. Again, there are major resource implications. The appointment of small research units would seem appropriate in this context.

These various proposals, then, are not exclusive to committee stage. Nor, in the context of committee scrutiny, are they exhaustive. I have elsewhere floated the idea of committee stage preceding plenary session (i.e. second reading).[1] Evidence from other legislatures suggests that commencing with committee deliberation serves as an independent variable in strengthening parliamentary influence.[2] I have not advanced it as a concrete recommendation in this memorandum. I think it is worth further consideration but I am not convinced that it would be a proposal that could muster a majority against the wishes of government. I have concentrated on proposals which may not necessarily prove acceptable, at least not immediately, but which have sufficient merit to garner support from Members in all parts of the House. As may be apparent, there is some implicit ranking within my proposals, ranging from the modest (limited use of SSCs, for example, and improvements in office cost allowances) to ambitious (SSC procedure as the norm, permanent or merged committees). The House will thus be able to determine how far down the road of improving its structures and procedures it wishes to go. It will be for the Commission to determine how much of a guiding framework it wishes to offer.

June 1992

M46   Rev Dr Ian Paisley MP, MEP

I would like to give a brief outline of my views on how Northern Ireland legislation should be handled.

First, I would like to put on record once again my Party's total opposition to the present arrangements whereby legislation concerning Northern Ireland is dealt with by way of Orders in Council. We believe this is entirely unsatisfactory as it is not subject to amendment on the floor of the House or to any detailed scrutiny at any stage of the Parliamentary process. This is totally unacceptable. Whatever the consultation period at the Draft Order stage there can be no substitute for detailed Parliamentary scrutiny of legislation as it goes through the House.

We recognise that the absence of a locally elected Assembly in Northern Ireland to deal with transferred matters is one of the reasons cited for the use of Orders in Council. My Party believes very strongly in a devolved administration and government in Northern Ireland which would be able to take these matters on board

---

1   P. Norton, "A Reform Parliament?" *The House Magazine*, No. 559, vol. 18, 22 June 1992, p. 15.
2   See especially M. Shaw, "Conclusion", in J. D. Lees and M. Shaw (eds), *Committees in Legislatures*, Oxford: Martin Robertson, 1979, pp. 361–434.

and give them the detailed attention that they deserve. The absence in the meantime of any such Assembly should not, however, preclude steps being taken to improve the way Northern Ireland is legislated for in the House of Commons. The duration of the consultation period needs to be extended and consultation must take place with as many interested bodies and people as possible.

If Orders in Council are to be proceded with in the meantime then more time should be given for their debate on the floor of the House and there must be an opportunity for them to be considered "line by line", as it were, rather than be subject to a blanket acceptance or a blanket rejection.

I would like to state, once again, my Party's desire that there should be a Select Committee on Northern Ireland which could scrutinise and monitor the work of the Northern Ireland Office. We believe that this would improve the situation as far as the conduct of Northern Ireland business is concerned although we would emphasise once again that we do not believe that this would be an adequate substitute for a democratically elected administration in Northern Ireland.

7 August 1992

M47　The Rt Hon Lord Renton PC, QC

(a) What is legislation for?

I agree that different purposes require different treatment and that tax legislation must be precise and detailed. Most other Bills however should be in more general terms. But both in tax legislation as well as in all other legislation *the intentions of Parliament should be made clear* even when detailed provisions are required.

(b) Are our present boundaries of legislation correct?

The UK Parliament sets little or no limit to the subject-matter of its legislation. Indeed Private Acts of Parliament may deal with very minor matters. Our Statutes and our secondary legislation are longer and more voluminous and detailed than those of any other country, and our Parliament spends more time each year on legislation than does any other Parliament. There is in my opinion a strong case for limiting the matters which require primary legislation by Parliament and making arrangements for delegating some legislation to Ministers, the Judiciary and Statutory Bodies. This is a big and complex part of the subject and a solution involving change would be controversial.

(c) Are changes needed in the processes by which legislation is prepared?

In the past 15 years, and partly as a result of recommendations made by the Committee on the Preparation of Legislation (hereafter called "the Renton Committee"), there is now a good deal more prior consultation than there used to be. Royal Commissions and Departmental Committees are of value because they take plenty of time to study the problems in depth after a great deal of enquiry involving taking evidence from experts. The Departmental Select Committees of the House of Commons should be encouraged to consider Bills in draft before they are presented.

I do consider that more effort should be made to obtain the views of those citizens most likely to be affected, although care has to be taken not to allow financial speculation as a result.

(d) Could the drafting procedures be improved?

I do consider that there should be more scope for consulting practising lawyers with relevant experience on early drafts of Bills. Parliamentary Counsel are obliged to accept the instructions of Departmental lawyers, but it is by tradition very much a "behind the scenes process" and one does not know to what extent Parliamentary Counsel are bold enough to tell the Departments when their instructions are impracticable, unworkable or unecessarily detailed. More draftsmen are always needed but under the present system it takes time to train them to the extent required for them to assume individual responsibility.

Acts could undoubtedly be more readily intelligible, and I would refer to recommendations (8) to (30) of the Renton Report. In Australia, Canada and New Zealand much more deliberate efforts have been and are being made to make Statutes more readily intelligible to those who are bound by them, or have to use them.

(e) Could the planning of the legislative programme be improved?

Yes. It is always over-loaded, not so much because of the number of Bills, but because of their detailed prolixity. It is perfectly clear from the vast number of Government amendments made during their passage through both Houses that not enough time has been spent on their preparation. At least two years of concentrated effort should be allowed before a Bill is presented to Parliament, unless it is urgent.

(f) To what extent should the detail of legislation be spelled out in Acts, or left to either delegated legislation or to Ministerial discretion not subject to parliamentary sanction?

As I have mentioned, our legislation is much too detailed and is much more so than that in most other countries. While agreeing that different solutions are needed for different purposes, it is quite clear that the purpose and principle should be stated in the sections of Statutes, but that any detail required to be in the primary legislation should be put into the Schedules. Whether, in order to keep pace with inflation and other changing circumstances, it would be desirable to change the law without troubling Parliament with a Statute for doing so, there is a strong case for doing so by Statutory Instrument. See also paras. 11.25&17.11 of the Renton Report.

(g) Are the arrangements for drafting delegated legislation satisfactory?

For the most part delegated legislation is well drafted in accordance with well established practice. It is a great advantage that each Statutory Instrument starts with a definition clause. Such legislation is drafted in the Legal Departments of the various Ministries and is generally well done.

I do not know who initiates the clauses of Bills containing power to make secondary legislation, but I assume that it is suggested by the people in each Ministry responsible for instructing Parliamentary Draftsmen. I do not consider that Parliamentary Counsel should play a bigger part, or any part, in the drafting of SIs.

There has been a deplorably excessive use of such powers in recent legislation. ee for example the Child Support Act 1991 which contains nearly 100 pportunities for Ministers to legislate by Statutory Instrument. Also there has been totally unacceptable increase in "Henry VIII clauses" enabling Ministers to amend rimary legislation, very often without restriction.

h) Is too much or too little time spent on legislation?

'oo much time is spent by our Parliament on legislation in spite of the fact that in 1e House of Commons at any rate MPs are so busy that they do not apply their ninds enough to the vast amount of primary legislation placed before them.

i) Is the balance between the two Houses properly struck?

'es. There has been a great improvement in that more Bills now start in the Lords.

j) Could the processes for the examination of bills be improved?

'es. More use should be made of Select Committees who should be required to xamine Bills affecting the Departments in which they are interested before Bills are resented to the House. I am not in favour of Joint Committees. The question of metables for major Bills in the Commons is a matter to be left to the Commons. I ee no need for small legislation committees in the Lords. There should be more irect consultation with outside experts and interests.

I leave open for the time being the question whether lessons could be learned rom the European Parliament, but I doubt it.

k) Could scrutiny of delegated legislation be improved?

ee above.

l) Should there be more or less Private Members' Bills?

'he present practice seems to me to be about right.

m) Should more use be made of select committees for post-legislative inquiry?

am doubtful. The better drafting of statutes would reduce the need.

n) Should there be a formal procedure for review by the courts of legislation in ractice?

'his is not necessary for judges have the opportunity of commenting on legislation /hen trying cases affected by it.

o) Is there sufficient and effective monitoring of the outcome of European Community law when it is translated into UK law?

am doubtful.

8 August 1991

M48   Mr Gareth Roscoe, Legal Adviser, BBC

.   I would like to make some observations drawn from my own experience as a government lawyer in the Department of the Environment from 1983 to 1989. During that period I was responsible for the raft of Local Government Finance legislation which was the subject of some cogent comment in Viscount Dilhorne's speech in the House of Lords on the topic of "Legislation: Scrutiny Proposal", Hansard 14 February 1990.

2. The legislative process prior to the introduction of a Bill falls into a number of stages. The first stage is to obtain approval in the bid for legislation prior to the Queen's Speech. The second consists of the preparation of a White or Green Paper followed by the consideration of comments arising from consultation. The third is the preparation by the Departmental lawyer, with administrators in the sponsoring department, of Instructions to Parliamentary Counsel. The fourth stage is the preparation of the draft bill which will be refined over time with the involvement of the departmental lawyer, Parliamentary Counsel and administrators. The fifth and final stage prior to Legislation Committee and introduction is the preparation of the Explanatory and Financial Memorandum and Notes on Clauses.

3. The critical factor is the time available to all concerned to complete these stages. It is obvious that in the case of a highly controversial measure, introduced to meet an immediate problem, these stages will be compressed and the time available for careful consideration of legislation prior to introduction will be short. And it is also true that where the legislation in question is not controversial that generally speaking there will be more time available prior to introduction.

4. In the first stage it is often the case that only the broad principles of the Bill have been developed; much more thought needs to be given to policy development prior to seeking approval for the bill. Only rough estimates can be given of the likely length of the bill, the time it will take to progress through both Houses and the resources which need to be allocated to its preparation. Another difficulty in my experience is the late involvement of the departmental lawyer in the development of policy. This leads to policy being set in stone as it were without any regard to whether it is achievable in legal terms. This can often store up problems for the future.

5. In the second stage it is frequently the case that the White or Green Paper is being prepared at the same time as instructions to Parliamentary Counsel. The effect of this is that it is often unlikely that departments will wish to change proposals in the light of comments received on the Green or White Papers since the preparation of the instructions is already at an advanced stage.

6. The third stage which involves 3 principal actors namely the departmental administrator, lawyer and Parliamentary Counsel is rather bizarre in the sense that the Bill appears to be developed by a process of "Chinese Whispers" with the departmental lawyer acting as a broker between Parliamentary Counsel and administrator over law and policy. It is unlikely that Parliamentary Counsel will simply be able to translate the instructions into legislation. If he or she encounters legal problems it is then often necessary to suggest a change in policy to circumvent them and often Ministers are committed to their original policy and not prepared to change it. Moreover Parliamentary Counsel has certain "duties to the Statute Book" and attempts if at all possible to keep the

detail of the legislation off the face of the Bill. The result of this is that there is often a large number of Statutory Instruments to be made which set out the fine details of the policy and indeed which have to be prepared and made or laid before the legislation can be implemented.

7. All these factors are compounded when the preparation of legislation proceeds at break-neck speed which is often the case. A classic example of this was the Local Government Finance Act 1988. There is also little chance of constructive comments made during the consultation process on the Green or White Papers being taken on board prior to introduction of the Bill since the principal actors are doing all that they can to get the basic bill in shape. Once the bill has been approved by Legislation Committee and a date confirmed for its introduction then most of the administrators' time is spent on handling the press release and other issues and little time is devoted to preparing helpful explanatory material to enable the ultimate consumers of the bill to understand what is being proposed. Indeed the Notes on Clauses which are usually made available to members of the Committee tend to be anodyne and merely repeat what the section says in non-legal words as far as that is possible.

14 January 1992

M49   Scottish Consumer Council

Introduction

The Scottish Consumer Council notes with interest the setting up of the Commission on the Legislative Process, to examine the whole process by which legislation is made in England and Wales. We are disappointed that the Commission's terms of reference do not extend to Scotland, or that a separate Scottish Commission has not been set up to examine the operation of the legislative process in relation to Scottish legislation.

The Scottish legal system has not been served well by the legislative process in recent years. We have a long backlog of unimplemented Scottish Law Commission reports, and, when parliamentary time is found for Scottish law reform, this is often kept to a minimum by adding Scottish provisions on to the end of legislation primarily intended for England and Wales, or a whole miscellany of issues are gathered together in a Law Reform (Miscellaneous Provisions) (Scotland) Bill. Bills are often strictly guillotined during their passage through committee.

Since there is no legislative forum in Scotland, individuals or organisations wishing to be present during debates involving Scottish legislation must visit London. Publicly funded or charitable organisations who represent the interests of the people affected by legislative change do not have the resources to mount a continued presence at Westminster during the passage of bills which are of interest to them, and their effective lobbying is thereby limited.

The Scottish Consumer Council, as Scotland's foremost consumer organisation, has been closely involved with the development of key pieces of reform in order to improve conditions for consumers in Scotland. We were instrumental in the introduction of the small claims procedure in Scotland's sheriff courts, we have been involved in lobbying on the community charge, the professional practice of the legal profession, education and school boards, and licensing law.

The Commission asks for views on such matters as the extent and nature of government consultation on proposed legislation (including delegated legislation and the implementation of EC directives); the form and drafting of bills and statutory instruments; parliamentary scrutiny of legislation; and the publication, and the accessibility to the public, of legislation passed by Parliament. With the exception of the last issue, the Scottish Consumer Council has direct experience of all of these matters and we shall deal with each of them in turn.

The Extent and Nature of Government Consultation on Proposed Legislation
The Scottish Consumer Council is consulted on a wide range of issues which are relevant to our work. In the last year, for instance, we responded to consultations on a wide range of subjects, from a number of different government departments, including the Scottish Office, the Department of Trade and Industry, the Ministry of Agriculture, Fisheries and Food, and the Department of Social Security. We have also responded to consultations from bodies closely linked to government – the Scottish Law Commission, the Scottish Health Service Advisory Committee, the Scottish Courts Administration and the Sheriff Court Rules Council.

The subject matter covered included structural warranties for new homes; the law of the tenement; tying-in of services to residential property loans; access to personal files; civil legal aid in Scotland; the development of community care; the council tax; court procedures like small claims; the management of ophthalmological services in Scotland; public registers of contaminated land; structure of local government in Scotland; pilot quality of wine scheme for the UK; abolition of the feudal system; performance in housing management; school reports; advice and information for tenants; and the provision of motorway service areas.

For an organisation with such a wide remit like the Scottish Consumer Council the amount of work in responding to consultation documents should not be underestimated. We are, however, delighted that we are now consulted so often and on such a wide range of subjects, but we have a growing concern that the periods allowed for preparation of responses to consultations are getting shorter. The Scottish Consumer Council has a committee structure which usually requires that draft responses are directed through a relevant committee, and if the response involves an issue on which we have no existing policy, it should not be submitted without the approval of our Council given at one of our monthly Council meetings. It is important that we retain a sound system of policy development.

Particularly with consultations on the content of delegated legislation, or on the implementation of EC directives through UK regulations, we regularly find difficulty in following this procedure. Recent examples of this are the consultation from the Department of Trade and Industry (DTI) on Articles 1 to 6 of the EC Directive on Package Travel, which was issued on 7 February with a deadline of 2 March; a similar consultation on Article 7 of the above Directive was received on 6 March with a 10 April deadline; another consultation from the DTI on regulation for tying-in residential property loans was received on 9 March, with a deadline of 24 April; a consultation from the Scottish Office Social Work Services Group on a Social Work Services Inspectorate for Scotland was dated 8 November, asking for comments by the end of December, but *preferably* the end of November; and a consultation from the Scottish Office Education Department on information for parents about school performance had a consultation period from 5 March to 30 April. It is imperative that if government wishes to consult others about its legislative proposals then it must allow a reasonable time for consultees to prepare their views. With our structure, the Scottish Consumer Council finds it very difficult to respond to anything if the deadline is less than three months unless we already have a very clear and detailed policy in the subject area concerned. The National Consumer Council has just produced *Involving the Community: Guidelines for Health Service Managers* (NCC, Spring 1992), which advises:

> *"Timetables and programmes for consultation must take into account the way CHC's [Community Health Councils] and voluntary groups work. Voluntary organisations are managed by a voluntary committee to whom staff, if any, are accountable. The committee in turn may be elected by a membership. Before giving views on proposals, staff consult the management committee who may in turn consult members....This means that consultation is often a slow process; the quality of comments makes it worthwhile."*

These constraints often affect those whom government consults about legislative proposals, and the advice about ensuring that timetable is equally relevant to government as it is to health service managers.

Some government departments include a list of consultees along with the letter or consultation paper. This is very useful because it allows consultees to advise the department of any organisations who may have an interest whose names do not appear on the list. We believe that all consultations should include a note of those invited to respond.

Another concern we have is when legislation appears without any consultation. This does not happen too often but when it does it can have far-reaching effects. The Bankruptcy (Scotland) Bill was published and had its First Reading on 8 May 1992, and will receive its Second Reading on 4 June, 1992. Committee stage should be completed by the end of June 1992. The Bill's primary purpose is to improve the efficient and effective administration of bankruptcy cases in Scotland, and we support this. However, prior to publication there was no consultation on the provisions contained in the Bill. It is likely that the resulting changes in bankruptcy law will have significant implications for consumers in debt, yet the Scottish Consumer Council has not had the opportunity to develop a considered policy on the issue. The Bill contains many complex issues on which we need to seek expert opinion. We will be unable to do this before Committee Stage. We are very concerned that this lack of consultation has meant that we are not able to represent the consumer view effectively in this area. In our view, detailed consultation should always precede the introduction of a significant piece of legislation.

We would also be quite happy to be asked to comment on draft Bills before they were formally published and entered their legislative stages. This is already possible when Scottish Law Commission reports have draft Bills appended to them. In many other cases, technical errors could be ironed out before the parliamentary stages of a Bill began, thereby allowing much more time for debate on questions of policy and principle.

The form and drafting of bills and statutory instruments

Our main concern about the form and drafting of bills is that there seems to be an increasing tendency for parliamentary draftsmen to create order-making powers in primary legislation instead of setting out the detailed provisions in the legislation. While there is certainly an argument that this is more efficient because statutory instruments are more readily amended or replaced and that it would be impossible to find parliamentary time to debate all the detailed issues necessary, we are concerned that this tendency should not become excessive. In some cases this could be regarded as an abuse of the parliamentary process because it does not allow adequate debate to take place in parliament on the regulations, or a line-by-line scrutiny of their provisions.

The Abolition of Domestic Rates Etc. (Scotland) Act, 1987 (the legislation which replaced the rates with the community charge or poll tax in Scotland) was one with which the Scottish Consumer Council had a great deal of involvement. It was a matter of great concern that the Act itself contained a large number of regulation-making powers, and over thirty separate sets of regulations were produced. The Scottish Consumer Council was particularly interested in the content of the Community Charges Registration Regulations because the procedures laid down in them for appeals against registration are very different and inferior to the system in England and Wales, and we thought that the language used in the prescribed forms to be used by the public was largely incomprehensible. Although we succeeded in having our views put forward forcibly by Donald Dewar MP and others in debate, it was impossible to have the regulations amended and they went through in their flawed state.

Another, completely separate concern is about information and training about new law, particularly when this is based in regulations rather than statute. Often a very short time elapses between the making of regulations and them coming into force. Those involved in giving advice to the public, including solicitors and advice workers, often have great difficulty in obtaining access to the information about new regulations in time to provide appropriate training to advisers.

Parliamentary scrutiny of legislation

Over the years, the Scottish Consumer Council has built up considerable experience in parliamentary lobbying. In recent years we have lobbied on the Education (No.2) Act, 1986, the Abolition of Domestic Rates Etc. (Scotland) Act, 1987, the Debtors (Scotland) Act, 1987, the Housing Act, 1988, the Law Reform (Miscellaneous Provisions) (Scotland) Act, 1990, and the Education (Schools) Act, 1992.

It has been a continuing source of frustration for us that often quite important changes in Scots law are appended to Bills which predominantly affect consumers in England and Wales. This was the case with the Education (Schools) Act 1992 which essentially deals with school inspections in England and Wales, yet has a section on the issuing of regulations on information for parents about school performance which affects Scotland. Parliamentary time was dominated by debate about the non-Scottish provisions, and since most of the MPs and members of the House of Lords involved with the Bill were English, we therefore found ourselves lobbying people with limited knowledge of the Scottish education system. Similar examples from earlier years include the Education (No. 2) Act, 1986, which was a piece of legislation for England and Wales, with a parallel clause for Scotland outlawing the use of corporal punishment; and the Housing Act, 1988, which clarified the rights of tenants in Scotland to be consulted about local authority voluntary transfers of their housing stock.

One of the most important issues which arises in relation to Scots law reform is the need to find parliamentary time to legislate on issues about which the Scottish Law Commission has produced reports in recent years. The Scottish Law Commission's 26th Annual Report, published in December 1991, lists thirteen reports which so far have not been implemented by legislation. The subject matter covered in many of the reports is not contentious, yet it has not been possible to find parliamentary time for them.

Many of the reports concern areas on which the Scottish Consumer Council has policy, and we are particularly concerned that the Report on the Sale and Supply of Goods (Scot Law Com No 104) (Cm 137) which was produced jointly with the Law Commission for England and Wales, has not yet been implemented. The report recommends important improvements in sale of goods legislation for the UK, but also recommends the extension of part of the 1982 Supply of Goods and Services Act to Scotland. This is a minor issue, but one which the Scottish Consumer Council has been urging since the Act was passed. Reports which have not yet been implemented are listed in the Annex to this paper.[1]

The Scottish Consumer Council is concerned about delays in law reform in Scotland because we consider it important that our laws are adapted to changes in our society. Life is now much more complicated for consumers and it is important that our laws protect them in their relationships with the providers of goods and services. We strongly support the comments of the Scottish Law Commission expressed in the latest Annual Report:

"In presenting this report to your Lordship we respectfully suggest that those responsible for the management of Parliamentary business would better serve the public interest were they to secure earlier consideration of draft Bills emanating from the Law Commissions as the bodies with the statutory responsibility to make recommendations for law reform."

The final concern we shall mention in this short paper is the tendency for a whole miscellany of issues to be gathered together in a Law Reform (Miscellaneous Provisions) (Scotland) Bill. The most recent Law Reform Act, the 1990 Act, contains provisions dealing with areas of law as diverse and distinct as charities, conveyancing by non-solicitors, solicitors' rights of audience, licensing law, evidence by children in criminal trials, drug trafficking, arbitration, and unfair

---

Not published.

contract terms. This type of legislation does have its benefits, because it allows campaigning organisations to lobby for the insertion of their pet reform. Indeed, the 1990 Act contains two reforms inserted by the Scottish Consumer Council – an amendment to the Unfair Contract Terms Act, and a provision to appoint two lay members to the Sheriff Court Rules Council. On the other hand, a Bill containing a wide range of reforms often does not allow enough parliamentary time for proper debate on all the issues, and the 1990 Act is a very good example of how law should not be made.

Conclusion

This paper does not attempt to suggest how the present problems with the processing of Scottish legislation might be solved. We have simply highlighted some of the difficulties we encounter in practice, and we believe that the present situation is serious enough to merit a separate Commission on the legislative process as it affects Scotland. We believe that problems of geographical remoteness from the legislature, and the lack of priority for Scots law reform make the issues we have raised even more crucial for Scotland than they are for England and Wales.

June 1992

M50 The Scottish Law Commission: Letter from Lord Davidson, Chairman

I note with some regret that your Commission's inquiry is restricted to the process by which legislation is made in England and Wales. In spite of the apparent exclusion of Scotland from the inquiry, I hope that time and resources will be sufficient to enable your Commission to give some attention to the position of the Scottish Law Commission.

Sir Peter [Gibson, Chairman of the Law Commission] was kind enough to let me have a copy of a note which was submitted to your Commission in advance of a meeting held with some of its members on 18 February[1]. This Commission shares the concern expressed by the English Commission about the difficulties which for some time now have been experienced in obtaining Parliamentary time for consideration of Law Commission recommendations. I endorse the main thrust of what is stated by Sir Peter in paragraph 5 of his note, and, for a summary of the current Scottish position, I refer to paragraphs 1.19 and 1.20 of this Commission's Twenty-Sixth Annual Report, a copy of which I enclose.[2]

I refer to the recently published Report of the Select Committee on the Committee Work of the House of Lords. The written evidence submitted to the Select Committee by this Commission is reproduced at page 253 of Volume 2 of the Report. In principle we welcome the proposals relating to a special standing committee which are set out in paragraph 132 of Volume 1 of the Report. We also

---

1   M35
2   Not published

hope that, if and when these proposals are developed further, it will be possible to take into account the important points of detail mentioned in our written evidence.

Although delays in implementation have been formally discussed within this Commission over recent months, our lack of firsthand experience of the workings of Parliament makes us diffident about suggesting solutions. The list of Commissioners attached to your letter encourages us to believe that, with the wealth of practical experience in the ways of Parliament that is available to it, your Commission will be able to formulate realistic proposals for the solution of this long-standing and hitherto intractable, problem.

27 February 1992

M51   Shelter

Shelter welcomes this Commission. Parliament has in recent years had to deal with a substantial increase in draft legislation, and we have seen a shift of emphasis from primary to secondary legislation. For most people the language of legislation is incomprehensible, and the sheer volume of legislation taxes the capacity even of experts to keep pace with it.

These trends have placed an increased burden on bodies concerned with social policy issues.

The Commission invites comments in particular under four headings concerning recent legislation. In our response we have kept to these where possible.

1. The extent and nature of Government consultation on proposed legislation (including statutory instruments and EC directives).

a) White Papers
The Queen's Speech of 25 June 1987 contained the words "Measures will be brought before you to effect major reform of housing legislation in England and Wales". Although the contents of that measure were likely to affect the budgets and living conditions of millions of households our understanding was that there was to be no formal statement of the proposals in the usual form of a Government White Paper before the legislation was drafted. This led to Shelter preparing its own document – "Not a White Paper" – which we published in September 1987. This document brought together known details of Government policy on housing in order to provide a framework for immediate discussion. Following this initiative the Department of the Environment on 29 September 1987 published a White Paper (Cm 214), followed by a series of consultation documents on specific legislative proposals. However, the consultation periods were very short, generally a month. There is a general problem caused by very short consultation periods. At a time when a great deal of legislation is being enacted this puts considerable pressure on the process of adequate consideration of policy proposals.

b) Publishing the results of consultation.
It would be good practice for Government to have to automatically publish the number of responses received in a consultation, the names of the respondents, and

where possible the proportions of respondents in favour or opposed to the Government's proposals.

2. The form and drafting of Bills and Instruments.

a) The language of legislation.
The language of Bills and Orders is still inaccessible. While we appreciate the difficulties involved in achieving plain English in legislation it must be a desirable aim, for much of current legislation is very difficult to decipher.

b) The shift to secondary legislation.
Government by Order has been an increasing and most unwelcome phenomenon throughout the 1980s and 1990s. It is common now for major Bills to be made up largely of powers granted to Secretaries of State to make delegated legislation, which Parliament does not have the power to amend. There is no effective opportunity for Parliament to oppose Statutory Instruments, for even if the Order is subject to the Affirmative procedure, and a Commons vote is required, a Government majority will make the outcome a foregone conclusion. Further, in the case of the Affirmative procedure, despite the convention which calls for a vote in both Houses, if the Commons votes for an Order the Lords cannot then hold a vote on it. We feel this situation should be rectified.

Interest groups outside Parliament find it much more difficult to mount effective campaigns against Bills which contain substantial delegated powers, and equally difficult to campaign effectively against draft Orders, which are often dealt with at a late hour or otherwise when few Parliamentarians are present.

c) Negative and Affirmative procedures re: Orders.
Sub-clauses in Bills enabling Ministers to make Orders frequently involve the Negative rather than the Affirmative procedure. This often appears to be an opening strategy on the part of Governments willing during passage of a Bill to accept amendments applying the Affirmative procedure. In that way it is a useful tool for them to indicate a willingness to be flexible. However, in view of the steady shift towards secondary legislation we feel that there should be a presumption for the Affirmative procedure unless it really is unnecessary.

3. Parliamentary scrutiny of legislation.

a) Standing, Select and Scrutiny Committees.
Clear information on how committees work, and public rights concerning them, would be welcome.

b) Select Committees
Select Committees were a very good innovation, but they should be used to examine regularly major legislation which has been passed.

We find it unsatisfactory that the Environment Select Committee has to deal with such a wide range of issues that it cannot give adequate time to housing issues, as the record shows.

Housing is of central importance in our society, and as such we urge the Commission to recommend that there should be a separate Housing Select Committee.

c) Passage of a Bill

The Standing Committee stage of a Bill is very important. It is the main opportunity for a "line by line" examination of a Government Bill. We are concerned that there is a tendency for the Government side to be Whipped into silence, and for Ministers to be content with speaking from briefs rather than answering critical points made, or providing information requested. This has the effect of devaluing this important stage of the scrutiny of a Bill, by lowering the quality of debate. Guidelines to Chairs of Committee would be welcome to ensure that issues raised are covered adequately.

4. The accessibility to the public of legislation passed by Parliament.

a) Redundant wording of Bills

We have already referred to the inaccessible language of Bills. There is a further point concerning accessibility. Published Acts of Parliament are not updated after amendment by subsequent legislation. They remain on sale at HMSO until repealed in their entirety. They should be updated at each susbtantial amendment, and an addendum published to deal with minor amendments.

b) Notes on Clauses.

It would be a welcome reform if Notes on Clauses were attached to Bills, or made available to the public separately. We propose that they should also be provided on the final wording of an Act, at the end of a Bill's passage, and then updated after cach amendment by subsequent legislation. Notes on Clauses should also give information on which other Acts affect and are affected by this Act, and in which way. In addition a list should be made in Notes on Clauses of any related Statutory Instruments.

14 January 1992

M52   Rt Hon Lord Simon of Glaisdale, PC

There was one matter which I omitted to mention [when giving oral evidence]. This is the situation which arises when a Minister is asked whether a provision in a Bill means so and so or covers such and such a situation. Unless the answer is too obvious to need inscription, it is desirable that the answer should be made the subject of specific amendment.

The point arose strikingly on one of the Race Relations Acts (I think 1968). Lord Strabolgi asked Lord Chancellor Gardiner, who was in charge of the Bill, whether it extended to working mens' clubs. He said something to this effect: "It is well known that a number of working men's clubs practice racial discrimination. Will the Act apply to them?" The Lord Chancellor answered "No". (I think a similar interpolation took place in the House of Commons.) But the Act was left unamended for obvious political reasons: one way the Race Relations lobby would be antagonised, the other way the working men's clubs' movement. So the Courts were left to do their best to determine whether a particular working men's club which had practised discrimination was in its context "a section of the public." The Court of Appeal decided it was; the House of Lords that it was not thereby giving an interpretation which coincided with the Lord Chancellor's assurance. But an enormous amount of public and private money was expended because the matter was not made explicit in the Statutes.

4 December 1991

M53   Society of County Secretaries

The Society of County Secretaries welcome the opportunity of commenting on the legislative process, insofar as it affects local authorities. There is a degree of concern about the nature of legislation, which we discuss more fully in Para.5. But in other respects we are not commenting on the content of legislation, but rather the procedure, which is, in our view, open to criticism in a number of important respects. These illustrations suggest that Parliament is not able to exercise the necessary detailed scrutiny over legislation made in its name.

1. Implementation, and the staged introduction of Legislation
It is often difficult to ascertain what particular legislation has been brought into effect at any one time. For example, the Local Government and Housing Act 1989 has to-date been the subject of 12 different Commencement Orders, and 13 different Commencement Dates. It is still not completely in force and the original timetable for implementation has fallen far behind, in some cases, because of difficulties encountered in drafting subordinate legislation.

2. Legislation by Statutory Instrument
Much important legislation is contained in statutory instruments, rather than primary legislation. The important General Development Orders and Use Classes Orders under the Town and Country Planning Acts are an example.

The Local Government and Housing Act 1989 is another important illustration. Among statutory instruments made under that Act are the following:

Local Authorities (Capital Finance) Regulations 1990 (No.432)
Local Authorities (Capital Finance) (Approved Investments)
  Regulations 1990 (No.426)
Local Government (Promotion of Economic Development)
  Regulations 1990 (No.763)
Local Authorities (Borrowing) Regulations 1990 (No.767)
Local Government (Promotion of Economic Development)
  (Amendment) Regulations 1990
Local Government Officers (Political Restrictions) Regulations 1990 (No.851)
Local Elections (Principal Areas) (Declaration of Acceptance of Office)
  Order 1990 (No.932)
Local Government (Politically Restricted Posts) (No.2)
  Regulations 1990 (No.1447)
Local Government (Committees and Political Groups)
  Regulations 1990 (No.1553)

Local Government (Assistants for Political Groups)
Remuneration Order 1990 (No.1636)
Local Authorities (Members' Allowances) Regulations 1991 (No.351)
Draft Regulations under Part V (Companies in which Local Authorities have Interests) have been circulated for consultation, but they have yet to be published in their final form.

Draft Regulations have also been published under ss.8 and 20 (Duty to Adopt Standing Orders).

The National Code of Local Government Conduct was approved by both Houses of Parliament (see Circular 8/90).

The details of this legislation, which is of great importance to local authorities, cannot be the subject of proper Parliamentary scrutiny, as the opportunity exists only to approve or reject, and not to amend.

3. Delayed Implementation

Certain provisions of the Children and Young Persons Act 1969 were never brought into effect, e.g. Section 4, which changed the age of criminal responsibility. Certain provisions in the Children Act 1975 were only implemented after a delay of 10 years. These constitute examples of the executive (or a new Government) acting in contravention of the will of Parliament.

An interesting example is the failure so far to bring into force Para.25 of Schedule 11 of the Local Government and Housing Act 1989, the Department of the Environment now being doubtful whether the provision achieves what was originally intended.

4. The Parliamentary Procedure

Some Bills are clearly introduced in far from final form. An early edition of the Children Bill, for example, contained 79 Clauses and 11 Schedules in 121 pages. As finally enacted, it was 108 Clauses, 15 Schedules in 218 Pages. The increase was primarily the result of Government amendments. Important parts of the legislation (Inspection of Independent Boarding Schools, and Child-minding) were after-thoughts. This is an increasing practice and makes virtually impossible the usual processes of consultation with the interested parties. It is worth adding that a number of drafting errors were corrected in the Courts and Legal Services Act 1990, Schedule 16, which contains 42 paragraphs amending the Children Act and other child-related legislation. Moreover, this was a measure which had all-party support!

5. Control of Local Authorities

It is a matter of some concern how far local authorities are finding themselves in the Courts. It must be questionable whether detailed statutory controls are the correct way to control local authorities (see, for example, Martin Loughlin in Public Law, 1990, Page 372 and 1991, Page 568) with the Audit Commission taking an increasingly high profile, or whether there should be, as Anthony Scrivener, Q.C. has argued, a general power of competence subject to not acting in contravention of any specific prohibition, or where the powers are allocated to another public body.

6. The Law Commission

Too many reports of the Law Commission have not been acted upon. There should be some simplified procedure when legislation is proposed in accordance with the recommendations of the Commission, just as there is for consolidating bills.

February 1992

M54 Study of Parliament Group: Memorandum Submitted by Professors David Myers and Alan Page

1. Two broad purposes may be attributed to the legislative process. The first is the erection of a series of obstacles to the exercise of what would otherwise be arbitrary power. Thus it is not enough that a majority be obtained for a legislative proposal on a single occasion: it must be obtained repeatedly if the proposal is to be invested with the force of law.

2. The second purpose that may be attributed to the process is the production of clear statements of the law in general and the rights and obligations of individual citizens in particular. It is for this reason that each of the stages of the legislative process has its own purpose and permitted range of debate. Thus the second reading provides an opportunity for the principle of the legislation to be approved or rejected, the committee stage an opportunity for line by line consideration of the individual clauses that make up the Bill, and so on.

3. But the legislative process is first and foremost a political process. In the absence of any enforceable canons of good law making there is no certainty that the provision of clear statements of the law will take precedence over the government's desire to get its proposals through or, in the extreme case, its opponents' desire to prevent the enactment of these proposals.

4. Complaints about the legislative process are not new. The last twenty five years have witnessed a steady increase in criticism of the quality of legislation emanating from that process. At times the legislative process has appeared to be in danger of being reduced to a caricature of itself with detailed thought sometimes being given to what a measure should contain only when a place has been secured for it in the legislative programme (rather than before a place in the programme is sought). The parliamentary stages of the legislative process are thus reduced to an opportunity for the government to work out the details of its proposals rather than for those proposals to be subjected to sustained scrutiny.

5. The history of the reform of legislation procedure provides little cause for optimism that this situation can be easily reversed. The driving force behind the reform of legislative procedure since the last century has been the need for government to secure the enactment of its legislative programme. Improving the scrutiny of individual measures, by contrast, has played only a limited part. Where it has been influential in reform, as in the introduction of the special standing committee procedure in the House of Commons, the results have been

regarded as disappointing from the standpoint of government because they have not yielded any saving in time.

6. Time is of crucial importance because historically the government's capacity to secure the enactment of its legislative programme has been closely linked to its control of the parliamentary timetable. It has therefore consistently opposed any proposals for reform which have threatened, no matter how slightly, its control of the timetable and with it its legislative capacity. In this stance it has been invariably supported by the official opposition, which benefits from the existing system because the parliamentary timetable is worked out in consultation with it. Both front benches have therefore opposed, for example, proposals for the automatic timetabling of the committee stage of Bills.

7. We are not of the view that there is some procedural innovation, as yet undiscovered, that would transform the situation just described, at least so long as the government's appetite for legislation shows no signs of diminishing. Nevertheless, a number of proposals for improved scrutiny of legislative proposals have been put forward in recent years which merit further examination. These include the extended use of special standing committee procedure, the insertion of fixed intervals between the various stages of the legislative process, the abolition of the rule against the carry over of legislation from one session to the next, and the automatic timetabling of the committee stage of Bills.

8. It is difficult to gainsay the proposition that the committee to which a Bill is referred should be sufficiently expert in its subject matter to test the premises on which it is based. The merit of special standing committee procedure is that it allows the members of a committee, if they so choose, to do this. Yet the extension of the procedure is opposed, presumably because at the very least it would involve delay if not the possibility of challenge to the effective monopoly the government currently enjoys in legislative policy making.

9. The suggestion has from time to time been made that fixed intervals should be introduced between the stages of the legislative process to allow affected interests as well as members the opportunity to digest and reflect on a proposal. The disadvantage of such a reform from the standpoint of the government is that it would diminish the flexibility it currently enjoys in the timetabling of legislation, though flexibility could be written into the standing orders governing the intervals.

10. A related reform that is sometimes proposed is that the first drafts of Bills should be published, say, one month before their second reading. Given the pressure under which measures are sometimes prepared it may be doubted whether this is practical politics.

11. The rule against the carry-over of legislative proposals from one session to the next provides one of the constants in the legislative process. As such it may be thought to provide a welcome source of discipline and its abolition to raise the prospect of legislation on a given topic as an almost unending process. At the same time, however, it has obvious disadvantages. Genuinely uncontroversial legislation may be lost and the opportunities for the consideration of measures

may be squeezed by the approach of the end of the parliamentary session. One way in which the disadvantages of the abolition of the rule could be minimised would be by providing that a measure not enacted within, say, one year of its introduction would automatically fail.

12. The most commonly made proposal for the reform of the legislative process is for the introduction of some form of automatic timetabling. The disadvantage of such a procedure, it may be thought, is that it would increase the government's autonomy and the predictability of the legislative process still further. Its advantage is that it would remove one of the most glaring inadequacies of the legislative process whereby the initial clauses of measures are discussed at length and the remaining clauses receive a more perfunctory examination or sometimes none at all. Creating the opportunities for scrutiny would not by itself ensure that measures are subject to any more effective scrutiny than at present.

13. Procedural reform by itself can achieve relatively little. The solution to the dissatisfaction currently being expressed lies with the government and also, it should be said, with the opposition who seldom display any real commitment to the effective scrutiny of legislation. For a government committed to citizens' charters, performance standards and quality control, it may be thought odd that it should not be equally prepared to take steps to improve the quality of legislation and its scrutiny.

June 1992

M55   Trades Union Congress

Introduction

1. As a major national institution which seeks to influence policy makers and which is often at the centre of political debate, the TUC has direct experience of all stages of the legislative process. We respond to Government proposals when they appear as Green/White Papers, we lobby Government, Opposition and Members of Parliament during the passage of a Bill and we seek to provide advice and assistance to TUC affiliates once legislation is brought into force. Although the TUC is broadly satisfied with the operation of the legislative process there are several specific points which we would wish to draw to the Commission's attention.

Consultation on Proposed Legislation

2. If a Government proposes to legislate in a particular area, then that should be because some need for changes has been identified. It would also appear sensible to seek to ensure that the contents of the legislation do respond to a genuine deficiency in the law and will produce the effects which the Government desires. This would suggest that before even a Green Paper appears the Government should have conducted extensive research to determine the shape of the problem in question and carried out some initial consultation with interested parties before reaching a preliminary view on the measures required.

Publication of a Green Paper could then be used to generate a more informed debate and enable the Minister concerned to refine the proposals. The whole process should be seen as "testing the water", with the Green Paper constituting an initial diagnosis to which interested organisations can respond. Extensive consultation is essential if informed policy making is to take place. Sufficient time should therefore be available to ensure that those with an interest can take a considered view of the Government's intention and produce a measured response.

3. Such an approach will ensure that the problem identified by the Government is a genuine one based upon substantial evidence, that the measures proposed actually address the problem and that there is a reasonable level of support for the measures outside Parliament. At this stage it is appropriate to publish a White Paper setting out the development of the Government's thinking, its response to the consultation process and final proposals on which the legislation will be based.

4. Clearly, it would not be necessary to have the most extensive pre-legislative consultation in all cases. The procedure adopted will depend no doubt on the complexity of the issues involved, the nature of the Government's plans and the responses received. In any event, it must be in the public interest to avoid hasty and ill-considered legislation which can only undermine respect for the law and the processes of democracy itself.

5. Unfortunately, recent experience demonstrates that the Government is some way from meeting the standards set out above. A good example is the Green Paper *Unofficial Action and the Law* which was published in 1989 and was later enshrined as a major part of the Employment Act 1990. The central thrust of the Green Paper was that the British economy was being undermined by "wildcat" action and that the best solution was to extend trade union liability in tort to civil wrongs resulting from such action. Leaving aside the merits or demerits of this analysis, it is clear from the Green Paper's eight pages of text that there is a great deal of assertion and very little evidence given to support the argument. Anecdotal examples are advanced which supposedly demonstrate that a "problem" exists, yet nothing is said about the *causes* of "unofficial" action, no indication is given that an examination has been undertaken of deficiencies in the British industrial relations system and no evidence provided that widening the scope of union liability is an appropriate remedy.

6. Intellectually, therefore, the arguments advanced in the Green Paper were unsupported by any substantial evidence. It might be thought that these weaknesses would become clear in the consultation process and that the Government would reconsider their proposals. Again, this was not to be the case. The Green Paper was published on October 11, 1989 and all responses had to be submitted to the Department of Employment by December 1. An Employment Bill drawing together the proposals in the Green Paper was published only a few weeks later, which surely demonstrates that the "consultation" process was a merely symbolic exercise.

Parliamentary Scrutiny of Legislation

7. In the TUC's view there are two major problems with the scrutiny of legislation by Parliament. The first concerns the use of the guillotine procedure to curtail the discussion of complex and controversial matters. No doubt any Government will wish to see legislation passed in line with its own timetable and will seek to prevent the use of filibustering as a tactic to hold up the process. There is however an impression that the guillotine is being used to avoid potential political embarrassment which might arise from detailed examination of the proposals. One recent example is the legislation creating the Council Tax which was rushed through by the Government to deal with the damaging consequences of the Community Charge. Although the TUC welcomes the demise of the Poll Tax, there is a danger that the undue haste with which it was replaced could lead to problems in the future.

8. Secondly, there is an increasing tendency for primary legislation to form the "bare bones" of a new legal framework which is fleshed out with delegated legislation. The current Local Government Bill is a good example which creates wide enabling powers for the Secretary of State for the Environment to extend compulsory competitive tendering and change the CCT rules by regulation. This may indicate that the Government have not thought clearly about the limits of CCT which is in itself a cause for concern, but it cannot be right for such significant changes in local government structures and procedures to be implemented by statutory instrument.

Volume and Complexity of Legislation

9. The langauge of parliamentary draughtsmanship is difficult enough for the layperson to understand and it would be sensible therefore for legislation regulating particular matters to be set out systematically in one easily accessible statute. In the field of labour law, for example, the International Labour Organisation Committee of Experts has criticised the legislation as unduly complex and voluminous. The relevant provisions are scattered across eight acts of parliament (although a consolidation is now taking place). There is a very strong argument for an overall simplification of the legislation in this area so that it can be readily understood by the majority of those people affected. The TUC would advocate that the law should not only be rendered more comprehensible, but should also conform with ILO Conventions which is of course a very different matter.

10. The TUC is also concerned about the pace of legislative change in several areas, particularly local government and labour law. This is symptomatic of a failure to adequately research a problem in advance and devise a comprehensive solution. Piecemeal or "step-by-step" approaches may have their political merits, but the consequences for people in the real world can be devastating. It is difficult to conceive of any organisation which could survive the pace of change recently enforced on local government without some dislocation or loss of efficiency. Similarly, there must be some question whether it was necessary

to legislate in various areas of industrial relations in 1988, 1989, 1990 and (potentially) 1992.

Conclusion

10. The TUC is concerned therefore that inadequate research is undertaken before legislation is proposed and that consultation is often a paper exercise. Guillotine procedures are being used to curtail the discussion of complex and controversial measures which could have damaging consequences in the future. There is also a disturbing reliance on enabling powers and delegated legislation which prevents full scrutiny of Government proposals. Finally, there is the point that in certain areas there is too much complex legislation which is not understood by those most directly affected and which can cause a high degree of administrative disruption through hasty implementation.

21 February 1992

M56   Trades Union Congress: Supplementary Memorandum from Mr David Coats, Assistant, Organisation and Industrial Relations Department

Implementation of EC Directives

In the course of giving oral evidence to the Commission I agreed that I would let you have a further note on the implementation of EC directives in the UK. Although Ms Tritton indicated that the Commission have a particular interest in public procurement I thought it would also be useful if I set out the TUC's position on those measures arising from the European Commission's Social Action Programme.

The Social Action Programme

At EC level there is extensive consultation before an instrument appears in draft form. Following the initial proposal to legislate, the Commission (DG V) will meet with the "social partners" (the European Trade Union Confederation, UNICE and the CEEP) and seek their preliminary views. Once the instrument in question is drafted a further discussion will take place so that the social partners can raise detailed points on the text. In general these arrangements work well, the Commission treats the views expressed with a degree of respect and will seek to ensure that they are incorporated in any further discussions at Commission level. Once the draft is referred to the Council of Ministers the ETUC loses any influence over the process and the discussions in the Council may bear little relationship to those which have taken place at an earlier stage.

Although the Government may formally seek the TUC's views on any proposed instrument which has been sent by the Commission to the Council there is no guarantee that these views will be reflected in the UK's final response. Nor is there any indication that, once the instrument has been approved by the Council, the Department of Employment will pay anything more than scant regard to the TUC's concerns relating to implementation in national legislation. At domestic level therefore, measures introduced under the Social Action Programme are not subject to adequate consultation.

Public Procurement

Public procurement is a rather more specialised area of policy for the TUC. First, it is important to note that the procurement directives are lengthy and technical. Many of the provisions do not directly relate to TUC policy and we have tended to concentrate on the social measures (eg contract compliance) and labour protection measures (eg wage protection, fair wages) contained in these instruments.

Again, the formal link between the TUC and the Commission (principally, DG III) is through the ETUC which is represented on the EC's Public Procurement Advisory Committee. The TUC also lobbies the Commission directly and we have good links with the European Parliament and Economic and Social Committee.

At domestic level the Treasury is the lead department on EC procurement matters. They have sent draft proposals to the TUC for comment in the past and respect our views in this area. Although the TUC would wish to play a greater part in the consultation process, our limited resources and the extent of our direct interest in the legislation means that this is not always possible.

The TUC has four representatives on the NEDC Working Party on EC Public Procurement. One of our representatives is the Chair of the NEDC Sub-Committee on public services procurement on which both Treasury and business representatives also serve.

In general therefore, compared with other policy areas public procurement is not a good example of poor consultation.

12 March 1992

M57   Mr David Trimble MP: Note on Northern Ireland Orders in Council

Outline of procedure

First, the Northern Ireland Office (NIO) may publish what is termed a "Proposal for a Draft Order."

This consists of a fully drafted Order which may be accompanied by a press release summarising the policy it embodies and a brief statement from the Legislative Draftman's Office of the effect of each clause. This proposal will be sent to certain interested bodies with a period, minimum usually six weeks, in which they may send in written observations on the Order.

This is described as "consultation" and the practice was adopted to counter criticism of Orders in Council, but is of course merely an opportunity to make representations. Meaningful consultation requires a genuine exchange of views based on prior information. The NIO does not generally provide any background briefings nor does it offer meetings with political parties, although it may receive delegations if they are sought.

Secondly the NIO will publish a "Draft Order."

This may be accompanied by a letter referring to some of the observations made during the first phase; such a letter will be general and not a specific response to particular objections a Party may have made.

Thirdly the Draft Order will be laid before both Houses of Parliament.

Orders are normally subject to affirmative resolution by each House of Parliament. Within the House of Commons there is a choice of procedure. The Order could be taken before the whole House it which case it normally comes on after ten o'clock and receives a minimum of 90 minutes debate. At least 30 and sometimes 40/45 minutes will be taken up with the Minister's speech, the leading opposition speech and winding up speeches. Consequently all the Northern Ireland members who wish to speak, must fit themselves into the limited period left. In our party we find that usually only one of our nine MPs can speak. Alternatively the Order can be referred to a standing Committee on Statutory Instruments. There two and a half hours are available for debate, but usually only one Northern Ireland member is appointed to the Committee so the full time is rarely used. Orders handled this way are not controversial in party political terms and I am not aware of any occasion when a Member not on the Committee has availed himself of his right to attend and speak.

In both cases the debate takes the form of a second reading in that it concentrates on generalities. There is no detailed debate on the clauses – Orders in Council sometimes run to 100 pages and no amendments can be tabled.

Fourthly the Order is then formally made at a Privy Council meeting and usually comes into effect 28 days later or on a prescribed day.

There are two ways in which the above procedure can be changed. In cases stated to be matters of urgency the Order can be made first and the resolutions passed later. This is very rare.

Much more frequent is the so-called Q procedure. A Great Britain Bill may include a clause that an Order to the same effect as all, or a specified part of the Bill, can be made subject to a negative resolution. In each year a significant proportion of Northern Ireland Orders are made this way. This means that there is no discussion of the NI Order at all. Sometimes the clause authorising the Q procedure is only added at the last moment – such a clause was added to the Planning and Compensation Act 1991 at the third reading. Northern Ireland members will have difficulty being called in a debate on such English or GB legislation and even if they were the English Ministers with carriage of the bill will be unable to respond to any query as to the practical application of the legislation to Northern Ireland.

Comments

The procedure is wrong in principle. There is a proper way to enact legislation. An inferior procedure debases that system. It says that Parliament has a cavalier attitude to the concept of law and is prepared to regard some citizens as not entitled to the full advantages of Parliamentary government.

The procedure is widely resented in Northern Ireland – see attached letter by the president of the Law Society for Northern Ireland, a former elected representative for the nationalist SDLP.[1]

The system puts delegated legislation beyond Parliamentary supervision. Orders in Council are primary legislation. They will contain powers to make delegated legislation subject to affirmative or negative resolutions of the "Northern Ireland Assembly." In the absence of such an Assembly, the Northern Ireland Act 1974 converts affirmative resolutions to negative resolutions at Westminster and removes negative resolution instruments from even that limited form of control. There is provision for a Northern Ireland Examiner of Statutory Instruments who should discharge the function exercised by the Joint and Select Committees on Statutory Instruments at Westminster. But the post became vacant some two years ago and has not been filled.

The system is inefficent. The bulk of Northern Ireland legislation today is parity legislation – exactly the same or very similar to GB legislation. But the Northern Ireland draftsman must wait until the Act has reached its final form (ie cleared third reading in the Lords) before he can begin the first stage in the procedure set out above. Delay therefore is built into the system. Perhaps as a result the system is becoming generally inefficient as well. The Planning and Compensation Act mentioned above increased home loss payments. It provides for a Q Order to same effect, but no such Order has yet been laid. So Northern Ireland taxpayers, who pay the same rates of tax as other citizens, will if their property is acquired compulsorily, receive on this matter lower levels of compensation. Examples could also be given of administrative confusion caused by the delays in the system.

Solutions

The obvious solution is that legislation for Northern Ireland be made in the normal way.

In passing it may be observed that if the United Kingdom had a written constitution which prescribed the method of enacting legislation the issue would simply never have arisen. It is also arguably a breach of the United Kingdom's obligations under international law to treat all its citizens equally. (See the writer's speech on the last renewal of the "direct rule" legislation.)

The Government argues that there is insuffcent time available for proper legislation. This arguement is bad. Most legislation today is parity. It would be easy to include a few clauses or a schedule modifying a GB Bill to apply it to Northern Ireland's different administrative structures and different legislative history. The Planning and Compensation Act 1991 is again a good example as it does precisely this with regard to the application of the Act in Scotland.

It is said that this would compromise the "integrity of the Northern Ireland Statute Book." Those who say that have no comprehension of Northern Ireland legislation. It consists of Acts of Parliament from five different Parliaments – those of England, Great Britain, the United Kingdom, Ireland and Northern Ireland – and

---

1 Not published

now European legislation as well. There is no volume or set of volumes that can be called the Northern Ireland Statute book. The annual volumes entitled "Northern Ireland Statutes" only contain Orders in Council, they do not include legislation applicable in Northern Ireland made through proper Act of Parliament (which includes all legislation which applies to the whole of the United Kingdom and occasional Acts applying to Northern Ireland only, such as the Northern Ireland (Emergency Provisions) Act and the Fair Employment Acts). Such a comprehensive statute book would be very welcome. "Statutes Revised" has done this for past legislation.

It is suspected that behind these inadequate excuses there lie political objections which Her Majesties' Government are reluctant to articulate.

There are other possible ameliorating measures.

Provision exists for a Northern Ireland Committee similar to the Scottish Grand Committee. This however has a majority of non Northern Ireland members, can only debate matters referred to it by the Government on a take note motion and appears to be subject to an agreent through the usual channels to four meetings a session.

The Committee was established in 1975. A fair degree of use was made of it until the creation of the "Prior" Assembly in Northern Ireland in 1982, when it was found that the select committees in that body, with their power to employ experts and send for persons and papers, provided a better forum for study of an Order in Council. Until 1985 it was the practice for Proposals for Draft Orders to be examined in such committees and debated in the Assembly. We revived the Northern Ireland Committee in the last session for discussion of the electricity privatisation legislation and a Fair Employment Order (which was amending the 1975 and 1989 Acts). The results, however, were not encouraging.

A Northern Ireland select committee could be created. This would not, however, directly affect the legislative process unless Douglas Hurd's interesting suggestion, made in a CPS speech at the last party conference, of referring bills to select committees for their committee stage is taken up.

A select committee would be very welcome on other grounds as it could begin to subject the NIO to proper scrutiny. The Second Report of the Procedure Committee on Select Committees in the last Parliament came very close to a firm recommendation on the matter, but Government, perhaps again for reasons it does not want to articulate, hesitates to act.

21 May 1992

Appendix 2 – Discussions Held with Bodies and Individuals

28 November, 1991
Rt Hon Lord Simon of Glaisdale, PC, and Rt Hon Lord Renton, PC, KBE, TD, QC

19 December, 1991
Rt Hon Tony Benn, MP

23 January, 1992
Dr John Cunningham, MP
Miss Betty Boothroyd, MP (then Chairman of Ways and Means, now Madam Speaker) and Mr Robert Rhodes-James, MP

30 January,1992
Mr Graham Allen, MP, Mr Andrew Bennett, MP, Mr Bob Cryer, MP (Chairman of the Joint Committee on Statutory Instruments), Sir Peter Emery, MP (Chairman of the Procedure Committee) and Sir John Wheeler, MP (Chairman of the Home Affairs Committee)

18 February, 1992
Hon Mr Justice Peter Gibson, Professor Brenda Hoggett, QC, and Mr Michael Collon, the Law Commission
Mr Peter Graham, CB, QC, First Parliamentary Counsel, and Sir James Nursaw, KCB, QC, Treasury Solicitor

25 February, 1992
Mr David Coates, Trades Union Congress
Mr Bill Nicolle, Mr David Elvidge, Mr Graham Mason, Mr Mervyn Woods and Ms Judith Vincent, Confederation of British Industry; and Mr Andrew Hutchinson and Miss Christine Prentice, Institute of Directors

19 March, 1992
Mr Alan Fraser and Mr Stephen Campbell, Society of County Secretaries; Mr Ian Wilson, National Trust; Mr M A Jones, Mr K E Loney, Mr A P O'Dowd and Miss B A Moss, Association of British Insurers and Lloyd's; and Mr M J Lowe, British Medical Association
Mr Gareth Roscoe, British Broadcasting Corporation; Mr Michael Redley, Independent Television Commission; Ms Vicky Chapman, Child Poverty Action Group; and Mr Les Burrows, Shelter

31 March, 1992
Hon Mr Justice Paul Kennedy (now Rt Hon Lord Justice Kennedy), Judges Council
Mrs Joyce Rose and Mr Toni Rudin, Magistrates' Association
Mr James Goudie, QC, General Council of the Bar; and Mr John Appleby, Mr Christopher Heaps, Miss Jane Hern and Ms Judy Foy, Law Society

19 May, 1992
Mr Alan Beith, MP
Mrs Margaret Ewing, MP, and Mr Dafydd Wigley, MP
Mr David Trimble, MP
Mr R M Le Marechal, National Audit Office

9 June, 1992
Rt Hon Lord Aberdare, PC, KBE
Lord Tordoff and Lord Williams of Elvel, CBE
Mr Michael Wheeler-Booth, Clerk of the Parliaments, and Mr Michael Davies, Clerk Assistant and Principal Clerk, Public Bills, House of Lords

17 June, 1992
Mr Richard White, Head of Legal Affairs Group, Lord Chancellor's Department, and Mr John Gibson, Head of Statutory Publications Office

18 June, 1992
Mr John Burrow, OBE, Chief Constable of Essex, Association of Chief Police Officers; and Mr Ken Wild and Mr John Jeffrey-Cook, Institute of Chartered Accountants in England and Wales
Mr Leonard Harris, Director of Inland Taxes, and Mr Geoffrey Butt, Principal Assistant Solicitor, H M Customs and Excise; and Mr Michael Johns, Director, Central Division, and Mr Richard Thornhill, Solicitor's Office, Board of Inland Revenue

2 July, 1992
Rt Hon Lord Howe of Aberavon, PC, QC – Sir Clifford Boulton, KCB, Clerk of the House of Commons
Professor David Miers and Professor Alan C Page, Study of Parliament Group; and Professor Philip Norton

28 October, 1992
Rt Hon Tony Newton, OBE, MP, Lord President of the Council and Leader of the House of Commons, and Rt Hon Lord Wakeham, PC, Lord Privy Seal and Leader of the House of Lords

APPENDIX 3 – Information from other Countries

Introduction

1. The Officers of certain other parliaments, with similar systems to that of the United Kingdom, were invited to provide information on the legislative processes in their countries and on how legislation is dealt with in their parliaments. We are extremely grateful for the helpful replies we received – some of which had involved a considerable amount of study to include up-to-date facts and statistics – from the parliaments of Australia (House of Representatives and Senate), Canada (House of Commons and Senate), Denmark, France (Senate), Germany (Bundestag and Bundersrat), Israel and New Zealand.

2. We also obtained information regarding legislative drafting in Australia (including the State of Victoria), Canada and New Zealand.

3. The Secretary to the Commission attended a Conference of the Statute Law Society, held at Fontevraud, France, from 27-29 September, 1991, on The Preparation and Accessibility of the Written Law in France. A report on some of the matters discussed at this Conference was circulated to the Commission.

4. All the documents containing the information referred to above have been deposited with the Hansard Society, St Philips Building, Sheffield Street, London WC2A 2EX (Tel. 071 995 7478), where they may be inspected by appointment. Unless otherwise stated, all the documents are in English.

5. One other document containing valuable information about the scrutiny of delegated legislation in Commonwealth parliaments is contained in the Report of the Third Commonwealth Conference on Delegated Legislation, held by the Commonwealth Parliamentary Association at Westminster in 1989 (London, HMSO).

6. The information we received is too voluminous to summarise, but we set out below a guide to the contents of these documents with special reference to the information which was most relevant to the conclusions we have reached in our Report.

Legislative Processes and Proceedings in Parliaments

A. AUSTRALIA

(i) The Australian Constitution.

(ii) Memorandum from the Department of the Clerk on Legislation in the House of Representatives. This covers:

- The procedures under which bills are debated, in the House and in committees and passed

- The extent to which interested bodies are consulted or otherwise involved in the legislative process;
- Time spent on legislation and the intervals between the various stages (with statistics);
- The extent to which bills are amended as a result of parliamentary scrutiny (with statistics); and
- The procedures for scrutinising delegated legislation.

(iii) Memorandum from the Clerk of the Senate on The Legislative Process in the Australian Senate. This covers:
- Procedures under which bills are considered;
- Consultation with interested outside bodies;
- Time spent on legislation and intervals between stages (with statistics);
- Extent to which bills are amended as a result of parliamentary scrutiny (with statistics); and
- Procedures for scrutinising delegated legislation.

(iv) Information about the Scrutiny of Bills Committee, with relevant documents and recent examples of reports:
- Legislative Scrutiny Manual, 1989
- Scrutiny of Bills Alert Digest, No. 1 of 1992
- Scrutiny of Bills Alert Digest, No. 3 of 1992
- Senate Standing Committee for the Scrutiny of Bills, Second Report for 1992
- Ten Years of Scrutiny: A seminar to mark the tenth anniversary of the Senate Standing Committee for the Scrutiny of Bills.

(v) Other documents relating to the Senate:
- Standing Orders
- Business of the Senate, 1989
- Business of the Senate, 1991
- References of Bills to Committees: Orders of the Senate of 5 December 1989
- Report of the Senate Select Committee on Legislation Procedures, 1988
- Senate Standing Committee on Regulations and Ordinances, Eighty-Eighth Report, May 1991
- Senate Standing Committee on Regulations and Ordinances, Ninetieth Report, Annual Report 1990-91.

(vi) A collection of Articles by The Clerk of the Senate and others on Referral of bills to Committees in the Senate.

B. CANADA

(i) The Federal Legislative Process in Canada.

(ii) Department of Justice Legal Awareness Program: The Federal Legislative Process in Canada (Instructors Manual).

(iii) Questionnaire on the Legislative Process in the House of Commons of Canada, prepared by the Department of the Clerk. This covers:
- Procedures for the debate and adoption of legislation;

- Consultation and involvement of outside bodies;
- Time spent on legislation and intervals between stages;
- Amendment of bills as a result of parliamentary scrutiny; and
- Procedures for scrutiny of delegated legislation.

(iv) Letter from the Clerk of the Senate. This covers:
- Procedures under which bills are debated and passed;
- Involvement of outside bodies in process;
- Time spent on legislation and intervals betweEn various stages;
- Time spent on study of bills in committee;
- Extent to which bills are amended as a result of parliamentary scrutiny; and
- Procedures for scrutinising delegated legislation.

(v) Background Notes on Parliamentary Scrutiny of Regulations and the Federal Regulatory Process.

(vi) Rules of the Senate of Canada.

C. DENMARK

(i) Note by the Legal Department of the Folketing on the Legislation Procedure of the Folketing.

(ii) Fact Sheet on the Constitutional Act.

(iii) Standing Orders of the Danish Parliament.

D. FRANCE

(i) Papers prepared by the Secretariat of the Secretary General of the Senate on:
- Procedures for debates and votes on legislative texts in committee and in public sittings;
- The involvement of bodies outside parliament in the legislative process;
- Time spent on legislative and other business (with detailed statistics);
- The importance and extent of amendments (with detailed statistics); and
- Procedures for the control and scrutiny of delegated legislation.

(These papers are in French).

(ii) The Preparation and Accessibility of the Written Law in France: A note by the Secretary to the Commission on the proceedings of a Conference of the Statute Law Society, in September, 1991. This covers:
- Preparation of Legislation, and in particular the functions, organisation and work of the Conseil d'Etat;
- Passage of legislation through Parliament;
- Codification of the law;
- The Cour de Cassation; and
- The accessibility of law to the citizen, including information about the automated publication of texts and access to them by the public.

E. GERMANY

(i) A book in German, English and French entitled Das Deutscher Parlament with many illustrations, dealing with:

- The parliamentary idea and the development of parliamentarianism in Germany from 1800 to 1945;
- The rebuilding and consolidation of democracy after World War II; and
- Organisation, Procedure and Functions of the German Bundestag.

(ii) A paper prepared for the Commission by the Parliamentary Law Section of the Bundestag covering:
- Procedures under which bills are debated in the plenary and in committees of the Bundestag:
- Involvement of outside bodies in legislation;
- Time frame of legislative deliberations;
- Amendments to bills during the deliberations in the Bundestag; and
- Participation of the Bundestag in the issuance of ordinances having the force of law.

(iii) The Rules of Procedure of the German Bundestag (in German and English).

(iv) A booklet, The German Bundesrat , covering:
- Constitutional Tradition;
- Constitutional Status;
- Organisation;
- Tasks;
- Decision-Making Process;
- The States in the Federal Republic of Germany; and
- Bundesrat -Statistical Record.

(v) A letter (in German with an English translation) from the Direktor of the Bundesrat on Deliberation Procedure of the Bundesrat. This covers:
- Procedures under which bills are debated in the House and in committees, and passed;
- The extent to which interested bodies are consulted or otherwise involved in the legislative process;
- The time spent on legislation and the intervals between the various stages of bills;
- The extent to which bills are amended as a result of parliamentary scrutiny; and
- The procedures for controlling or scrutinising delegated legislation.

F. ISRAEL

(i) A paper prepared by the Secretary General of the Knesset, covering:
- Procedures under which bills are debated in the House and in committees, and passed;
- The extent to which interested bodies are consulted or otherwise involved in the legislative process;
- The time spent on legislation and the intervals between the various stages of bills;
- The extent to which bills are amended as a result of parliamentary scrutiny; and
- The procedures for controlling or scrutinising delegated legislation.

G. NEW ZEALAND

(i) Extensive papers, prepared by the Clerk of the House of Representatives, covering:
- Procedures under which bills are considered and passed in the House (including an article, published in Statute Law Review, on The Influence of Parliamentary Procedure on the Form of Legislation in New Zealand, by D G McGee, Clerk of the House of Representatives);
- Procedures under which bills are considered by select committees (including a full description of the way bills are examined by select committees after first reading, and specimen reports from such committees);
- Comment on the extent to which interested bodies are consulted or otherwise involved in the legislative process;
- The extent to which bills are amended as a result of parliamentary scrutiny;
- The procedures for scrutinising delegated legislation (including specimen reports from the Regulation Review Committee); and
- Tables and schedules on the Houses legislative workload.

Legislative Drafting

A. AUSTRALIA

(i) Clear Legislative Drafting: New Approaches in Australia, paper prepared in October 1990 by Mr Ian Turnbull, First Parliamentary Counsel. This covers:
- Background: The complexity of statute law;
- The plain English movement;
- Drafting in general terms;
- Towards a simpler (Australian) Commonwealth style;
- Clarity: the balance between simplicity and precision; and
- The three elements of the Commonwealth approach: – Rules of simple writing – Traditional expressions – Aids to understanding – Examples of new approach

The Office of Parliamentary Counsel were preparing a Clear Drafting Manual.

(ii) The Acts Interpretation Act 1901 (Reprinted as at 31 January 1990).

(iii) Plain English and the Law, Report No. 9 of the Law Reform Commission of Victoria.

(iv) Access to the Law: the structure and format of legislation, Report No 33 of the Law Reform Commission of Victoria.

(v) Law Reform Agenda – Special edition of quarterly newsletter published by the Law Reform Commission of Victoria on producing a computerised up-dated and consolidated statute book.

(vi) The Occupational Health and Safety Legislation (Amendment) Bill 1990 of New South Wales.

B. CANADA

(i) Letter from Mr Peter E Johnson, Chief Legislative Counsel, Department of Justice, describing recent developments in the drafting and printing of federal legislation. It covers:
  – The establishment of a Review Committee of drafters to review all draft bills nearing completion:
  – The Deskbook Committee to maintain a record of precedents etc.;
  – Drafting notes issued by the Chief Legislative Counsel;
  – Bi-weekly meetings of all drafters in the Legislation Section;
  – Plain language drafting;
  – Amending formulae;
  – Loose-leaf statutes; and
  – Speedier production of Assent copies of Acts.
(ii) Note to Drafters on amendments to bills in Parliament, issued by the Chief Legislative Counsel, February 1990.
(iii) The Interpretation Act.
(iv) Two specimen bills.
(v) Legislative Drafting Practices and Other Factors Affecting the Clarity of Canada's Laws, article by Peter E Johnson, QC, Chief Legislative Counsel, Department of Justice, published in Statute Law Review.

C. NEW ZEALAND

(i) Legislative Change: Guidelines on Process and Content (revised edition), Report No. 6 by the Legislation Advisory Committee, December 1991.
(ii) Three articles by Mr Walter Iles, CMG, QC, Chief Parliamentary Counsel, New Zealand, published in Statute Law Review:
  – Legislative Drafting Practices in New Zealand (Vol. 12, No. 1 Summer 1991)
  – New Zealand Experience of Parliamentary Scrutiny of Legislation (Vol. 12, No. 3 Winter 1991)
  – The Responsibilities of the New Zealand Legislation Advisory Committee (Vol. 13, No. 1 Summer 1992).

Appendix 4 – Government Bills Introduced in the House of Lords

This paper examines the extent to which Government bills begin their Parliamentary life in the House of Lords. In addition to a statistical breakdown of such bills for the three Parliaments 1979-83, 1983-87 and 1987-92, an analysis is made of the political saliency of the bills (measured by inclusion in the Queen's Speech). The role of the House of Lords in the passage of consolidation legislation is also examined.

Government Bills Introduced in HL: 1979-80 to 1991-92

Session	Total Govt. Bills	GB in HL	Consol*	Other**	Q.S.***
1979-80	71	24	16	8	3
1980-81	55	24	12	12	3
1981-82	47	17	8	9	4
1982-83	48	16	5	11	4
1983-84	60	28	13	15	4
1984-85	56	23	11	12	7
1985-86	50	20	5	15	7
1986-87	38	15	1	14	6
1987-88	49	14	6	8	3
1988-89	37	16	4	12	3
1989-90	36	13	5	8	5
1990-91	52	18	8	10	5
1991-92	39	16	11	5	4

  *   Consolidation Bills
 **   Substantive Bills
*** Announced in Queen's Speech

A majority of bills announced in the Queen's Speech and introduced in the House of Lords are either related to the criminal and civil justice systems, or are complicated technical issues (such as the Children Bill 1989-90, the Copyright, Designs and Patents Bill 1987-88, or the Cable and Broadcasting Bill 1983-84). Few of the bills could be said to be at the forefront of party political struggle, although some, such as the Human Fertilization and Embryology Bill 1989-90 and the Shops Bill 1985-86, excited considerable cross – party controversy.

Substantive Government bills not announced in the Queen's Speech vary considerably in importance. They range from such arcane legislation as the Irish Sailors and Soldiers Land Trust Bill (1986-87) and the Outer Space Bill (1985-86) to the more widely relevant Energy Conservation Bill (1979-80) and Legal Aid Bill (1981-82).

The table also indicates the importance of the House of Lords in the process of consolidating the statute book, although the number of consolidation bills introduced in each session varies considerably.

Some idea of the issues covered in consolidation measures can be gained by examining the bills introduced in the 1985-86 session. The following measures were introduced: Agricultural Holdings Bill, Company Directors Disqualification Bill, Insolvency Bill, Parliamentary Constituencies Bill, Statute Law (Repeals) Bill.

(Information derived from Sessional Digests 1983-84 to 1991-92 and HC Weekly Bulletins 1979-80 to 1982-83).

Appendix 5 – The Broadcasting Act 1990: A Case Study

Summary of Findings

This study traces the formulation and parliamentary passage of the Broadcasting Act 1990. Four points emerge of particular relevance to the concerns of the Commission.

First, there was extensive pre-legislative consultation; an official report, a Select Committee Report, a Green Paper and a White Paper. However, the forms of consultation involved were fragmented and only the White Paper was wholly authoritative. Some of the White Paper proposals which attracted the most criticism still appeared in the Bill. Consultation is not an end in itself, and the failure to meet the concerns of those affected was perhaps the most significant cause of the length of the Parliamentary process.

Second, the parliamentary process was lengthy, and the Bill was heavily amended. Seventeen full days of Parliamentary debate and 38 sessions of the Standing Committee took place, 2,673 amendments were discussed and 1,300 amendments were made to the Bill. This may indicate that the Bill was inadequately prepared, or that parliamentary scrutiny worked well. The Government not only introduced a large number of departmentally generated amendments, but also tabled a large number embodying commitments made to the Opposition parties and Government back benchers.

Third, the House of Commons Committee Stage of the Bill was widely hailed as being unusually constructive. The Minister, David Mellor, was prepared to amend the Bill where the arguments were convincing, and the Labour and SLD Opposition (and the Government back bench MPs) took the process seriously and tabled amendments designed to improve rather than wreck the Bill.

Fourth, the Government was compelled to introduce a large number of amendments, including new clauses and schedules during the House of Lords stage of the Bill, some at very short notice and leaving inadequate time for full consultation with affected interests. The Sessional system meant that by the end of the Bill's progress, a large amount of work had to be undertaken by the House of Lords in the October "spill over" period. There was no evidence of filibustering, and the Bill was not guillotined at any stage. Detailed consideration of a complicated technical measure is necessarily a time consuming activity, especially if it is politically controversial and affects well organised and funded groups.

Introduction

The Broadcasting Act 1990 provides an interesting case study of the contemporary legislative process in action. Despite extensive consultation, the Bill as published encountered harsh criticism, and was significantly amended during its passage through Parliament. The Independent Television Commission in its evidence to the Commission criticised the fact that no comprehensive inquiry on the future

mmercial broadcasting was established; the alternative of a number of piecemeal
estigations and consultations was inadequate, especially when the Government
ored many of their findings. The result was that "many details remained to be
rked out in the Bill as it was introduced" (M 27).

mmary of Main Provisions as Enacted

e Broadcasting Act 1990 established a flexible "light touch" system of regulation
· the independent broadcasting sector. More reliance was placed on market
chanisms than previously, with consumer choice taking precedence over the
blic service ethos. The main provisions of the Act were:

The establishment of a looser system of regulation for the independent
broadcasting sector, replacing the IBA with the Independent Television
Commission and the Radio Authority. The ITC was to regulate commercial
television, satellite and cable television companies, and teletext services. The
RA was to regulate national and local commercial radio and community radio
stations.

The re-franchising of Channel Three companies, with licenses being awarded to
the person submitting the highest cash bid, subject only to an "exceptional
circumstances" provision. The same system was to be followed for Television
Channel Five, cable television franchises and national radio. A "quality
threshold" would act both as an initial hurdle, and as a benchmark for
programme output throughout the duration of the license. (Both the exceptional
circumstances and quality hurdle provisions were amended in Parliament).

The removal of the public service broadcasting obligation to disseminate
information, education and entertainment from Channel Three licence holders.

The publication of codes on impartiality by the ITC and the RA, relating to
matters of political or industrial controversy, or to current public policy.
(Strengthened in the course of Parliamentary passage).

The placing on a statutory basis of the Broadcasting Standards Council (BSC),
established in 1988, with a duty to draw up draft codes on the portrayal of sex
and violence for the broadcasters to adopt, and the ability to initiate its own
investigations.

The application of the Obscene Publication Act 1959 to broadcasting.

The transformation of the IBA transmission network into a company, Transcom,
initially Government owned, but with increasing private sector involvement.

The establishment of a fifth television channel.

A requirement that both the BBC and ITV have a minimum of 25% of
programmes made by independent production companies.

Channel Three companies being forced to divest themselves of a majority
shareholding in ITN.

Targets set for the number of programmes to be subtitled for the deaf and
hearing impaired, leading to 50% of all programme output being subtitled by

1997. (Greatly strengthened as a result of Parliamentary pressure and interest group activity).

The lifting of restrictions on religious broadcasting, allowing Christian and other groups to own television and radio stations, provided that they did not exploit the susceptibilities of the audience, or abuse the beliefs of other religions or denominations. (Amended in Parliament to further relax the rules).

Powers for the Secretary of State to proscribe the reception of unacceptable foreign satellite stations.

The establishment of a Gaelic Television Fund to support the broadcasting of programmes in the Gaelic language in Scotland.

The establishment of a National Television Archive.

The strengthening of powers against pirate broadcasting, especially relating to offshore pirate radio stations.

The removal of the monopoly of programme providers on the publication of programme listings, opening up the Radio Times and TV Times to greater competition.

Outline Chronology of Act

7/86   Publication of the Peacock Report on the financing of the BBC (Cmnd 9824).

2/87   Publication of Green Paper, Radio: Choices and Opportunities, (Cm 92). Comments to be submitted by 30/6/87.

5/87   Conservative Party General Election Manifesto pledges a policy of "more competition, variety and innovation" in broadcasting, committing the Government to bringing in a 25% quota for independent productions for both BBC and ITV, to bringing broadcasting under the Obscene Publications Act 1959 and to strengthening controls over the portrayal of sex and violence on television.

19/1/88   Written answer c. 647-649 announces Government response to consultations on Green Paper.

16/5/88   HC Statement announces the establishment of the BSC, c. 689-698. The BSC was put on a statutory basis in the Bill, and played a part in the passage of the Bill.

11/88   Publication of White Paper Broadcasting in the 90s: Competition, Choice and Quality (Cm 517). It was described as "white with green edges", and comments to be in by 28/2/89. Included Government responses to consultation over the Green Paper on radio broadcasting.

7/11/88   HC Statement launching the White Paper, c. 29-46.

8/2/89   HC Debate on White Paper, c. 1006-1080. Approved after Labour amendment rejected 275 – 203.

19/5/89   HC Statement on radio, c. 317-9w.

13/6/89 HC Statement on plans for commercial television following responses to White Paper.

6/12/89 Bill published and received First Reading.

18/12/89 HC Second Reading of Bill. Approved 310 – 238.

1/1/90 ITC established on a non – statutory basis. Played a major role in the Parliamentary passage of the Bill.

9/1/90 HC Committee Stage began; 38 sittings held until 15/3/90.

8-9/5/90 HC Report Stage held.

10/5/90 HC Third Reading held. Approved 259 – 180.

5/6/90 HL Second Reading held.

9/7/90 HL Committee stage began. Seven days of debate held until 26/7/90.

9/10/90 HL Report Stage held over three full days until 16/10/90.

22/10/90 HL Third Reading held.

25/10/90 HC consideration of HL amendments.

30/10/90 HL consideration of HC response to HL amendments.

1/11/90 Royal Assent given to Broadcasting Act.

16/10/91 Results of franchise auction announced. Thames, TSW, TVS and TV-AM all lost their franchise.

Extent of Consultation

The Bill was preceded by an extensive public debate, which had included the publications of an official report (The Peacock Report on the Financing of the BBC), a Green Paper (Radio: Choices and Opportunities Cm 92), a major Select Committee inquiry (3rd Report of Home Affairs Committee, The Future of Broadcasting 1987-88 HC 262), and a White Paper (Broadcasting in the 90s: Competition, Choice and Quality Cm 517). The Minister responsible, David Mellor, observed that "no Bill has had a longer gestation period: it makes that of an elephant seem flimsy by comparison". (Ctte Debs, 15/2/90 c. 923).

Despite this, the nature of the pre-legislative consultation came under attack. The ITC told the Commission that whereas previous comparable legislation had been based on a Committee of Enquiry given specific terms of reference to examine the areas upon which it was proposed to legislate, it did not happen in this case. "The foundations of the Bill were not based on a thorough and considered examination of the evidence for inadequacies in the existing statutory provision and of the case for change....In consequence of this, many details remained to be worked out in the Bill as it was introduced". They considered that "the Bill as it was eventually presented to Parliament would undoubtedly have benefited from a period of prior exposure to scrutiny as a totality, with the opportunity for informed opinion to comment on it" (M 27).

Because of the scope of the proposals it offered, the Broadcasting White Paper attracted over 3,000 responses. They ranged from the reactions of those in the industry to the comments of individual members of the public. A large number of public and national bodies made submissions. These included charities (such as t Parkinson's Disease Society, the Royal National Institute for the Blind, and t National Eczema Society), commercial companies (Thorn EMI, British Telecom a British Nuclear Fuels), political parties, a number of churches and religio denominations, and a large variety of miscellaneous bodies ranging from t Campaign for Press and Broadcasting Freedom and the Campaign for Quali Television, to the Family Planning Association, the Grand Orange Lodge Scotland, the Mothers Union, the Royal Mission to Deep Sea Fishermen, a Wireless for the Bedridden. (See Deposited Paper NS 4908). David Mellor told t HC Committee considering the Bill that he had held over 100 meetings with inter groups on the measure. (Ctte Debs 9/1/90 c. 5).

Some groups continued to play a particularly active role during the Parliamenta passage of the Act. A number of religious groups (such as the Christi Broadcasting Campaign and the Evangelical Alliance) campaigned vigorous against the proposed restrictions on religious broadcasting, and with the support MPs and Peers won considerable concessions in the course of the passage of t Bill. MPs also received material from the Broadcasting Consortium (a gro including Age Concern, the British Council of Churches and Oxfam), broadcasti trade unions, commercial interests, and pressure groups established in the wake the White Paper, such as the Campaign for Quality Television (which David Mel acknowledged had persuaded the Government to amend the franchise proce Independent 5/6/90). A Labour member of the Standing Committee (Tony Ban MP) recalled that the opposition "received from various organisations excelle briefings that we were able to put to effective use. .. Many a speech was ridd home on the IBA briefings and the support that we got from the BBC and vario advisors" (10/5/90, c 440).

The IBA and the shadow ITC played a prominent part in the shaping of t legislation when it was before Parliament. The IBA produced over 30 briefing no for MPs and Peers, and occasionally amendments were put down throu sympathetic Parliamentarians. The Cable Authority did the same (See M27). T ITC and the Radio Authority both existed in shadow form from 1/1/90, and we frequently required to explain the likely implementation of particular clauses. (occasion they called for, and got, amendments to the Bill. In particular, the I strongly criticised Government amendments on impartiality introduced at HL Rep Stage, and were influential in having them withdrawn and redrafted.

In its evidence to the Commission, the BBC criticised the quality of t consultation that occurred during the passage of the Bill. It was "often too late, ga insufficient time for a considered response and many of the observations we ma were ignored.... it was another example of a Bill prepared in haste, policy r properly thought through and it became a matter of getting the policy right duri the passage of the Bill rather than improving it and refining it" (M 11).

Changes Between Proposals and Bill

As a result of the consultation process, a number of changes were made to proposals between the release of the White Paper in November 1988 and publication of the Bill in December 1989. The Government abandoned plans to franchise the night hours of Channel Three separately, to assign the BBC's night hours to the ITC, to launch a Sixth Channel, and to make Channel Four compete for advertising revenue with Channel Three. It also rejected the suggestion of amalgamating the pre-existing Broadcasting Complaints Commission (BCC) and the BSC, and relaxed some of the proposed restrictions on cable operators. Two further changes were of particular significance.

First, the Government strengthened the proposed controls on concentration of ownership, limiting individuals to two Channel Three franchises, and banning the ownership of two geographically contiguous companies. Cross ownership of terrestrial national/regional and satellite television companies, national independent radio licences and newspapers was restricted to a 20% holding. (Except for non-domestic satellites such as Rupert Murdoch's SKY TV). (HC Debs Vol 153 c. 317-19W 19/5/89).

Second, the White Paper proposed that franchise applicants would have to meet a quality threshold of consumer protection standards, and would then be judged on the basis of a cash bid. As a result of concerns that programme quality would be adversely affected, the Government announced that it would strengthen the quality threshold to emphasise both quality and the diversity of tastes and interests catered for. Although the ITC would ordinarily be expected to allocate the franchise to the highest bidder, an "exceptional circumstances" clause would allow the ITC to favour a lower bid, subject to judicial review. (HC Debs Vol 154 c. 710-13, 13/6/89).

The Bill "was greeted with almost universal opposition". (Times 8/12/89). Criticism was not confined to industry and the Opposition, or to the substance of the Bill. The quality of drafting also came in for attack, with solicitor Michael Ridley warning that there was much "uncertain language" in the Bill "we may think that we know what it means because of the way that ministers explain it, but the courts may take a different view". (Times 30/1/90).

Government Case and Opposition Views

The debate on the Second Reading of the Bill on 18/12/89 set out the fundamental attitudes of the Government and the Opposition parties on the major issues.

For the Government, Home Secretary David Waddington commended the Bill as creating "a sensible regulatory framework for a new age in broadcasting in which technical change has brought vastly increased choice" (c. 40). The Bill would guarantee wider consumer choice by establishing Channel Five, three new national radio channels, and deregulating local cable and radio services. It would maintain programme quality and diversity and ensure widespread ownership by "sharply focussed statutory safeguards" (c. 41). It would also protect viewers through "safeguards for programme standards on taste, decency, accuracy and balance" (c. 41). The tendering process would be fairer and more objective than in the past, and would produce a good return for the tax payer.

For the Opposition, Shadow Home Secretary Roy Hattersley argued that the Bill would lead to a decline in quality and a fall in the standards of UK television. The Bill contained no adequate protection for programme quality, without which choice was illusory. "Real choice for viewers depends on a diversity of programmes, not simply on the proliferation of the number of buttons on a set that it is possible to press" (c 53). In particular, he attacked the franchising arrangements; the higher the bid necessary to win a franchise, the less money available for programmes. The proposals for diversity of ownership were also inadequate and offered a threat to democracy by favouring Rupert Murdoch. Labour strongly opposed the existence of the BSC: it was not sinister but ridiculous. A Labour motion to commit the Bill to a Special Standing Committee was rejected by 303 to 237.

For the SLD, Robert Maclennan pointed out that the vast majority of the responses to the White Paper had criticised the Government's proposals for the franchise auctions, but the proposals were still in the Act. The Government had treated the views of those involved in the industry "with complete contempt" (c.89).

Labour back bencher Bob Cryer attacked the number of powers which the Bill gave to the Secretary of State. These included a Henry VIII clause in Clause 163 and a number of other powers which did not require subsequent Parliamentary approval. (A number of these powers were removed by Government amendment at the House of Commons Committee Stage).

Main Features of the Parliamentary Proceedings

When the Bill was published, it was noted that "even the Government seems far from certain that its legislative package is the correct formula, and appears resigned to big changes to the Bill before it reaches the statute book" (Times 8/12/89). This proved to be the case. Perhaps the most significant feature of the parliamentary passage of the Bill was the sheer length of the process and the volume of amendments considered. Seventeen full days of Parliamentary debate in the HC and HL were held, in addition to 38 sessions of the HC Standing Committee. In all, a total of 2,673 amendments were discussed, and 1,356 amendments were made to the Bill. Of the amendments made, 1,322 were tabled by the Government. The Bill as published was made up of 167 clauses and 12 schedules. By the time it gained Royal Assent, it had grown to comprise 204 clauses and 22 schedules.

Two views can be taken of this. Either the legislation had been inadequately prepared and was not ready for parliamentary scrutiny, or else Parliament worked as it should and played a significant role in the shaping of the Bill. Both views were expressed in the course of proceedings.

An unusual feature of the process was the fact that the ITC, RA and the BSC already existed in shadow form, and played a significant role in shaping the legislation, giving information about the likely implementation of particular provisions, and sometimes calling for amendments. The ITC in particular was frequently cited by the Government in support of specific elements of the Bill. Lord Chalfont (chairman designate of the RA) and Lord Rees-Mogg (chairman of the BSC) contributed to debates in the House of Lords.

Equally unusual was the constructive use of the House of Commons Committee stage, which won widespread praise for David Mellor and was acknowledged as having greatly improved the quality of the Bill. (See below).

House of Commons Committee Stage

The Committee Stage of the Bill took place in Standing Committee F, comprised of 38 sittings and lasted from 9/1/90 to 13/3/90. The Committee had 30 members, reflecting the political balance in the House as a whole (17 Conservative, 11 Labour, 1 SLD and one PC MP), and including a number of MPs with experience of working in broadcasting. Leading Tory critic George Walden was excluded from the Committee. A total of 652 amendments and New Clauses were discussed (46 New Clauses and 606 amendments), of which 72 were agreed. Table One below gives the details.

Table One: Amendments/New Clauses tabled at HC Committee Stage

Amendments	Govt	Govt BB	Lab FB	Lab BB	SLD	PC
Tabled	59	95	295	53	120	30
Called	16	22	90	11	33	8
Not Called	-	25	42	15	21	-
Gpd. & disc.*	43	48	163	27	66	22
Moved**	42	4	8	2	2	1
Not Moved**	1	44	155	25	64	21
Withdrawn	-	20	70	7	26	7
Negatived	-	1	23	6	5	2
Agreed	58	5	5	-	4	-

  *   Amendments grouped and discussed.
**   Relates only to amendments grouped and discussed.

There were Opposition complaints that the membership of the Committee had not been announced until the last day before the Christmas recess, with the first Committee session taking place immediately on the return of the House. This made it very difficult for the Opposition to meet with interest groups. Both Labour and the SLD considered that the Standing Committee system was not the ideal forum for examining a lengthy and detailed technical measure of this nature, and argued that the Bill should have been committed to a Special Standing Committee able to take expert evidence and cross examine witnesses. As a result, Labour established an informal Special Standing Committee, allowing Labour Committee members to meet and discuss the issues involved with leading figures in the industry and other experts.

The table suggests that the impact of the Opposition parties was minimal. It does not reflect the fact that the Minister, David Mellor, made a number of concessions both to the Opposition parties and to his own back benchers, which he pledged to redeem in Government amendments at Report of in the House of Lords stages of the Bill. Mellor accepted the principle of 30 Labour front bench amendments (on issues such as the size of the ITC, training, subtitling, greater openness in the tendering process by the RA and ITC, and the order – making powers of the Secretary of State), 2 Labour backbench amendments (on SC4 and defences against obscenity changes), 6 SLD amendments (on HC scrutiny of the powers of the Secretary of State, C3 news, and the removal of Clause 87 giving the RA powers to ban programmes), 4 Conservative backbench amendments (on C3 licence conditions, and the relationship of the ITC and SKY), and one, on SC4, from PC.

Table One shows that the Government introduced a number of amendments. These included a batch of 21 new clauses and schedules tabled only a week to ten days before the end of the Committee stage. Most were technical (relating to the division of assets of the IBA, the privatisation of the IBA transmission system, and copyright), but there were complaints at the lack of time given for consultation. As a result, Mellor offered the Opposition access to civil service advice on the matter before the Report Stage (13/3/90). Indeed, one Labour back bencher, Gwyneth Dunwoody, earlier criticised the number of major changes which the Government had committed itself to make to the Bill, arguing that the Government "(had) not presented legislation that (was) in a fair state for the House of Commons to consider". (23/1/90 c. 254). Some Government new clauses were not ready until the Report Stage.

A number of important changes were made to the Bill. These included the abandonment of powers for the police to demand the handing over of programmes and to search broadcasters and seize programmes before transmission, the strengthening of the quality hurdle for C3 license applicants, and the addition of further controls on cross media ownership.

Committee members received extensive lobbying from concerned groups. At one point, a Labour MP complained that they were "being bombarded, indeed buried, by submissions from interest groups and television companies". (6/2/90 c 527). These ranged from material from commercial interests through to constituency bodies such as schools concerned over educational programmes. Labour was also assisted by a number of full time research assistants provided by broadcasting trade unions. (See Ctte c. 1517, 15/3/90).

Speaking on Third Reading, Conservative back bencher Roger Gale characterised the Committee Stage as "one of the most constructive and creative Committees on which any of us are likely to serve in this place" (10/5/90 c. 421). The Chairman of the Committee felt that it was "an example that many Committees could follow" (Ctte Debs c. 1520 15/3/90).

House of Commons Report Stage

The Report Stage of the Bill was spread over two full days, May 8th and 9th 1990, and totalled 17 hours of debate on the floor of the House. The Commons considered 730 amendments and 33 New Clauses, a total of 763, and agreed 509. The table below gives the combined statistics.

The significant factor to note is that the Government tabled and had approved 503 amendments to the Bill. These ranged from minor drafting amendments to significant changes to the structure of the Bill (some a result of concessions during the Ctte Stage, and some due to further consultations and representations). Mellor considered this "a sign of the success of parliamentary processes, not a criticism of them" (8/5/90, c. 50).

Among the major changes made were: the strengthening of the quality threshold, the enhancement of the regional nature of C3, the clarification of the exceptional circumstances requirement, the relaxation of restrictions on religious broadcasting and the ownership of cable / satellite television and local radio stations by religious groups (a result of representations by the Evangelical Alliance, Christian Standards in Society and other groups, and the support of MPs): and an increase in the targets for subtitling (a response to pressure in Committee and from the Deaf Broadcasting Association and Jack Ashley MP).

Pressure group activity was again in evidence. A group of MPs acting for the cable industry sought changes to this aspect of the Bill. An amendment by Conservative MP John Watts to bring Rupert Murdoch's SKY TV under tighter regulation (A8) proved to have been drafted with the assistance of BSB, SKY's main competitor (9/5/90 c. 227).

Table Two: Amendments / New Clauses Tabled at HC Report Stage

Amendments	Govt.	Cons BB	Lab FB	Lab BB	SLD
Tabled	508	79	104	28	44
Called	290	8	13	4	3
Not Called	5	24	58	16	24
Gpd. & Disc.	213	47	33	8	17
Moved	213	-	4	1	-
Not Moved	-	47	29	7	17
Withdrawn	-	6	7	4	-
Negatived	-	2	5	-	3
Agreed	503	-	5	1	-

The raw figures give the impression that the Opposition parties and Conservative back benchers had very little impact on the Bill. Just 6 amendments were accepted. This however is misleading. The Government accepted to varying degrees a number of Opposition and back bench amendments. From the Labour front bench, they accepted the principle of three amendments, on public consultations over C3 franchises, on equal opportunity policies for ITC and the RA, and on the role of the ITC with C5. From the Labour back benches, two amendments on SC4 and Welsh language broadcasting were accepted in principle, as were two restricting the powers of the Secretary of State. From the Conservative back benches, the Government accepted the need to clarify the definition of "exceptional circumstances" for franchise bids, to change the rules on Christian broadcasting, to limit the funding of ITC by the cable industry, and to protect the franchises of current cable licence holders. All these these areas would be subject to Government amendments in the HL. No concessions were made towards SLD amendments.

As during the Committee Stage, the Opposition attacked some of the time constraints under which they had to operate. For example, the final selection of amendments to be discussed was not made available until the first day of the Report Stage itself.

House of Commons Third Reading

The Bill as amended in the House of Commons received its Third Reading on 10/5/90. Labour welcomed the changes made in the Bill but still opposed it as being too market oriented. For the Government, Mellor underlined his willingness to listen to arguments for changes to the Bill, and summarised the concessions already made.

A considerable part of the debate was given over to praising the flexibility and responsiveness of Mellor. He set out his view of the role of Parliament in legislation; it was "not an optional extra in the process of Government or some kind of tedious and necessary excursion to fill time between the Government conceiving an idea and carrying it through, but a vital part in the process of ensuring that legislation has a fair chance of being coherent and convincing in its detail and hopefully fairly broadly acceptable in its principle". (c. 412).

House of Lords Second Reading
The Bill received its Second Reading in the House of Lords on 5/6/90. The debate lasted over 9 hours, until 12.30am, and 42 peers spoke, many of them (including Lord Grade, Lord Boston of Faversham, the Earl of Glasgow and Lord Forbes) having extensive personal experience of the broadcasting industry.

For the Government, Earl Ferrers promised five major changes to the Bill as a result of the HC stages: a relaxation of restrictions on religious broadcasting, changes to the rules for the renewal of licenses, tighter measures against subscription piracy, additions to the transitional arrangements, and a role for the ITC in safeguarding National Television Archive arrangements. The Government had not yet decided whether to include clauses on C3 networking and needle time.

For Labour, Baroness Birk congratulated the Government for listening to criticism, but condemned the Bill for its "obsession with the marketplace". It contained four major flaws which the Opposition would address: the need for a moratorium on C3 takeovers, powers for the ITC to enforce networking, tighter controls on cross media ownership, and the need to prohibit multiple bidding for C3 licenses.

For the SLD, Lord Thomson of Monifieth praised Mellor's handling of the Bill in the HC, but attacked the measure for undermining public service broadcasting and called for the strengthening of role of the ITC and RA in maintaining standards. Changes were required on networking, the position of ITN, cross media ownership and the coverage of sporting events.

An important feature of the Second Reading debate, which greatly influenced the HL stages of the Bill, was a vigorous attack on bias in the media launched by Lord Wyatt of Weeford (Independent) and Lord Orr-Ewing (Conservative). They considered the existing provisions of the Bill inadequate, and promised to attempt to amend the Bill in Committee.

House of Lords Committee Stage
The House of Lords Committee stage was held over seven days from 9/7/90 to 26/7/90, giving a month for consultation after the Second Reading. A total of 714 amendments were discussed, of which 368 were agreed. The Government was heavily criticised by the Opposition parties for tabling 46 pages of detailed technical amendments late on Friday 20th July for discussion on Tuesday 24th July. It gave little time for the Opposition to digest the amendments, let alone for outside parties to make representations upon them. In response, Earl Ferrers apologised, but argued that if necessary they could be amended on Report. (24/7/90, c. 1324-26). Even before this, Labour leader Lord Cledwyn of Penrhos warned that the HL was

"overworked due to the Government's insistence on overloading the legislative programme". (18/7/90 c. 863). The timetable for the Committee Stage was constrained by the fact that the HL was due to rise for the summer recess on 27/7/90.

An important feature of all the HL stages of the Bill was the close co-operation evident between the Labour and SLD front benches. Each frequently seconded amendments tabled by the other, spoke in support of each others amendments, and voted together. The coherence and impact of the Opposition benefited from this.

The key feature of the stage was a heated debate on bias and impartiality initiated by Lord Wyatt (Independent). In place of the "due impartiality" rule which had applied to independent television since the 1950s, the amendments attempted a far more detailed and specific requirement of balance. As a result, the Government abandoned its previous stance that it was a matter for the ITC, and pledged to amend the Bill on Report to reflect these concerns. Great controversy ensued.

As before, the Government made a number of concessions to opposition parties and others. The Government accepted the principle of 6 amendments from Government back benchers, 3 from the Labour front bench, 6 from the SLD benches, and 2 amendments from Independent peers. Two Government amendments (on the research powers of the ITC and the RA) were dropped as a result of opposition from the House. A series of Government amendments removing the obligation for C3 licensees to provide performance bonds were tabled following discussions with the IBA. The Government also amended the Bill to include a moratorium on takeovers as a result of pressure from the HC and the HL Second Reading debate (19/7/90 c. 1011). Lord Monson (Independent) attempted to relax some of the powers to seize and search pirate radio stations, but was defeated. He returned to the subject at Report and Third Reading, but without success.

The Government suffered one defeat, by 91 – 64, over a Labour back bench amendment concerning programme diversity. It was reversed in the HC.

Table Three: Amendments / New Causes Tabled at HL Ctte Stage

Amendments	Govt	Govt BB	Lab FB	Lab BB	SLD	Others
Tabled	361	105	99	36	74	39
Called	52	23	24	12	33	10
Not Called	-	32	13	1	11	2
Gpd. & Disc.	309	50	62	23	30	27
Moved	307	5	3	3	1	-
Not Moved	2	45	59	20	29	27
Withdrawn	-	23	21	10	29	9
Negatived	-	1	6	1	4	1
Agreed	359	4	-	4	1	-

House of Lords Report Stage

The House of Lords Report Stage of the Bill was held over three days, October 9th, 11th and 16th. A total of 416 amendments were discussed, of which 288 were agreed. (Table Four below gives the details). Consideration began with Labour and SLD protests over the late arrival of Government amendments. Despite a pledge that all Government amendments would be tabled by 19/9/90, some (including highly controversial amendments on impartiality) were not available until 1/10/90, and others not until 4/10/90. The Opposition did not have the necessary facilities to cope with this, and the time for consultation was inadequate. The Government explained that 203 amendments had been tabled in time, but that others had required further extensive consultation. It was now ten months since the Bill began its Parliamentary life. (9/10/90 c 154-56).

The main feature of the Report stage was that the Government was forced not to move its new amendments relating to impartiality as a result of widespread opposition, coming not just from opponents but also from senior Conservative peers such as Lords Whitelaw and Peyton. There had already been widespread criticism of the amendments. Broadcasters had been consulted but were unhappy over the position (See Independent 21/9/90). The IBA had denounced the amendments as "unworkable" and considered that they would bring the law into disrepute. (Independent 6/10/90). The Government offered to further amend the amendments at Third Reading, but were instead persuaded to table redrafted amendments at Third Reading.

Table Four: Amendments / New Clauses Tabled at HL Report Stage

Amendments	Govt	Govt BB	Lab FB	Lab BB	SLD	Other
Tabled	293	33	36	5	29	20
Called	62	9	13	4	13	7
Not Called	-	5	5	-	4	7
Gpd. & Disc.	231	19	18	1	12	6
Moved	223	-	1	-	4	1
Not Moved	8	19	17	1	8	5
Withdrawn	-	8	9	2	15	6
Negatived	-	1	2	2	2	2
Agreed	285	-	3	-	-	-

Their Lordships also discussed definitions of "pop music", causing considerable hilarity in the press. A number of highly technical amendments were discussed concerning needle time, prompting Lord Ferrers to comment that, "Some of Your Lordships who are not deeply familiar with the intricacies of the subject matter which we are now considering might have obtained an equally clear understanding of the debate had it been conducted in ancient Greek". (16/19/90 c. 839).

The Government accepted three Labour amendments; one inserted a "high quality" condition on radio licences, and the other two strengthened safeguards over IBA pensions.

The legislative timetable was again criticised at the end of the Report Stage. The opposition argued that an extra day should have been made available, after the proceedings on the last day of consideration continued until 12.57 am.

House of Lords Third Reading

The House of Lords Third Reading of the Bill was held on 22/10/90. A total of 12? amendments were tabled for discussion, of which 119 were agreed. As can be see from Table Five below, the vast majority of the amendments were tabled by th

Government, and were predominantly technical changes or acted on commitments given earlier.

The most important debate occurred over the Government's new amendments on impartiality, redrafted from those attacked on Report. Despite a battery of legal critiques quoted by the opposition, the amendments were accepted. The Government accepted an SLD amendment on the ownership by overseas nationals, and a back bench Conservative proposal that defaulting licensees paid the costs of any measures taken against them. Some issues, such as the copyrighting of programme formats, the amendment of proposed powers over pirate radio stations and the funding of the National Television Archive were raised again, but without any further concessions from the Government.

Table Five: Amendments/New Clauses Tabled at HL Third Reading

Amendments	Govt	Govt BB	Lab FB	Lab BB	SLD	Other
Tabled	117	1	-	-	2	8
Called	14	1	-	-	1	4
Not Called	-	-	-	-	-	-
Gpd. & Disc.	103	-	-	-	1	4
Moved	103	-	-	-	1	-
Not Moved	-	-	-	-	-	4
Withdrawn	-	-	-	-	-	4
Negatived	-	-	-	-	-	-
Agreed	117	1	-	-	1	-

At the end of the debate, Earl Ferrers observed that the House of Lords had sat long and late on the Bill, often with "an uncomfortably short time in which to absorb late waves of often highly technical amendments". This he attributed to the fact that "the Bill affects an enormous range of interests who have, naturally enough, continued to comment and to urge various changes right up until the last moments". (22/10/90, c 1209-10). For Labour, Lady Birk commented on the difficulties which the Opposition experienced in handling technical bills with a very limited number of researchers. She listed ten areas in which the Opposition had been able to modify the Bill, but identified six elements (cross media ownership, the BSC, the remit for C5, access to listed sporting events, impartiality, and the C3 franchise system) where the Opposition still had problems. For the SLD, Lord Thomson observed that he could not in his Parliamentary experience "remember a Bill that has changed so greatly between its original introduction and its final passage through the Second Chamber" (c. 1216).

House of Commons Consideration of House of Lords Amendments

The House of Commons examined the amendments made during the House of Lords stages of the passage of the Bill on 25/10/90. There were 676 amendments to consider, taking up 141 pages. The debate was structured to suit the priorities of the Opposition, with over three hours devoted to the most controversial amendments, those concerning impartiality. These were eventually agreed by 268-181, with four Conservative MPs voting with the opposition. The Government succeeded by 52-92 in rejecting the amendments in Clause 15 on diversity which Labour had carried against Government opposition at the House of Lords Committee stage, thus reversing the only defeat which the Government had experienced in the whole course of the Bill. The Government accepted all the other amendments made in the House of Lords, and the rest of the debate was spent in eliciting explanations from the Government over the meaning of particular amendments. It also emerged that the Government had inadvertently reversed in the House of Lords a concession which they had earlier made to Labour. The Government apologised for the mistake.

House of Lords Consideration of House of Commons Amendments to House of Lords Amendments

The House of Lords considered the House of Commons response to the House of Lords amendments on 30/10/90, the final day of the 1989-90 Session. Baroness David, the Labour back bench sponsor of the amendments which the HC opposed, put down five new alternative amendments with the same effect. Earl Ferrers warned that if the amendments were carried and the HC resisted them then the whole Bill could be lost. As a result, the amendments were defeated, and the Bill received Royal Assent the next day.

Provision for Secondary Legislation

In a brief debate on the Money Resolution for the Bill immediately after Second Reading on 18/12/89, the Chairman of the Joint Committee on Statutory Instruments, Labour MP Bob Cryer, criticised the extent of the delegation of powers to the Secretary of State, and particularly attacked the inclusion of a Henry VIII clause at Clause 163, allowing the Government to vary the provisions of the Bill without reference to Parliament.

A number of these powers were removed or brought under parliamentary scrutiny in the course of the passage of the Bill. The Henry VIII clause was deleted at the House of Lords Committee Stage. The Secretary of State retained a wide range of powers, mainly concerned with amending regulations (such as on advertising in s.8), or updating financial provisions (as in the percentage of qualifying revenue for C4 (s. 29). Some of the Government powers to control the media (as in s.10 and s.94) were modelled on earlier provisions and were simply carried over into the Act.

Statutory Instruments Promulgated since Royal Assent

Approximately 15 S.I.s have been promulgated under the Act since Royal Assent. Some of them are simply administrative, being Commencement Orders (such as 1990/2347 and 1990/2566) or dealt with the transition to the new regime under the Act (such as 1990/2579 on the BCC and misleading advertisements). Others provided definitions for certain sections of the Act, such as 1990/2388 which laid down the number of houses to be served for a cable service to come under the provisions of Schedule 12, or 1991/1820 which specified those countries from which satellite services were licensable.

Steps Taken to Implement the Act

The implementation of parts of the Act has proved controversial. In particular, the decisions made by the ITC in licensing the new Channel Three franchises were contentious and subject to requests for judicial review. (See T. Jones, "Judici

Review of the Independent Television Commission", Public Law Autumn 1992 P372-377). The application of the exceptional circumstances provision was challenged, and the operation of the preference for the highest bidder gave rise to some anomalies. Central TV was unopposed, and so retained its franchise with a bid of £2000 only, whereas TVS, bidding £59 million, lost its licence. Because of the operation of the quality hurdle, eight of the successful companies were not the highest bidders for their licences. Four existing C3 companies (TV-AM, TSW, TVS and Thames Television) were beaten by new applicants. The new set of franchise holders will begin transmitting on 1/1/93. A code of practice on impartiality has been drawn up, and as yet has proved relatively uncontroversial. The franchise for Channel Five attracted just a single applicant, and has not yet been awarded (November 1992). The C3 franchise holders agreed a draft networking agreement in May 1992, which was agreed after consultation with the ITC and others, and is being implemented by the Independent Television Association. By July 1992, 55 cable services had been franchised (with over 300,000 homes receiving cable TV). Two teletext services (one the replacement of Oracle, the other a commercial teletext service for banks and finance houses) had also been franchised.

The Radio Authority has received around 100 applications for local radio licenses. For the three new national commercial radio stations, three applications were received for the first license. It was awarded to Classic FM, who started broadcasting in September 1992. Five applications have been received for the second channel to start in March 1994, and a third channel, for which tenders have not yet been opened, will begin transmitting in the Spring of 1995.

The BSC received 2,662 complaints for the year 1/4/91 – 31/3/92. Of these, 1,130 were within its remit, and findings were reached on 627 complaints. The BSC upheld 117, and rejected 510. The reason that so many of the complaints received were outside the remit of the BSC is primarily due to the fact that it has no ability to preview programmes. In 1991-92, 1,054 of these complaints related to a planned screening of the film "The Last Temptation of Christ". The BSC was unable to consider any complaints until the film had been transmitted. Its role has been that of a watchdog, not a censor (See BSC Annual Report 1991-92).

Appendix 6 – The Dangerous Dogs Act 1990: A Case Study

Summary of Main Provisions as Enacted

The Dangerous Dogs Act 1991 imposed a ban, with certain tightly controlled exemptions, on the ownership of two particular breeds of fighting dog, the American pit bull terrier and the Japanese tosa, and provided for restrictions to be imposed by order on other breeds of fighting dogs or on other particularly dangerous breeds. It created the offence of having a dog dangerously out of control in a public place, and enabled magistrates to specify the types of control measures to be applied to dangerous dogs. It strengthened existing police powers over the seizure of dangerous dogs, and gave the Secretary of State the power to prescribe by order the kinds of lead or muzzle to be used to comply with the Act.

Outline Chronology of the Act

24/5/88 Dog licensing abolished under s.38 of Local Government Act 1988.

14/6/89 House of Commons (HC) Statement by Home Secretary Douglas Hurd announced a package of dog control measures, including the strengthening of existing penalties for dangerous dogs. An attempt to reinstate dog registration as part of the Local Government and Housing Bill defeated, 159 – 146.

15/6/89 Adjournment debate on dangerous dogs brought by John McAllion (Lab) following the death of a 12 year old girl in his Dundee constituency after an attack by two rottweilers. Home Office Minister Douglas Hogg rejected as unworkable a ban on dangerous breeds, saying that "the idea of simply prohibiting an American pit bull terrier is a non runner". (c1188).

4/7/89 Government proposals for dangerous dogs (see 14/6/89) taken up in a Private Members Bill by Dame Janet Fookes (Conservative) and Lord Houghton of Sowerby. Supported by the Government. Received Royal Assent as the Dangerous Dogs Act 1989 at the end of July 1989.

10/8/89 Government consultation document Action on Dogs (Deposited Paper 5256) published. Proposed no further action on dangerous dogs.

30/4/90 Attempt to re-introduce dog registration as part of the Environmental Protection Bill defeated 275 – 263.

6/90 Government consultation document The Control of Dogs (Deposited Paper 6158) published. Suggested creating new offence of "allowing a dog to be dangerously out of control", giving further powers to local authorities and the police to seize and detain dogs after an incident, and to destroy a dog which appeared to be dangerously out of control. Courts could specify how dangerous dogs should be controlled, perhaps by ordering that the dog should be kept on a lead or muzzled. The consultation paper also discussed controls over particular breeds of fighting or particularly vicious dogs. Such controls might include a requirement that such dogs should always be on a lead or muzzled outside the home, that breeds should be banned altogether, with breeding made an offence, the spaying and neutering of existing dogs enforced, and an import ban imposed. It recognised the difficulties inherent in identifying particular breeds, especially when dealing with cross breeds such as the American pit bull terrier, and the need for flexible controls to allow for additions and deletions to the types of dogs on the list. The Government welcomed comments on the proposals, and gave respondents until 15/11/90 to submit their views.

1 – 5/91 Series of heavily publicised attacks on humans by rottweilers and pit bull terriers in particular. Mounting pressure in the press for action from the Government.

15/4/91 Early Day Motion (No. 691) tabled by John Fraser MP (Labour) calling for an import ban on the Japanese Tosa fighting dog. Attracted 64 signatories; 47 Labour, 13 Conservative, 3 SLD, 1 SDP.

8/5/91 Savage attacks on Mr Frank Tempest by two pit bull terriers.

14/5/91 Early Day Motion (No. 840) tabled by Terry Lewis MP (Labour) calling for an import ban on dangerous breeds, a dog registration scheme, compulsory third party insurance, and the destruction of all dogs of breeds raised for illegal dog fighting, in particular the Japanese tosa and the American pit bull terrier. Attracted the support of 57 members, including two Conservative MPs.

18/5/91 Savage attack on six year old Ruchsana Khan by a pit bull terrier in Bradford.

19/5/91 Home Secretary Kenneth Baker appeared on the David Frost Show, and said that the Government would not be taking any further action beyond the 1989 Act.

20/5/91 Government attacked in the press for inaction. The Daily Star addressed Kenneth Baker with the headline, "YOU WET WINDBAG".

21/5/91 John Major announced in Prime Minister's Question Time that the Government would act; an immediate import ban on pit bull terriers and Japanese tosa dogs was imposed, and the likelihood of legislation was hinted at. (c 776).

22/5/91 Statement by Kenneth Baker announcing that legislation would be brought before the House as quickly as possible to ban the breeding and ownership of such dogs. (See below for details).

4/6/91 Bill published. (See below for differences between it and the 22/5/91 Statement).

10/6/91 Bill passed through all its HC stages, having been guillotined from the beginning. Guillotine approved 280-56. No division on Second Reading.

Out of thirty five New Clauses and amendments, only four were moved and 15 discussed in Committee. No Report Stage or Third Reading was held.

25/6/91 House of Lords (HL) Second Reading held.

10/7/91 HL Committee Stage held.

18/7/91 HL Report Stage held.

23/7/91 HL Third Reading held.

24/7/91 HC consideration of HL amendments held.

25/7/91 Royal Assent.

12/8/91 Majority of Act came into force.

30/11/91 Ban on pit bull terriers and tosas came into force.

It should be noted that there were only four working days between the publication of the Bill and its HC stages, giving very limited time for both MPs and for interest groups and the public to respond. There were a further eleven working days before HL Second Reading, ten more days before HL Committee stage, a further six working days before the Report stage, and four working days more before HC consideration of HL amendments.

Extent of Consultation

Extensive consultation took place on the Control of Dogs document in 1990, but no Government response was published prior to the announcement of legislation on 22/5/91.

Once the decision was taken to legislate, on 21/5/91 the Home Office held consultations with the RSPCA, the Kennel Club and the veterinary associations. They all supported the ban on fighting dogs, but suggested exemptions. The RSPCA advocated a compensation scheme, while both the RSPCA and the Kennel Club opposed extending the ban to include rottweilers. (See Statement, 22/5/91).

During the Second Reading debate, Baker stressed the extent of the consultations undertaken. In addition to those listed above, talks had been held with the Canine Defence League and the Association of British Insurers, the Joint Association for the Care of Pets in Society, the All Party Animal Welfare group, and representatives of the pit bull owners. The RSPCA and the Kennel Club were giving assistance over the problem of conclusively identifying pit bull terriers.

The Police Federation supported the Bill, having initially been concerned that the police might have to administer it and complained of a lack of consultation. Interestingly, the Police Federation through their advisor Lord Bethell, sought to amend the bill at HL Committee Stage so as to extend the new "dangerous dog" offence to cover private premises as well as public areas (A23), to allow the costs of destroying dogs to be recoverable by the court (A45), and to allow magistrates to make compensation orders against the owners of dangerous dogs (A46). The first was covered in a Government amendment, the second was accepted in principle and agreed on Report, and the third was already the case.

At the HL stages, supporters of fox hunting sought to protect themselves from having the Act used against them by hunt saboteurs. (Ctte A36, Rep. A12). The Government re-assured those concerned and promised to look at the issue. The Government also held discussions with the Association of Chief Police Officers concerning the administration of the exemption scheme.

As far as can be ascertained, the impact of lobbying on the Parliamentary stages of the Bill was limited. With the exception of the HL amendments from the Police Federation there was little evidence of any impact. The main lobbying, which succeeded in obtaining considerable modification to the original proposals, came between Baker's statement on 22/5/91 and the publication of the Bill on 4/6/91.

Changes Between the Statement and the Bill

In the 22/5/91 Statement, the Government was unconvinced that the neutering of pit bull terriers was sufficient, and made it clear that unless expert opinion could convince them otherwise, all such dogs would have to be destroyed. At the request of the RSPCA the Government was considering whether to compensate owners of destroyed dogs, and whether there should be an exemption scheme.

Some concerns emerged following Baker's statement. In particular, it was not clear who was going to be responsible for rounding up and killing the 10,000 pit bull terriers in the country, since both the RSPCA and the British Veterinary Association refused to be involved and the police were reluctant to take part. Following an outcry from pit bull owners and the RSPCA, the Government was said to be re-thinking the compulsory destruction of dogs where the owners could look after them responsibly (Guardian, 30/5/91). The RSPCA was also said to be pressing for a neutering programme as a less drastic way of reducing the risk posed by the dogs, and was concerned that irresponsible owners would simply abandon dogs rather than pay for their destruction or neutering. (Times 31/5/91).

The Bill when published met some of the concerns expressed about the original proposals. Rather than require that all pit bull terriers be immediately destroyed, a licensing scheme would be established allowing the retention of banned dogs so long as they were neutered, had third party insurance cover, and were muzzled and on a lead in public places. If these were not met by the end of November 1991, the dog would be destroyed. It also contained reserve powers to add further dogs to the list of banned breeds. Following the Control of Dogs proposals, it created the new offence, not mentioned in the initial statement, of allowing a dog to be dangerously out of control in a public place, which would address the danger from dogs outside the banned categories.

Government Case and Opposition Views

The Government case for the Bill, set out at Second Reading, was that public concern about irresponsible dog owners and the increase in the number of serious attacks made action necessary. The aim of the Bill was to remove the menace of fighting dogs, and it would also tackle the more general threat from dangerous dog along the lines indicated in The Control of Dogs, which had been widely welcomed in consultations with the relevant bodies.

The Labour Party and the Liberal Democrats supported the Bill in principle, but attacked the handling of the issue by the Home Secretary. Both argued that the Bill should have included compulsory third party insurance for all "other especially dangerous dogs" under Clause Two, and a national dog registration scheme.

Features of the Parliamentary Proceedings

Table One below indicates the way in which time was spent in the House of Commons stages of the Bill.

Table One: Time Spent in the HC Stages.

Guillotine Debate	2 hours 24 minutes
Second Reading	3 hours 52 minutes
Money Resolution	22 minutes
Committee Stage	4 hours 32 minutes
(Debate on Dog Registration Scheme	2 hours 47 minutes)
(Rest of Committee Stage	1 hour 45 minutes)
Third Reading	Not debated
Total	11 hours 16 minutes

(No Report Stage is held for an unamended Committee of the Whole House Bill).

The House of Commons stages of the Bill were subject to a guillotine from the start of the Second Reading, and the whole Bill passed through the House in one day, 10/6/91. The reasons given for this were the public demand for immediate action, and the need for the Bill to gain Royal Assent by the end of July 1991 if the ban on unexempted dogs was to take effect by the end of November. Labour attacked this as unnecessary since the Bill enjoyed all party support. The Government, Labour claimed, was trying to prevent a back bench revolt in favour of a universal dog registration scheme.

House of Commons Committee Stage

The HC Committee ` .age was taken on the floor of the House. Five New Clauses and thirty amendments were tabled. Of these 35 amendments, just four were called, a further 10 were grouped and discussed, and 21 were not called or not reached. (See Table Two). Consideration failed to get beyond Clause 1.

Table Two: Amendments and New Clauses tabled on HC Ctte Stage

	Govt	Cons BB	Lab FB	Lab BB	SLD	Others
Tabled	-	3	12	17	1	2
Called	-	1	2	1	-	-
Not Called*	-	1	7	11	-	2
Gpd. & Disc.**	-	1	3	5	1	-
Moved	-	-	-	-	-	-
Not Moved	-	1	3	5	1	-
Withdrawn	-	-	2	-	-	-
Negatived	-	1	-	1	-	-
Agreed	-	-	-	-	-	-

   *   Not reached for debate because of guillotine.
  ** Grouped under another amendment and discussed, rather than called in its own right.

The main feature of the HC Committee Stage was the debate under New Clause 1 (tabled by an all party group under Conservative back bencher Dame Janet Fookes) to re-introduce a universal dog registration scheme. This occupied over half of the time available, and was defeated by 303 to 260 (including 17 Conservative MPs voting against the Government). As a result of this, under the guillotine the debate did not extend past Clause 1, the majority of amendments received no consideration, and the Bill had no Report Stage or debated Third Reading in the House of Commons.

House of Lords Second Reading
The House of Lords Second Reading was held on 26/6/91. The Government commended the Bill to the House. The Labour Opposition supported the Bill in principle, but Lord Richard criticised the Bill as being "far from faultlessly drafted" as a result of the speed with which the Bill was produced, and listed a number of omissions and defects which Labour would seek to redress. Conservative back benchers Lords Kimball and Dulverton were worried about the impact of the Clause 3 "dangerously out of control" offence on fox hunting, and would bring amendments forward to safeguard it. Lord Hayter (Independent) was worried that Clause 3 might be applied to police dogs in the course of their duty. Lord Houghton (Labour) attacked the whole basis of the Bill as fundamentally flawed because of the rushed way in which it was introduced, and argued that it should have been sent to a special Select Committee for evidence to have been taken on the issue.

House of Lords Committee Stage
The House of Lords Committee stage took place on 10/7/91. Sixty two amendments and new clauses were tabled. Four major groups of Government amendments, largely based on concerns expressed in the HC debates and at HL Second Reading, were agreed in the course of the proceedings.

First, the running of the exemption and compensation schemes were put out to tender (Ctte. A11,14,17,19).

Second, the offence of letting a dog be dangerously out of control was extended to cover places not open to the public (Ctte A28, 30, 31, 40, 41).

Third, a new Clause (section 6 of the Act) relating to the muzzling and control of listed dogs was introduced, ordering that clause 1 dogs should be in the care of someone over the age of 16. (This was partly based on HC Ctte A18, a back bench Labour amendment that had not been reached in the Commons).

Fourth, the definition of "public place" was extended to include the common parts of buildings in multiple occupation. This too was based on a back bench Labour amendment from the HC Committee stage (A14), and on pressure at HL Second Reading.

Table Three: Amendments / New Clauses at HL Ctte Stage

	Govt	Cons BB	Lab FB	Lab BB	SLD	Other
Tabled	20	13	13	9	7	-
Called	10	9	5	5	4	-
Not Moved	-	-	-	4	-	-
Gpd. & Disc.	10	4	6	-	3	-
Moved	10	4	-	-	-	-
Not Moved	-	-	6	-	3	-
Withdrawn	-	9	5	5	4	-
Negatived	-	-	-	-	-	-
Agreed	20	-	-	-	-	-

As can be seen in Table Three, no amendment were agreed other than those emanating from the Government. In addition, the Government accepted the principle of A45, a Conservative back bench amendment supported by the Police Federation, which made the cost of destroying a dog recoverable by the courts. Government amendment A12 was based on Labour bench bench HC amendment A7, which had not been reached, and said that dogs to be destroyed must be put down by a vet. Labour Front Bench A6 on the age at which a person was permitted to be in possession of a Clause 1 dog, was accepted by the Government and embodied in Rep St. A256 and 3R A10. The Government was pressed on Labour Front Bench A39 on compensation for victims, and agreed to look at the measure again.

Another feature of the Committee stage was the attempt by Lord Houghton of Sowerby (Lab) to amend the act in favour of the dog owners concerned. All nine Labour back bench amendments were tabled by him. Table Four indicates the reasons for the withdrawal of the amendments shown above.

Table Four: Amendments Withdrawn at HL Ctte Stage

Party	Wdn.	Satisfied	Not Satisfied	Raised Again
Govt BB	9	5	4	2*
Lab FB	5	2	3	2**
Lab BB	5	3	2	-
SLD	4	3	1	-

*   The issues concerned were the protection of fox hunting, and the reversal of the burden of proof in cases of the contested identification of dogs as pit bull terriers, whereby the onus lay on the owner to prove that the dog was not a pit bull. In addition A52 which was not moved related to this. The mover, Lord Campbell of Alloway, attacked the Government explanation as "neither understood nor ... accepted". The issue of the onus of proof was raised again at both Report and Third Reading.

**   The issues were third party insurance for all dogs and compensation for the victims of attacks if the owner of the dog could not be traced.

House of Lords Report Stage

The House of Lords Report Stage of the Bill was held on 18/7/91. Twenty eight amendments and New Clauses were tabled. See Table Five below.

Table Five: Amendments / New Clauses at HL Report Stage

	Govt	Cons BB	Lab FB	Lab BB	SLD	Others
Tabled	6	9	2	6	2	3
Called	4	4	1	6	1	2
Not Called	-	-	1	-	-	1
Gpd. & Disc.	2	5	-	-	-	-
Moved	2	-	-	-	-	-
Not Moved	-	5	-	-	-	-
Withdrawn	1*	4	1	4	1	2
Negatived	-	-	-	1	-	-
Agreed	5	-	-	1**	-	-

    *   Government A25, a New Clause "Offences by Young Persons", contained drafting problems, and the Government agreed to withdraw it and return at Third Reading with a new amendment.

    **   Labour back bench A1 was a drafting amendment, which the Government accepted and was agreed.

A number of amendments elicited Government concessions. Conservative back bench A11 extending the powers of the courts was duplicated by Government A10. Government A27 duplicated SLD A14, which exempted police dogs and military dogs from the "dangerously out of control" offence. (This reflected concerns at 2R and also SLD A38 on HL Ctte, which the Government had then opposed as unnecessary). Conservative back bench A12 again sought to exempt fox hounds from the "dangerously out of control" offence (raised at HL 2R and with Ctte A36), and the Government promised to look at the problem.

Table Six: Amendments Withdrawn at HL Report Stage

Party	Wdn.	Satisfied	Not Satisfied	Raised Again
Govt BB	4	2	2*	1
Lab FB	1	1	-	-
Lab BB	4	2	2**	-
SLD	1	1	-	-
Others	2	-	2***	-

    *   The issues concerned were the burden of proof in identifying banned dogs (also raised without satisfaction in Committee, and returned to on Third Reading), and whether to use the word "injures" or "attacks".

    **   The issues concerned were the date for the enforcement of the ban on pit bull terriers, and a clarification of the differences in penalties applicable for Clause 1 and Clause 2 dogs.

    ***   The amendments concerned both related to third party insurance for exempted dogs.

House of Lords Third Reading

The Bill received its House of Lords Third Reading on 23/7/91. Ten amendments were tabled, all reflecting concerns or undertakings given earlier in the passage of the Bill. One of the two Government amendments was tabled only the day before the debate.

Two Government amendments were tabled. One, New Clause A10, was a revised version of Report Stage A25, which was itself a Government redraft of Labour Front Bench HL Committee A6. The second, A8, was a compromise on the question of the onus of proof in the identification of banned dogs. The issue had been strongly pressed by Conservative Back Bench peer Lord Campbell of Alloway throughout the HL stages of the Bill. This did not placate him, and he pressed his own A5 on the issue, which was rejected. (The burden of proof has proved to be a problem in practice; see below). Independent peer Lord Monson returned to the subject of third party insurance for exempted dogs, which had again been raised throughout the stages of the Bill. A1 was rejected, and the further amendments on the issue were not moved.

In the debate both Labour and independent speakers criticised the lack of a mandatory third party insurance scheme for exempted dogs. Lord Houghton condemned the lack of information available about the administration of the Bill and about how it would be implemented. He argued that the Bill had not been thought out in detail before being introduced.

Table Seven: Amendments / New Clauses at HL Third Reading

	Govt	Cons BB	Lab FB	Lab BB	SLD	Others
Tabled	2	4	1	-	-	3
Called	1	1	-	-	-	1
Not Called	-	-	1	-	-	2
Gpd. & Disc.	1	3	-	-	-	-
Moved	1	-	-	-	-	-
Not Moved	-	3	-	-	-	-
Withdrawn	-	-	-	-	-	-
Negatived	-	1	-	-	-	1
Agreed	2	-	-	-	-	-

HC Consideration of HL Amendments

The House of Commons considered the House of Lords amendments on 25/7/91. There was little debate, with Labour and the SLD simply welcoming some of the concessions made by the Government towards their concerns. The Bill received Royal Assent that day, just over two months after the Government had announced its intention to legislate.

Provisions for Secondary Legislation

Section 1 of the Act contains five provisions for secondary legislation, giving powers to the Secretary of State to bring further breeds of fighting dogs under the section; to fix the date under which the restrictions on fighting dogs came into force and to create a compensation scheme; to fix the conditions for an exemption scheme; and to let the exemption and compensation schemes be operated by "such persons or bodies as the Secretary of State thinks appropriate".

Other provisions for secondary legislation enable the Secretary of State to apply some of the restrictions under section 1 to other dangerous breeds (section 2); to specify the kinds of muzzles and leads to be used in order to comply with the A (section 7); to make the Order applying the Act to Northern Ireland open annulment rather than to affirmative resolution (section 8); and to fix the date on which the Act came into force (section 10).

Statutory Instruments Promulgated Since Royal Assent

Three statutory instruments were made on the day of the Royal Assent to the Bill. S.I.1991/1742 brought the Act into force on 12/8/91, and fixed the deadline for registering and exempting pit bull terriers at 30/11/91. S.I. 1991/1743 added the Dogo Argentina and the Fila Braziliera to the list of dogs banned under section 1. S.I. 1991/1744 set out the details of the compensation and exemption schemes. On 16/10/91, S.I.1991/2297 set down the conditions to be complied with for exempted dogs, and S.I.1991/2636 modified the timescale for having exempted dogs tattooed.

Steps Taken to Implement the Act

The majority of the Act came into force on 12/8/91. The prohibition on the ownership of unexempted fighting dogs under section 1 came into effect on 30/11/91. Responsibility for the operation of the exemption scheme was put out to tender, and was won by the Index of Exempted Dogs, a part of Wood Green Animal Shelters.

The owners of banned dogs under section 1 were required to collect notification forms from local police stations, giving details of the provisions of the Act. They were then required to register their dogs at the local police station, and to send their notification forms to the Index of Exempted Dogs, which was responsible for ensuring that the conditions for exemption were fulfilled, and for paying compensation to owners who chose to have their dogs destroyed.

Details of the operation of the Act were set out in Home Office Circular 67/1991. No statistics are yet available on the number of prosecutions under the Act. In a written answer on 12/2/92 (c 522), Home Office Minister Angela Rumbold said that 8,000 dogs had been registered. Some 400 claims for compensation had been made by owners who had had their dogs destroyed. 3,200 exemption certificates had been issued, with a further 1,100 applications being processed.

Working of the Act

As yet, no official statistics are available on the working of the Act. However, recent newspaper articles have suggested that the Act is encountering difficulties and is proving to be more expensive than expected. The key problem seems to be the inadequate definition of pit bull terriers contained in section 1. It simply refers to "the type of dog known as the pit bull", and leaves identification to vets. In a test case in June 1992 at Knightsbridge Crown Court, it was ruled that any dog which had the "substantial characteristics" of a pit bull came under the definition. This brought thousands of previously unregistered mongrels within the ambit of the Act, and has resulted in a large number of appeals. Vets are experiencing problems in identifying pit bull terriers, as was predicted throughout the Parliamentary passage of the Bill (Independent 26/10/92).

In addition, the police are concerned at the cost of holding suspected dogs (9 per day) and at the time cases take to come to court. The Metropolitan Police has brought about 700 prosecutions in the year that the Act has been in force, but they

have received no additional funding to cover the costs of enforcing the A
(Independent 26/10/92).

The Kennel Club believes that the Act should be revised, with its Executi
Officer, Bill Edmond, arguing that the difficulties over identifying pit bull terrie
had been foreseen. As he commented, "All emergency legislation has flaws in i
The RSPCA has stopped helping prosecutions except in cases of cruelty, and wan
the Act amended to lift the mandatory death penalty on unexempted dog
(Independent 26/10/92).

An adjournment debate on the operation of the Act was held on 4/11/92 (H
Debs c. 387-392). Conservative MP Andrew Bowden asked for a review of the A
on the grounds that it had been "unfair and a disaster for many responsible d
owners". (c. 387). He called for amendments to give more discretion to the cour
especially in cases where identification of the dog as a pit bull terrier was conteste
A review was supported by the RSPCA, the BVA, the Royal College of Veterina
Surgeons, the Kennel Club, and also by many magistrates and lawyers. In respons
the Minister (Charles Wardle MP) argued that the Act was working well and that
changes were required, but that the operation of the Act would be kept under revie

Appendix 7 – Volume of Legislation

This paper examines the raw figures for legislative growth in Public General Acts and Statutory Instruments since 1900, and points to some of the methodological inadequacies of utilising the main statistics most popularly used.

1. Table 1 shows the growth of Public General Acts in this century –

Table 1 – Volume of all Public General Acts, 1901-1991

Year	No. of Acts	Pages	No. of Sections and Schedules
1901	40	247	400
1911	58	584*	701
1921	67	569	783
1931	34	375	440
1941	48	448	533
1951	66	675	803
1961	65	1048	1087
1971	81	2107	1963
1981	72	2276	2026
1991	69	2222*	1985

*   The paper size in 1911 was somewhat larger than the paper used in 1901, 1921 and subsequent years. The size of the paper was also increased to A4 in 1987, so requiring fewer pages.

2. Table 2 gives fuller statistics on the pages of statutes in more recent years, and also shows the volume of genuinely new primary legislation by excluding consolidation Acts –

Table 2 – Volume of Public General Acts 1985-1991, showing effect of excluding consolidation Acts

Year	No. of Acts	Pages	No. of Acts excluding Cons. Acts	Pages excluding cons. Acts
1985	76	3233	65	1860
1986	68	2780	64	2310
1987	57	1538*	56	1269*
1988	55	3385	49	2047
1989	46	2489	43	2399
1990	46	2391	42	1743
1991	69	2222	61	2012

*   The statute book from 1987 onwards has been printed on A4 paper which is larger than the size previously used, so requiring fewer pages.

3. A number of points ought to be made in putting the data into context. First, the differing political circumstances of the time have an effect on the output of legislation. 1901, as the second full year of the 1900-05 Salisbury/Balfour Parliament, can be taken as fairly typical of the period. (However, the 1901 figures are dominated by the Factories and Workshops Act, which contained 102 pages, and 170 sections and Schedules). 1911 was effectively the first year of the 1910 to 1915 Asquith Liberal administration, and so one would expect a substantial output, both because of its position in the life of the Parliament and because the Government was a radical and reforming one. Indeed, the 1911 figures are boosted by the National Insurance Act (141 pages, 124 clauses and Schedules) and the Coal Mines Act (85 pages, 131 sections and Schedules). 1921 also contained a few major Acts, such as the Education Act (111 pages, 180 sections and Schedules). The figures for 1931 reflect the quiescence of the second Macdonald administration, and the fact that the Government fell in August and that a General Election was held in October. 1951 saw the tail-end of the Attlee administration, which was clearly running out of steam and coping with a much reduced majority after the 1950 election.

4. Second, the stage in the Parliament has a significant impact on the amount of legislation enacted. For 1913, Lord Renton (The House Magazine 11/12/91) quotes figures of 38 statutes and 301 pages, a significant reduction from 1911. The figure for 1951 does not reflect the volume of legislation enacted by the Attlee Government. At its high point in 1949, 2288 pages of legislation was added to the statute book. 1987 was an election year and less legislation was enacted. Similarly, 1991 was late in the 1987-92 Parliament and was expected to be an election year, so that the legislative programme was not particularly heavy. The total figures for 1988, also quoted by Lord Renton as evidence of the extent of legislative growth, are rather deceptive, in that they include the Income and Corporation Taxes Act, an enormous consolidation measure of 1038 pages, 845 sections and 31 Schedules. When this is removed, the figures for 1988 appear less of a leap in volume than they do on face value.

5. Third, the figures in Table 1 are somewhat distorted by the inclusion of consolidation measures; this adds to the apparent volume, while taking no account of the amount of legislation removed from the statute book each year by repeal or consolidation. As a result, the total annual volume of legislation exaggerates the amount of growth in the statute book as a whole.

6. Fourth, the figures for the number of sections and Schedules enacted do not tell the whole story, as they can be of greatly differing length. In the Broadcasting Act 1990, section 191 is only four lines long, whereas Schedule 12 is sixteen pages long. In addition, length is no indication of significance, and ignores the extent to which provision is made for delegated legislation.

Delegated Legislation

7. Table 3 shows the growth of delegated legislation in this century –

Table 3 – Volume of Statutory Instruments

Year	No. of General SIs	Pages
1901	156	N/A
1911	172	N/A
1921	727	N/A
1951	2335	3523
1961	2515	4524
1971	2167	6338
1981	1892	6521
1983	1966	6405
1984	2065	6062
1985	2082	6476
1986	2332	9048
1987	2279	6266*
1988	2311	6294
1989	2510	N/A **
1990	2569	N/A
1991	2945	N/A

*   Statutory Instruments from 1987 onwards have been printed on A4 paper which is larger than the size previously used, so requiring fewer pages.

** The figures for pages from 1989 onwards are unavailable because the bound volumes of Statutory Instruments are not yet published; individual SIs are not paginated culmulatively.
(Figures for 1901 to 1921 drawn from memorandum by C.T. Carr to the Committee on Ministerial Powers (the Donoughmore Report), Minutes of Evidence, Volume Two, p. 204).

8. The number of pages occupied by general S.I.s for years before the Second World War is not available because certain categories of general S.I.s were not published. An important point to note is that throughout the earlier period, there were always more local S.I.s than general S.I.s, except during the two World Wars. The 1946 Act revised the classification of S.I.s, so that the figures before and after 1948 are not strictly comparable.

9. However the figures do indicate the trend. The start of the welfare state had an impact on the figures, with Carr noting that the National Insurance Act 1911 increased the number of general S.I.s by at least 50 per year. A great expansion occurred during the First World War, up to a maximum of 1204 general orders in 1918, before declining to just above pre-war levels by 1929. Since 1945, the S.I.s withdrawn in the "bonfire of controls" were replaced by those resulting from the establishment of the welfare state.

10. As with Public General Acts, some problems arise in quantifying the growth of S.I.s. First, as C.T. Carr observed in his evidence to Donoughmore (Minutes of Evidence, Vol. Two, p. 104), "A mere numerical test, of course, is of limited value; it is not a test of liberty or tyranny . . . But the annual comparison of

registered totals is probably a better guide than the annual comparison of bulk reckoned by pages of text".

11. Second, in addition to the definitional problems mentioned above, the size of paper was increased to A4 in 1987.

12. Third, as with Public General Acts, the number of pages used is no indication of the scope or significance of the S.I. The figures also fail to indicate the number of S.I.s of temporary duration or which replace existing S.I.s. An increase in the number of S.I.s issued per year does not necessarily mean that the overall number of S.I.s in force is increasing.

Appendix 8 – Use of Green Papers and other Consultative Documents

The following Table shows the numbers of Green Papers and departmental consultative documents issued by Governments in recent years.

Year	Green Papers	Other Consultative Documents
1976	8	11
1977	12	27
1978	9	48
1979	9	63
1980	15	85
1981	8	76
1982	3	76
1983	5	112
1984	7	146
1985	15	140
1986	10	191
1987	14	208
1988	10	288
1989	-	276
1990	-	267
1991	-	232

These documents covered a wide range of matters, ranging from "Scallop dredging in the 12 mile inshore zone" to "Local Government Review: the internal management of local authorities in England". It was not feasible to distinguish those concerned with proposed legislation.

THE HANSARD SOCIETY
FOR PARLIAMENTARY GOVERNMENT

The principal objective of the Hansard Society, which was founded in 1944, is to promote knowledge of and interest in Parliamentary Government. Its work ranges over research, commissions on topical issues and an active schools programme.

Recent publications include:

Paying for politics: the Report of the Commission on the Financing of Political Parties (1981) £2.50

Company Donations to Political Parties: a Suggested Code of Practice (1985) £2.50   ISBN 0 948419 00 8

The Report of the Hansard Society Commission on Women at the Top (1990) £7.50 (£6 to members)   ISBN 0 900432 21 7

Cameras in the Commons, a research study by Alastair Hetherington, Kay Weaver and Michael Ryle (1990) £10 (£8 to members)   ISBN 0 900432 22 5

Agenda for Change: the Report of the Hansard Society Commission on Election Campaigns (1991) £10 (£7.50 schools, £6.50 members)   ISBN 0 900432 23 3

All the above titles are available direct from the Society, or through bookshops. The following title, which is published by Oxford University Press in association with the Society, is available only through bookshops: Parliament at Work, by Derek Heater (1989) £4.95   ISBN 0 19 832921 0

The Society's quarterly journal, 'Parliamentary Affairs', is sent free to Subscribing, School and Overseas Members, and to Corporate Supporters, and is also available in the UK and Europe on annual subscription of £52 from: Journal Subscriptions Dept., Oxford University Press, Walton Street, Oxford OX2 6DP. Other subscription rates are available on request.

map of Parliamentary Constituencies, published by Stanfords in association with the Society, is available price £4.95 from Stanfords, 12 Long Acre, London C2E 9LP   ISBN 0 9519231 0 2

Membership Categories
(with annual minimum subscription rates as at 1 January 1993)

Ordinary	£10
School	£25
Subscribing	£30
Overseas	£37
Corporate Supporters	£250

The Hansard Society for Parliamentary Government, St Philips Building North, Sheffield Street, London WC2A 2EX   Tel 071-955 7478   Fax 071-955 7492